CONTENTS

PRIMER

Welcome to the official game guide for *Battlefield 3*. If you're a veteran of Wake Island, Karkand, Verdun, or Arica Harbor, you know why we're starting with multiplayer. While the new single-player campaign offers a great story and plenty of memorable moments, it's only a small part of *Battlefield 3*. The multiplayer experience is the other part. Playing against others and working together as a team with members of your squad adds an entirely new dimension of intensity and fun. Plus, earning new ranks and unlocks is incredibly addictive, making hours melt away. So before jumping into a multiplayer match, make sure you've set aside plenty of free time. After all, who needs sleep?

WHAT'S NEW?

If you're a grizzled *Battlefield* veteran, then you can jump online now and feel right at home among the whizzing bullets and exploding shells. But before rushing into action, here's a quick summary of the some of the new features and gameplay mechanics.

LOADOUT CUSTOMIZATION

Take a moment to customize your soldier and vehicle loadouts before joining a game.

While veteran *Battlefield* players are accustomed to being rewarded with new weapons and gear as they progress through their multiplayer career, there has never before been so many customization options available. Each class, weapon, and vehicle has its own unlock progression, allowing you to unlock a variety of upgrades, accessories, gadgets, and specializations. When choosing your soldier's loadout, you can choose a primary weapon, a sidearm, up to two gadgets, and a specialization. Taking customization even deeper, each primary weapon can be outfitted with a scope, as well as primary and secondary attachments. You can even choose loadouts for vehicles, selecting from a mix of unlocked upgrades, gadgets, and weapons. The more you play, the more unlocks you acquire. So don't forget to visit the loadout screen to make adjustments that best fit your style of play and the current needs of your team.

PRONE

Make a habit of dropping prone, especially if you find yourself in an area with no cover.

Okay, this really isn't a new feature. But it's back by popular demand and it really changes the pace of the game, especially if you're used to the *Bad Company* series. By lying prone you not only make yourself a smaller target, but you also greatly increase the accuracy and stability of your weapon, particularly when using a Bipod. The ability to go prone also makes it much easier to conceal yourself within high grass and shrubs, making it extremely difficult for opponents to spot you. To better conceal your position, consider equipping a Suppressor or Flash Suppressor to minimize muzzle flash.

SUPPRESSION

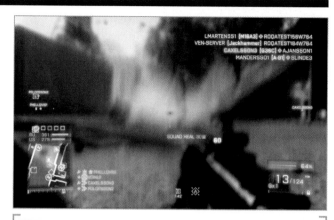

If this is what your screen looks like, find cover fast!

The new suppression system will definitely make you think twice before exposing yourself to incoming fire. If incoming rounds hit you or strike anywhere close by, you become suppressed. When you're suppressed, your vision is blurred and your weapon accuracy is greatly diminished. However, the effects of suppression pass quickly if you get out of the line of fire and seek cover. The new suppression mechanic can work in your favor, too. Even if you don't have a clear shot at an opponent, open fire in an attempt to suppress them. Any class or weapon is capable of suppressing, but the support kit's light machine guns are the most effective. The large magazine capacities of these weapons allow you to lay down sustained heavy fire, which is ideal for keeping an opponent's head down. Each player has an invisible suppression radius around them. Simply landing rounds within this small radius suppresses the target. The new Suppression Assist score (50 points) is awarded if a teammate kills an opponent you've suppressed.

VEHICLE DAMAGE

A single rocket hit no longer destroys light vehicles like this Vodnik—but it may kill some of the occupants.

In *Battlefield 3*, vehicle damage has been completely overhauled. Now if vehicles take light damage, they slowly regenerate health on their own, assuming the vehicle stays out of danger and avoids taking damage for several seconds. However, if a vehicle takes heavy damage, it catches fire and becomes disabled. At this point, vehicle speed and mobility are greatly reduced, but the weapons still function—the loss of speed and control is extremely dangerous when piloting a jet or chopper. While disabled, a vehicle's health slowly declines until it eventually explodes. A disabled ground vehicle can be repaired only by engineers. Jets and helicopters in flight have the benefit of deploying the Fire Extinguisher upgrade to put out the flames and restore control. As a result of these changes, destroying vehicles outright is much more difficult; you must disable a vehicle before it can be destroyed. Meanwhile, the crew of a disabled vehicle have a critical choice to make: Do they stay with the burning vehicle and try to score more kills? Or do they bail out and attempt to find cover before their ride explodes?

REVIVAL DECLINE

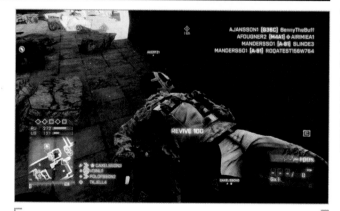

Even if a player declines your revive attempt, you still get points.

The ever-popular defibrillator returns, this time as part of the assault kit. Reviving fallen teammates with the defibrillator remains a great way to keep your squad and teammates alive while scoring some big points for yourself. But this time, the soldier you revive has a choice. They can either rejoin the action or return to the spawn screen and deploy from a new location. This allows fallen troops to avoid being revived in a hot spot only to get killed as soon as they come back to life. Regardless of the decision made, the soldier who performed the revive still gets the standard Revive (100 points) or Squad Revive (110 points) score. But if a revive is declined, the team loses a ticket instead of being refunded one.

JETS

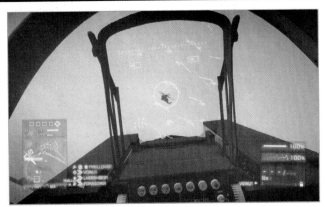

Feel the need for speed? Spawn directly into the pilot's seat of a waiting jet.

Like the ability to drop prone, jets aren't new to the *Battlefield* series. But they're back, adding a new layer of intensity to the conflict. Initially, jets are equipped with only a cannon that useful for performing strafing runs and shooting down enemy aircraft. Like all the vehicles, jets have their own reward progression; you unlock more powerful air-to-air and air-to-ground weapons including heat-seeking missiles, Rocket Pods, and Guided Missiles. So choose your weapons carefully based on your team's needs. If they need help knocking out tanks, choose Rocket Pods or Guided Missiles. If your team is constantly being harassed by enemy helicopters or jets, choose Heat Seekers to shoot down these threats. Veterans will be happy to know that all aircraft (jets and helicopters) have their own spawn points. So instead of lingering on a runway waiting for a jet to spawn, simply hold in the spawn screen and spawn directly into the pilot's seat when a jet or helicopter is available.

SQUAD LEADER

Be ready to issue attack/defend orders when you become the squad leader.

Each squad now has one squad leader who is tasked with issuing attack and defend orders. Squad leaders are assigned at random and are the only squad members who can issue orders. When you've been selected as the squad leader, a message appears on the screen informing you of your new job. Your name also appears at the top of the squad list on the left side of the HUD and is marked with a star icon. As squad leader, you can better direct your squad by placing attack or defend orders on control points and M-COM stations. Once an order has been placed at a location, any kills that occur within a wide radius of the given order results in points for both you and your squad. It's a simple mechanic, but it's a great way to keep your squad focused on one location.

BATTLEFIELD BOOT CAMP

Are you new to *Battlefield*? If so, jumping into a well-established online community can be a bit intimidating. But there's really nothing to fear. Regardless of your experience or skill level, there is a role for everyone in *Battlefield*. In fact, this is one of the only online shooters where you can post a big score without even firing a single bullet. In this section we take a look at the basic gameplay mechanics as well as the different multiplayer game modes.

INTERFACE

The heads up display, or HUD, is the way that vital information is displayed on your screen. None of the items on your HUD are there for aesthetics. Rather, they are there to help you accomplish your objectives and keep you alive. Here's a brief explanation of every item on the HUD.

Game Mode Information: The icons and meters above the minimap relate to the current game mode. The diamond shaped icons represent control points in Conquest mode and M-COM stations in Rush mode. The two meters below these icons track how many tickets each team has.

Objectives: The square and diamond-shaped icons on the HUD represent objectives. Blue square icons are held by your team while red diamond icons are held by the opposing team. Beneath each of these icons is a number showing the distance to each objective in meters.

Reticle: The reticle is always located in the center of the screen. The reticle is the aiming point for your selected weapon. To hit a target, place the reticle over it and fire. The reticle may change based on the weapon you're using. When firing at an enemy, watch for diagonal lines flashing around the perimeter of the reticle. This bloom animation means you are hitting the target. This is especially useful when making long-range shots.

Kill Notifications: The text in the top right corner of the screen reports recent deaths, showing who killed whom and with what weapon or vehicle.

Score Notification: Every time you earn points, text appears in the middle of the screen describing what action you're being rewarded for and how many points you gain.

Minimap: The minimap provides a top-down, 360-degree view of the environment through which you are moving. The view rotates as you change direction so that the top of the minimap is always the direction you are currently facing. The minimap also shows the location of all detected enemies as red triangles or red vehicle icons. Teammates show up as blue icons while squad members are green. Empty vehicles are represented by white icons. It is a good idea to constantly refer to the minimap to keep track of all detected enemies. Even if you can't see them visually, the minimap lets you know where they are, even if they are behind a hill or inside a building. Finally, red-and-blue diamond icons show you the location of objectives—these same objective icons also appear on the HUD. The terrain shaded red is out of bounds. If you move into this area, you have ten seconds to get back on the map or else you will die.

Squad List: Shown in green text on the right side of the minimap, the squad list shows every member of your squad as well as the kit and specialization they currently have equipped. The squad leader appears at the top of the list with a star icon next to their name.

Compass: The compass is located just beneath the minimap and shows the direction you're currently facing.

Ammo: The ammo count box in located in the bottom right corner of the screen. Your ammo is represented by three numbers. The large number to the left is the number of rounds you currently have loaded in the weapon's magazine while the small number to the right is the amount of ammo available in unloaded magazines. As you reload your weapon, the number on the right decreases as the number on the left increases up to the maximum amount the weapon's magazine can hold. The third number, below the ammo reserves, represents how many grenades you have.

Health: By default your health is at 100 percent. But if you take damage, your health will drop—if it reaches 0 percent, you die. You can slowly regenerate health by staying behind cover and avoiding injury. But the fastest way to heal is with a Medic Kit dropped by an assault player. Stand (or lay) close to a Medic Kit to rapidly restore your health.

Fire Mode: This icon represents the selected fire mode of you weapon. Some weapons allow you to switch fire modes, choosing from single shot, automatic, and burst modes.

Weapon Unlock Status: This status bar represents how close you are to the next unlock for the selected weapon. The more enemies you kill with a specific weapon, the more accessories you unlock.

SPAWN SCREEN

Before spawning on a squad member, make sure they're in a relatively safe location.

When you first join a game, the spawn screen is where it all begins. Before immediately jumping into the game, take a few seconds to choose your class and gear. It's possible to switch primary weapons from the spawn screen, but if you want to make more adjustments to your kit, choose the Customize option. This opens a new screen allowing you to select different sidearms, gadgets, and specializations. You can also customize your primary weapon with accessories you've unlocked. Once you're finished adjusting your loadout, return to the spawn screen and figure out where you want to join the fight. If you're in a squad, you can spawn on any living squad member. Or if a recon squad member as deployed a Radio Beacon, you can spawn at its location. Depending on the game mode, there are also bases, deployment areas, and control points where you can spawn. New to *Battlefield 3*, if there are jets or helicopters available, you can spawn directly into the pilot's seat of these idle aircraft. US troops can also spawn directly into the AAV-7A1 AMTRAC, an armored vehicle that serves as a mobile spawn point. As you can see, the spawning options are numerous. In most instances you should spawn on or close to your squad so you can provide support. But if your squad is in a tense firefight, sometimes it's safest to spawn at a less dangerous location, otherwise you may get killed as soon as you spawn into the game.

MOVEMENT FUNDAMENTALS

Sprinting is essential at the beginning of match as players race to capture and defend key locations.

Moving your soldier around the battlefield is simple, especially if you've played the earlier installments or other first-person shooters. When standing, your soldier jogs at moderate pace, which is ideal for getting around areas where threats are minimal. While crouched, you move slower, and while prone, your movement is literally reduced to a crawl. However, since you are lower, you make a smaller target for the enemy to hit and you can more easily duck behind cover. When advancing against an enemy position, it is best to move while crouched or prone, as it is harder for the enemy to detect you. These lower stances also cause the reticle to tighten up, indicating an increase in your weapon accuracy. So make a habit of dropping to a knee or down on your belly before firing a shot.

At times, it is better to move fast, by sprinting. You can't use weapons or equipment while sprinting, but you are much more difficult for the enemy to hit. Sprint when you have to cross a dangerously open piece of ground as you move from one position of cover to another. But never sprint in tight, confined spaces where you're likely to encounter enemy troops. If you encounter an enemy at close range while sprinting, chances are you won't have time to stop and aim your weapon, giving the enemy a huge advantage.

■ [CAUTION]

Some maps feature deep bodies of water, allowing you to swim. Avoid swimming at all costs. While you're in the water you can't access your weapons; you are a sitting duck.

PARACHUTES

If you bail out of a plane or helicopter, make sure you do so within the map's boundary.

Whether jumping out of a damaged aircraft of hopping off a tall building, you can avoid cratering into the ground by deploying your parachute. While in free fall, press the jump button/key once to open your parachute. You can slightly steer the parachute with standard movement inputs. But don't expect to travel great distances in your parachute, as the descent is rapid. It's possible to fire your weapons during the descent, but your accuracy is greatly diminished. If you're descending directly over an enemy position, consider dropping grenades—just make sure they explode before you reach the ground. But the longer you're in the air, the more attention you're likely to attract. For this reason, free fall for as long as possible and open the parachute just before you reach the ground. This is a great way to sneak into enemy-held territory.

COMBAT

While moving about the battlefield is a major part of gameplay, the sole purpose of movement is to place yourself in a position where you can use your weapons to engage and eliminate the enemy. You have access to different types of weapons. However, the controls for using these weapons are fairly common.

SPOTTING TARGETS

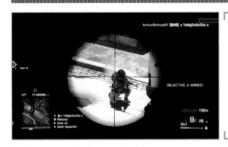

Always spot a target before opening fire to alert your teammates of an enemy's presence.

Before you attack your first enemy, you must first learn how to spot them. When you have an enemy player or vehicle in your sight, press the spot button/key to highlight it for your team. This places a red icon on the HUD and minimap, showing your entire team where the enemy unit is. Enemy infantry show up as red triangle icons while vehicles are represented by red vehicle icons. Targets only remain spotted for approximately five seconds, but that's usually more than enough time for your team to take notice of the threat. Also, once the icon disappears, you can spot the target again as long as you've maintained a line of sight. If a teammate kills the target you tagged, you earn a Spot Bonus worth 10 points. So consider playing as recon with a high-powered scope and simply spot enemy units for your team. Even if you don't fire a shot, you can still rack up a decent score.

KNIFE

Ouch! Turn around periodically to avoid getting knifed in the back.

The knife is a standard-issue weapon available to all players, regardless of their class or rank. When approaching an enemy from behind you can kill them instantly by attacking with the knife. But if you attack an enemy head-on, it now takes at least two swipes with the knife to score a kill from the front—a new gameplay mechanic introduced in *Battlefield 3*. So if an enemy is looking in your direction, think twice before attempting a knife kill. Chances are they'll shoot you in the face before you can get within striking range. Instead, always look for opportunities to flank and sneak up behind unsuspecting opponents and knife them from behind. As in *Battlefield 2142* and every installment since, scoring knife kills earns you the victim's dog tags, a permanent trophy. In addition to scoring stealthy kills, the knife is also great for slicing through chain link fences and other obstacles.

FIREARMS

A subtle bloom animation appears at the center of the reticle, scope, or ironsight when your bullets strike your target.

As mentioned earlier, the reticle in the center of the screen is your aiming point for using weapons. Most of the weapons you use are direct fire, meaning that the projectile you fire travels in a basically straight line from your weapon to the target. Using these weapons is simple. Place the reticle directly over the target and then press the fire button. For semiautomatic or single-shot weapons such as pistols, shotguns, and sniper rifles, each time you press the fire button/key, you fire a single round. However, for automatic weapons such as submachine guns, assault rifles, and light machine guns, the weapons will continue to shoot as you hold down the fire button/key until they run out of ammo. Most weapons in *Battlefield 3* have selectable fire modes, allowing you to choose from single-shot, burst, and automatic modes. So experiment with each weapon's fire modes in an effort to increase accuracy and reduce recoil. When firing automatic weapons, the longer the burst, the less accurate your fire. Therefore, to maintain greater accuracy and still put a lot of lead on target, fire in short bursts. You are more likely to kill your target, especially at medium to long range, with a few accurate rounds rather than by spraying an entire magazine over a wide area. If recoil is still a problem, consider switching to burst or single-shot mode.

IRONSIGHTS AND SCOPES

The reticle disappears when aiming through ironsights or a scope, but the bloom animation still appears when hitting a target.

When you fire a weapon using the reticle to aim, you are essentially firing from the hip, with the butt of your weapon in the crook of your arm. This is not very accurate and should be used only at close range. To increase your accuracy, press the zoom button/key. This will bring up the ironsight view, where you are actually looking through the weapon's sight to aim. The butt of the weapon is brought up to your shoulder to give you greater accuracy. If your weapon is equipped with a scope, the zoom button/key will provide a view through the scope rather than ironsight. It is a good idea to get in the habit of pressing the zoom button to bring up your ironsight before firing. This is not only more accurate, but it also provides a zoomed-in view of the target. To further increase accuracy, crouch or drop prone and remain stationary while firing. When peering through high-powered scopes, there is noticeable sway that makes it difficult to aim. You can temporarily reduce this sway by holding your breath—hold down the sprint button/key. But this lasts only for a few seconds. You can completely eliminate scope sway by using a Bipod.

■ [TIP]

Gravity affects all firearms, causing bullets to drop over distance. When engaging targets at long range, compensate for gravity by aiming high.

GRENADES

If you suspect an opponent is hiding in a building or other confined space, toss a grenade inside before entering.

Grenades require a bit more skill to use effectively since they are either thrown or launched. Unlike a bullet or rocket that travels in a straight line, grenades travel in a parabolic arc due to their lower speed and the effect of gravity. In the case of a grenade launcher, the farther away you are from the target, the higher you need to aim. That is why the reticle for a grenade launcher has several horizontal line aiming points. For a short-range shot, use the top line. The farther away your target is, use the lower lines. By using a lower aiming point, you are essentially aiming the weapon up higher to lob the grenade toward the target.

Hand grenades work a bit differently. They are thrown rather than launched and you don't get a separate reticle for aiming. Instead, use your weapon's reticle to best judge where you want to throw a grenade. One press of the grenade button/key causes the grenade to be thrown, which is shown as a orange flashing icon on the HUD. But hand grenades have limited range, so you may need to aim high to get them near your intended target—the farther your target, the higher you should aim your throw. When using grenades, it is important to understand how they work. Rifle grenades fired from a launcher explode on impact. Hand grenades, in contrast, have a five-second fuse. As a result, you can bounce hand grenades around corners or roll them down inclines. Like your own grenades, enemy grenades show up as flashing orange icons on the HUD. So if you see one of these flashing icons nearby, sprint in the opposite direction before it explodes.

VEHICLES

When driving a vehicle, consider slowing or stopping while your passengers are targeting enemies—you get points if they score a kill.

The maps in *Battlefield 3* are massive. It can take a while to walk them on foot. Therefore, use vehicles to get around. There are several types of vehicles in the game, yet they all are driven with similar controls. All vehicles have more than one seat. When you get into an empty vehicle, you are placed in the driver's seat by default. However, you can move to another position inside the vehicle with the press of a button/key, cycling through all seats until you find the seat you want. The driver has control of a vehicle's movement and, in the tanks and IFVs, also controls the vehicle's turret-mounted main weapon. Most vehicles even have gunner and passenger positions, allowing teammates to man other vehicle-mounted weapons. So make sure all crew positions are filled before leaving a base or deployment area. For more information on the various types of vehicles in the game, see the Vehicles chapter.

[KILL CAM]

Every time you die you get a brief glimpse of your killer through the kill cam. This screen appears briefly immediately after your death, providing a shot of the player who killed you as well as their name, rank, health, kit, weapon, specialization, and dog tags. The kill cam also shows any kit, weapon, or vehicle service stars your killer has obtained. It may seem like a a frivolous feature, but the kill cam has larger implications for how the game is played. Snipers can no longer camp one spot and kill from an undisclosed location throughout the entire match. Through the kill cam, victims can see approximately where an enemy player is camping and exact revenge once they respawn. So make a habit of moving frequently, or else you're likely to find one of your angry victims sneaking up behind you with a knife.

GAME MODES

There are five game modes spread across nine different maps, offering plenty of variety for all. Most of the game modes are familiar classics, but the addition of Team Deathmatch ramps up the intensity for those who prefer nonstop action.

CONQUEST/CONQUEST 64

In Conquest, you must be within a flag's capture radius to raise or protect your team's flag.

Max Players: 24 Console/64 PC

This classic *Battlefield* game mode is back. Your team must dominate the area of operations by capturing control points and holding them. Simply stand next to a flag pole at a control point to raise your team's flag—the more teammates there are in the flag's capture radius, the faster the flag is raised. Once captured, some control points provide vehicles and stationary weapons, so leave some personnel back to defend these locations. Both teams have a limited number of reinforcements known as tickets. The ticket count for both teams appears just above the minimap—the team who runs out of tickets first, loses the match. You can drain the enemy ticket count by holding more than half of the control points on the map. So if there are four control points, all you need to do is hold three to initiate a ticket drain. So capture a majority of the control points early on and stay put, thereby forcing the enemy to attack your defended positions.

[HARDCORE MODE]

Hardcore mode is back, available on all game modes. This setting removes most of the HUD elements, including the reticle. Therefore, you must aim using the weapon's ironsight or scope view. Friendly fire is turned on, so watch your fire around teammates, especially when using explosive weapons. The weapons also inflict much more damage, making for a hyper-realistic Battlefield experience designed specifically for experts.

RUSH

Destroying and defending objectives known as M-COM stations is the focus of Rush matches.

Max Players: 24 Console/32 PC

In this game mode, one team is the attacker while the other is the defender. On the map there are several bases controlled by the defender—the US team always attacks and the RU team always defends. The attacker's objective is to destroy the two M-COM stations at each base. Once both stations have been destroyed, that base is considered destroyed and the defender receives a new base to defend with two more M-COM stations. The attacker has a limited number of tickets at the beginning of a match, which is shown just above the minimap. Whenever an attacking soldier dies, it costs a ticket for the soldier to respawn on the map. Once the tickets run out, the attackers can't spawn new soldiers back onto the map and the defenders win. However, once the attacker destroys a base, the team gets more tickets as well as a new set of vehicles. The defenders do not have to worry about tickets—they have an unlimited number of respawns. The defender wins by eliminating all attackers and reducing their tickets before they can destroy all the M-COM stations on the map.

■ [NOTE]

M-COM stations can no longer be destroyed by explosive weapons or falling debris from collapsed buildings. Therefore soldiers must approach each objective and physically plant a charge on it; stand next to an M-COM station and hold down the interact button/key to arm or disarm a charge.

SQUAD RUSH

Despite the low player count, always approach an M-COM station cautiously in Squad Rush.

Max Players: 8

Squad Rush is a modified version of Rush that pits two squads against each other in a compact attack/defend style game. In this mode there are only two zones, with only one M-COM station positioned at each. It's the job of the defending team's four-player squad to defend each base's M-COM station against the four-player attacking squad. The gameplay is identical to Rush, but on a much smaller scale that emphasizes infantry combat. Teamwork is essential if you wish to come out on top, so stay together and keep the lines of communication open at all times.

SQUAD DEATHMATCH

In Squad Deathmatch, try to take control of the IFV to give your team a big score boost.

Max Players: 16

In this mode there are four four-player squads, each representing a different team: A, B, C, and D. The team that scores 50 kills first wins—the score is listed on the left side of the screen above the minimap. To make things more interesting, each Squad Deathmatch map contains one Infantry Fighting Vehicle (IFV) that spawns in one of four possible locations. Whoever can take control of this vehicle gains a huge advantage in firepower. But while manning the vehicle, be aware that there are three other squads gunning for you. As you can imagine, this is a very fast-paced game mode that is best played with good squad mates you can rely on to watch your back. Stay together, and stay alive!

TEAM DEATHMATCH

If you can't find any teammates nearby, immediately seek cover— this game mode does not favor solo players.

Max Players: 24 Console/32 PC

Team Deathmatch is a no-holds-barred infantry-only battle in a confined area. The two teams struggle to score the most kills to win the match. Each kill is counted, so take down your enemies to increase your team's score, which is represented by the numbers and status bars above the minimap. It's your choice whether to stick with your team or to go on a solo hunt. But be warned, the tempo is high and enemies can pop up from behind almost any corner. Monitor the scoring status bars to see how the fight is going, and make tactical adjustments as necessary. For example, if both teams are close to scoring the requisite points for a win, play it safe to avoid giving the enemy team the kills they need. Squads are still available in Team Deathmatch, but you can't spawn on squad members.

SQUAD PLAY

If you've played past installments of *Battlefield*, you know the benefits of joining a squad. A squad is a four-player unit that can communicate with each other over headsets. Being able to talk to the other players in your squad allows you to discuss each situation and respond as a single, unified fighting force. Beyond the obvious tactical advantages, being in a squad allows you to earn the squad bonus points that boost your score and fast-track promotions. But if you're new to *Battlefield* and the squad system, let's take a look at how they work.

JOINING A SQUAD

You can join a random squad while a multi-player map is loading.

At the start of any match, while the map is loading, you're asked if you want to join a squad. Always choose yes. In this instance, you'll be automatically assigned a squad randomly. Chances are your new squad mates are complete strangers, so say hi and ask what kit they will use before spawning into the game.

If you prefer playing with friends, you can create a squad from your friend's list before even joining a game. Choose the *Invite a Friend* option from the multiplayer Quickmatch menu and send invitations to anyone on your friend's list who is online. You don't need four players to form a squad, so feel free to join a game once you have at least one friend on your side. However, if you have less than four players in your squad, the extra slots could be filled by strangers. When your squad is formed and ready for action, choose the *Find a Game* option to begin a match.

SQUAD SPAWN

If you spawn on a squad mate who is prone, you'll enter the game prone as well.

One of the huge benefits of playing in a squad is the ability to spawn on any squad mate. In the spawn screen you can see a number of spawning options, including your team's base and control points. If you don't want to spawn at one of those static locations, select the name of one of your squad members. As you select their name, a blue circle icon appears on the map and the camera view switches, showing exactly where they are. Before spawning on a squad member, make sure they're in a safe location. The last thing you want to do is spawn in the middle of an enemy kill zone. You can also spawn on any squad member who is in a vehicle with unoccupied seats. New to *Battlefield 3* are Radio Beacons, which are deployed by recon troops. Radio Beacons can be placed almost anywhere on the map and serve as forward spawn points for your squad. This is a great way for attackers to maintain a presence close to an objective, especially in Rush matches. But don't let enemies see where your Radio Beacon is placed, otherwise they may camp nearby and pick off your squad mates as they enter the game.

TEAMWORK

Issuing and following squad orders is a simple way to boost your score.

Once in the game, you can identify your squad mates by the green name tags above their heads accompanied by their kit icon—they also show up as green triangles on the minimap. Other teammates have blue name tags above their head while enemies appear as red. Stay close to your squad so you can support one another. But don't cluster around each other too tightly or else all four of you can be eliminated by an explosive attack. Instead, try to stay within each others' line of sight. By simply communicating and working together you can gain a huge advantage over your opponents, especially those that wander off by themselves.

In addition to talking to each other over your headsets, use the target spotting system to tag enemies and issue attack/defend orders. Only the squad leader can issue orders so watch for blinking boxes around objectives like M-COM stations and control points. If no order has been issued, ask your squad leader to place an order on an objective. Kills performed within close proximity of an objective marked with an attack/defend order result in a Squad Attack Order (20 points) or Squad Defend Order (20 points) bonuses. So if you're the squad leader, don't forget to issue orders to help your squad's scores.

■ [NOTE]

You can gauge your squad's performance on the scoreboard during or at the end of a round. Each of your squad mates is highlighted by a green bar—your name is highlighted with an orange bar.

MULTIPLAYER TACTICS

Tactics is the combining of maneuvers and firepower to achieve an objective. Both movement and weapons have already been covered, so this section focuses on using the two together.

PLAN AHEAD

Before a round begins, take a few seconds to discuss tactics with your teammates. Any game plan is better than none.

There is an old saying that those who fail to plan, plan to fail. You need to come up with a plan before the bullets start flying. The best place to start is to look at your game mode's objectives, since those determine victory or defeat. While killing the enemy is always a goal, it is often a means to an end. Instead, focus on the objectives. Do you have to destroy a target, defend a position, or just get to a certain point on the map?

Once you know what you must do, look at the map and examine the terrain. Where are you located? Where is the objective? How will you get there? Are there any vehicles you can use? These are all questions you need to ask yourself. Once you have determined how to get to the target, you must then consider how to accomplish your orders. Will you need to get in close to plant an explosive charge on the target? If so, how will you secure the perimeter? Finally, you need to take into account your opposition. What does the enemy have and where are they located? Usually you will not know that type of information until you get in close to the target and can see the enemy with your own eyes. Therefore, planning continues on the fly as you learn new information about enemy positions and actions.

COVER

If you can't find suitable cover nearby, drop prone in an attempt to avoid detection, and crawl to a piece of cover.

Combat is very dangerous. Bullets and other deadly projectiles fly through the air and can kill you outright if they make contact. The concept of cover is to place something solid between you and the enemy that will stop those projectiles and keep you safe. The multiplayer maps are filled with objects that you can use as cover—buildings, walls, trees, rocks, earthen mounds, and so on. Some types of cover will stop small arms fire such as rifle bullets, but not stop the heavier machine gun fire. Walls of buildings will stop machine gun fire, but not rockets or tank rounds. Therefore, pick cover that will protect you from the current threat—objects constructed from wood or flimsy sheet metal won't stop a bullet.

Cover should become ingrained in your combat thinking. In addition to looking for enemies, you also need to be looking for cover. During a firefight, always stay behind cover. The only reason you leave cover is to move to another position with cover. If the cover is low, you may need to crouch down or drop prone to get behind it, standing only to fire over it. When moving from cover to cover, sprint to get there quicker.

While you want to stay behind cover, you also want to try to deny the benefit of cover to your enemies. Destroying their cover is a way to do that. Another way is to reduce the effect of their cover by moving to hit them from a direction for which they have no cover. This is called flanking. For example, if an enemy is taking cover behind a wall, move around to the side of the wall so that the wall is no longer between you and your target. Or, if you have an explosive weapon, you can simply blow a hole in the wall, taking out your target in the process.

DESTRUCTIBLE ENVIRONMENTS

Tanks are great for dishing out destruction. Use their cannons to blow holes in walls and other pieces of cover.

One of the awesome features in *Battlefield 3* is that many of the structures and objects can be damaged or outright destroyed. This presents a large range of possibilities and opportunities that will affect the tactics you use. For example, if the enemy is holed up in a house and taking shots at you from the windows, you could try to throw a grenade through the window or rush into the house via the doorway and clear out the threat with close-range combat. However, with destruction as an option, you can launch a rocket at a wall of the structure and blow a hole in it. If an enemy was on the other side of the wall, that threat might be killed. Otherwise, you can then use direct fire to kill the enemy, since you destroyed the wall that was providing cover.

Often, structures can funnel you into a kill zone the enemy has set up. But you can blast your way through walls or other objects and come at the enemies from different directions that they might not expect. While this may seem to favor the attacker, the defender can also use this as an advantage. Destroy potential cover the attacker may use to approach your position. Call in mortar strikes on groves of trees or shoot out wooden fences to deny the enemy a place to hide. As a result, you can create your own kill zones of open land that the enemy must traverse—all the while under the fire of your weapons.

■ [TIP]

Some structures that take heavy damage can completely collapse, killing everyone inside. Target a building's exterior walls until you hear a series of creaking and moaning sounds that indicate an imminent collapse. This can be a fun (yet inefficient) way to take out a pesky sniper hiding in an attic or upper floor. Obviously, if you find yourself in a creaking and moaning building, get out fast!

LONG-RANGE COMBAT

When sniping, try to focus your fire down narrow choke points like streets, alleys, and bridges.

If possible, it is best to try to attack the enemy at long range before they're even aware of your presence. While sniper rifles work great for this type of combat, you can even use assault rifles, light machine guns, or rocket launchers to hit targets at long range. The key to winning at long range is to take your time. Drop prone, stay still, and use ironsights or scopes to increase your magnification and accuracy. As always, make sure you have some good cover in case the enemy decides to shoot back—if you can see them, they can see you. Also remember to fire in short bursts to ensure that more of your bullets hit the target.

CLOSE-QUARTERS COMBAT

Quick reflexes trump accuracy in close-quarters gun battles like this. This is why shotguns are so effective.

This type of combat is the exact opposite of long-range combat. In close quarters, such as in a town or even within a building, you don't have a lot of time to aim before shooting. However, at such short ranges, accuracy is not really a factor. Instead, you need a weapon that puts out a lot of firepower with some spread so you are more likely to get a hit while moving. Shotguns and PDWs are great for close-quarters combat. Your minimap is also an important tool, especially if teammates have spotted targets. Since you can see where enemies are located, use this info to set up shots while strafing around corners. Your weapon will already be aimed at the target as it appears on the minimap, which saves you just enough time to have the advantage and make the kill rather than be killed. Don't forget to use grenades, which can be thrown around corners or over walls to hit enemies who think they are safe behind cover.

■ [TIP]

Have you just run out of ammo in the middle of a close-quarters duel? It's much faster to draw your pistol than to reload your main weapon. Or if your opponent is reloading too, rush in for a melee kill.

ENGAGING VEHICLES

If you don't have the firepower to kill a tank, don't draw its attention. Instead, seek cover and spot the tank for teammates who are capable of taking it out.

Attacking vehicles is dangerous—especially when you are an infantryman on foot. However, modern soldiers have a lot of firepower they can use to disable and destroy vehicles. This role usually falls to the engineer, who carries anti-tank rocket launchers and mines. It takes only a single rocket to disable most light vehicles. However, tanks and IFVs require at least two rocket hits to disable, and even more to destroy. Always try to attack tanks from the rear, where their armor is the weakest. Rocket launchers are most effective, but grenade launchers can work in a pinch, too, assuming the vehicle is already heavily damaged. Of course, the best way to kill a tank is with another tank.

Even if you don't have those powerful weapons or gadgets, you can still damage light vehicles with small arms fire. The gunners on the Growler ITV and VDV Buggy are completely exposed—shoot them and the vehicles lose their firepower. For those who are really daring, engineers can place mines in the path of moving vehicles. C4 (now carried by the support kit) is also very effective against vehicles, but you have to get very close to slap on a charge.

[SERVICE STARS]

As you advance through your multiplayer career you can earn service stars for every class, weapon, and vehicle type. For classes and vehicles, you must meet certain point thresholds to achieve a service star. Weapon service stars are awarded for every 100 kills. A maximum of 100 service stars can be earned for every class, weapon, and vehicle type. A service star is also awarded when reaching the rank of Colonel.

PERSISTENCE SYSTEM

A message appears at the top of the screen each time you earn a new promotion.

Almost every action performed in a multiplayer match can earn you points. Points not only determine which players are listed at the top of the scoreboard after a round, but they also help you unlock new weapons, gadgets, specializations, and even achieve new ranks. So at the end of a round, check out your overall performance in the *End of Round* screens. These screens show your current rank as well as your progress toward achieving the next rank. It also has statistical breakdowns of your score, showing how many points were earned with each kit, vehicles, and awards. Speaking of awards, any dog tags, medals, or ribbons earned during the round are shown in the *Unlocks* and *Awards* sections. The *Kits* screen shows how much progress you've made toward unlocking new equipment for each kit.

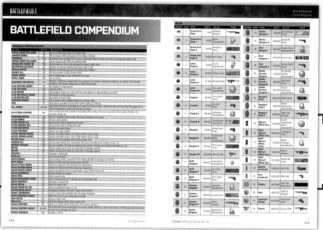

■ [NOTE]

For complete information on the game's scoring system and ranks, flip to the Battlefield Compendium chapter at the back of the guide. There you'll find scoring details for each action as well as criteria for earning every rank, medal, ribbon, and dog tag. All rank, class, weapon, and vehicle unlocks are also listed in this chapter.

BATTELOG

Review your multiplayer stats, awards, and unlocks from the Battlelog website.

URL: battlelog.battlefield.com

The new Battelog website allows you to keep tabs on everything happening in *Battlefield 3*, even when you're away from the game. Log in to the Battlelog using the e-mail address and password associated with your EA.com or Origin.com account. The Battlelog keeps track of every stat imaginable and also offers social networking features that allow you to see what your friends have been up to. By creating or joining a platoon, you can guarantee you always have a reliable group of friends to play with. PC players can even access a server browser and join games directly from the Battlelog.

[BATTLEFIELD VETERAN PROGRAM]

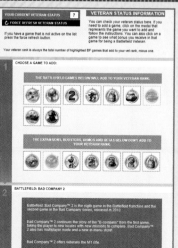

Have you owned at least one Battlefield *game before* Battlefield 3*? If so, then you're eligible for* Battlefield *veteran status. Becoming a veteran unlocks special dog tags you can use to customize your soldier, one for each* Battlefield *game you own. Simply log in to veteran. battlefield.com with your EA.com or Origin.com account and register all the* Battlefield *games that you own. In addition to the dog tags, you're also assigned a* Battlefield *veteran rank based on how many games you register. Each title is worth one point—expansions,* Battlefield Heroes*, and* Battlefield 1943 *are not worth points, but you can still register them. Your veteran rank is displayed on the* Battlelog *website as well as next to your profile name on the scoreboard during multiplayer matches. So let your opponents know that they're facing a veteran!*

COMMUNITY

The *Battlefield* community is very active, and always a good source of information for game news, software updates, and even unorthodox tactics. Here's a few good sources to check-out for the latest *Battlefield* news:

BATTLEFIELD BLOG

blogs.battlefield.ea.com

This is the official blog maintained by employees of DICE. Go here for all the latest information on the game straight from the developers.

OFFICIAL BATTLEFIELD TWITTER

twitter.com/Battlefield

Go here for the latest tweets from the game's developers.

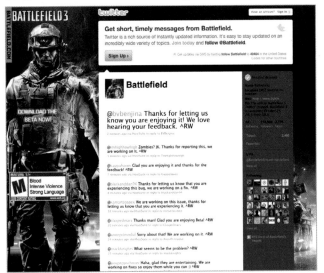

PLANET BATTLEFIELD

planetbattlefield.com

This site is unofficial, but is one of the most comprehensive and frequently updated *Battlefield* sites on the web. Check it for news, updates, as well as details on upcoming tournaments. The forums are also an excellent source of information frequented by some of the most experienced players in the world. Bookmark this one!

CLASSES

Succeeding during multiplayer often comes down to choosing the right tools for the job. That's where the classes come in, also known as troop kits. Before spawning into a game, you're prompted to choose which class you wish to play. If you're a team player, your choice should be based on what is needed by your team instead of which kit you want to use. For example, if your base is being overrun by enemy tanks, choose the engineer kit and use rockets or mines to eliminate the threats. Although there are only four troop kits to choose from, the options for customizing it are more elaborate than in any *Battlefield* game to date, allowing you to mix and match weapons, accessories, gadgets, and specializations to create a unique kit that compliments your style of play.

➕ ASSAULT

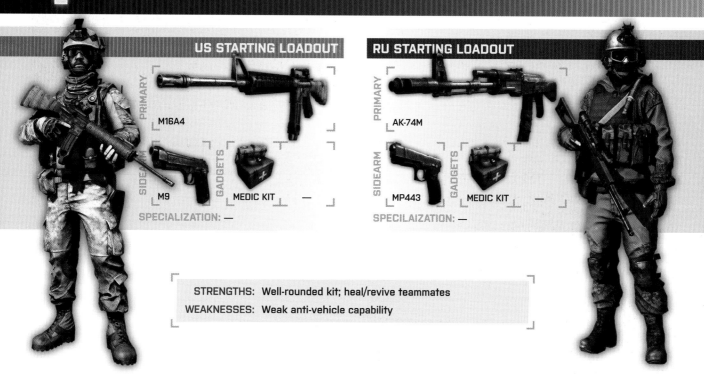

US STARTING LOADOUT

PRIMARY — M16A4
SIDEARM — M9
GADGETS — MEDIC KIT —
SPECIALIZATION: —

RU STARTING LOADOUT

PRIMARY — AK-74M
SIDEARM — MP443
GADGETS — MEDIC KIT —
SPECILAIZATION: —

> **STRENGTHS:** Well-rounded kit; heal/revive teammates
> **WEAKNESSES:** Weak anti-vehicle capability

The assault class is the most versatile of the four, effective in both offensive and defensive situations. When you're not sure what kit to choose, you can't go wrong with this one. The assault rifles associated with this kit are excellent at any range, with great damage output and impressive rates of fire. Each assault rifle can also be equipped with the M320 40mm grenade launcher, which is great for blasting infantry, light-skinned vehicles, and even structures. The M26 MASS assault rifle attachment is a powerful shotgun, capable of firing a variety of devastating ammo. Beyond their impressive offensive capabilities, the assault class is now responsible for healing injured teammates with the Medic Kit and reviving recently deceased teammates with the Defibrillator. The Defibrillator isn't immediately available, so keep playing as the assault class to unlock it—it's the first item unlocked.

[ASSAULT SERVICE STARS]

 You earn a service star for every 220,000 points you score with the assault class. 100 assault service stars are available.

➕ Unlock Progression

UNLOCK	NAME	IMAGE	ASSAULT SCORE
1	Defibrillator		4,000
2	M320		11,000
3	M416		22,000
4	M26 MASS		38,000
5	AEK-971		60,000
6	M16A3		89,000
7	F2000		124,000
8	AN-94		166,000
9	M16A4 (for RU)		220,000
9	AK-74M (for US)		220,000

SPECIAL EQUIPMENT

MEDIC KIT

Unlock: Assault Kit Start

Description: A deployable medical kit provides healing over time to soldiers near the kit, greatly speeding the body's natural healing processes.

FIELD NOTES

The Medic Kit is commonly referred to as a medkit. These function similar to the support kit's Ammo Box, only they replenish health instead of ammo. Simply drop a Medic Kit on the ground near wounded teammates to heal them. The longer you (or an injured teammate) stand next to a Medic Kit, the more health they'll receive. The Medic Kit has a small healing radius, so players must stand very close to the medkit. Healing teammates and squad mates earns you a Heal bonus. Critically injured teammates have a white cross icon flashing above their head—the same icon appears on the minimap. These icons are visible only to friendly assault players so look for them to locate and heal teammates before they die. All players (including enemies) have a life meter below their name, allowing you to see exactly how much health they have. So even if a wounded teammate isn't critical, offer them a Medic Kit to fully replenish their health.

DEFIBRILLATOR

Unlock: 4,000 Assault score

Description: Automated External Defibrillator (AED) allows an assault soldier with proper medical training to revive a downed teammate within a short time after his apparent death.

FIELD NOTES

The shock paddles make their triumphant return! Use the Defibrillator to bring recently deceased teammates back to life. Simply aim at their dead body (at close range) and pull the trigger to deliver a lifesaving jolt of electricity. After each use, the Defibrillator must recharge for a few seconds before being deployed again. Reviving teammates earns you a Revive bonus, boosting your score significantly, especially if you make the resurrection business a full-time job. Dead teammates have a jagged horizontal line icon above their body, resembling the line on an electrocardiogram. The same icon appears on the minimap so that you can find dead teammates. But you must act quickly. Once a teammate has been down for a while, the body will disappear, preventing you from saving them. The Defibrillator can be used as an offensive weapon, too. Try sneaking up behind an opponent and shocking them for an instant, chuckle-inducing kill.

■ **[NOTE]**

For information on the M302 and M26 MASS, flip ahead to the "Assault Rifle" section.

[ASSAULT TACTICS]

› Most of the kit's assault rifles are fully automatic. But go easy on the trigger when firing automatically, as the rifle's recoil can pull your aim skyward. Instead, tap the trigger, firing in short bursts, to keep the weapon on-target. Many of the assault rifles have single-shot and burst fire modes you can select if recoil becomes a problem.

› Pestered by an enemy firing from a window? Using the M320, launch a grenade just below the window to take out the entire wall and the shooter standing behind it.

› Grenades cause very little damage to heavy vehicles like tanks and IFVs. Don't bother attacking these vehicles unless you see fire and smoke pouring out, indicating they have suffered heavy damage. If you do attack a heavy vehicle, always strive to hit their weak rear armor to maximize damage.

› Once you unlock the M320's smoke ammo, use it to cover your squad's advances or obscure defensive positions. Smoke causes no damage, but it can greatly increase the survivability of your teammates by hindering the visibility—if the enemies can't see you, they'll have a hard time hitting you.

› Assault troops can earn a ton of points by simply healing and reviving teammates. Drop Medic Kits near injured teammates to earn Heal (10) and Squad Heal (20) points. Also, keep an eye open for dead teammates lying on the ground. Zap them with the Defibrillator to score Revive (100) and Squad Revive (110) points. Healing and reviving can be a full-time job, particularly when defending on Rush maps.

› Revived teammates don't have to respawn, and thus don't use up the team's precious tickets. Conserving tickets in this manner can give your team a huge advantage in tightly contested Conquest matches, so keep those shock paddles buzzing. As veterans know, the Defibrillator can also be used to kill opponents with consistently hilarious results.

› Did an assault teammate just die in front of you? You can save him, even if you're not playing as the assault class. Grab his kit, then equip the Defibrillator to revive your teammate before his body disappears. Any kit can be grabbed off a dead enemy or teammate. This is a good way to test weapons and equipment you haven't unlocked yet.

ENGINEER

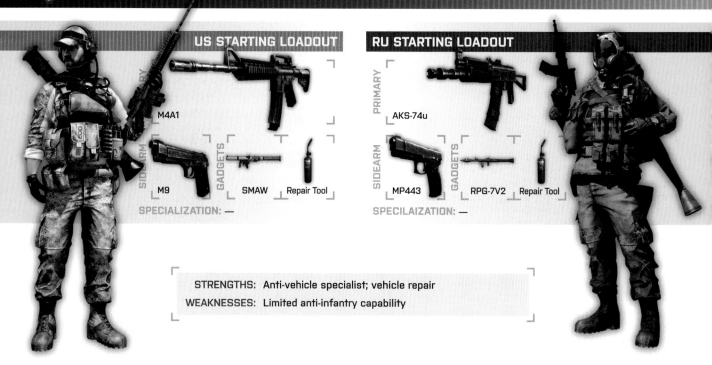

US STARTING LOADOUT

PRIMARY

M4A1

SIDEARM

M9

GADGETS

SMAW | Repair Tool

SPECIALIZATION: —

RU STARTING LOADOUT

PRIMARY

AKS-74u

SIDEARM

MP443

GADGETS

RPG-7V2 | Repair Tool

SPECILAIZATION: —

STRENGTHS: Anti-vehicle specialist; vehicle repair

WEAKNESSES: Limited anti-infantry capability

Engineers are great at taking out vehicles as well as fixing them. Out of the gate, the engineer is equipped with the SMAW or RPG-7V2 rocket launcher. Use this weapon (and the kit's unlockable FGM-148 Javelin) to take out enemy vehicles, including heavily armored tanks and IFVs. The first unlocks available to this class are the FIM-92 Stinger and SA-18 IGLA shoulder-fired anti-aircraft missiles, which are perfect for shooting down helicopters and jets. While the engineer is strong against vehicles, the kit's carbines are a bit underpowered, particularly at long range. So when you're not facing tons of vehicles, consider choosing a different kit with better performance against infantry. In addition to demolishing vehicles, the engineer can also repair them with the Repair Tool. Repairing manned friendly vehicles can earn you Repair points, a great way to supplement your score. Try to use the vehicle you're repairing as cover to avoid getting picked off by enemies.

Unlock Progression

UNLOCK	NAME	IMAGE	ENGINEER SCORE
1	FIM-92 Stinger (for US)		3,000
1	SA-18 IGLA (for RU)		3,000
2	M15 AT Mine		7,000
3	SCAR-H		14,000
4	EOD Bot		25,000
5	M4		40,000
6	A-91		58,000
7	FGM-148 Javelin		82,000
8	G36C		110,000
9	M4A1 (for RU)		145,000
9	AKS-74u (for US)		145,000

SPECIAL EQUIPMENT

REPAIR TOOL

Unlock: Engineer Kit Start

Description: A handheld oxy-fuel welding and cutting torch provides the engineer with the ability to both repair friendly vehicles and damage enemy vehicles.

FIELD NOTES

The engineer kit's Repair Tool is the only way to repair disabled vehicles. To deploy it, simply stand next to a damaged vehicle (while aiming at it) and hold down the trigger. Watch the circular meter in the center of the HUD fill in a clockwise fashion. Once the meter is filled completely, the vehicle is fully repaired. You're vulnerable while using this tool, so make sure you have adequate cover. During tank duels, stand behind a friendly tank and repair it as it takes damage. Repairing vehicles manned by a teammate or squad mate earns you Repair points—a great way to boost your score while playing as an engineer.

[ENGINEER SERVICE STARS]

You earn a service star for every 145,000 points you score with the engineer class. 100 engineer service stars are available.

SMAW

Unlock: US Engineer Kit Start

Description: Developed especially for the US Marine Corps to defeat light armor and enemy bunkers, the Mark 153 SMAW is capable of defeating both modern armor and emplacements. Unguided 83mm rockets are loaded individually at the back of the launcher from disposable, sealed, one-time use units.

FIELD NOTES

The SMAW (shoulder-launched multipurpose assault weapon) is the default rocket launcher for US engineers. The launcher fires an 83mm high-explosive dual purpose (HEDP) rocket that is ideal for targeting tanks, IFVs, and light vehicles. In a pinch, the rockets can also be fired at enemy infantry, but don't expect a large blast radius—the rocket must impact and detonate close to your target to produce lethal results. The rocket has no guidance system and tends to lose altitude as it travels. Therefore, when firing at a distant target, compensate for range by aiming slightly above the intended impact point.

RPG-7V2

Unlock: RU Engineer Kit Start

Description: A widely produced, anti-tank rocket-propelled grenade weapon, the RPG-7 has been used in almost all conflicts across all continents since the mid-1960s. Modernized into the RPG-7V2, which is lighter and more accurate than the original RPG-7, and firing GP-7VL rocket-propelled grenades, the RPG-7V2 is effective against both fortifications and armor.

FIELD NOTES

RU engineers begin their tank-busting career by toting around the RPG-7V2 rocket launcher. Like the SMAW, this rocket launcher has no optical sighting system. Instead you must use the ironsight view to aim the weapon prior to launch. As with the SMAW, aim high when firing at distant infantry or vehicles because the rocket tends to dip when traveling great distances. Since the weapon lacks a guidance system, don't bother firing at jets and helicopters—the chances of scoring a hit against these fast-moving targets are incredibly slim.

FIM-92 STINGER

Unlock: 3,000 Engineer score

Description: The FIM-92 Stinger is a portable infrared homing surface-to-air missile (SAM). The Stinger is capable of locking on and engaging a large variety of craft, from small UAVs up to low-flying helicopters and jets. The Stinger requires a locked target to fire.

FIELD NOTES

The Stinger is only available to US engineers—RU engineers get the SA-18 IGLA at the same time the Stinger is unlocked. With helicopters and jets firing rockets and missiles from above, the battlefield is much more dangerous for troops on the ground. Fortunately, engineers now have a powerful way to counter these airborne threats. Simply aim the missile at an enemy jet or helicopter and wait for a red bouncing box to surround the aircraft while peering through the weapon's sight. When a circle appears within the box and the word "LOCK" appears above, the missile has attained a lock and is ready to fire. At this point, the missile tracks the targeted aircraft and slams into it, dealing heavy damage.

SA-18 IGLA

Unlock: 3,000 Engineer score

Description: Russian man-portable infrared homing SAM. Labeled the 9K38 by the Russians and SA-18 IGLA by the US, the IGLA is capable of engaging a wide range of threats from UAV-sized aircraft up to helicopters and low flying jets. The IGLA requires a locked target to fire.

FIELD NOTES

The IGLA functions identically to the Stinger and is only available to RU engineers. This shoulder-fired surface-to-air missile is capable of locking onto jets and helicopters. One hit from this will disable a healthy aircraft or potentially destroy a damaged one. Pilots can break missile locks by deploying IR Flares or by breaking line of sight with the missile prior to launch. So once you lock on to an aircraft, wait for it deploy its Flares, then achieve a new lock before firing the missile. Both the Stinger and IGLA can be fired only at enemy aircraft—they can't be used against ground vehicles or infantry.

M15 AT MINE

Unlock: 7,000 Engineer score

Description: Proximity-triggered anti-tank mine. Multiple mines may be required to defeat heavily armored vehicles. Equipped with a friend-or-foe recognition system.

FIELD NOTES

This is a powerful anti-tank mine, effective against any ground vehicle. It requires a couple of these mines to take out a tank, but one mine instantly disables all other vehicles. Scatter these M15 AT Mines around high-traffic areas such as control points or M-COM stations. Choke points like bridges or narrow urban streets are also good ambush spots. However, when carrying these mines, you cannot carry a Repair Tool. So weigh the pros and cons before entering the battle. Enemy mines can be destroyed with explosives, such as grenades or tank rounds. Although they're only triggered by enemy vehicles, an anti-tank mine can still be lethal to all nearby infantry. So keep your distance, or else you may be killed by your own detonating mine.

EOD BOT

Unlock: 25,000 Engineer score

Description: A remotely controlled explosive ordinance disposal robot allows the engineer to repair and damage vehicles like a normal Repair Tool, but can also arm and disarm explosives and MCOM stations in Rush.

FIELD NOTES

When you don't want to expose yourself to incoming fire, send an EOD Bot to do the dangerous work. However, before deploy an EOD Bot, find a very good hiding spot. While controlling this robot you're completely vulnerable to attacks. So drop prone behind some cover to make yourself as invisible as possible. Once the EOD Bot is deployed, the camera switches to the robot's vantage point. The EOD Bot controls just like a vehicle. Drive next to a friendly vehicle and repair it. Or drive next to an enemy vehicle and damage it with the EOD Bot's own Repair Tool. The EOD Bot is most effective in Rush matches, where it can be used to arm and disarm charges on M-COM stations. But don't expect your new friend to go unnoticed by enemies. Although this little robot can absorb some damage, it won't last long when exposed to high concentrations of enemy fire.

FGM-148 JAVELIN

Unlock: 82,000 Engineer score

Description: A shoulder-launched, anti-tank missile with both a direct and top attack mode. Its fire-and-forget system requires a lock on before launch; it is exceptionally powerful against enemy armor.

FIELD NOTES

Firing a 127mm high explosive anti-tank (HEAT) missile, the Javelin takes tank killing to whole new level. The weapon is aimed through a small TV-screen that totally blocks all peripheral vision. So make sure a buddy is watching your back while you're aiming this weapon system. When you place the green crosshairs icon over a vehicle, a red bracket appears and you'll hear a beeping sound. When the bracket becomes a solid red box and the beeps transition into a solid, high-pitched tone, the missile has acquired a lock on the targeted vehicle. Fire the missile to score a hit. When launched, the missile flies straight up then comes crashing down on the target. This is the best way to score hits on the weak top armor of a tank. However, tanks can break locks by deploying IR Smoke. So consider waiting for a tank to use their smoke before firing a missile. The tank's Thermal Camo upgrade increases the time it takes for Javelins to lock on.

[ENGINEER TACTICS]

› The carbines associated with this kit are excellent during close-quarters firefights. Consider equipping a Tactical Light or Laser Sight to these weapons in an effort to blind your opponents and give you a slight advantage.

› Make friends with the support class. You'll need Ammo Boxes dropped at your feet if you want to keep firing rockets and missiles.

› The engineer's Stinger and IGLA help to even the playing field when enemy jets and helicopters are present. But you must maintain line of sight with the target to achieve a missile lock. If your target flies behind a hill or line of trees before a lock is achieved, the missile cannot be fired. The missile cannot be dumb-fired at any other targets, either. So don't bother equipping these missiles unless there's plenty of air traffic.

› Never attack tanks or IFVs head-on with a rocket launcher. For one, the driver will probably see you and return fire, sending you back to the spawn screen. Secondly, the front armor on these vehicles is very thick, reducing the effectiveness of your weapon's warhead. Instead, try to hit the vehicle from the side or rear, where you're less likely to be spotted. Furthermore, the side armor is weaker than the front and the rear armor is weakest of all. If you hit the side or rear, you'll ensure that your rocket inflicts maximum damage—it takes two rockets to kill a tank from the rear and three to kill it from the front.

› Try to hit tanks and IFVs at perpendicular angles when attacking with the rocket launchers. Glancing shots may deflect, and therefore inflict considerably less damage. A rocket striking armor at a perpendicular angle ensures maximum penetration by the warhead's shaped charge. The vertical surfaces covering the wheels and treads on the side are good targets, as is the engine compartment at the back of each vehicle.

› Anti-tank mines are extremely powerful explosives capable instantly disabling any ground vehicle. However, the mines fill the gadget slot, meaning you can't carry a Repair Tool while they're equipped. Consider deploying mines when defending a static position with predictable avenues of attack. Otherwise, stick with a rocket launcher.

[TACTICAL LIGHT VS. LASER SIGHT]

The intense red beam of the Laser Sight can blind opponents in both dark and bright environments.

You can now customize your weapons with a wide variety of scopes, muzzle, and rail attachments. Among these accessories are the Tactical Light and Laser Sight. The Tactical Light is essentially a small flashlight attached to the end of your weapon that is ideal for illuminating dark spaces such as tunnels. This light can also temporarily blind opponents, giving you a slight advantage in close-quarters duels. While the Laser Sight doesn't illuminate, it does increase weapon accuracy when firing from the hip. Like the Tactical Light, it can also temporarily blind opponents, making it difficult for them to return fire. But these accessories have one major drawback—they give away your position. Use these accessories sparingly, turning them off whenever you want to remain concealed.

So which one is better? The Tactical Light works well for blinding opponents at close range in dark environments. But beyond that, the light only serves as an aiming point for your opponents. The Laser Sight, on the other hand, can blind opponents (and teammates) at both close and intermediate ranges. Plus, the Laser Sight also increases your weapon's accuracy.

[STANDARD-ISSUE EQUIPMENT]

Each player is issued a knife and at least one grenade, regardless of class or rank. You can carry more grenades by unlocking and selecting the Grenades specialization.

COMBAT KNIFE

Description: Standard-issue combat knife based on the M9 Bayonet.

Field Notes

The combat knife isn't only useful for acquiring an opponent's dog tags. Use it to silently break open doorways or slice through chain-link fences to access new areas where your opponents are less likely to expect you. But if you are going after an enemy, stab them from behind, denying them the opportunity to retaliate. If you charge directly at an enemy with your knife, you're likely to get shot in the face.

M67 GRENADE

Description: A common defensive hand grenade, the M67 has a 3.5-second fuse and can be thrown approximately 30 meters by the average soldier. The lethal effect of this grenade is limited against targets with modern body armor.

Field Notes

Frag Grenades are most effective against infantry, but they can cause significant damage to light-skinned vehicles, too. But don't bother trying to take out a tank with them. Grenades don't explode on impact, instead, they tend to roll around until the timed fuse triggers the explosion. So keep this in mind when tossing a frag—they will bounce off surfaces and roll down slopes. Make a habit of tossing grenades in buildings prior to entering, especially if you suspect an enemy presence.

SUPPORT

US STARTING LOADOUT

PRIMARY: M27 IAR

SIDEARM: M9

GADGETS: Ammo Box —

SPECIALIZATION: —

RU STARTING LOADOUT

PRIMARY: RPK-74M

SIDEARM: MP443

GADGETS: Ammo Box —

SPECILAIZATION: —

> **STRENGTHS:** Solid anti-infantry kit; ammo resupply
>
> **WEAKNESSES:** Limited anti-armor capability

The support class is back! With the introduction of the new suppression mechanic, the support kit is a crucial member of any squad, regardless of the tactical situation. These guys carry the large, cumbersome light machine guns that are capable of laying down high volumes of sustained fire, which is great for suppressing enemy infantry. The support class also has access to some of the most devastating weapons in the game, including C4, Claymores, and the new M224 Mortar. When they're not busy scoring kills, support troops should supply teammates using the Ammo Box. The Ammo Box dispenses ammunition to all friendly troops within a small radius. There are no ammo crates in multiplayer, so it's up to the support players to replenish everyone's ammo. You earn a Resupply bonus (10 points) whenever a teammate retrieves ammo from an Ammo Box, so don't be stingy with these things. Scatter them around your teammates to boost your score. Since this is the only kit equipped with explosives, support players are also effective at taking out enemy vehicles with C4, either through direct application or through the creation of car bombs. So if you're not satisfied laying down suppressive fire from a distance, take the fight to close range and do some damage with your explosives. But such attacks are extremely dangerous, so you better have an assault buddy nearby to revive you.

Unlock Progression

UNLOCK	NAME	IMAGE	SUPPORT SCORE
1	C4 Explosives		4,000
2	M249		11,000
3	M18 Claymore		23,000
4	M224 Mortar		40,000
5	PKP Pecheneg		60,000
6	M240B		90,000
7	M60E4		130,000
8	M27 IAR (for RU)		170,000
8	RPK-74M (for US)		170,000

[SUPPORT SERVICE STARS]

You earn a service star for every 170,000 points you score with the support class. 100 support service stars are available.

SPECIAL EQUIPMENT

AMMO BOX

Unlock: Support Kit Start

Description: The deployable Ammo Box refills ammunition for nearby soldiers. Explosives and grenades take longer to be resupplied than standard magazines.

FIELD NOTES

Carried exclusively by the support class, the Ammo Box is the only source of ammo during multiplayer matches. There are no ammo crates, so it's up to support players to provide ammo to their teammates. Simply stand next to one of these Ammo Boxes for a few seconds to replenish the ammo for all of your weapons, including grenades and rockets. When playing as support, drop Ammo Boxes around clusters of teammates—each time someone retrieves ammo from a pack you earn a Resupply bonus. This is a great way to supplement your score while supporting your team and squad mates. If a teammate or squad mate is low on ammo, an icon depicting three bullets appears above their head. Get them some ammo fast!

C4 EXPLOSIVES

Unlock: 4,000 Support score

Description: Remotely detonated Composition 4 explosive packs provide anti-material, anti-vehicle and antipersonnel abilities.

FIELD NOTES

C4 is the first unlock for the support kit and undeniably one of the most powerful weapons in the game. Initially, up to three explosive charges can be placed at a time and detonated simultaneously with this device. However, the support class can replenish their C4 using an Ammo Box, so they can set elaborate C4 deathtraps involving more than three simultaneously detonated charges. Explosives are great for taking out vehicles. Simply stick a couple of charges on the back of a tank and step back a safe distance to watch the fireworks. When attacking vehicles, no matter the size, always plant at least two charges. One C4 charge will only disable a vehicle—it takes at least two to instantly destroy it. Charges can also be used as booby traps when placed around critical high-traffic areas like control points or M-COM stations—but it's up to you to detonate them when enemies are nearby. When defending in Rush matches, use the alarm sound of an armed M-COM station to alert you to nearby enemies—detonate your charges before they can move away from the kill zone. Don't worry about damaging an M-COM station with C4, as these objectives can no longer be damaged with anything other than a manually placed charge applied by the attackers.

M18 CLAYMORE

Unlock: 23,000 Support score

Description: The M18 Claymore is a directional antipersonnel mine that is detonated by motion in front of the mine. The mine can be passed safely if the target is moving at low speeds.

FIELD NOTES

Adding to the support kit's deadly arsenal is the M18 Claymore antipersonnel mine. Unlike traditional land mines, the Claymore is a directional mine that sprays shrapnel in the direction it's facing upon detonation. So think carefully before dropping one of these. From what direction is your enemy likely to approach? Once you have figured out where you want to place this mine, orient yourself in the proper direction before dropping the Claymore. Claymores are triggered by fast enemy movement. You can avoid triggering a Claymore by crawling past it. But it's much safer to take out a Claymore from a distance by tossing a grenade at it or shooting it with an explosive weapon such as a rocket or grenade launcher. The support class can carry one Claymore at a time. But more can be retrieved from the support kit's own Ammo Box. Like C4, Claymores are great for defending flags in Conquest and M-COM stations in Rush. Unlike C4, these weapons trigger on their own, so you don't have to constantly babysit them while waiting for an enemy to enter the kill zone.

M224 MORTAR

Unlock: 40,000 Support score

Description: The M224 60mm Mortar is capable of firing high-explosive and smoke rounds to provide suppressing fire and visual cover from indirect fire positions.

FIELD NOTES

A unique weapon introduced in *Battlefield 3* is the support kit's M224 Mortar—the kit's fourth unlock. This is a powerful, indirect fire weapon capable of lobbing high-explosive and smoke rounds great distances. When you first select the weapon, you must find a flat piece of terrain to deploy it. But before setting it down, take into account your surroundings—you're extremely vulnerable while crouched behind this weapon, so find cover in a remote area of the map. Also take into account the direction you want to fire; aim it toward a problematic control point or M-COM station. Once you've found a good spot and have oriented the weapon in the proper direction, set it down and begin firing. At this point, an enlarged minimap appears on the left side of the HUD. You can see friendly (blue) and enemy (red) units spotted by your teammates. The white crosshairs icon placed over the minimap shows you where you're aiming the mortar. Simply place the crosshairs over an enemy target and fire. By default, high-explosive rounds are chosen, but you can switch to smoke by pressing the corresponding button/key shown on the right side of the HUD. Don't expect to score tons of kills with this weapon, but it's great for softening up enemy positions prior to or during an assault on a fixed position. When you're finished firing, don't forget to pick up the mortar before moving on.

[SUPPORT TACTICS]

› With the introduction of the new suppression system, the support class plays a pivotal role in any squad. When playing as support, lay down covering fire while the rest of your squad advances. Even if you can't see the enemy, fire rounds in the area around them to keep their heads down. The support kit's light machine guns have a greater suppressive effect than most firearms, and cause your suppressed opponents to suffer from blurred vision and poor accuracy. If your teammates kill an enemy you suppressed, you get a Suppression Assist bonus worth 50 points.

› The belt-fed light machine guns take a long time to reload, so make sure a teammate has your back while you load fresh rounds into your weapon. At the very least, find an isolated piece of cover before initiating a reload. The magazine-fed weapons (M27 IAR and RPK-74M) have much faster reload times. To prevent frequent reloads, consider equipping the Extended Mag accessory once it's unlocked. This doubles the amount of ammo in each magazine. So, when firing a weapon like the M249 or M240B, you have 200 rounds per magazine instead of 100. This makes a huge difference when laying down suppressive fire.

› Use the light machine guns to target light vehicles like the Growler ITVs and VDV Buggies. The occupants of these vehicles are completely exposed, so it is easy to score a few kills with a prolonged burst. You may even disable the vehicle. Light machine guns can also inflict damage on the HMMWV and the Vodnik. These rapid-firing weapons are also great for shooting down MAVs deployed by enemy recon troops.

› The support kit should never run out of ammo, so don't forget to toss an Ammo Box at your feet if you're running low on ammo, grenades, C4, or Claymores. Also, make sure the recon and engineer players on your team have plenty of ammo. Sniper rifles and rocket launchers run dry quickly, so supplying these players with their own Ammo Box can become quite lucrative in terms of scoring Resupply points.

› When attacking an M-COM station in Rush, plant three C4 charges around the objective before setting the main charge on the station itself. Then seek cover at a distance and set off the charges as your opponents rush in to disarm the M-COM station. Not only does this prevent the objective from being disarmed, it also nets you some easy kills.

› The M224 Mortar is effective only if your team spots targets. Otherwise you'll be firing blind, with no enemy icons appearing on the minimap. The recon kit's T-UGS motion sensor can automatically place targets on the minimap as well. But even when you have enemy icons to shoot at, don't expect to score tons of kills. Like the light machine guns, the mortar is a great suppressive weapon. You're more likely to suppress and injure enemies with this weapon than kill them.

US STARTING LOADOUT

PRIMARY — MK11 MOD 0

SIDEARM — M9

GADGETS — Radio Beacon

SPECIALIZATION: —

RU STARTING LOADOUT

PRIMARY — SVD

SIDEARM — MP443

GADGETS — Radio Beacon

SPECILAIZATION: —

STRENGTHS: Long-range/spotting specialist

WEAKNESSES: Slow-firing; vulnerable in close quarters

The recon class is much more than just a sniper. New equipment like the Radio Beacon, SOFLAM, and MAV put a greater emphasis on team play, allowing the recon player to fill a more supportive role. It's up to the recon class to spot targets for infantry and vehicles, informing teammates of enemy movement and designating targets for laser-guided munitions. But this doesn't mean recon troops can't still crack skulls at long range. The sniper rifles offered by this kit require the greatest amount of skill and patience of any weapon type, and are best reserved for players willing to put in the practice to master them. Unless you score headshots every time, it will take two or three hits to down an opponent. Accuracy and stability can be improved significantly by firing from a prone position with a Bipod.

⊕ Unlock Progression

UNLOCK	NAME	IMAGE	RECON SCORE
1	T-UGS		5,000
2	SV98		13,000
3	SOFLAM		26,000
4	MAV		45,000
5	SKS		71,000
6	M40A5		104,000
7	M98B		146,000
8	MK11 MOD 0 (for RU)		195,000
8	SVD (for US)		195,000

SPECIAL EQUIPMENT

RADIO BEACON

Unlock: Recon Kit Start

Description: The AN-PRC-117F radio allows the recon soldier to deploy an additional squad spawn position. The recon soldier must be part of a squad for this item to function.

FIELD NOTES

Remember the Squad Leader Spawn Beacon (SLSB) from *Battlefield 2142*? Well, the Radio Beacon works the same way, only it's carried by the recon class. Use this device as a forward spawn point for getting your squad back into the action. This is particularly helpful for attackers during Rush matches, allowing squads to spawn close to the objectives. The Radio Beacon can be placed on any flat surface. However, pay close attention to where you're placing it. You don't want to place it anywhere enemy troops can easily spot. Otherwise your spawning squad mates may be killed before they get a chance to defend themselves. So place these devices behind large rocks or other pieces of solid cover that provide both protection and concealment. The Radio Beacon emits a constant beeping sound. Enemies can use this distinct sound to home in on the device and either destroy it or camp it. If your Radio Beacon is being camped, immediately notify your squad, warning them not to spawn on it. You can retrieve the Radio Beacon by interacting with it. Alternately, it can be destroyed with explosives or disabled with the MAV's jamming feature.

T-UGS

Unlock: 5,000 Recon score

Description: The T-UGS (tactical unattended ground sensor) uses motion sensors to detect the presence of vehicles and infantry. The sensor emits an audible beep on detection and can be avoided by moving at low speed.

FIELD NOTES

The T-UGS motion sensor is a great way to keep tabs on enemy movement in high traffic areas, such as around flags in Conquest or near M-COM stations in Rush matches. To deploy this device, you must find a piece of even terrain. An icon of the device appears in front of you when selected. The icon turns green when you're standing over a suitable area—it turns red when standing on rough terrain. Since the device is visible, try to place it in high grass or vegetation to better conceal it from enemy troops. Once deployed, enemy units that move within the motion sensor's detection radius show up on each teammate's minimap to guide units toward hostile intruders. However, enemies can avoid detection by crawling. Like the Radio Beacon, the T-UGS makes a beeping sound, potentially warning enemies of its presence. If you find an enemy T-UGS, you can destroy it with explosives or jam it with a MAV and render it inoperable.

SOFLAM

Unlock: 26,000 Recon score

Description: The AN/PEQ-1 SOFLAM allows the recon soldier to designate enemy vehicles for precision strikes. The SOFLAM is semiautonomous and will designate targets even when unattended.

FIELD NOTES

The SOFLAM (special operations forces laser acquisition marker), unlocked by the recon kit, is a laser target designator. This tripod-mounted device is used to target vehicles for guided munitions fired by IFVs, tanks, helicopters, and jets. Both the Guided Shell and Guided Missile vehicle weapon unlocks rely on the SOFLAM to acquire targets. Once a target is painted with a laser, teammates in vehicles equipped with these guided weapons get an indication on their HUD. At that point, all they have to do is fire and the shell or missile automatically zeros in on the target and scores a hit. While behind the device, you can pan and zoom in on targets at will. But if you leave the SOFLAM behind, it can still acquire targets on its own, but only within a limited viewing arc. So if you leave the SOFLAM behind, point it down a street or other narrow passage that is frequented by enemy vehicles. Unattended SOFLAMs can be destroyed with explosives or jammed by an enemy MAV.

MAV

Unlock: 45,000 Recon score

Description: A remotely operated micro air vehicle equipped with a suite of motion sensors and a camera with IRNV capabilities for aerial reconnaissance.

FIELD NOTES

The MAV is a small unmanned reconnaissance drone deployed by the recon class. It effectively takes the place of the UAV made popular in *Bad Company 2*. While operating the MAV, you're vulnerable to attack, so only deploy this device when you're in a relatively secure area. You must also find a relatively flat piece of terrain from which the MAV can take off. Once activated, the view switches to the MAV's camera, allowing you to control the small vehicle like a small helicopter. Equipped with an infrared camera, the MAV makes it easy to spot enemy troops and vehicles by highlighting their heat signatures, which appear bright white on the black-and-white screen. Using the spotting function, call out the positions of enemies for your teammates. The MAV also has the ability to disable enemy Radio Beacons, T-UGS motion sensors, SOFLAMs, and EOD Bots with its electronic jamming function. But the MAV is very fragile and susceptible to small arms fire. So either keep it high above the battlefield or use trees and hills to mask its location.

[RECON TACTICS]

> Equip the Bipod accessory as soon as you unlock it for your selected sniper rifle. The Bipod stabilizes the rifle, eliminating all lateral and horizontal scope drift. This makes it much easier to engage targets, especially at long range. On bolt-action sniper rifles, the Straight Pull Bolt occupies the same slot as the Bipod, so you must make a tough choice. While the Straight Pull Bolt allows you to view through scope while loading a new round, it does nothing to stabilize the weapon.

> Gravity greatly affects the trajectory of your bullets when sniping, causing each round to drop over distance. At long range, simply placing an enemy's head in your crosshairs isn't enough to score the instant kill. Instead, compensate for range by aiming high, just above the target's head. Use the black mil dots on the scope's vertical crosshair line to gauge proper barrel elevation before gently squeezing the trigger. After scoring a kill or two, move to a new location—the kill cam gives away your sniping spot, so don't wait around for reprisals.

> Choose your sniping location carefully, paying close attention to how you appear to enemy snipers. To avoid presenting your enemies with a clearly defined silhouette, avoid sniping from rooftops and the crests of hills. Instead, snipe from lower elevations, using bushes and other objects behind you to break up your visible outline. If you must snipe from a high elevation, make sure you have adequate cover and concealment, as you're likely to draw plenty of attention in such a predictable spot. And always drop prone. This not only reduces your chances of being spotted, but it also increases accuracy and stability.

> You'll never capture a flag or destroy an M-COM station by sniping. The powerful sniper rifles make the recon class extremely popular. But a well-rounded squad should never have more than one recon soldier. While the recon class is great for long-range combat, the other classes are better suited for taking and holding ground.

> The recon kit isn't restricted to using sniper rifles. Consider equipping a shotgun or PDW for better close-quarters performance. This is a great way to boost your recon score if your sniping skills are lacking. If you prefer keeping a sniper rifle, always switch to your pistol before moving around for quicker close-range target acquisition and rate of fire. If playing in a match with friendly jets and helicopters, take it upon yourself to serve as the team's spotter. Using the high-powered scopes attached to the sniper rifles, it's easy to zoom in on distant enemy troops and vehicles and spot them for your teammates. The MAV and SOFLAM are equally effective for spotting and designating targets for destruction. Due to their high speeds, aircraft have a tough time identifying ground targets. Spotting enemies greatly enhances their ability to identify and target enemy units.

[RECON SERVICE STARS]

You earn a service star for every 195,000 points you score with the recon class. 100 support service stars are available.

WEAPONS

Throughout the course of your multiplayer career you have access to a variety of weapons. In *Battlefield 3*, every primary weapon has its own unlock progression, allowing you to equip new accessories such as scopes and rail attachments. For a complete list of every weapon accessory, see the table below. No two weapons are exactly the same, so get to know them and select ones that best reflect your style of play.

Weapon Accessories

IMAGE	NAME	DESCRIPTION
OPTICS		
	ACOG (4x)	The Advanced Combat Optic Gunsight is a medium-speed, medium-range scope that magnifies at 4x. A ballistic reticle makes gauging bullet drop at longer ranges easier.
	Ballistic (12x)	The Ballistic Scope's 12x magnification allows for the greatest accuracy for extremely long-range engagements. Ballistic Scope reflections can reveal your position when aimed at enemies.
	Holographic (HOLO)	A Holographic Sight provides a fast, open sighting picture for mid- to close-range engagements. The reticle features a circle and dot configuration.
	IRNV (IR 1x)	An IR Enhanced Night Vision Scope for low- and no-light situations, the IRNV scope can be steadied by holding the sprint button when aimed, or by using a Bipod.
	KOBRA (RDS)	Russian Red Dot Sight used by military and police organizations on AK-style mounts, adapted to fit standard accessory rails; features a single red dot reticle.
	M145 (3.4x)	Originally developed for the Canadian Army, the M145 is commonly mounted on the M240 and M249 with a 3.4x zoom. A ballistic reticle helps with longer range engagements.
	PK-A (3.4x)	Common Russian mid-range scope for AK and Saiga-style receivers with a chevron reticle and 3.4x zoom; faster aiming than the PSO-1 with less zoom.
	PKA-S (HOLO)	Russian advanced Holographic Sight featuring a circle and dot reticle for fast sighting. Great for mid- to close-range engagements with an open sight picture.
	PKS-07 (7x)	A Russian high magnification 7x scope with ballistic reticle. The PKS-07 can be steadied by holding the sprint button when aimed, or by using a Bipod. PKS-07 scope reflections can reveal your position when aimed at enemies.
	PSO-1 (4x)	Standard-issue Russian medium-speed, medium-range scope with a 4x magnification originally developed for the SVD; adapted to fit on standard rails with a ballistic reticle.
	Reflex (RDS)	American made Red Dot Sight for extremely fast and clear target acquisition in close quarters. The single red dot in this sight makes getting on target easy.
	Rifle Scope (6x)	A high-magnification 6x scope available for most rifles, the Rifle Scope can be steadied by holding the sprint button when aimed, or by using a Bipod, but can reveal your position when aimed at enemies.
	Rifle Scope (8x)	A high-magnification 8x scope available for sniper rifles, the Rifle Scope can be steadied by holding the sprint button when aimed, or by using a Bipod, but can reveal your position when aimed at enemies.
PRIMARY & SECONDARY ATTACHMENTS		
	Bipod	Bipods allow the shooter to support their gun on flat horizontal surfaces, or when prone to gain an increased accuracy and reduced recoil. By default, aiming will enter supported shooting.
	Extended Mag	Extended Magazines increase the total amount of bullets in each magazine, giving more shots before you need to reload.
	Flash Suppressor	The Flash Suppressor hides muzzle flash but has no effect on sound. Flash Suppressors decrease aimed and automatic accuracy.
	Foregrip	A Foregrip decreases the amount of horizontal muzzle drift when firing a weapon, giving better control over long bursts. Vertical muzzle climb is not affected.
	Heavy Barrel	A Heavy Barrel gives greater accuracy for aimed fire, but increases the total vertical muzzle climb due to the use of heavy match ammunition. Match rounds do not increase the overall damage of the weapon.
	Laser Sight	The Laser Sight adds a visible laser aiming dot to the weapon, which increases accuracy from the hip. The Laser Sight can dazzle enemies when turned on, but also reveals your position.
	Straight Pull Bolt	A Straight Pull Bolt allows the recon soldier to chamber another round in his bolt-action sniper rifle without having to first zoom out.
	Suppressor	A Sound Suppressor significantly reduces the sound signature and eliminates muzzle flash. However, the cold-loaded ammunition used by Suppressed weapons travels slower and does less damage at long range.
	Tactical Light	A Tactical Light lights up the dark environments with white light. In close quarters, the Tactical Light can disorient and temporarily blind others, but can also reveal your position.
SPECIAL AMMO		
	12G Flechette	Flechette rounds have increased penetration ability but a reduced damage potential compared to buckshot.
	12G Slug	SABOT Slug rounds fire a single fin-stabilized projectile for longer range than standard shot. Slugs are not accurate at extreme ranges, and have less stopping power in CQB than standard buckshot.
	12G Frag	An advanced explosive round, Frag rounds provides enhanced suppression but lack accuracy or stopping power.
	40MM SHG	The 40mm Flechette round fires tungsten steel darts for excellent close-combat lethality and penetration ability, but lacks damage at long range.
	40MM SMK	40mm Smoke rounds provide visual screening and prevent soldiers and vehicles in the smoke's effect range from being spotted or laser designated for a short time.

ASSAULT RIFLES

Assault rifles are the most versatile primary weapon available, useful in a variety of situations. All assault rifles can be equipped with a grenade launcher, offering even more firepower that is capable of knocking down walls and damaging light-skinned vehicles. An underslung shotgun attachment is also available. These rifles can only be accessed by the assault kit. Continue playing as the assault kit to boost your assault score and lead to more assault rifle unlocks.

M16A4

AMMO: 5.56x45mm NATO

RATE OF FIRE: 800 rpm

MAGAZINE CAPACITY: 30

UNLOCK: Assault Start (US)/220,000 Assault score (RU)

Fire Modes		
SINGLE-SHOT	X
BURST	X
AUTOMATIC	X

The fourth generation of M16 is equipped with a removable carry handle, a RIS (rail interface system) for mounting accessories, and is capable of automatic, 3-round burst, and semiautomatic fire. The original flaws of the M16 design have all but been eliminated and the AR15 platform upon which it is built is the standard rifle of the USMC. With low recoil and a high rate of fire, the M16 is a good medium-range weapon.

Unlock Progression

IMAGE	ACCESSORY	SLOT	KILLS	IMAGE	ACCESSORY	SLOT	KILLS
	ACOG (4x)	Optics	10		IRNV (IR 1x)	Optics	100
	Heavy Barrel	Secondary	20		Rifle Scope (6x)	Optics	125
	Foregrip	Underslung Rail	30		M145 (3.4x)	Optics	150
	Tactical Light	Secondary	40		Flash Suppressor	Secondary	175
	Reflex (RDS)	Optics	50		PSO-1 (4x)	Optics	200
	Bipod	Underslung Rail	60		KOBRA (RDS)	Optics	235
	Suppressor	Secondary	70		PKA-S (HOLO)	Optics	270
	Holographic (HOLO)	Optics	80		PKS-07 (7x)	Optics	300
	Laser Sight	Secondary	90		PKA-A (3.4x)	Optics	350

AK-74M

AMMO: 5.45x39mm WP

RATE OF FIRE: 650 rpm

MAGAZINE CAPACITY: 30

UNLOCK: Assault Start (RU)/220,000 Assault score (US)

Fire Modes		
SINGLE-SHOT	X
BURST	
AUTOMATIC	X

The AK-74M is the latest modernized version of the classic AK-47. Fielded as the standard assault rifle by the Russian Army, the M variant includes a side-folding polymer stock and a scope mount rail on the left side of the weapon. Recent developments allow the AK series of weapons to field many of the accessories typically seen on Western guns. The AK-74M is a reliable and rugged medium-range weapon.

Unlock Progression

IMAGE	ACCESSORY	SLOT	KILLS	IMAGE	ACCESSORY	SLOT	KILLS
	PSO-1 (4x)	Optics	10		IRNV (IR 1x)	Optics	100
	Heavy Barrel	Secondary	20		PKS-07 (7x)	Optics	125
	Foregrip	Underslung Rail	30		PKA-A (3.4x)	Optics	150
	Tactical Light	Secondary	40		Flash Suppressor	Secondary	175
	KOBRA (RDS)	Optics	50		ACOG (4x)	Optics	200
	Bipod	Underslung Rail	60		Reflex (RDS)	Optics	235
	Suppressor	Secondary	70		Holographic (HOLO)	Optics	270
	PKA-S (HOLO)	Optics	80		Rifle Scope (6x)	Optics	300
	Laser Sight	Secondary	90		M145 (3.4x)	Optics	350

M320

AMMO: 40mm HE

RATE OF FIRE: N/A

MAGAZINE CAPACITY: 1

UNLOCK: 11,000 Assault score

Fire Modes
- SINGLE-SHOT ☒
- BURST
- AUTOMATIC

A single-shot 40mm grenade launcher, the M320 replaced the old M203 in service with the US military. Initially developed for the G36 assault rifle, the M320 allows a larger variety of ammunition to be used with the weapon, including Fragmentation, Flechette, and Smoke rounds. The M320 can be equipped on some assault rifles with the Underslung Rail.

Unlock Progression

IMAGE	ACCESSORY	SLOT	KILLS	IMAGE	ACCESSORY	SLOT	KILLS
	40mm SHG	Ammo	10		40mm SMK	Ammo	20

M416

AMMO: 5.56x45mm NATO

RATE OF FIRE: 750 rpm

MAGAZINE CAPACITY: 30

UNLOCK: 22,000 Assault score

Fire Modes
- SINGLE-SHOT ☒
- BURST ☒
- AUTOMATIC ☒

The M416 was developed by a famous German weapons manufacturer as a more reliable version of the classic M16. The weapon is essentially a fusion of the M16 and the G36 assault rifles. The M416 is reliable and accurate, with a moderate recoil and rate of fire that make an effective all-around weapon.

Unlock Progression

IMAGE	ACCESSORY	SLOT	KILLS	IMAGE	ACCESSORY	SLOT	KILLS
	ACOG (4x)	Optics	10		IRNV (IR 1x)	Optics	100
	Heavy Barrel	Secondary	20		Rifle Scope (6x)	Optics	125
	Foregrip	Underslung Rail	30		M145 (3.4x)	Optics	150
	Tactical Light	Secondary	40		Flash Suppressor	Secondary	175
	Reflex (RDS)	Optics	50		PSO-1 (4x)	Optics	200
	Bipod	Underslung Rail	60		KOBRA (RDS)	Optics	235
	Suppressor	Secondary	70		PKA-S (HOLO)	Optics	270
	Holographic (HOLO)	Optics	80		PKS-07 (7x)	Optics	300
	Laser Sight	Secondary	90		PKA-A (3.4x)	Optics	350

[WEAPON SERVICE STARS]

Weapon service stars are awarded for all weapons. You earn a service star for every 100 kills you score with a specific weapon. A maximum of 100 service stars can be earned for each weapon.

M26 MASS

AMMO: 12G Buckshot
RATE OF FIRE: Semi-Auto
MAGAZINE CAPACITY: 5
UNLOCK: 38,000 Assault score

Fire Modes	
SINGLE-SHOT	[x]
BURST	
AUTOMATIC	

The M26 Lightweight Shotgun System was developed to replace older, more cumbersome breaching shotguns. Available as a standalone shotgun, or capable of being mounted on some assault rifles with Underslung Rails, the M26 is able to fire Buckshot, Flechette, Frag, and Slug rounds.

Unlock Progression

IMAGE	ACCESSORY	SLOT	KILLS	IMAGE	ACCESSORY	SLOT	KILLS
	12G Frag	Ammo	10		12G Slug	Ammo	30
	12G Flechette	Ammo	20				

AEK-971

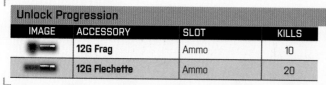

AMMO: 5.45x39mm WP
RATE OF FIRE: 750 rpm
MAGAZINE CAPACITY: 30
UNLOCK: 60,000 Assault score

Fire Modes	
SINGLE-SHOT	[x]
BURST	[x]
AUTOMATIC	[x]

The AEK-971 was developed as a possible successor to the AK-74 series of assault rifles and features a unique recoil reduction system. The AEK-971's high rate of fire makes it excellent in close quarters but difficult to control. Shooters should switch to semi-automatic or the included 3-round burst mode for longer ranges.

Unlock Progression

IMAGE	ACCESSORY	SLOT	KILLS	IMAGE	ACCESSORY	SLOT	KILLS
	PSO-1 (4x)	Optics	10		IRNV (IR 1x)	Optics	100
	Heavy Barrel	Secondary	20		PKS-07 (7x)	Optics	125
	Foregrip	Underslung Rail	30		PKA-A (3.4x)	Optics	150
	Tactical Light	Secondary	40		Flash Suppressor	Secondary	175
	KOBRA (RDS)	Optics	50		ACOG (4x)	Optics	200
	Bipod	Underslung Rail	60		Reflex (RDS)	Optics	235
	Suppressor	Secondary	70		Holographic (HOLO)	Optics	270
	PKA-S (HOLO)	Optics	80		Rifle Scope (6x)	Optics	300
	Laser Sight	Secondary	90		M145 (3.4x)	Optics	350

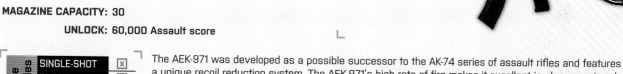

M16A3

AMMO: 5.56x45mm NATO

RATE OF FIRE: 800 rpm

MAGAZINE CAPACITY: 30

UNLOCK: 89,000 Assault score

Fire Modes	
SINGLE-SHOT	[X]
BURST	
AUTOMATIC	[X]

The third generation of M16A3 has been upgraded with a RIS (rail interface system) for mounting accessories and is capable of automatic and semi-automatic fire. Available to frontline units engaged in urban combat, the M16A3's low recoil makes for a capable all-around weapon.

Unlock Progression

IMAGE	ACCESSORY	SLOT	KILLS	IMAGE	ACCESSORY	SLOT	KILLS
	ACOG (4x)	Optics	10		IRNV (IR 1x)	Optics	100
	Heavy Barrel	Secondary	20		Rifle Scope (6x)	Optics	125
	Foregrip	Underslung Rail	30		M145 (3.4x)	Optics	150
	Tactical Light	Secondary	40		Flash Suppressor	Secondary	175
	Reflex (RDS)	Optics	50		PSO-1 (4x)	Optics	200
	Bipod	Underslung Rail	60		KOBRA (RDS)	Optics	235
	Suppressor	Secondary	70		PKA-S (HOLO)	Optics	270
	Holographic (HOLO)	Optics	80		PKS-07 (7x)	Optics	300
	Laser Sight	Secondary	90		PKA-A (3.4x)	Optics	350

F2000

AMMO: 5.56x45mm NATO

RATE OF FIRE: 850 rpm

MAGAZINE CAPACITY: 30

UNLOCK: 124,000 Assault score

Fire Modes	
SINGLE-SHOT	[X]
BURST	
AUTOMATIC	[X]

A Belgian manufactured bullpup assault rifle configured in the tactical setup with top and forward rails for mounting a variety of accessories. The rifle is in use with a variety of Special Forces units including Pakistani, Peruvian, Chilean, Indian and Polish. It has also been adapted as the standard rifle of Saudi Arabia and Slovenia. The bullpup configuration prevents it from mounting underslung weapons, but a high fire rate makes it lethal in CQB.

Unlock Progression

IMAGE	ACCESSORY	SLOT	KILLS	IMAGE	ACCESSORY	SLOT	KILLS
	ACOG (4x)	Optics	10		IRNV (IR 1x)	Optics	100
	Heavy Barrel	Secondary	20		Rifle Scope (6x)	Optics	125
	Foregrip	Underslung Rail	30		M145 (3.4x)	Optics	150
	Tactical Light	Secondary	40		Flash Suppressor	Secondary	175
	Reflex (RDS)	Optics	50		PSO-1 (4x)	Optics	200
	Bipod	Underslung Rail	60		KOBRA (RDS)	Optics	235
	Suppressor	Secondary	70		PKA-S (HOLO)	Optics	270
	Holographic (HOLO)	Optics	80		PKS-07 (7x)	Optics	300
	Laser Sight	Secondary	90		PKA-A (3.4x)	Optics	350

AN-94

AMMO: 5.45x39mm WP

RATE OF FIRE: 600 rpm

MAGAZINE CAPACITY: 30

UNLOCK: 166,000 Assault score

Fire Modes	
SINGLE-SHOT	
BURST	☒
AUTOMATIC	☒

In service with elite Russian forces, the AN-94 offers a unique, highly accurate, 2-round burst feature. Compared to the standard AK series, the AN-94 requires a significantly higher degree of training. A skilled shooter can effectively engage targets at a longer range than typical assault rifles.

Unlock Progression

IMAGE	ACCESSORY	SLOT	KILLS	IMAGE	ACCESSORY	SLOT	KILLS
	PSO-1 (4x)	Optics	10		IRNV (IR 1x)	Optics	100
	Heavy Barrel	Secondary	20		PKS-07 (7x)	Optics	125
	Foregrip	Underslung Rail	30		PKA-A (3.4x)	Optics	150
	Tactical Light	Secondary	40		Flash Suppressor	Secondary	175
	KOBRA (RDS)	Optics	50		ACOG (4x)	Optics	200
	Bipod	Underslung Rail	60		Reflex (RDS)	Optics	235
	Suppressor	Secondary	70		Holographic (HOLO)	Optics	270
	PKA-S (HOLO)	Optics	80		Rifle Scope (6x)	Optics	300
	Laser Sight	Secondary	90		M145 (3.4x)	Optics	350

KH2002

AMMO: 5.56x45mm NATO

RATE OF FIRE: 850 rpm

MAGAZINE CAPACITY: 30

UNLOCK: 126,000 Co-Op score

Fire Modes	
SINGLE-SHOT	☒
BURST	☒
AUTOMATIC	

This Iranian developed assault rifle is essentially a bullpup conversion of the M16. The KH2002 is intended to replace the G3 in service with the Iranian armed forces, though there is speculation that it may be years before the rifle is ready for full deployment. The KH2002's short length lends itself well to close combat, but prevents it from mounting any underslung weapons.

Unlock Progression

IMAGE	ACCESSORY	SLOT	KILLS	IMAGE	ACCESSORY	SLOT	KILLS
	PSO-1 (4x)	Optics	10		IRNV (IR 1x)	Optics	100
	Heavy Barrel	Secondary	20		PKS-07 (7x)	Optics	125
	Foregrip	Underslung Rail	30		PKA-A (3.4x)	Optics	150
	Tactical Light	Secondary	40		Flash Suppressor	Secondary	175
	KOBRA (RDS)	Optics	50		ACOG (4x)	Optics	200
	Bipod	Underslung Rail	60		Reflex (RDS)	Optics	235
	Suppressor	Secondary	70		Holographic (HOLO)	Optics	270
	PKA-S (HOLO)	Optics	80		Rifle Scope (6x)	Optics	300
	Laser Sight	Secondary	90		M145 (3.4x)	Optics	350

G3A3

AMMO: Ammo: 7.62x51mm NATO

RATE OF FIRE: Rate of Fire: 500 rpm

MAGAZINE CAPACITY: Magazine Capacity: 20

UNLOCK: Unlock: 441,000 Co-Op score

Fire Modes

SINGLE-SHOT	☒
BURST	
AUTOMATIC	☒

The G3 rifle is one of the most widely fielded assault rifles in the world. Multiple versions of the G3 exist, and it has been used in countries around the world, including Sweden where it was known as the AK4. This particular G3 is the A3 variant, with a fixed stock. The long barrel and firing heavy 7.62x51mm NATO rounds enable the G3A3 to reach longer ranges than most other assault rifles, but at the cost of heavy recoil.

Unlock Progression

IMAGE	ACCESSORY	SLOT	KILLS	IMAGE	ACCESSORY	SLOT	KILLS
	ACOG (4x)	Optics	10		IRNV (IR 1x)	Optics	100
	Heavy Barrel	Secondary	20		Rifle Scope (6x)	Optics	125
	Foregrip	Underslung Rail	30		M145 (3.4x)	Optics	150
	Tactical Light	Secondary	40		Flash Suppressor	Secondary	175
	Reflex (RDS)	Optics	50		PSO-1 (4x)	Optics	200
	Bipod	Underslung Rail	60		KOBRA (RDS)	Optics	235
	Suppressor	Secondary	70		PKA-S (HOLO)	Optics	270
	Holographic (HOLO)	Optics	80		PKS-07 (7x)	Optics	300
	Laser Sight	Secondary	90		PKA-A (3.4x)	Optics	350

CARBINES

Carbines bridge the gap between assault rifles and submachine guns; they are ideal for a variety of combat situations. Their compact design makes them easy to maneuver in tight quarters. The shorter barrel length mean less muzzle velocity, accuracy, and range than their assault rifle counterparts, But they still have the stopping power to take down opponents quickly. The carbines are available to only the engineer class. So rack up your engineer score to unlock more carbines.

M4A1

AMMO: 5.56x45mm NATO

RATE OF FIRE: 800 rpm

MAGAZINE CAPACITY: 30

UNLOCK: Engineer Start (US)/145,000 Engineer score (RU)

Fire Modes

SINGLE-SHOT	☒
BURST	
AUTOMATIC	☒

Essentially a shortened version of the M16, the M4A1 carbine traces its roots to weapons designed for US Special Operations Command (SOCOM) during the Vietnam War. The M4A1 variant is capable of automatic fire and includes rails that allow the user to equip a large number of accessories. The carbine has seen heavy use at the front lines of Iraq and Afghanistan in close quarters and urban environments.

Unlock Progression

IMAGE	ACCESSORY	SLOT	KILLS	IMAGE	ACCESSORY	SLOT	KILLS
	Reflex (RDS)	Optics	10		IRNV (IR 1x)	Optics	100
	Laser Sight	Secondary	20		Rifle Scope (6x)	Optics	125
	Foregrip	Primary	30		M145 (3.4x)	Optics	150
	Tactical Light	Secondary	40		Flash Suppressor	Secondary	175
	Holographic (HOLO)	Optics	50		KOBRA (RDS)	Optics	200
	Suppressor	Secondary	60		PKA-S (HOLO)	Optics	235
	ACOG (4x)	Optics	70		PSO-1 (4x)	Optics	270
	Heavy Barrel	Secondary	80		PKS-07 (7x)	Optics	300
	Bipod	Primary	90		PKA-A (3.4x)	Optics	350

AKS-74U

AMMO: 5.45x39mm WP

RATE OF FIRE: 650 rpm

MAGAZINE CAPACITY: 30

UNLOCK: Engineer Start (RU)/145,000 Engineer score (RU)

Fire Modes
SINGLE-SHOT	X
BURST	
AUTOMATIC	X

Derived from the AKS-74, the AKS-74u is a shortened carbine with the power of a rifle cartridge but the size of a submachine gun. Often called by its nickname "Krinkov," the shortened barrel makes the weapon inaccurate at medium ranges but extremely effective in close quarters. Due to its incredibly short length, the AKS-74u cannot mount a Bipod.

Unlock Progression

IMAGE	ACCESSORY	SLOT	KILLS	IMAGE	ACCESSORY	SLOT	KILLS
	KOBRA (RDS)	Optics	10		PKS-07 (7x)	Optics	100
	Laser Sight	Secondary	20		IRNV (IR 1x)	Optics	125
	Foregrip	Primary	30		Rifle Scope (6x)	Optics	150
	PKA-A (3.4x)	Optics	40		M145 (3.4x)	Optics	175
	Tactical Light	Secondary	50		Flash Suppressor	Secondary	200
	PKA-S (HOLO)	Optics	60		Reflex (RDS)	Optics	235
	Suppressor	Secondary	70		Holographic (HOLO)	Optics	270
	PSO-1 (4x)	Optics	80		ACOG (4x)	Optics	300
	Heavy Barrel	Secondary	90				

SCAR-H

AMMO: 7.62x51mm NATO

RATE OF FIRE: 600 rpm

MAGAZINE CAPACITY: 20

UNLOCK: 14,000 Engineer score

Fire Modes
SINGLE-SHOT	X
BURST	
AUTOMATIC	X

Developed for the US SOCOM, the SCAR is a modular series of weapons available in multiple interchangeable calibers, barrel lengths, and configurations. This particular model has been configured as a SCAR-H CQB (SCAR-Heavy Close Quarters Battle), with a shortened barrel and is chambered for the hard-hitting 7.62mm NATO round. This gives the SCAR-H a greater range than typical Carbines at the expense of some serious recoil.

Unlock Progression

IMAGE	ACCESSORY	SLOT	KILLS	IMAGE	ACCESSORY	SLOT	KILLS
	Reflex (RDS)	Optics	10		IRNV (IR 1x)	Optics	100
	Laser Sight	Secondary	20		Rifle Scope (6x)	Optics	125
	Foregrip	Primary	30		M145 (3.4x)	Optics	150
	Tactical Light	Secondary	40		Flash Suppressor	Secondary	175
	Holographic (HOLO)	Optics	50		KOBRA (RDS)	Optics	200
	Suppressor	Secondary	60		PKA-S (HOLO)	Optics	235
	ACOG (4x)	Optics	70		PSO-1 (4x)	Optics	270
	Heavy Barrel	Secondary	80		PKS-07 (7x)	Optics	300
	Bipod	Primary	90		PKA-A (3.4x)	Optics	350

M4

AMMO: 5.56x45mm NATO

RATE OF FIRE: 800 rpm

MAGAZINE CAPACITY: 30

UNLOCK: 40,000 Engineer score

Fire Modes: SINGLE-SHOT [X] / BURST [X] / AUTOMATIC

Visually and mechanically similar to the M16, the M4 carbine was developed to replace pistols and submachine guns at the front lines. The M4 is capable of semi-automatic and 3-round burst fire and is equipped with accessory rails for end user customization. The rifle has largely replaced the M16A2 previously used by the US Marine Corps.

Unlock Progression

IMAGE	ACCESSORY	SLOT	KILLS	IMAGE	ACCESSORY	SLOT	KILLS
	Reflex (RDS)	Optics	10		IRNV (IR 1x)	Optics	100
	Laser Sight	Secondary	20		Rifle Scope (6x)	Optics	125
	Foregrip	Primary	30		M145 (3.4x)	Optics	150
	Tactical Light	Secondary	40		Flash Suppressor	Secondary	175
	Holographic (HOLO)	Optics	50		KOBRA (RDS)	Optics	200
	Suppressor	Secondary	60		PKA-S (HOLO)	Optics	235
	ACOG (4x)	Optics	70		PSO-1 (4x)	Optics	270
	Heavy Barrel	Secondary	80		PKS-07 (7x)	Optics	300
	Bipod	Primary	90		PKA-A (3.4x)	Optics	350

A-91

AMMO: 5.56x45mm NATO

RATE OF FIRE: 800 rpm

MAGAZINE CAPACITY: 30

UNLOCK: 58,000 Engineer score

Fire Modes: SINGLE-SHOT [X] / BURST / AUTOMATIC [X]

An unusual weapon, even by Russian standards, the A-91 is a bullpup carbine chambered for the 5.56mm NATO round, instead of a Russian caliber. Made from polymers, it features a forward shell ejection system that keeps shells well clear of the shooter's face upon ejection. The bullpup configuration prevents the A-91 from mounting a bipod.

Unlock Progression

IMAGE	ACCESSORY	SLOT	KILLS	IMAGE	ACCESSORY	SLOT	KILLS
	KOBRA (RDS)	Optics	10		PKS-07 (7x)	Optics	100
	Laser Sight	Secondary	20		IRNV (IR 1x)	Optics	125
	Foregrip	Primary	30		Rifle Scope (6x)	Optics	150
	PKA-A (3.4x)	Optics	40		M145 (3.4x)	Optics	175
	Tactical Light	Secondary	50		Flash Suppressor	Secondary	200
	PKA-S (HOLO)	Optics	60		Reflex (RDS)	Optics	235
	Suppressor	Secondary	70		Holographic (HOLO)	Optics	270
	PSO-1 (4x)	Optics	80		ACOG (4x)	Optics	300
	Heavy Barrel	Secondary	90				

G36C

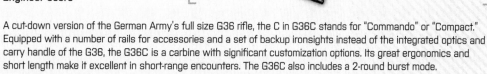

AMMO: 5.56x45mm NATO

RATE OF FIRE: 750 rpm

MAGAZINE CAPACITY: 30

UNLOCK: 110,000 Engineer score

Fire Modes	
SINGLE-SHOT	[X]
BURST	[X]
AUTOMATIC	[X]

A cut-down version of the German Army's full size G36 rifle, the C in G36C stands for "Commando" or "Compact." Equipped with a number of rails for accessories and a set of backup ironsights instead of the integrated optics and carry handle of the G36, the G36C is a carbine with significant customization options. Its great ergonomics and short length make it excellent in short-range encounters. The G36C also includes a 2-round burst mode.

Unlock Progression

IMAGE	ACCESSORY	SLOT	KILLS	IMAGE	ACCESSORY	SLOT	KILLS
	Reflex (RDS)	Optics	10		IRNV (IR 1x)	Optics	100
	Laser Sight	Secondary	20		Rifle Scope (6x)	Optics	125
	Foregrip	Primary	30		M145 (3.4x)	Optics	150
	Tactical Light	Secondary	40		Flash Suppressor	Secondary	175
	Holographic (HOLO)	Optics	50		KOBRA (RDS)	Optics	200
	Suppressor	Secondary	60		PKA-S (HOLO)	Optics	235
	ACOG (4x)	Optics	70		PSO-1 (4x)	Optics	270
	Heavy Barrel	Secondary	80		PKS-07 (7x)	Optics	300
	Bipod	Primary	90		PKA-A (3.4x)	Optics	350

SG553

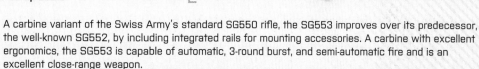

AMMO: 5.56x45mm NATO

RATE OF FIRE: 700 rpm

MAGAZINE CAPACITY: 30

UNLOCK: 378,000 Co-Op score

Fire Modes	
SINGLE-SHOT	[X]
BURST	[X]
AUTOMATIC	[X]

A carbine variant of the Swiss Army's standard SG550 rifle, the SG553 improves over its predecessor, the well-known SG552, by including integrated rails for mounting accessories. A carbine with excellent ergonomics, the SG553 is capable of automatic, 3-round burst, and semi-automatic fire and is an excellent close-range weapon.

Unlock Progression

IMAGE	ACCESSORY	SLOT	KILLS	IMAGE	ACCESSORY	SLOT	KILLS
	Reflex (RDS)	Optics	10		IRNV (IR 1x)	Optics	100
	Laser Sight	Secondary	20		Rifle Scope (6x)	Optics	125
	Foregrip	Primary	30		M145 (3.4x)	Optics	150
	Tactical Light	Secondary	40		Flash Suppressor	Secondary	175
	Holographic (HOLO)	Optics	50		KOBRA (RDS)	Optics	200
	Suppressor	Secondary	60		PKA-S (HOLO)	Optics	235
	ACOG (4x)	Optics	70		PSO-1 (4x)	Optics	270
	Heavy Barrel	Secondary	80		PKS-07 (7x)	Optics	300
	Bipod	Primary	90		PKA-A (3.4x)	Optics	350

LIGHT MACHINE GUNS

When it comes to laying down high volumes of fire, few weapons are as effective as the light machine guns. Thanks to their large magazine capacities and high rates of fire, these hulking weapons can fire long bursts of automatic fire, sending your opponents diving for cover. This is the support kit's primary weapon, ideal for suppressing opponents. Continue playing as the support class to unlock new light machine guns. All light machine guns come equipped with a Bipod for greater stability while firing automatic bursts.

M27 IAR

AMMO: 5.56x45mm NATO

RATE OF FIRE: 750 rpm

MAGAZINE CAPACITY: 45

UNLOCK: Support Start (US)/170,000 Support score (RU)

Fire Modes
SINGLE-SHOT	☒
BURST	
AUTOMATIC	☒

This beefed-up M416 entered service alongside the M249 in the Marine Corps in 2011. The M27 infantry automatic rifle (IAR) features a heavier, longer barrel and an extended magazine to enable greater amounts of suppressive fire while retaining some of the mobility of a standard M416. The M27 features a Bipod by default for supported shooting.

Unlock Progression

IMAGE	ACCESSORY	SLOT	KILLS	IMAGE	ACCESSORY	SLOT	KILLS
	Holographic (HOLO)	Optics	10		ACOG (4x)	Optics	90
	Laser Sight	Secondary	20		IRNV (IR 1x)	Optics	100
	Foregrip	Primary	30		Rifle Scope (6x)	Optics	125
	Tactical Light	Secondary	40		PKA-S (HOLO)	Optics	150
	M145 (3.4x)	Optics	50		PKA-A (3.4x)	Optics	175
	Flash Suppressor	Secondary	60		KOBRA (RDS)	Optics	200
	Reflex (RDS)	Optics	70		PSO-1 (4x)	Optics	235
	Suppressor	Secondary	80		PKS-07 (7x)	Optics	270

RPK-74M

AMMO: 5.45x39mm WP

RATE OF FIRE: 600 rpm

MAGAZINE CAPACITY: 45

UNLOCK: Support Start (RU)/170,000 Support score (US)

Fire Modes
SINGLE-SHOT	☒
BURST	
AUTOMATIC	☒

The RPK-74M is an improved version of the original RPK developed in the 1950s. Essentially a heavy-barreled AK-74, the RPK fires from a longer magazine and has been equipped with polymer furniture to lighten the weapon. The RPK-74M also features the same scope mount as the AK-74M and is equipped with a Bipod by default for supported shooting.

Unlock Progression

IMAGE	ACCESSORY	SLOT	KILLS	IMAGE	ACCESSORY	SLOT	KILLS
	PKA-S (HOLO)	Optics	10		PSO-1 (4x)	Optics	90
	Laser Sight	Secondary	20		IRNV (IR 1x)	Optics	100
	Foregrip	Primary	30		PKS-07 (7x)	Optics	125
	Tactical Light	Secondary	40		Holographic (HOLO)	Optics	150
	PKA-A (3.4x)	Optics	50		M145 (3.4x)	Optics	175
	Flash Suppressor	Secondary	60		Reflex (RDS)	Optics	200
	KOBRA (RDS)	Optics	70		ACOG (4x)	Optics	235
	Suppressor	Secondary	80		Rifle Scope (6x)	Optics	270

M249

AMMO: 5.56x45mm NATO
RATE OF FIRE: 800 rpm
MAGAZINE CAPACITY: 100
UNLOCK: 11,000 Support score

Fire Modes	
SINGLE-SHOT	
BURST	
AUTOMATIC	☒

An adapted version of the Belgian original, the M249 was modified to conform to the United States' design requirements. The M249 has seen action in every major conflict since the 1989 invasion of Panama and has earned a reputation as a reliable weapon. A single M249 can supply suppressive fire equivalent to 15 riflemen. The M249 comes equipped with a Bipod for supported shooting by default.

Unlock Progression

IMAGE	ACCESSORY	SLOT	KILLS	IMAGE	ACCESSORY	SLOT	KILLS
	M145 (3.4x)	Optics	10		Suppressor	Secondary	90
	Flash Suppressor	Secondary	20		IRNV (IR 1x)	Optics	100
	Extended Mag	Primary	30		ACOG (4x)	Optics	125
	Tactical Light	Secondary	40		PKA-A (3.4x)	Optics	150
	Holographic (HOLO)	Optics	50		PKA-S (HOLO)	Optics	175
	Foregrip	Primary	60		KOBRA (RDS)	Optics	200
	Laser Sight	Secondary	70		PSO-1 (4x)	Optics	235
	Reflex (RDS)	Optics	80				

PKP PECHENEG

AMMO: 7.62x54mm R
RATE OF FIRE: 650 rpm
MAGAZINE CAPACITY: 100
UNLOCK: 60,000 Support score

Fire Modes	
SINGLE-SHOT	
BURST	
AUTOMATIC	☒

Another modernization of a traditional Russian weapon, the PKP Pecheneg replaces the PKM machine gun in service with Spetsnaz units. Firing a heavier round than the RPK-74M the Pecheneg is able to supply greater suppressive fire, thanks to its greater power and belt feed. The Pecheneg comes equipped with a Bipod for supported shooting by default.

Unlock Progression

IMAGE	ACCESSORY	SLOT	KILLS	IMAGE	ACCESSORY	SLOT	KILLS
	PKA-S (HOLO)	Optics	10		Suppressor	Secondary	90
	Flash Suppressor	Secondary	20		IRNV (IR 1x)	Optics	100
	Extended Mag	Primary	30		PSO-1 (4x)	Optics	125
	Tactical Light	Secondary	40		M145 (3.4x)	Optics	150
	PKA-A (3.4x)	Optics	50		Holographic (HOLO)	Optics	175
	Foregrip	Primary	60		Reflex (RDS)	Optics	200
	Laser Sight	Secondary	70		ACOG (4x)	Optics	235
	KOBRA (RDS)	Optics	80				

M240B

AMMO: 7.62x51mm NATO

RATE OF FIRE: 750 rpm

MAGAZINE CAPACITY: 100

UNLOCK: 90,000 Support score

Fire Modes
SINGLE-SHOT
BURST
AUTOMATIC ☒

The M240 is a general purpose machine gun (GPMG) that was first developed in Belgium and adopted by the USMC in 1991. The M60 was replaced first by the M240G, and subsequently by the M240B, which provides commonality between the Marines and the US Army. Firing the heavier 7.62mm NATO round, the M240B has greater power than the M249. The M240 is equipped with a Bipod for supported shooting by default.

Unlock Progression

IMAGE	ACCESSORY	SLOT	KILLS	IMAGE	ACCESSORY	SLOT	KILLS
	M145 (3.4x)	Optics	10		Suppressor	Secondary	90
	Flash Suppressor	Secondary	20		IRNV (IR 1x)	Optics	100
	Extended Mag	Primary	30		ACOG (4x)	Optics	125
	Tactical Light	Secondary	40		PKA-A (3.4x)	Optics	150
	Holographic (HOLO)	Optics	50		PKA-S (HOLO)	Optics	175
	Foregrip	Primary	60		KOBRA (RDS)	Optics	200
	Laser Sight	Secondary	70		PSO-1 (4x)	Optics	235
	Reflex (RDS)	Optics	80				

M60E4

AMMO: 7.62x51mm NATO

RATE OF FIRE: 500 rpm

MAGAZINE CAPACITY: 100

UNLOCK: 130,000 Support score

Fire Modes
SINGLE-SHOT
BURST
AUTOMATIC ☒

"The Pig," as it was commonly referred to when it was introduced in Vietnam, has served with every branch of the US military and continues to serve with Special Forces groups. All though the M60 has been mostly replaced by the M240, the upgraded M60E4 features modern accessory rails, a shortened barrel, and improved reliability, and reduced weight. The M60E4 features a Bipod for supported shooting by default.

Unlock Progression

IMAGE	ACCESSORY	SLOT	KILLS	IMAGE	ACCESSORY	SLOT	KILLS
	M145 (3.4x)	Optics	10		Suppressor	Secondary	90
	Flash Suppressor	Secondary	20		IRNV (IR 1x)	Optics	100
	Extended Mag	Primary	30		ACOG (4x)	Optics	125
	Tactical Light	Secondary	40		PKA-A (3.4x)	Optics	150
	Holographic (HOLO)	Optics	50		PKA-S (HOLO)	Optics	175
	Foregrip	Primary	60		KOBRA (RDS)	Optics	200
	Laser Sight	Secondary	70		PSO-1 (4x)	Optics	235
	Reflex (RDS)	Optics	80				

TYPE 88 LMG

AMMO: 5.8x42mm DAP-87

RATE OF FIRE: 700 rpm

MAGAZINE CAPACITY: 100

UNLOCK: Physical Warfare Pack (Pre-Order)

Fire Modes
- SINGLE-SHOT
- BURST
- AUTOMATIC [X]

A Chinese general purpose machine gun, the Type 88 is also known by its Chinese designation QJY-88. Despite the Type 88 name (referring to 1988 as the year of adoption), the weapon has only recently entered wide service with the People's Liberation Army. The Type 88 fires a special, heavy version of the Chinese 5.8x42mm round and is equipped by default with a Bipod for supported shooting.

Unlock Progression

IMAGE	ACCESSORY	SLOT	KILLS	IMAGE	ACCESSORY	SLOT	KILLS
	PKA-S (HOLO)	Optics	10		Suppressor	Secondary	90
	Flash Suppressor	Secondary	20		IRNV (IR 1x)	Optics	100
	Extended Mag	Primary	30		PSO-1 (4x)	Optics	125
	Tactical Light	Secondary	40		M145 (3.4x)	Optics	150
	PKA-A (3.4x)	Optics	50		Holographic (HOLO)	Optics	175
	Foregrip	Primary	60		Reflex (RDS)	Optics	200
	Laser Sight	Secondary	70		ACOG (4x)	Optics	235
	KOBRA (RDS)	Optics	80				

SNIPER RIFLES

If you prefer engaging enemies at extreme distances, the sniper rifles are the choice for you. These are the most powerful and accurate weapons available, but they also require the most skill and patience to master. Sniper rifles are only available to the recon kit. So rack up your recon score to unlock new sniper rifles and their associated unlocks.

MK11 MOD 0

AMMO: 7.62x51mm NATO

RATE OF FIRE: Semi-Auto

MAGAZINE CAPACITY: 10

UNLOCK: Recon Start (US)/195,000 Recon score (RU)

Fire Modes
- SINGLE-SHOT [X]
- BURST
- AUTOMATIC

Essentially an M16 chambered for the heavy 7.62mm NATO caliber, the MK11 Mod 0 features a longer, heavier, free-floating barrel, enhanced rail system and provisions to mount a sound suppressor. Everything about the MK11 Mod 0 is designed to enhance accuracy and provide a squad-level unit accurate, long-range semi-automatic fire. The MK11 Mod 0 is equipped with a Rifle Scope (8x) by default.

Unlock Progression

IMAGE	ACCESSORY	SLOT	KILLS	IMAGE	ACCESSORY	SLOT	KILLS
	ACOG (4x)	Optics	10		Reflex (RDS)	Optics	90
	Laser Sight	Secondary	20		IRNV (IR 1x)	Optics	100
	Foregrip	Primary	30		PKS-07 (7x)	Optics	125
	Tactical Light	Secondary	40		M145 (3.4x)	Optics	150
	Holographic (HOLO)	Optics	50		PSO-1 (4x)	Optics	175
	Bipod	Primary	60		PKA-S (HOLO)	Optics	200
	Suppressor	Secondary	70		KOBRA (RDS)	Optics	235
	Ballistic (12x)	Optics	80		PKA-A (3.4x)	Optics	270

BATTLEFIELD 3

SVD

AMMO: 7.62x54mm R

RATE OF FIRE: Semi-Auto

MAGAZINE CAPACITY: 10

UNLOCK: Recon Start (RU)/195,000 Recon score (US)

Fire Modes: SINGLE-SHOT [X] / BURST / AUTOMATIC

Designed as a squad support weapon, the SVD Dragunov enhances a squad's ability by providing long-range, rapid, accurate semi-automatic fire. Although the SVD seems similar to an AK-style weapon, the similarity is merely cosmetic. When paired with specially designed sniper cartridges, the SVD Dragunov is a deadly and accurate marksman's weapon. The SVD is equipped with a PKS-07 (7x) scope by default.

Unlock Progression

IMAGE	ACCESSORY	SLOT	KILLS	IMAGE	ACCESSORY	SLOT	KILLS
	PSO-1 (4x)	Optics	10		KOBRA (RDS)	Optics	90
	Laser Sight	Secondary	20		IRNV (IR 1x)	Optics	100
	Foregrip	Primary	30		Rifle Scope (6x)	Optics	125
	Tactical Light	Secondary	40		PKA-A (3.4x)	Optics	150
	PKA-S (HOLO)	Optics	50		ACOG (4x)	Optics	175
	Bipod	Primary	60		Holographic (HOLO)	Optics	200
	Suppressor	Secondary	70		Reflex (RDS)	Optics	235
	Ballistic (12x)	Optics	80		M145 (3.4x)	Optics	270

SV98

AMMO: 7.62x54mm R

RATE OF FIRE: Bolt-Action

MAGAZINE CAPACITY: 10

UNLOCK: 13,000 Recon score

Fire Modes: SINGLE-SHOT [X] / BURST / AUTOMATIC

Similar to its Western counter parts, the SV-98 began life as a proven bolt-action sporting rifle. The SV-98 is equipped with a 10-round detachable box magazine, a muzzle brake that can be swapped for a suppressor, and backup ironsight. The SV-98 is standardly equipped with a PKS-07 (7x) for very long-range shooting.

Unlock Progression

IMAGE	ACCESSORY	SLOT	KILLS	IMAGE	ACCESSORY	SLOT	KILLS
	Ballistic (12x)	Optics	10		KOBRA (RDS)	Optics	90
	Laser Sight	Secondary	20		IRNV (IR 1x)	Optics	100
	Bipod	Primary	30		Rifle Scope (6x)	Optics	125
	Tactical Light	Secondary	40		PKA-A (3.4x)	Optics	150
	PSO-1 (4x)	Optics	50		ACOG (4x)	Optics	175
	Straight Pull Bolt	Primary	60		Holographic (HOLO)	Optics	200
	Suppressor	Secondary	70		Reflex (RDS)	Optics	235
	PKA-S (HOLO)	Optics	80		M145 (3.4x)	Optics	270

SKS

AMMO: 7.62x39mm WP

RATE OF FIRE: Semi-Auto

MAGAZINE CAPACITY: 20

UNLOCK: 71,000 Recon score

Fire Modes: SINGLE-SHOT [X] / BURST / AUTOMATIC

Millions of SKS rifles were produced originally for the Soviet Army in 1945 and in China as the Type 56. The SKS is a popular rifle with civilian shooters, and can still be found in a number of arsenals around the world. A number of aftermarket upgrades are available for the SKS; this model is equipped with a synthetic stock, detachable 20-round magazine, and a PKS-07 (7x) scope by default.

Unlock Progression

IMAGE	ACCESSORY	SLOT	KILLS	IMAGE	ACCESSORY	SLOT	KILLS
	PSO-1 (4x)	Optics	10		KOBRA (RDS)	Optics	90
	Laser Sight	Secondary	20		IRNV (IR 1x)	Optics	100
	Foregrip	Primary	30		Rifle Scope (6x)	Optics	125
	Tactical Light	Secondary	40		PKA-A (3.4x)	Optics	150
	PKA-S (HOLO)	Optics	50		ACOG (4x)	Optics	175
	Bipod	Primary	60		Holographic (HOLO)	Optics	200
	Suppressor	Secondary	70		Reflex (RDS)	Optics	235
	Ballistic (12x)	Optics	80		M145 (3.4x)	Optics	270

M40A5

AMMO: 7.62x51mm NATO

RATE OF FIRE: Bolt-Action

MAGAZINE CAPACITY: 5

UNLOCK: 104,000 Recon score

Fire Modes: SINGLE-SHOT [X] / BURST / AUTOMATIC

Developed around the bolt-action of a proven American hunting rifle, the M40A5 has been upgraded with a lightened fiberglass stock, a detachable magazine, and the provisions for mounting suppressors. An incredibly accurate rifle, the M40A5 currently serves as the primary sniper rifle for the USMC. The M40A5 is equipped with a Rifle Scope (8x) by default.

Unlock Progression

IMAGE	ACCESSORY	SLOT	KILLS	IMAGE	ACCESSORY	SLOT	KILLS
	Ballistic (12x)	Optics	10		Reflex (RDS)	Optics	90
	Laser Sight	Secondary	20		IRNV (IR 1x)	Optics	100
	Bipod	Primary	30		PKS-07 (7x)	Optics	125
	Tactical Light	Secondary	40		M145 (3.4x)	Optics	150
	ACOG (4x)	Optics	50		PSO-1 (4x)	Optics	175
	Straight Pull Bolt	Primary	60		PKA-S (HOLO)	Optics	200
	Suppressor	Secondary	70		KOBRA (RDS)	Optics	235
	Holographic (HOLO)	Optics	80		PKA-A (3.4x)	Optics	270

M98B

AMMO: .338 Magnum

RATE OF FIRE: Bolt-Action

MAGAZINE CAPACITY: 5

UNLOCK: 146,000 Recon score

Fire Modes: SINGLE-SHOT [X] / BURST / AUTOMATIC

A precision tactical rifle, the M98B was uniquely developed from the ground up as a bolt-action sniper rifle. Firing the .338 Magnum round from a detachable box magazine, the M98B is capable of impressive accuracy and great stopping power even at extreme ranges. The M98B is currently being evaluated by US SOCOM in a modified form. The M98B is equipped with a Rifle Scope (8x) by default.

Unlock Progression

IMAGE	ACCESSORY	SLOT	KILLS	IMAGE	ACCESSORY	SLOT	KILLS
	Ballistic (12x)	Optics	10		Reflex (RDS)	Optics	90
	Laser Sight	Secondary	20		IRNV (IR 1x)	Optics	100
	Bipod	Primary	30		PKS-07 (7x)	Optics	125
	Tactical Light	Secondary	40		M145 (3.4x)	Optics	150
	ACOG (4x)	Optics	50		PSO-1 (4x)	Optics	175
	Straight Pull Bolt	Primary	60		PKA-S (HOLO)	Optics	200
	Suppressor	Secondary	70		KOBRA (RDS)	Optics	235
	Holographic (HOLO)	Optics	80		PKA-A (3.4x)	Optics	270

M39 EMR

AMMO: 7.62x51mm NATO

RATE OF FIRE: Semi-Auto

MAGAZINE CAPACITY: 20

UNLOCK: 252,000 Co-Op score

Fire Modes: SINGLE-SHOT [X] / BURST / AUTOMATIC

The M39 EMR (Enhanced Marksman Rifle) is a highly modernized M14 designed to be utilized by USMC designated marksmen. Issued with match-grade 7.62mm NATO long-range ammunition, the M39 is significantly lighter and more accurate than the original M14. The M39 is limited to semi-automatic fire, but supports a number of accessories, including a standard Rifle Scope (8x).

Unlock Progression

IMAGE	ACCESSORY	SLOT	KILLS	IMAGE	ACCESSORY	SLOT	KILLS
	ACOG (4x)	Optics	10		Reflex (RDS)	Optics	90
	Laser Sight	Secondary	20		IRNV (IR 1x)	Optics	100
	Foregrip	Primary	30		PKS-07 (7x)	Optics	125
	Tactical Light	Secondary	40		M145 (3.4x)	Optics	150
	Holographic (HOLO)	Optics	50		PSO-1 (4x)	Optics	175
	Bipod	Primary	60		PKA-S (HOLO)	Optics	200
	Suppressor	Secondary	70		KOBRA (RDS)	Optics	235
	Ballistic (12x)	Optics	80		PKA-A (3.4x)	Optics	270

PERSONAL DEFENSE WEAPONS (PDWS)

These compact and lightweight weapons are best deployed in close quarters due to their short range. But what they lack in accuracy and damage output, they make up for in rate of fire. In *Battlefield 3*, the PDWs are available to all classes. So consider choosing one of these weapons when tasked with assaulting or defending a building interior or other confined space. These weapons are unlocked with promotions in rank. So the more you play (with any kit), the more PDWs you'll unlock.

PP-2000

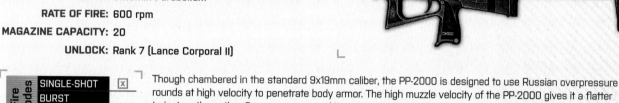

AMMO: 9x19mm Parabellum

RATE OF FIRE: 600 rpm

MAGAZINE CAPACITY: 20

UNLOCK: Rank 7 (Lance Corporal II)

Fire Modes	
SINGLE-SHOT	☒
BURST	
AUTOMATIC	☒

Though chambered in the standard 9x19mm caliber, the PP-2000 is designed to use Russian overpressure rounds at high velocity to penetrate body armor. The high muzzle velocity of the PP-2000 gives it a flatter trajectory than other 9mm weapons, and its compact size make it ideal as a personal defense weapon. When equipped with the 40-round extended magazine, the PP-2000 also functions admirably in a CQB assault role.

Unlock Progression

IMAGE	ACCESSORY	SLOT	KILLS	IMAGE	ACCESSORY	SLOT	KILLS
	KOBRA (RDS)	Optics	10		PKA-A (3.4x)	Optics	70
	Laser Sight	Primary	20		ACOG (4x)	Optics	80
	Suppressor	Secondary	30		Reflex (RDS)	Optics	90
	PKA-S (HOLO)	Optics	40		IRNV (IR 1x)	Optics	100
	Tactical Light	Primary	50		Holographic (HOLO)	Optics	125
	Extended Mag	Secondary	60		M145 (3.4x)	Optics	150

UMP-45

AMMO: .45ACP

RATE OF FIRE: 600 rpm

MAGAZINE CAPACITY: 25

UNLOCK: Rank 16 (Sergeant III)

Fire Modes	
SINGLE-SHOT	☒
BURST	☒
AUTOMATIC	☒

The German-built UMP-45 is a fully automatic personal defense weapon noted for its versatility and optimal mobility. Essentially an improved version of the MP5, the UMP-45 is functionally similar but substantially cheaper to manufacture and includes several modern upgrades such as the top and forward accessory rails. The UMP-45 is well-rounded and capable as a personal defense weapon.

Unlock Progression

IMAGE	ACCESSORY	SLOT	KILLS	IMAGE	ACCESSORY	SLOT	KILLS
	Reflex (RDS)	Optics	10		M145 (3.4x)	Optics	70
	Laser Sight	Primary	20		ACOG (4x)	Optics	80
	Suppressor	Secondary	30		KOBRA (RDS)	Optics	90
	Holographic (HOLO)	Optics	40		IRNV (IR 1x)	Optics	100
	Tactical Light	Primary	50		PKA-S (HOLO)	Optics	125
	Flash Suppressor	Secondary	60		PKA-A (3.4x)	Optics	150

PDW-R

AMMO: 5.56mmx45mm NATO

RATE OF FIRE: 600 rpm

MAGAZINE CAPACITY: 30

UNLOCK: Rank 32 (Sergeant Major)

Fire Modes	
SINGLE-SHOT	[X]
BURST	
AUTOMATIC	[X]

Developed as a personal defense weapon, the PDW-R differs from most others by utilizing the standard 5.56mm NATO rounds of the M16 or M4. This allows the PDW-R to share magazines and supply lines with standard troops, while its short length and bullpup configuration allow the PDW-R to be easily operated in CQB. Though it lacks the accuracy of a rifle, the PDW-R has a greater punch at longer ranges than other PDWs.

Unlock Progression

IMAGE	ACCESSORY	SLOT	KILLS	IMAGE	ACCESSORY	SLOT	KILLS
	Reflex (RDS)	Optics	10		M145 (3.4x)	Optics	70
	Laser Sight	Primary	20		ACOG (4x)	Optics	80
	Suppressor	Secondary	30		KOBRA (RDS)	Optics	90
	Holographic (HOLO)	Optics	40		IRNV (IR 1x)	Optics	100
	Tactical Light	Primary	50		PKA-S (HOLO)	Optics	125
	Extended Mag	Secondary	60		PKA-A (3.4x)	Optics	150

P90

AMMO: 5.7x28mm

RATE OF FIRE: 900 rpm

MAGAZINE CAPACITY: 50

UNLOCK: Rank 40 (Second Lieutenant)

Fire Modes	
SINGLE-SHOT	[X]
BURST	
AUTOMATIC	[X]

Developed in Belgium as a personal defense weapon for vehicle crews, Special Forces and counter-terrorist groups, the P90 is a compact and capable weapon system. The three forward rails allow an operator to mount a wide variety accessories, and the 5.7x28mm special armor-piercing ammunition is fired at nearly rifle velocity. With a standard 50-round magazine, the P90 is an effective offensive CQB weapon for highly mobile personnel.

Unlock Progression

IMAGE	ACCESSORY	SLOT	KILLS	IMAGE	ACCESSORY	SLOT	KILLS
	Reflex (RDS)	Optics	10		M145 (3.4x)	Optics	70
	Laser Sight	Primary	20		ACOG (4x)	Optics	80
	Suppressor	Secondary	30		KOBRA (RDS)	Optics	90
	Holographic (HOLO)	Optics	40		IRNV (IR 1x)	Optics	100
	Tactical Light	Primary	50		PKA-S (HOLO)	Optics	125
	Flash Suppressor	Secondary	60		PKA-A (3.4x)	Optics	150

AS VAL

AMMO: 9x39mm

RATE OF FIRE: 900 rpm

MAGAZINE CAPACITY: 30

UNLOCK: Rank 45 (Colonel)

Fire Modes		
SINGLE-SHOT	X
BURST	
AUTOMATIC	X

The AS VAL is an integrally suppressed, Soviet-designed assault rifle developed for use in the Spetsnaz. Chambered for a special high-performance armor-piercing 9x39mm round, the AS VAL includes mounts for using optical, red dot, or even night vision scopes. The AS VAL is designed to be fired only with the suppressor attached, and this therefore prevents the rifle from mounting underslung attachments.

Unlock Progression

IMAGE	ACCESSORY	SLOT	KILLS	IMAGE	ACCESSORY	SLOT	KILLS
	PSO-1 (4x)	Optics	10		PKA-A (3.4x)	Optics	80
	Tactical Light	Primary	20		ACOG (4x)	Optics	90
	KOBRA (RDS)	Optics	30		Reflex (RDS)	Optics	100
	PKA-S (HOLO)	Optics	40		Holographic (HOLO)	Optics	125
	Laser Sight	Primary	50		Rifle Scope (6x)	Optics	150
	IRNV (IR 1x)	Optics	60		M145 (3.4x)	Optics	175
	PKS-07 (7x)	Optics	70				

MP7

AMMO: 4.6x30mm

RATE OF FIRE: 950 rpm

MAGAZINE CAPACITY: 20

UNLOCK: 189,000 Co-Op score

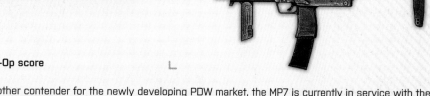

Fire Modes		
SINGLE-SHOT	X
BURST	
AUTOMATIC	X

Another contender for the newly developing PDW market, the MP7 is currently in service with the German Bundeswehr and the Norwegian Armed Forces. The MP7 includes an improved stock, additional safeties, and added rails for mounting lights, lasers, and sights. The weapon is also capable of being suppressed, and therefore has excellent close-combat stealth performance.

Unlock Progression

IMAGE	ACCESSORY	SLOT	KILLS	IMAGE	ACCESSORY	SLOT	KILLS
	Reflex (RDS)	Optics	10		M145 (3.4x)	Optics	70
	Laser Sight	Primary	20		ACOG (4x)	Optics	80
	Suppressor	Secondary	30		KOBRA (RDS)	Optics	90
	Holographic (HOLO)	Optics	40		IRNV (IR 1x)	Optics	100
	Tactical Light	Primary	50		PKA-S (HOLO)	Optics	125
	Extended Mag	Secondary	60		PKA-A (3.4x)	Optics	150

SHOTGUNS

Nobody misses with a shotgun. Although these weapons lack the accuracy and finesse of the other weapons, their brutal power is a worthwhile trade-off. At close range, these weapons are unmatched, capable of killing with one shot. Like the PDWs, shotguns can be equipped by every kit and their unlocks are tied to your global score. So the more promotions your earn, the more shotguns you'll unlock.

870MCS

AMMO: 12 gauge

RATE OF FIRE: Pump-Action

MAGAZINE CAPACITY: 4

UNLOCK: Rank 1 (Private First Class)

Fire Modes
- SINGLE-SHOT [X]
- BURST
- AUTOMATIC

The 870MCS is an American-made pump-action shotgun that has been used by Special Forces units for decades. In urban environments, the 870MCS is especially effective due to its high stopping power at close range. The ability to load different types of shells makes the 870MCS able to adapt to a wide variety of situations, while a narrow choke gives the 870MCS slightly more range than other shotguns.

Unlock Progression

IMAGE	ACCESSORY	SLOT	KILLS	IMAGE	ACCESSORY	SLOT	KILLS
	Reflex (RDS)	Optics	10		IRNV (IR 1x)	Optics	100
	12G Flechette	Secondary	20		Rifle Scope (6x)	Optics	125
	Extended Mag	Primary	30		M145 (3.4x)	Optics	150
	Holographic (HOLO)	Optics	40		Flash Suppressor	Primary	175
	Tactical Light	Primary	50		KOBRA (RDS)	Optics	200
	12G Frag	Secondary	60		PKA-S (HOLO)	Optics	235
	ACOG (4x)	Optics	70		PSO-1 (4x)	Optics	270
	Laser Sight	Primary	80		PKS-07 (7x)	Optics	300
	12G Slug	Secondary	90		PKA-A (3.4x)	Optics	350

M1014

AMMO: 12 gauge

RATE OF FIRE: Semi-Auto

MAGAZINE CAPACITY: 4

UNLOCK: Rank 22 (Gunnery Sergeant II)

Fire Modes
- SINGLE-SHOT [X]
- BURST
- AUTOMATIC

An Italian semi-automatic shotgun, delivered to USMC in 1999, the M1014 fires 12 gauge rounds without the need for the pump action seen on the M870. A reliable and versatile weapon, the M1014 is also equipped with a rail for the mounting of various accessories and an open choke that results in a wide pellet spread.

Unlock Progression

IMAGE	ACCESSORY	SLOT	KILLS	IMAGE	ACCESSORY	SLOT	KILLS
	Reflex (RDS)	Optics	10		IRNV (IR 1x)	Optics	100
	12G Flechette	Secondary	20		Rifle Scope (6x)	Optics	125
	Extended Mag	Primary	30		M145 (3.4x)	Optics	150
	Holographic (HOLO)	Optics	40		Flash Suppressor	Primary	175
	Tactical Light	Primary	50		KOBRA (RDS)	Optics	200
	12G Frag	Secondary	60		PKA-S (HOLO)	Optics	235
	ACOG (4x)	Optics	70		PSO-1 (4x)	Optics	270
	Laser Sight	Primary	80		PKS-07 (7x)	Optics	300
	12G Slug	Secondary	90		PKA-A (3.4x)	Optics	350

SAIGA 12K

AMMO: 12 gauge

RATE OF FIRE: Semi-Auto

MAGAZINE CAPACITY: 6

UNLOCK: Rank 34 (Sergeant Major II)

Fire Modes
- SINGLE-SHOT [X]
- BURST
- AUTOMATIC

This Russian-made magazine-fed 12 gauge shotgun is based on the proven AK-47 action and equipped with a folding stock. It is reliable, fast to reload, and capable of mounting a variety of accessories. The Saiga 12K is popular with Russian police and security services, and it is an effective close-combat weapon with a wide pellet spread.

Unlock Progression

IMAGE	ACCESSORY	SLOT	KILLS	IMAGE	ACCESSORY	SLOT	KILLS
	KOBRA (RDS)	Optics	10		IRNV (IR 1x)	Optics	100
	12G Flechette	Secondary	20		PKS-07 (7x)	Optics	125
	Extended Mag	Primary	30		PKA-A (3.4x)	Optics	150
	PKA-S (HOLO)	Optics	40		Flash Suppressor	Primary	175
	Tactical Light	Primary	50		Reflex (RDS)	Optics	200
	12G Frag	Secondary	60		Holographic (HOLO)	Optics	235
	PSO-1 (4x)	Optics	70		ACOG (4x)	Optics	270
	Laser Sight	Primary	80		Rifle Scope (6x)	Optics	300
	12G Slug	Secondary	90		M145 (3.4x)	Optics	350

DAO-12

AMMO: 12 gauge

RATE OF FIRE: Semi-Auto

MAGAZINE CAPACITY: 12

UNLOCK: Rank 38 (Chief Warrant Officer Four)

Fire Modes
- SINGLE-SHOT [X]
- BURST
- AUTOMATIC

A *Battlefield 2* classic, originally developed in South Africa, the DAO-12 is essentially the combination of a revolver and a shotgun. The fixed drum magazine is made of individual chambers, each holding a single round, which are fired only when placed in line with the barrel. A spring winding mechanism makes reloading an empty weapon a time-consuming process and the short barrel results in a wide pellet spread.

Unlock Progression

IMAGE	ACCESSORY	SLOT	KILLS	IMAGE	ACCESSORY	SLOT	KILLS
	Reflex (RDS)	Optics	10		IRNV (IR 1x)	Optics	100
	12G Flechette	Secondary	20		Rifle Scope (6x)	Optics	125
	Extended Mag	Primary	30		M145 (3.4x)	Optics	150
	Holographic (HOLO)	Optics	40		Flash Suppressor	Primary	175
	Tactical Light	Primary	50		KOBRA (RDS)	Optics	200
	12G Frag	Secondary	60		PKA-S (HOLO)	Optics	235
	ACOG (4x)	Optics	70		PSO-1 (4x)	Optics	270
	Laser Sight	Primary	80		PKS-07 (7x)	Optics	300
	12G Slug	Secondary	90		PKA-A (3.4x)	Optics	350

USAS-12

AMMO: 12 gauge

RATE OF FIRE: 600 rpm

MAGAZINE CAPACITY: 6

UNLOCK: Rank 43 (Major)

Fire Modes		
SINGLE-SHOT	☒
BURST	
AUTOMATIC	☒

A South Korean-produced automatic shotgun, the USAS-12 was specifically developed for the combat shotgun role. Feeding from a box magazine and capable of both automatic and semi-automatic fire, the USAS-12's high weight makes recoil manageable. The open choke results in a wide pellet spread.

Unlock Progression

IMAGE	ACCESSORY	SLOT	KILLS	IMAGE	ACCESSORY	SLOT	KILLS
	KOBRA (RDS)	Optics	10		IRNV (IR 1x)	Optics	100
	12G Flechette	Secondary	20		PKS-07 (7x)	Optics	125
	Extended Mag	Primary	30		PKA-A (3.4x)	Optics	150
	PKA-S (HOLO)	Optics	40		Flash Suppressor	Primary	175
	Tactical Light	Primary	50		Reflex (RDS)	Optics	200
	12G Frag	Secondary	60		Holographic (HOLO)	Optics	235
	PSO-1 (4x)	Optics	70		ACOG (4x)	Optics	270
	Laser Sight	Primary	80		Rifle Scope (6x)	Optics	300
	12G Slug	Secondary	90		M145 (3.4x)	Optics	350

PISTOLS

Don't write off these sidearms as mere peashooters. The pistols pack a serious punch and can save your life during desperate close-quarters duels—remember, it's faster to draw your pistol than it is to load a fresh magazine in your primary weapon. Also, when suppressed, the pistols do not suffer from a loss of accuracy, making them a great weapon to equip when you're under heavy fire. Like the PDWs and shotguns, the pistols can be equipped by any kit, and fill the sidearm slot in the loadout screen. New pistols are unlocked as you earn promotions.

M9

AMMO: 9x19mm Parabellum

RATE OF FIRE: Semi-Auto

MAGAZINE CAPACITY: 15

UNLOCK: Standard-Issue (US)

Fire Modes		
SINGLE-SHOT	☒
BURST	
AUTOMATIC	

The M9 was selected as the primary sidearm of the entire United States military in 1985. Developed in Italy, the M9 was selected in a series of often-disputed trials, only narrowly beating out other contenders, because of its high quality and low price. The M9 is the primary sidearm of the USMC.

M9 Variants

NAME	ATTACHMENT	UNLOCK CRITERIA
M9 TACT.	Tactical Light	Rank 10 (Corporal I)
M9 SUPP.	Suppressor	Rank 25 (Master Sergeant II)

■ [NOTE]

RU players can unlock the M9 by obtaining the first Service Star for the MP443.

MP443

AMMO: 9x19mm Parabellum

RATE OF FIRE: Semi-Auto

MAGAZINE CAPACITY: 18

UNLOCK: Standard-Issue (RU)

Fire Modes	
SINGLE-SHOT	☒
BURST	
AUTOMATIC	

Designed to replace the dated PMM pistol, the MP443 Grach pistol was developed in 1993 and fires high powered armor-piercing 9mm Russian rounds. The pistol is a combined construction of polymers and steel and has been adopted by select Special Forces units in the Russian military.

MP443 Variants

NAME	ATTACHMENT	UNLOCK CRITERIA
MP443 TACT.	Tactical Light	Rank 13 (Sergeant)
MP443 SUPP.	Suppressor	Rank 28 (First Sergeant II)

■ [NOTE]

US players can unlock the MP443 by obtaining the first Service Star for the M9.

G17C

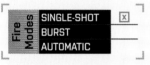

AMMO: 9x19mm Parabellum

RATE OF FIRE: Semi-Auto

MAGAZINE CAPACITY: 17

UNLOCK: Rank 4 (Private First Class III)

Fire Modes	
SINGLE-SHOT	☒
BURST	
AUTOMATIC	

The G17C pistol is part of a large series of pistols from an Austrian manufacturer. Chambered in 9mm, this full-size combat pistol features a polymer frame and anticorrosion surfaces that make it incredibly reliable. The G17C is popular with both police and military units worldwide. This G17C has been equipped with an integral Laser Sight that makes unaimed fire more accurate.

G17C Variants

NAME	ATTACHMENT	UNLOCK CRITERIA
G17 SUPP.	Suppressor	Rank 19 (Staff Sergeant II)

G18

AMMO: 9x19mm Parabellum

RATE OF FIRE: 1,100 rpm

MAGAZINE CAPACITY: 20

UNLOCK: Rank 41 (First Lieutenant)

Fire Modes	
SINGLE-SHOT	☒
BURST	
AUTOMATIC	☒

Essentially an automatic version of the G17C, the G18 was developed for the Austrian EKO Cobra counterterrorist force. Classified as a machine pistol, the G18 has been equipped with a number of modifications to allow greater control over its very rapid fire. Regardless, the G18 in automatic mode is incredibly difficult to fire effectively at anything other than extremely short ranges.

G18 Variants

NAME	ATTACHMENT	UNLOCK CRITERIA
G18 SUPP.	Suppressor	Rank 30 (Master Gunnery Sergeant I)

.44 MAGNUM

AMMO: .44 Magnum

RATE OF FIRE: Semi-Auto

MAGAZINE CAPACITY: 6

UNLOCK: Rank 36 (Chief Warrant Officer Two)

A .44 Magnum, the most powerful handgun in the world; this particular model features a ported barrel, a compact frame for easy carry, and of course, a round that will blow your head clean off. The .44 Magnum is the most powerful side arm available, but the recoil and weight of the weapon makes fast follow-up shots extremely difficult.

.44 Magnum Variants

NAME	ATTACHMENT	UNLOCK CRITERIA
.44 SCOPED	3x Scope	Rank 44 (Lieutenant Colonel)

MP412 REX

AMMO: .357 Magnum

RATE OF FIRE: Semi-Auto

MAGAZINE CAPACITY: 6

UNLOCK: 63,000 Co-Op points

Developed for export in Russia (REX stands for revolver for export), the MP443 is a compact .357 Magnum handgun with an interesting tilt open and auto extraction design. While not as powerful as the .44 Magnum, the .357 Magnum round from the MP412 offers excellent stopping power and the compact package offers a slightly higher rate of accurate fire.

93R

AMMO: 9x19mm Parabellum

RATE OF FIRE: 1,100 rpm

MAGAZINE CAPACITY: 20

UNLOCK: 315,000 Co-Op points

A modified version of the M9 pistol, the 93R is able to fire in 3-round bursts. The 93R is equipped with a forward-folding foregrip and an extended barrel that is ported to reduce recoil. Trained shooters are able to fire busts in rapid succession, and the pistol is typically seen in service only with elite special-purpose units.

M1911

AMMO: .45ACP

RATE OF FIRE: Semi-Auto

MAGAZINE CAPACITY: 9

UNLOCK: BF Veteran Status

The M911 is one of the most popular pistols in the world. Adopted in 1911 for the US armed forces, the M1911 served as the primary side arm until 1985. Many clones and copies of the M1911 exist, and the internal action is used in nearly all modern pistols. Modernized and updated versions of the M1911 are still in use by MEU(SOC) US Marine Corps Special Forces.

M1911 Variants

NAME	ATTACHMENT	UNLOCK CRITERIA
M1911 SUPP.	Suppressor	BF Veteran Status
M1911 TACT.	Tactical Light	BF Veteran Status
M1911 S-TAC	Suppressor/Tactical Light	BF Veteran Status

■ [NOTE]

Battlefield veterans gain access to the M1911 automatically. If you don't own any previous *Battlefield* games you can unlock this weapon by becoming a member of the EA Gun Club, at http://gunclub.ea.com. Simply log in to the website using your EA.com or Origin.com account.

SPECIALIZATIONS

As you progress through your multiplayer career you unlock a variety of specializations. These perks provide varying bonuses to your kit. But you can only equip one specialization at a time, so pick the bonus that best fits your style of play. The squad specializations are very powerful, as they apply a bonus to your entire squad. All specializations are tied to ranks. So the more promotions you earn, the more specializations you'll have to choose from.

Weapon Accessories

IMAGE	NAME	UNLOCK CRITERIA	DESCRIPTION
	Sprint	Rank 2 (Private First Class I)	Lightweight load-bearing equipment that reduces soldier fatigue and allows a higher sprint speed.
	Ammo	Rank 5 (Lance Corporal)	Additional MOLLE tactical ammunition pouches allow the player to carry a greater amount of primary and sidearm ammunition.
	Flak Jacket	Rank 8 (Lance Corporal III)	Reduces the damage taken from explosives and shrapnel by providing additional coverage to high-risk body parts.
	Explosives	Rank 11 (Corporal II)	An EOD vest that increases the total amount of explosive and rocket ammunition.
	Suppression Resist	Rank 14 (Sergeant I)	The combined effect of field experience and advanced training reduces the suppressive effect of incoming rounds.
	Suppression	Rank 17 (Staff Sergeant)	Advanced marksman training gives the soldier's rounds a greater suppressive effect on his targets.
	Grenades	Rank 20 (Gunnery Sergeant)	Additional MOLLE grenade pouches allow the soldier to carry a larger amount of hand grenades and 40mm grenades.
	Squad Sprint	Rank 23 (Master Sergeant)	Lightweight load-bearing equipment that reduces soldier fatigue and allows a higher sprint speed. This specialization will be granted to your entire squad.
	Squad Ammo	Rank 26 (First Sergeant)	Additional MOLLE tactical ammunition pouches allow the player to carry a greater amount of primary and sidearm ammunition. This specialization will be granted to your entire squad.
	Squad Flak Jacket	Rank 29 (Master Gunnery Sergeant)	Reduces the damage taken from explosives and shrapnel by providing additional coverage to high-risk body parts. This specialization will be granted to your entire squad.
	Squad Explosives	Rank 31 (Master Gunnery Sergeant II)	An EOD vest that increases the total amount of explosive and rocket ammunition. This specialization will be granted to your entire squad.
	Squad Suppression	Rank 33 (Sergeant Major I)	Advanced marksman training gives the soldier's rounds a greater suppressive effect on his targets. This specialization will be granted to your entire squad.
	Squad Suppression Resist	Rank 35 (Warrant Officer One)	The combined effect of field experience and advanced training reduces the suppressive effect of incoming rounds. This specialization will be granted to your entire squad.
	Squad Grenades	Rank 37 (Chief Warrant Officer Three)	Additional MOLLE grenade pouches allow the soldier to carry a larger amount of hand grenades and 40mm grenades. This specialization will be granted to your entire squad.

CAMO PATTERNS

Don't like the look of your outfit? You can customize that, too, with a variety of camouflage patterns. Like specializations, new camo patterns are unlocked when you achieve new ranks. The look of each camo pattern differs whether you're on the US or RU teams. You can switch between the default and unlocked camo patterns by choosing the Appearance option from the Loadout screen. Your selected camo is then applied to all classes. When playing with a squad, consider choosing the same camo pattern to make it easier to identify each other.

Weapon Accessories

IMAGE	NAME	UNLOCK CRITERIA	IMAGE	NAME	UNLOCK CRITERIA
	Woodland	Rank 3 (Private First Class II)		Jungle	Rank 21 (Gunnery Sergeant I)
	Ranger	Rank 6 (Lance Corporal I)		Desert Khaki	Rank 24 (Master Sergeant I)
	Army Green	Rank 9 (Corporal)		Urban	Rank 27 (First Sergeant I)
	Expeditionary Force	Rank 12 (Corporal III)		Veteran Kit	Rank 39 (Chief Warrant Officer Five)
	Paratrooper	Rank 15 (Sergeant II)		Spec Ops Black	Rank 42 (Captain)
	Navy Blue	Rank 18 (Staff Sergeant I)			

VEHICLES

One of the highlights of any *Battlefield* game are the vehicles. Nothing can be more entertaining than hopping into a tank and cruising across the landscape, laying waste to both enemy vehicles and structures alike. *Battlefield 3* continues this rich tradition and lets you hop aboard boats, tanks, helicopters, and jets to quickly move across the battlefield with speed and devastating firepower.

VEHICLE CUSTOMIZATION

Before spawning into a game, take a moment to customize your vehicle loadouts.

In *Battlefield 3*, most of the vehicles can be customized by means of unlockable upgrades, gadgets and weapons. The more you use a vehicle from a particular class, the more points you earn. Unlocks are awarded at regular intervals in a linear progression. Once an unlock is awarded, you can assign it through the same loadout screen you use to customize the soldier classes. With the exception of attack helicopters, all vehicles have three assignable slots: one upgrade slot, one gadget slot, and one weapon slot. Attack helicopters benefit from six slots, three for the pilot and three for the gunner. Upgrades are passive and require no action to take advantage of their benefits. Meanwhile, gadgets and weapons require some interaction on the part of the driver or pilot to deploy. So as you progress through your multiplayer career, you will have to make some tough decisions as to what unlocks you wish to equip. Some unlocks improve offensive capabilities while others impact survivability. Experiment with the different options until you find a combination that best suits the tactical situation and your style of play. The unlock progression for each vehicle type is provided in this chapter. We list the point requirements for each as well as a brief description of every upgrade, gadget, and weapon. There are no unlocks available for light vehicles and transport helicopters.

LIGHT VEHICLES

The light vehicles are the fastest land vehicles in the game, and are useful for rushing control points and M-COM stations at the start of a battle. But their light armor and exposed positions make them death traps if driven into heavy action. Most explosive munitions can disable these vehicles with one hit, potentially killing the driver and passengers. Their greatest defensive asset is their speed and off-road capability. To ensure survival, use these vehicles to traverse terrain on a map's periphery; stay away from heated battles near control points and M-COM stations. Although these vehicles can attain high speeds on roads, most roads are traveled by larger and more deadly vehicles like tanks and IFVs. So stay off-road and out of sight. Such tactics are essential when staging raids on distant enemy-held control points or M-COM stations. There are no vehicle unlocks or loadout options for the light vehicles.

GROWLER ITV

NATIONALITY: US

DESRIPTION: Used by the USMC starting in 2009, the Growler is the only transport vehicle that fits in the V-22 Osprey.

Vehicle Performance

SPEED					
ARMOR					
FIREPOWER					

Vehicle Occupancy

SEAT	POSITION	WEAPON
1	Driver	None
2	Gunner	12.7mm Machine Gun
3	Passenger	Troop Kit

FIELD NOTES

The Growler ITV is fast and maneuverable, but the open-cockpit design leaves the driver and passengers vulnerable to incoming small arms fire. Never drive this vehicle into the middle of an intense firefight. Instead, use it for quick raids on distant control points.

VDV BUGGY

NATIONALITY: RU

DESRIPTION: Russian paratrooper light buggy.

Vehicle Performance

SPEED					
ARMOR					
FIREPOWER					

Vehicle Occupancy

SEAT	POSITION	WEAPON
1	Driver	None
2	Gunner	12.7mm Machine Gun
3	Passenger	Troop Kit

FIELD NOTES

Like the US Growler ITV, the VDV Buggy is a fast attack vehicle ideal for launching sneaky flanking attacks on lightly defended enemy positions. Due to its lack of armor, take extra steps to keep this vehicle out of the line of fire. While the machine gun turret is great for suppressing enemy infantry, the gunner position is completely exposed.

M1114 HMMWV

NATIONALITY: US

DESRIPTION: This vehicle has served in every division of the US Armed Forces for 20 years; increased armor was added as a response to urban threats.

Vehicle Performance

SPEED					
ARMOR					
FIREPOWER					

Vehicle Occupancy

SEAT	POSITION	WEAPON
1	Driver	None
2	Gunner	HMG .50
3	Passenger	None
4	Passenger	None

FIELD NOTES

The familiar HMMWV is the most common light vehicle when playing as the US. The vehicle's body and doors can repel most small arms fire, but the windows leave the driver and passengers somewhat exposed. Consider keeping this vehicle back from the action and using its machine gun turret (with zoom capability) to engage enemy infantry and helicopters.

GAZ-3937 VODNIK

NATIONALITY: RU

DESRIPTION: Dependable armored 4x4 that was introduced in 1997.

Vehicle Performance

SPEED	
ARMOR	
FIREPOWER	

Vehicle Occupancy

SEAT	POSITION	WEAPON
1	Driver	None
2	Gunner	HMG .50
3	Passenger	None
4	Passenger	None

FIELD NOTES

The Vodnik performs much like the HMMWV, but has a slightly taller profile making it a bit unstable on uneven terrain. Watch your speed, particularly when turning. Otherwise you may roll the vehicle, forcing you to find another ride or continue your journey on foot.

RHIB

NATIONALITY: US and RU

DESRIPTION: The Rigid Hull Inflatable Boat (RHIB) is a vessel whose hull is partially rigid and partially inflatable to allow it to traverse long distances at high speed.

Vehicle Performance

SPEED	
ARMOR	
FIREPOWER	

Vehicle Occupancy

SEAT	POSITION	WEAPON
1	Driver	None
2	Gunner	Light Machine Gun
3	Passenger	Troop Kit
4	Passenger	Troop Kit

FIELD NOTES

The RHIB is used by both teams and usually spawns next to bodies of water or within the lower deck of US aircraft carriers. Despite its light machine gun mounted on the bow, this is a transport vehicle, not a gunboat. The boat cannot sustain heavy damage. Even worse, it provides zero protection for its occupants. Instead of launching frontal assaults, circumvent the enemy's defenses and launch surprise attacks on rear positions.

[LIGHT VEHICLE TACTICS]

- The roof-mounted machine guns found on most of these vehicles are excellent anti-aircraft guns. Fire a steady burst of automatic fire at enemy helicopters to make them spin out of control. On the HMMWV and Vodnik, the gunner operates the machine gun turret from within the vehicle, which protects the gunner from small arms fire. Each turret also has a zoom function, making them great weapons for spotting and engaging enemies at long range.

- Think twice before loading your entire squad into one of these vehicles. All it takes is one hit from a tank or rocket launcher to disable your ride, potentially killing a large number of your squad members. If the vehicle becomes disabled, bail out and seek cover before the flaming wreck explodes.

- Given their speed, the light vehicles are great for scoring road kills. Simply drive directly toward enemy troops at high speed and run them down before they can dash out of your way.

- Passengers in the Growler ITV and VDV Buggy can fire the weapons from their troop kits. But accurately targeting enemies while driving in moving vehicle is tough. It's often better to save your ammo for when the vehicle reaches its destination.

- At the start of a battle, don't drive off in one of these vehicles until a few teammates hop inside. On most maps, these vehicles serve as your team's primary means of transportation. Stranding teammates at your base won't win you any fans. However, your squad mates can spawn into the vehicle if there are open seats.

INFANTRY FIGHTING VEHICLES (IFVS)

The Infantry Fighting Vehicles are the most versatile vehicles in the game; they are sometimes referred to as light tanks. They lack the heavy armor of tanks, but still have a lot of firepower. Their main weapon is an auto-cannon, that fires high-explosive rounds in quick succession as long as you hold down the fire button. But the auto-cannon can only fire six rounds before a new rack must be loaded, resulting in a brief interruption. The IFVs also have a machine gun turret—the driver controls the auto-cannon while the gunner controls the machine gun. The four passenger seats are equipped with port- and starboard-mounted machine guns, making it ideal for hauling around your entire squad.

IFV Unlock Progression

IMAGE	NAME	LOADOUT SLOT	POINTS	DESCRIPTION
	IR Smoke	Gadget	800	Smoke grenades enhanced with metal filaments that when launched remove laser designation, spoof incoming guided missiles, and prevent enemies from revealing your position to teammates.
	ATGM Launcher	Weapon	2,300	Wire-guided anti-tank missile launchers are mounted on the turret.
	Belt Speed	Upgrade	4,700	An enhanced mechanism decreases the minimum time between firing bursts with your main weapon.
	Coaxial LMG	Weapon	8,300	A light machine gun mounted coaxially to your main weapon.
	Thermal Optics	Gadget	13,100	A secondary weapon sight with thermal optics that highlights soldiers and vehicles for efficient target identification.
	Proximity Scan	Upgrade	19,200	External sensors detect and reveal enemy units on your minimap.
	Zoom Optics	Gadget	26,900	A secondary weapon sight with up to 3x magnification.
	Maintenance	Upgrade	36,000	Preventative maintenance procedures improve your vehicle's recovery from damage.
	APFSDS-T Shell	Weapon	47,000	Armor-piercing fin-stabilized discarding sabot (with tracer) ammo that deals more direct damage but has no explosive element.
	Thermal Camo	Upgrade	60,000	Antireflective coating on your vehicle increases enemy locking and tracking difficulty, and decreases the time you are revealed to the enemy when spotted.
	Guided Missile	Weapon	74,000	Laser-guided anti-tank missile launchers are mounted on the turret; they lock on to and track enemy land vehicles and can acquire laser-designated targets even if they are out of line of sight.
	Reactive Armor	Upgrade	90,000	Reactive armor panels and/or slats absorb the impact from anti-tank weapons, protecting you from damage but becoming destroyed in the process.

LAV-25

NATIONALITY: US

DESRIPTION: The LAV-25 is an eight-wheeled amphibious Infantry Fighting Vehicle (IFV) used by the United States Marine Corps.

Vehicle Performance

SPEED	
ARMOR	
FIREPOWER	

Vehicle Occupancy

SEAT	POSITION	WEAPON
1	Driver	25mm Chain Gun
2	Gunner	HMG .50
3	Passenger	Machine Gun
4	Passenger	Machine Gun
5	Passenger	Machine Gun
6	Passenger	Machine Gun

FIELD NOTES

Sporting thick armor and bristling with weapons, the LAV-25 is the ideal troop transport for the US team. While the vehicle is very effective against enemy infantry, it is vulnerable to attacks by tanks, helicopters, and jets. So if such threats are in the area, consider dropping off your passengers as soon as possible.

BMP-2M

NATIONALITY: RU

DESRIPTION: Description: The BMP-2M is a second-generation, amphibious infantry fighting vehicle introduced in the 1980s in the Soviet Union.

Vehicle Performance

SPEED	
ARMOR	
FIREPOWER	

Vehicle Occupancy

SEAT	POSITION	WEAPON
1	Driver	30mm Auto-Cannon
2	Gunner	12.7mm Machine Gun
3	Passenger	Machine Gun
4	Passenger	Machine Gun
5	Passenger	Machine Gun
6	Passenger	Machine Gun

FIELD NOTES

The Russian BMP-2M has a sleek, low profile when compared to its boxy American counterpart. This makes it a little easier to conceal the vehicle behind low hills and other pieces of cover. Hold back from the front lines and pepper enemy infantry (and helicopters) with the vehicle's auto-cannon and machine gun.

AAV-7A1 AMTRAC

NATIONALITY: US

DESRIPTION: The AAV-7A1 is the current amphibious troop transport of the United States Marine Corps.

Vehicle Performance

SPEED	
ARMOR	
FIREPOWER	

Vehicle Occupancy

SEAT	POSITION	WEAPON
1	Driver	None
2	Gunner	7.62mm Machine Gun
3	Passenger	None
4	Passenger	None
5	Passenger	None
6	Passenger	None

FIELD NOTES

Technically the AMTRAC is not an IFV, so it does not benefit from the unlocks associated with the vehicle class. However, it performs just like an IFV, as it's capable of carrying six players. It also serves as a mobile spawn point for the US team. Park this vehicle anywhere, and as long as seats are available, any teammate can spawn directly into the AMTRAC.

[IFV TACTICS]

- Never charge into a group of enemy infantry. IFVs are well armored, but they can't withstand more than two or three rocket hits, not to mention mines. Instead, hold back and engage infantry from a safe distance, where they can't sneak up behind you. The auto-cannon and machine gun turrets on these vehicles are devastating against infantry.

- All the IFVs are amphibious and can travel across deep bodies water. Use this to your advantage by staging attacks from unpredictable directions. This is a great way to take enemies by surprise. But these vehicles move very slow while in the water, so watch out for helicopters and jets overhead.

- When engaging an IFV, try to maneuver so you can score a side or rear hit, where the vehicle's armor is thinnest. Likewise, when driving one of these vehicles, be mindful of these weak spots and try to keep the vehicle's front armor facing the enemy at all times.

- Be careful when transporting your entire squad in an IFV. A hit from a helicopter or jet's Guided Missile could send your whole squad back to the respawn screen.

- Like jets and helicopters, IFVs can fire a Guided Missile capable of locking on to targets designated with the recon kit's SOFLAM. So once you've unlocked this weapon, keep your IFV back from the action and wait for enemy vehicles to be painted with a laser. A red diamond icon appears on the HUD when an enemy target has been designated.

- Completely different tactics apply when driving the AMTRAC. This slow troop transport only has a light machine gun for defense, making it vulnerable against tanks and other heavy vehicles. When using this vehicle as a forward spawn point, park it in a relatively safe location that's still close to the action. This is very effective when attacking M-COM stations during Rush matches because the attacking team can maintain a presence close to the objectives.

MOBILE AA

Despite their rugged armored appearance, these vehicles aren't intended for toe-to-toe slugfests with enemy tanks. In fact, their armor isn't different from that found on the IFVs. But these vehicles are designed for the sole purpose of shooting down enemy aircraft. Move them to strategically advantageous locations to provide your forces protection from air strikes. The auto-cannons on these vehicles are great for shredding helicopters and jets alike. But these weapons can also be very effective when targeting infantry and light vehicles. These vehicles are rare, so take steps to protect them by keeping them repaired.

Mobile AA Unlock Progression

IMAGE	NAME	LOADOUT SLOT	POINTS	DESCRIPTION
	IR Smoke	Gadget	400	Smoke grenades enhanced with metal filaments that when launched remove laser-designation, spoof incoming guided missiles, and prevent enemies from revealing your position to teammates.
	Anti-Air Missile	Weapon	1,200	Anti-aircraft missile launchers are mounted on the turret and will lock on to and track enemy air vehicles.
	Belt Speed	Upgrade	2,500	An enhanced mechanism decreases the minimum time between firing bursts with your main weapon.
	Zoom Optics	Gadget	4,400	A secondary weapon sight with up to 3x magnification.
	Proximity Scan	Upgrade	7,000	External sensors detect and reveal enemy units on your minimap.
	Thermal Optics	Gadget	10,000	A secondary weapon sight with thermal optics that highlights soldiers and vehicles for efficient target identification.
	Air Radar	Upgrade	14,000	The range of your minimap increases greatly and reveals all friendly and enemy aircraft.
	Maintenance	Upgrade	19,000	Preventative maintenance procedures improve your vehicles recovery from damage.
	Thermal Camo	Upgrade	25,000	Antireflective coating on your vehicle increases enemy locking and tracking difficulty and decreases the time you are revealed to the enemy when spotted.
	Reactive Armor	Upgrade	32,000	Reactive armor panels and/or slats absorb the impact from anti-tank weapons, protecting you from damage but becoming destroyed in the process.

LAV-AD

NATIONALITY: US

DESRIPTION: The LAV-AD includes the Avenger anti-air system on a LAV-25 chassis.

Vehicle Performance

SPEED	
ARMOR	
FIREPOWER	

Vehicle Occupancy

SEAT	POSITION	WEAPON
1	Driver	25mm AA Cannon

FIELD NOTES

The LAV-AD looks just like the LAV-25, but it performs quite differently. For one, it has only a driver seat and cannot be used to transport troops. But the five-barreled 25mm cannon attached to its turret is great for tearing apart enemy helicopters or jets. The weapon is equally devastating against infantry and light vehicles. It can even damage tanks.

[MOBILE AA SERVICE STARS]

You earn a service star for every 32,000 points you score with the mobile AA vehicles. 100 mobile AA service stars are available.

9K22 TUNGUSKA-M

NATIONALITY: RU

DESRIPTION: This mobile surface-to-air gun and missile system has been in service since 1982. It was developed in response to range shortcomings in the ZU-23 Shilka design.

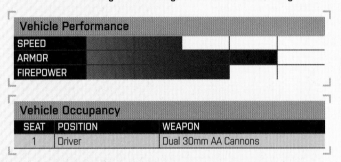

Vehicle Performance

SPEED			
ARMOR			
FIREPOWER			

Vehicle Occupancy

SEAT	POSITION	WEAPON
1	Driver	Dual 30mm AA Cannons

FIELD NOTES

Offensively, the Tunguska performs identically to the LAV-AD and is ideal for ripping apart aircraft, light vehicles, and infantry with its rapid-firing 30mm cannons. However, this hulking tracked vehicle is a bit more sluggish than its wheeled counterpart, and therefore a bit more difficult to maneuver in tight spaces.

[MOBILE AA TACTICS]

- Before moving out, analyze your team's air defenses and move the vehicle to an area where it can protect your team. Make an effort to park it in a well-protected area that is out of sight from advancing enemy tanks and infantry. While scanning the skies for targets, it's easy to lose sight of the battle happening around you.

- Instead of constantly rotating the turret looking for targets, rely on the minimap to spot enemy jets and helicopters. If your vehicle is spotted by teammates, these threats appear as red icons on the minimap. So rotate the turret in the direction of these icons, then scan the sky for the target—if still spotted, a red icon appears above the aircraft, making it easy to track. The Air Radar upgrade automatically marks the positions of all enemy aircraft on the minimap.

- The mobile AA vehicles have unlimited ammo, but the cannons tend to overheat when fired for long, uninterrupted bursts. To prevent overheating, fire in bursts that last no longer than four seconds. A brief pause in firing allows the guns to cool down.

- When attacking one of these vehicles, try to hit them from the side or rear, where their armor is weakest. Although they fill a very specialized role, these vehicles have thick armor capable of withstanding heavy damage. Tanks and IFVs are best suited for taking out these vehicles.

- These vehicles have only one weapon unlock in the form of the Anti-Air Missile. This is a heat-seeking missile similar to those fired by the Stinger and IGLA missiles carried by engineers. When selected, these missiles automatically track targets in the center of your screen, indicated by a red bounded box. Keep tracking the target across the sky until a lock is achieved, then fire the missile. The pilot you're tracking is made aware of the missile lock and may deploy IR Flares in an effort to break the lock. So consider waiting for the pilot to dump their flares before reacquiring a lock and firing a missile. If the lock is achieved quickly, the pilot won't have a chance to deploy a second set of flares.

MAIN BATTLE TANKS (MBT)

While tanks are still at the top of the food chain during ground combat, they're far from invincible. Rockets fired by infantry, helicopters, and jets pose a big threat, as do other tanks. A tank's side and rear armor are the weakest. For this reason, keep the front armor facing a threat at all times, especially when engaging other tanks. The rounds fired by a tank's main gun travel in an arced trajectory. So compensate for range by elevating the barrel and aiming above your target. Use the horizontal lines on the tank's HUD to determine the proper elevation setting to score a hit.

MBT Unlock Progression

IMAGE	NAME	LOADOUT SLOT	POINTS	DESCRIPTION
	IR Smoke	Gadget	800	Smoke grenades enhanced with metal filaments that when launched remove laser-designation, spoof incoming guided missiles, and prevent enemies from revealing your position to teammates.
	Coaxial LMG	Weapon	2,100	A light machine gun mounted coaxially to your main weapon.
	Autoloader	Upgrade	4,400	An enhanced mechanism decreases the minimum time between firing rounds in your main weapon.
	Zoom Optics	Gadget	7,600	A secondary weapon sight with up to 3x magnification.
	Maintenance	Upgrade	12,000	Preventative maintenance procedures improve your vehicles recovery from damage.
	Coax HMG	Weapon	17,700	A heavy machine gun mounted coaxially to your main weapon.
	Proximity Scan	Upgrade	24,700	External sensors detect and reveal enemy units on your minimap.
	Guided Shell	Weapon	33,200	A smart target-activated fire and forget shell that can lock on to and track enemy land vehicles and can acquire laser-designated targets even if they are out of line of sight.
	Thermal Optics	Gadget	43,200	A secondary weapon sight with thermal optics that highlights soldiers and vehicles for efficient target identification.
	Thermal Camo	Upgrade	54,800	Antireflective coating on your vehicle increases enemy locking and tracking difficulty and decreases the time you are revealed to the enemy from being spotted.
	Canister Shell	Weapon	68,100	A tank shell encasing thousands of tungsten balls that is fired though the cannon muzzle like a shotgun.
	Reactive Armor	Upgrade	83,200	Reactive armor panels and/or slats absorb the impact from anti-tank weapons, protecting you from damage but becoming destroyed in the process.
	CITV Station	Gadget	100,000	Access to a third turret position in the tank from which you can laser-designate targets and use a proximity scanner. You can enter a tank in this seat even if other players are occupying both the driver and remote gunner positions.

M1 ABRAMS

NATIONALITY: US

DESRIPTION: The M1 Abrams is the principal battle tank of the US Marine Corps.

Vehicle Performance

SPEED				
ARMOR				
FIREPOWER				

Vehicle Occupancy

SEAT	POSITION	WEAPON
1	Driver	120mm Cannon
2	Gunner	HMG .50

FIELD NOTES

Powered by a turbine engine that produces a distinct whining sound, the M1 Abrams sounds more like a jet than a tank. The green horizontal lines in the center of the tank's HUD can be used to gauge barrel elevation when firing at distant targets. But hitting targets at extreme ranges requires more guesswork, as there are no lines to reference. Fire a shot, watch where it lands, then either elevate or lower the barrel to zero in on your target.

T-90A

NATIONALITY: RU

DESRIPTION: The T-90A is derived from the T-72, and is the most modern tank in service with the Russian Ground Forces and Naval Infantry.

Vehicle Performance

SPEED					
ARMOR					
FIREPOWER					

Vehicle Occupancy

SEAT	POSITION	WEAPON
1	Driver	125mm Cannon
2	Gunner	12.7mm Machine Gun

FIELD NOTES

The T90A is well balanced when countering the US M1 Abrams, but its HUD offers a bit more help when engaging targets at long range. Use the green vertical line beneath the tank's center crosshairs to better gauge barrel elevation. The horizontal notches on this line can be used as reference points when firing the main gun—if the first notch was too low, elevate your aim to the second notch, and so on.

[MBT TACTICS]

- Tanks are designed for one purpose: killing other tanks. Statistically, the M1 Abrams and T-90A are identical, providing an even playing field for both drivers during tank duels. But there are a few tactics you can use to gain the upper hand. For one, try to maneuver so you can target the enemy tank's weaker side or rear armor. Likewise, rotate your tank so both the chasis and turret are facing the enemy tank's main gun. This allows the thick front armor to absorb the majority of the damage. Unlocks like the Autoloader and Reactive Armor upgrades can also make a huge difference in a tank duel.

- Tanks are best deployed as stand-off weapons. Use the power and range of the cannon to engage enemy vehicles at long range. This is easiest when firing the Guided Shell weapon unlock. These shells are capable of locking onto laser-designated targets painted by the SOFLAM or CITV Station.

- When the CITV Station gadget is unlocked, a third seat is added to the tank. The crew member occupying this third seat mans a laser-designator. When used in combination with the Guided Shell, a tank with a CITV Station can paint and engage their own targets without having to rely on a recon soldier's SOFLAM.

- The Canister Shell unlock is a devastating antipersonnel weapon, effectively turning a tank's main gun into a massive shotgun. But like a shotgun, this shell is most effective at close to intermediate range. Only use this in defensive situations. Never go hunting for infantry in a tank, especially in urban environments. If you spot enemy infantry on the periphery, immediately back up while firing before one of them can toss a mine or C4 in your direction.

- Consider playing as an engineer when driving a tank. As you take damage, retreat, hop out, and use the repair tool to fix your ride. Better yet, have your engineer gunner get out and repair while you continue firing the main gun. This tactic gives you a huge advantage during tank duels and is the only way to keep a disabled tank in the fight.

- Helicopters and jets are a tank's worst enemy. However, the machine gun turret is completely capable of damaging these airborne threats. But when counterattacking, stay on the move so as to not give your opponent an easy target to strafe. If you have the IR Smoke gadget unlock, use it to conceal your position and break the locks of laser-guided munitions.

- The tank's driver seat offers poor visibility. Unless a teammate is manning the machine gun turret and actively scanning the perimeter for threats, switch to an external view when driving a tank through city streets. This allows you to spot enemy troops attempting to sneak up on your tank—support troops can ruin your day by sticking C4 to the back of your ride.

[MBT SERVICE STARS]

You earn a service star for every 100,000 points you score with the MBTs. 100 MBT service stars are available.

ATTACK HELICOPTERS

The attack helicopters are the most devastating vehicles in the game, but only when crewed by a capable pilot and gunner. A two-man crew is essential for each attack helicopter to live up to its deadly potential. The pilot can fire the chopper's unguided rockets, which are ideal for taking out tanks and other ground vehicles. But it's the gunner who benefits from the awesome firepower provided by the chin-mounted turret. Like the auto-cannons found on the IFVs, the cannons on attack helicopters fire small explosive rounds. The gunner can use this weapon to rack up dozens of infantry kills. Despite their impressive offensive capability, attack helicopters are vulnerable to heavy machine gun fire and heat-seeking missiles fired by engineers or other aircraft. But with some fancy flying and the aid of upgrades and gadgets, it's possible to minimize the danger posed by these threats. Unlike other vehicles, attack helicopters have six loadout slots—three for the pilot and three for the gunner. This allows an experienced crew to become more powerful with each attained unlock.

Attack Helicopter Unlock Progression

IMAGE	NAME	LOADOUT SLOT	POINTS	DESCRIPTION
	IR Flares	Gadget	300	Infrared flare launchers that when launched will distract incoming missiles and cause them to miss their locked target.
	Heat Seekers	Pilot Weapon	800	Heat-seeking missiles launched by the pilot that lock on to and track enemy aircraft.
	Stealth	Upgrade	1,600	Engine tuning and fuselage coating materials disguise your vehicle's infrared signature, thereby increasing enemy locking and tracking difficulty and decreasing the time you are revealed to the enemy when spotted.
	Autoloader	Upgrade	2,800	An enhanced mechanism decreases the minimum time between firing bursts with your main weapon.
	Zoom Optics	Gunner Gadget	4,400	A secondary weapon sight for the gunner position with up to 3x magnification.
	Proximity Scan	Upgrade	6,500	External sensors detect and reveal enemy units on your minimap.
	Air Radar	Upgrade	9,000	The range of your minimap increases greatly and reveals all friendly and enemy aircraft.
	Guided Missile	Gunner Weapon	12,000	Guided missiles launched by the helicopter gunner that lock on to and track enemy land vehicles and can acquire laser-designated targets even if they are out of line of sight.
	Extinguisher	Pilot Gadget	16,000	A controlled air pressure release in the engine compartment will extinguish engine fires when activated, helping a disabled aircraft return to normal operation and recover from damage.
	Maintenance	Upgrade	20,000	Preventative maintenance procedures improve your vehicles recovery from damage.
	Thermal Optics	Gunner Gadget	25,000	A secondary weapon sight for the gunner position using thermal optics that highlights soldiers and vehicles for efficient target identification.
	Laser Painter	Pilot Upgrade	30,500	Nose-mounted targeting systems designate an enemy vehicle in your line of sight automatically, painting them as a target for teammates using laser-guided weapons.
	Below Radar	Upgrade	37,000	When flying at low altitudes your heat signature is decreased, hiding you from enemy radar and preventing enemy air-to-air missile systems from locking on to you.
	ECM Jammer	Pilot Gadget	44,000	Electronic countermeasures including chaff launchers and deceptive transmitters prevent your aircraft from being locked on to by enemy weapon systems for a short time when activated.
	Guided Rocket	Upgrade	51,000	The pilot's rockets are equipped with semi-active guidance systems, increasing accuracy and thereby range of effectiveness.
	TV Missile	Gunner Weapon	60,000	TV-guided missiles launched by the helicopter gunner that are flown by direct-feed video.

AH-1Z VIPER

NATIONALITY: US

DESRIPTION: The AH-1Z Viper (also called SuperCobra or Zulu Cobra) is a twin-engine helicopter based on the AH-1W.

Vehicle Performance

SPEED	
ARMOR	
FIREPOWER	

Vehicle Occupancy

SEAT	POSITION	WEAPON
1	Driver	70mm Rockets
2	Gunner	20mm Cannon

FIELD NOTES

When piloting the Viper, use the I-shaped reticle in the middle of the HUD to aim your rockets. You can fire up to 14 rockets in one salvo, but then the rockets must reload. Likewise, the gunner can fire only 30 cannon rounds in quick succession before the weapon must be reloaded. The time it takes to reload these weapons can be reduced by applying Autoloader to both the pilot and gunner upgrade slots.

MI-28 HAVOC

NATIONALITY: RU

DESRIPTION: The Mil Mi-28 (NATO reporting name Havoc) is a Russian all-weather day or night, two-seat anti-armor attack helicopter.

Vehicle Performance

SPEED				
ARMOR				
FIREPOWER				

Vehicle Occupancy

SEAT	POSITION	WEAPON
1	Driver	S-8 Rockets
2	Gunner	30mm Chain Gun

FIELD NOTES

The Havoc performs identically to the US team's Viper, even utilizing the same HUD layout. In the default configuration, the pilot can fire rockets while the gunner controls the chin-mounted chain gun. Both weapons are effective against infantry as well as light and armored vehicles. When not firing, the gunner position is great for spotting targets, particularly when the Zoom Optics or Thermal Optics gadgets are selected.

[ATTACK HELICOPTER TACTICS]

- If you're planning to fly an attack helicopter, discuss loadouts with your gunner before spawning into the game. Make sure you don't have any duplicate upgrade or gadget loadout slots assigned. For example, there is no benefit for both the pilot and gunner to have the Stealth upgrade selected. So mix up your loadouts to maximize the effectiveness of this powerful vehicle.

- With the new vehicle damage system, it's possible to recover from light damage simply by flying away from danger. If you stay away from enemy fire for a few seconds, you chopper automatically returns to full health. However, if your helicopter catches fire, there are only two ways to repair it. You can land and have an engineer use their Repair Tool or you can use the Extinguisher gadget to put out the flames.

- Add Heat Seekers to the pilot's weapon loadout slot when you're confronted with enemy jets and choppers. This gives the attack helicopter the ability to shoot down enemy aircraft. Heat-seeking missiles can only lock on to enemy aircraft in flight. Once a lock is achieved, fire the missile and watch it streak toward the target.

- The Below Radar and IR Flares upgrades greatly increase your chances of survival. Both upgrades make it difficult for heat-seeking missiles to achieve a lock. If you haven't unlocked these upgrades, stay low to the ground, utilizing nap-of-the-earth (NOE) flight to put objects such as hills and trees between your chopper and hostile missile launchers. By breaking line of sight with a heat-seeking missile, you can prevent a lock prior to launch.

- The chin turrets on the Viper and Havoc are absolutely devastating against infantry. So when piloting these choppers, try to give your gunner a stable firing platform to increase the weapon's accuracy. Instead of dipping the chopper's nose forward, fly laterally, keeping the nose pointed toward the enemy. Strafing left and right keeps the chopper moving while allowing your gunner to accurately engage enemy ground targets.

- The Guided Missile is very effective but requires a laser target designator, such as the recon kit's SOFLAM, to paint a target. Once the Laser Painter upgrade is unlocked, the pilot of an attack helicopter can paint their own targets, allowing the gunner to fire a Guided Missile. The gunner can fire the TV Missile without having to wait for a lock or laser designation, but it must be manually guided into a target.

- As soon as it's available, choose the Extinguisher unlock for your gadget slot. If your chopper ever becomes disabled, it's incredibly difficult to control, potentially leading to a crash. But if you immediately deploy the Extinguisher, the controls are restored. Still, you may want to seek cover while the helicopter regenerates health.

[ATTACK HELICOPTER SERVICE STARS]

You earn a service star for every 60,000 points you score with the attack helicopters. 100 attack helicopter service stars are available.

SCOUT HELICOPTERS

The scout helicopters bridge the gap between the attack helicopters and the transport helicopters. Initially the scout helicopters have only light armament in the form of gun pods that are ideal for strafing infantry and light vehicles. But new and more powerful weapons can be unlocked to turn these small, agile helicopters into formidable weapons platforms. Over time, both Heat Seekers and Guided Missiles can be unlocked and equipped, allowing these helicopters to serve a more active role in shooting down enemy aircraft and destroying enemy armor. But with three passenger seats, the scout helicopter is best utilized as a quick way to move troops around the battlefield.

Scout Helicopter Unlock Progression

IMAGE	NAME	LOADOUT SLOT	POINTS	DESCRIPTION
	IR Flares	Gadget	400	Infrared flare launchers that when launched will distract incoming missiles and cause them to miss their locked target.
	Heat Seekers	Weapon	1,200	Heat-seeking missiles launched by the pilot that lock on to and track enemy aircraft.
	Stealth	Upgrade	2,500	Engine tuning and fuselage coating materials disguise your vehicle's infrared signature, thereby increasing enemy locking and tracking difficulty and decreasing the time you are revealed to the enemy when spotted.
	Autoloader	Upgrade	4,400	An enhanced mechanism decreases the minimum time between firing bursts with your main weapon.
	Proximity Scan	Upgrade	7,000	External sensors detect and reveal enemy units on your minimap.
	Air Radar	Upgrade	10,000	The range of your minimap increases greatly and reveals all friendly and enemy aircraft.
	Extinguisher	Gadget	14,000	A controlled air pressure release in the engine compartment will extinguish engine fires when activated, helping a disabled aircraft return to normal operation and recover from damage.
	Maintenance	Upgrade	19,000	Preventative maintenance procedures improve your vehicle's recovery from damage.
	Guided Missile	Weapon	25,000	Guided missiles launched by the pilot that lock on to and track enemy land vehicles and can acquire laser-designated targets even if they are out of line of sight.
	Below Radar	Upgrade	32,000	When flying at low altitudes your heat signature is decreased, hiding you from enemy radar and preventing enemy air-to-air missile systems from locking on to you.
	Laser Painter	Upgrade	40,000	Nose-mounted targeting systems designate an enemy vehicle in your line of sight automatically, painting them as a target for teammates using laser-guided weapons.
	ECM Jammer	Gadget	48,000	Electronic countermeasures including chaff launchers and deceptive transmitters prevent your aircraft from being locked on to by enemy weapon systems for a short time when activated.

AH-6J LITTLE BIRD

NATIONALITY: US

DESRIPTION: This is an improved attack version of the MH-6.

Vehicle Performance

SPEED					
ARMOR					
FIREPOWER					

Vehicle Occupancy

SEAT	POSITION	WEAPON
1	Pilot	Gun Pod
2	Passenger	Troop Kit
3	Passenger	Troop Kit
4	Passenger	None

FIELD NOTES

When piloting the Little bird, be mindful of your passengers in the second and third positions riding on the helicopter's landing skids. These passengers are completely exposed to incoming fire. So fly low and fast to prevent these troops from being hit. Consider dropping these passenger off before performing any strafing runs.

Z-11W

NATIONALITY: RU

DESRIPTION: This is an armed military version of the Z-11 Chinese light utility helicopter.

Vehicle Performance

SPEED	
ARMOR	
FIREPOWER	

Vehicle Occupancy

SEAT	POSITION	WEAPON
1	Pilot	Gun Pod
2	Passenger	Troop Kit
3	Passenger	Troop Kit
4	Passenger	None

FIELD NOTES

The Z-11W is slightly larger than the Little Bird, but it still possesses the same speed and maneuverability. In this chopper, the passengers in the second and third positions ride within the cargo compartment in the back. This gives them a bit more protection from incoming fire than riding on the landing skid.

[SCOUT HELICOPTER TACTICS]

- On some maps, the scout helicopters are the fastest way to transport troops. So don't take off until every seat is full. Instead of landing, fly over your destination so you passengers can bail out and parachute down to the ground. This is the best way to quickly secure control points during Conquest matches. For more precise troop insertions, these helicopters are small and agile enough to land on rooftops or other elevated positions usually inaccessible to infantry. So consider dropping recon troops on high perches so they can monitor the battlefield from above.

- The reticle in the center of the pilot's HUD is the aiming point for the chopper's gun pods. The gun pods are fixed and always fire straight ahead. This requires you to dip the nose of the chopper while engaging targets on the ground. When pitching the nose down, the chopper will lose altitude. Applying full rotor speed can reduce the speed of descent, but you will still need to pitch the nose of the chopper up to avoid crashing. So when performing strafing runs, don't get greedy. Fire a quick burst then pull away before you crash.

- The gun pods are best deployed against infantry and light vehicles. But with sustained, accurate fire, they can damage armored vehicles, too, including IFVs and tanks. As usual, try to hit these vehicles from the side or rear to inflict the most damage.

- Once the Laser Painter is unlocked a scout helicopter becomes a self-sufficient tank killer. The Laser Painter upgrade allows the chopper to designate its own targets and fire on them with the Guided Missile weapon unlock. It's up to the pilot to both designate the target and fire the missile. Start by orienting the chopper within line of sight of an enemy vehicle to automatically attain a lock. At this point a Guided Missile can be fired, which will automatically home in on the laser.

- Given their speed and maneuverability, the scout helicopters serve as great air-to-air weapons platforms when armed with the Heat Seekers unlock. When an enemy aircraft is within view, instead of chasing it, simply rotate the chopper so you're always facing the target. This gives the missile enough time to lock on. While carrying these missiles, the pilot can still switch back to the gun pods for strafing runs. So once unlocked, there's no reason not to have the Heat Seekers unlock assigned to the weapon slot. But when the Guided Missile is unlocked, you'll have to make a choice between the two.

[SCOUT HELICOPTER SERVICE STARS]

You earn a service star for every 48,000 points you score with the scout helicopters. 100 scout helicopter service stars are available.

TRANSPORT HELICOPTERS

Each transport helicopter is capable of holding five players, making them ideal for transporting squads to any spot on the battlefield. During Conquest matches, these large choppers are the best way to capture neutral control points at the start of a battle. But the transport helicopter's impressive troop capacity is also its weakness, and may result in a big score for a fighter pilot or any other unit armed with heat-seeking missiles. To avoid such threats, fly low and fast, using trees, hills, and buildings to mask you movements. As long as you avoid line of sight with your enemies, they can't attain a lock and fire a missile. There are no vehicle unlocks or loadout options for transport helicopters.

UH-1Y VENOM

NATIONALITY: US

DESRIPTION: The modern version of the Twin Huey helicopters used by the Marines since the 1970s, this new variant was introduced in 2008.

Vehicle Performance

SPEED	
ARMOR	
FIREPOWER	

Vehicle Occupancy

SEAT	POSITION	WEAPON
1	Pilot	None
2	Gunner	Minigun
3	Gunner	Minigun
4	Passenger	Troop Kit
5	Passenger	Troop Kit

FIELD NOTES

The Venom is the US team's fastest high-capacity troop transport. It is also armed with port and starboard mounted miniguns. The miniguns have a blazing rate of the fire, ideal for engaging troops and light vehicles. With sustained fire, they can even damage armored vehicles such as tanks and IFVs.

KA-60 KASATKA

NATIONALITY: RU

DESRIPTION: This new utility helicopter from Kamov is entering service with the Russian Air Force to replace the aging Mi-8.

Vehicle Performance

SPEED	
ARMOR	
FIREPOWER	

Vehicle Occupancy

SEAT	POSITION	WEAPON
1	Pilot	None
2	Gunner	Minigun
3	Gunner	Minigun
4	Passenger	Troop Kit
5	Passenger	Troop Kit

FIELD NOTES

The KA-60 performs much like the US team's Venom, but the pilot sits on the starboard side. This can be a bit disorienting at first, compared to piloting the other choppers where the pilot either sits in the middle or on the port side. So when maneuvering the chopper at low altitude, be mindful of the port side to avoid clipping trees, towers, and other objects.

[TRANSPORT HELICOPTER TACTICS]

- Unless you have experience flying helicopters, don't try to fly a transport helicopter filled with teammates. This is the wrong time to take a flying lesson. If you want more experience flying, find a server with a low player count and experiment taking off, flying, and landing.

- It takes a few seconds for a transport helicopter's rotor to spin up before takeoff. So after securing an enemy base in Rush matches, watch for enemies lurking about during these vulnerable seconds as you can die fast if you get hit with a rocket or tank round. Also, take steps to ensure the enemy doesn't steal your choppers.

- The transport helicopters can be used to quickly capture control points during Conquest matches—hover over the flag to convert it. The more players onboard, the faster it will be captured. However, watch out for defenders below. A hovering chopper makes a juicy target. It's much safer to drop troops via parachute onto a control point.

- Use the miniguns to blow apart light cover offered by walls and rooftops. This is a great way to expose M-COM stations located inside small structures during Rush matches.

- The miniguns are capable of high rates of fire, but they have a tendency to overheat, rendering them inoperable for a few seconds. So lay off the trigger occasionally to give the barrels a chance to cool down. For a better view of distant targets, use the minigun's zoom function.

- When piloting a transport helicopter, orbit around a contentious point so the gunners on the port and starboard sides can provide supporting fire with the miniguns. While orbiting around one location, usually only one gunner has the best view. So consider switching directions so both gunners get a chance to lay down some fire. A transport helicopter spitting out thousands of rounds is likely to draw attention so be prepared to escape to a safe distance if you detect a missile lock. Drop altitude fast in an attempt to break line of sight with a missile before it is launched.

JETS

The jets make their triumphant return in *Battlefield 3*, providing air superiority as well as close air support. Jets are the fastest vehicles in the game and can travel a significant distance outside the map's combat zone, along with helicopters. This is useful when engaged in a dogfight with an enemy jet. But eventually a jet must turn around to avoid flying off the map. If your jet is heavily damaged, make sure you're within the map's combat zone before bailing out. Initially, each jet is equipped only with a cannon that is useful for strafing ground targets or peppering enemy aircraft with rapid fire. But as you score more points with the jets, more weapon unlocks become available, including Heat Seekers, the Guided Missile, and Rocket Pods. Only one of these weapons can be assigned to the weapon slot, so you must decide what kind of role your jet will fill before spawning into the game.

Jet Unlock Progression

IMAGE	NAME	LOADOUT SLOT	POINTS	DESCRIPTION
	IR Flares	Gadget	300	Infrared flare launchers that when launched will distract incoming missiles and cause them to miss their locked target.
	Heat Seekers	Weapon	700	Heat-seeking missiles launched by the pilot that lock on to and track enemy aircraft.
	Stealth	Upgrade	1,500	Engine tuning and fuselage coating materials disguise your vehicle's infrared signature, thereby increasing enemy locking and tracking difficulty and decreasing the time you are revealed to the enemy when spotted.
	Autoloader	Upgrade	2,700	An enhanced mechanism that decreases the minimum time between firing bursts with your main weapon.
	Proximity Scan	Upgrade	4,200	External sensors detect and reveal enemy units on your minimap.
	Rocket Pods	Weapon	6,200	A set of unguided FFAR Rocket Pods mounted under the wings.
	Air Radar	Upgrade	8,600	The range of your minimap increases greatly and reveals all friendly and enemy aircraft.
	Extinguisher	Gadget	11,600	A controlled air pressure release in the engine compartment will extinguish engine fires when activated, helping a disabled aircraft return to normal operation and recover from damage.
	Below Radar	Upgrade	15,000	When flying at low altitudes, your heat signature is decreased, hiding you from enemy radar and preventing enemy air-to-air missile systems from locking on to you.
	Maintenance	Upgrade	19,000	Preventative maintenance procedures improve your vehicles recovery from damage.
	Guided Missile	Weapon	24,000	Laser-guided missiles launched by the pilot which lock on to and track enemy land vehicles and can acquire laser-designated targets even if they are out of line of sight.
	Beam Scanning	Upgrade	29,000	A computer upgrade for advanced weapon systems that helps you lock on to enemy targets faster when using heat-seeking or laser-guided missiles.
	ECM Jammer	Gadget	35,000	Electronic countermeasures including chaff launchers and deceptive transmitters prevent your aircraft from being locked on to by enemy weapon systems for a short time when activated.

A-10 WARTHOG

NATIONALITY: US

DESRIPTION: Designed for a USAF requirement to provide Close Air Support (CAS) of ground forces by attacking ground targets with limited AA capability.

Vehicle Performance		
SPEED		
ARMOR		
FIREPOWER		

Vehicle Occupancy		
SEAT	POSITION	WEAPON
1	Pilot	30mm Cannon

FIELD NOTES

Designed as a tank killer, the A-10 excels in a ground attack role. Its massive 30mm cannon can pierce the thick armor of tanks and IFVs, disabling them with a single strafing pass. The aircraft benefits from a relatively low stall speed, allowing you to reduce speed during strafing runs, giving you more time to fire the cannon and rockets.

SU-25TM FROGFOOT

NATIONALITY: RU

DESRIPTION: Soviet-designed Close Air Support (CAS) plane nicknamed Grach. NATO reporting name is Frogfoot.

Vehicle Performance		
SPEED		
ARMOR		
FIREPOWER		

Vehicle Occupancy		
SEAT	POSITION	WEAPON
1	Pilot	30mm Cannon

FIELD NOTES

Like the A-10, the RU team's SU-25TM is best deployed as a ground attack aircraft. However, with the addition of the Heat Seekers weapon unlock, the aircraft can also serve as a fighter. While banking, apply the air brake to perform tight turns. But don't forget to apply throttle after the turn to prevent stalling.

F/A-18E SUPER HORNET

NATIONALITY: US

DESRIPTION: A multi-role jet fighter aircraft introduced in 1983 and used today by the USMC.

Vehicle Performance		
SPEED		
ARMOR		
FIREPOWER		

Vehicle Occupancy		
SEAT	POSITION	WEAPON
1	Pilot	20mm Cannon

FIELD NOTES

The Super Hornet is a high-speed multi-role aircraft capable of serving as an air superiority fighter or a ground attack jet. Like the other aircraft, its cannon is well suited for strafing ground targets as well as shooting down enemy aircraft. Use the jet's afterburner to produce a quick jolt of speed that is ideal during takeoffs.

SU-35BM FLANKER-E

NATIONALITY: RU

DESRIPTION: A long-range multi-role fighter, modernized and deployed starting in 2011. The last of the Flanker series by Sukhoi.

Vehicle Performance

SPEED		
ARMOR		
FIREPOWER		

Vehicle Occupancy

SEAT	POSITION	WEAPON
1	Pilot	30mm Cannon

FIELD NOTES

The Flanker-E is always deployed opposite of the Super Hornet. So consider choosing the Heat Seekers weapon upgrade and hunting down the US jet. Wait until you're behind the enemy aircraft before switching to missiles. This gives you a better chance of achieving a lock, allowing you to follow closely behind as the Super Hornet tries to escape.

[JET TACTICS]

- There's no longer a need to camp runways waiting for jets to spawn at your base. You can spawn directly into a waiting jet (or helicopter) from the spawn screen. Simply choose the name of a jet from the list of available spawn points to hop in the pilot's seat.

- Pay close attention to the floating circle icon in the center of the jet's HUD. This is the angle of attack indicator, representing the true direction your aircraft is traveling. If the icon is firmly in the center of the HUD, you are traveling straight ahead. However, if the icon drifts to the bottom of the HUD, you're experiencing a stall. Immediately apply throttle and gently lift the nose of the aircraft to increase lift before you crash.

- All jets are equipped with afterburners. Press and hold the sprint key/button to activate the afterburners, producing a sudden increase in speed. Apply afterburners when taking off or when trying to prevent a stall. Do not use the afterburner when attempting to make tight turns. This increases the turn radius of the aircraft, putting you at a disadvantage during dogfights. Instead, decrease throttle during tight turns to reduce the aircraft's turn radius.

- Jets travel so quickly that it's difficult for them to identify both air and ground targets. Teammates on the ground or in slower moving helicopters can greatly aid jets by spotting ground targets such as tanks and IFVs. This temporarily marks targets on the HUD, making it much easier for jets to set up strafing runs. Recon troops equipped with SOFLAMs are equally important when firing the Guided Missile weapon unlock. This weapon requires a laser-designated target before it can be fired.

- When aligning your aircraft prior to a strafing run, use the strafe controls to apply left and right rudder. Making these slight lateral adjustments makes it much easier to align your jet with the target. After making a strafing pass, continue flying straight for a couple of seconds, then perform a half loop. If you made no lateral adjustments, you'll still be lined up with you target, assuming it hasn't moved.

- IR Flares or Extinguisher? This is a choice you'll have to make when assigning an unlock to the jet's gadget slot. Since the IR Flares are the first unlock, stick with them until the Extinguisher is available. IR Flares make it tough for heat-seeking missiles to acquire a lock, allowing you to escape. But the Extinguisher practically repairs any damage dealt by a heat-seeking missile or any other weapon by putting out the flames.

- Due to the jets' high speed, it's difficult to lock on to a slow chopper with the Heat Seekers weapon unlock. Your jet will often zoom past the helicopter before it can acquire a lock. Therefore, consider using the cannon when engaging enemy choppers. This requires more skill, but if your aim is true, the enemy helicopter is toast. The cannon is also a good option when dog fighting enemy jets, because IR Flares can't fool this weapon.

- The Rocket Pods weapon unlock works similar to the rockets fired by the attack helicopters. When selected, an I-shaped reticle appears at the center of the HUD. Use this reticle to aim the rockets during strafing runs. You can fire up to 14 rockets per salvo, at which point the weapon must reload. So when making a pass, simply hold down the trigger to fire all 14 rockets. By the time you circle around for another pass, a new salvo of rockets should be ready to fire. The Autoloader upgrade significantly reduces the reload time for the Rocket Pods.

[JET SERVICE STARS]

You earn a service star for every 35,000 points you score with the jets. 100 jet service stars are available.

STATIONARY ANTI-VEHICLE WEAPONS

When the weapons you're carrying aren't enough to hold back the enemy vehicles, look for stationary weapons to gain some extra firepower. Anti-tank missile launchers and anti-air guns are available on most multiplayer maps. These weapons are fixed and can't be relocated, but each can rotate 360 degrees. Simply stand next to one of these weapons and interact with it to take control. All stationary weapons have unlimited ammo.

M220 TOW LAUNCHER

NATIONALITY: US

DESRIPTION: The Tube-launched, Optically-tracked, Wire guided missile (TOW) has been in service with the US military since the 1970s.

FIELD NOTES

The TOW launcher fires a wire-guided anti-tank missile capable of inflicting heavy damage to any vehicle it strikes. Once launched, the missile must be guided manually into the target. This leaves the operator vulnerable to attack while operating the weapon system. So make sure a squad or teammate has your back while using this weapon.

CENTURION C-RAM

NATIONALITY: US

DESRIPTION: Land-based version of the Phalanx CIWS, deployed in Iraq to protect against missile and airborne attacks.

FIELD NOTES

The Centurion C-RAM is usually deployed at US bases and on US aircraft carriers. Man this weapon station at the start of a round to protect advancing troops and vehicles from air strikes by enemy jets and helicopters. The cannon is similar to the one attached to the LAV-AD, capable of intense rapid fire. The weapon also has a zoom function making it easier to engage distant targets.

9M133 KORNET LAUNCHER

NATIONALITY: RU

DESRIPTION: The Kornet is a modern anti-tank missile system developed in Russia and deployed by armed forces around the world.

FIELD NOTES

The Kornet launcher functions identically to the TOW launcher and can usually be found at bases and other defensive positions, particularly during Rush matches. When engaging tanks or other armored vehicles, don't attack their front armor. Not only does this inflict minimal damage, but the tank crew is likely to spot the launch of the missile, resulting in a quick retaliation. Instead, try to hit the side or rear armor of a tank where you can inflict more damage and stand a better chance of remaining undetected.

PANTSIR S-1

NATIONALITY: RU

DESRIPTION: Russia's SA-19/SA-N-11 (Tunguska) mobile AA artillery system parked on a stationary platform.

FIELD NOTES

The Panstsir S-1 functions identically to the 9K22 Tunguska-M, but it can't move. So you must make the most of this weapon's platform wherever it is parked, usually at the RU team's base. Use it to protect vulnerable helicopters and aircraft sitting on the tarmac—these are popular targets for enemy pilots. To improve your field of view, consider chopping down nearby trees with the rapid firing cannons.

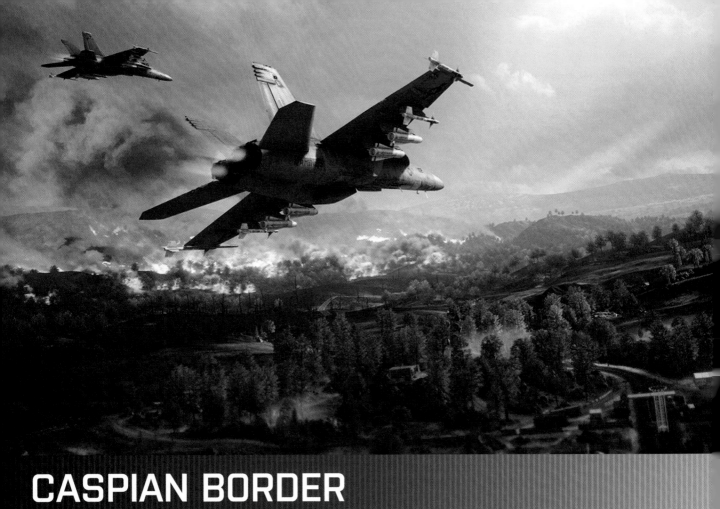

CASPIAN BORDER

After the death of Al-Bashir, Russia moves into Northern Iran to police its borders, telling the US to stay out or risk Russian retribution. A recon Russian force has set up camp on the Turkmenistan side of the border and has proceeded to take over the heavily built-up Iranian border checkpoint. The checkpoint regulates traffic across the border and through a highway that leads into Tehran.

US Marines, attempting to cut of the Russian advance towards the inland, need to push the Russians out of the border and destroy their nearby base.

The lush green valley represents a welcome change of scenery for advancing American forces accustomed to the dry desert plains. However, the Russian forces are better acquainted with the local terrain and will prove a tenacious foe.

CONQUEST

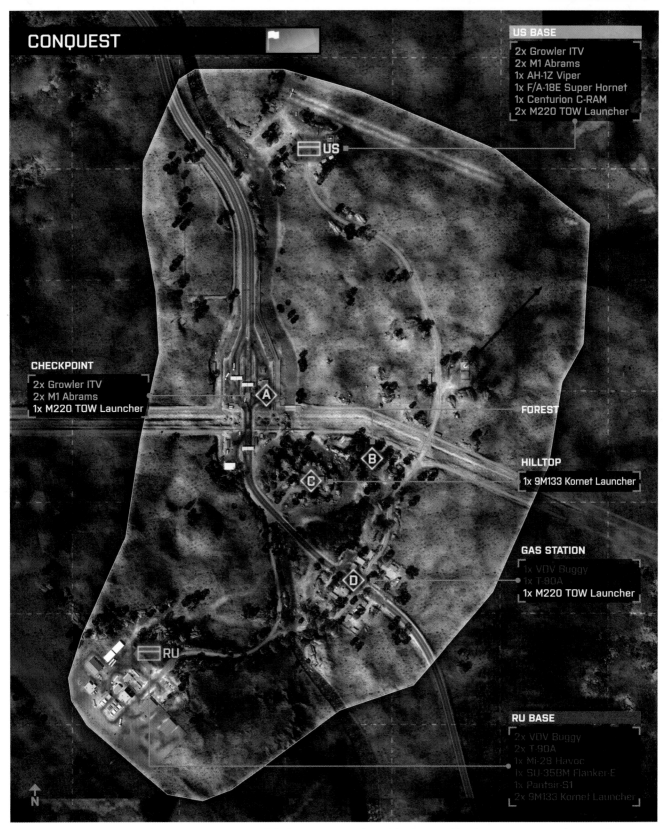

US BASE

2x Growler ITV
2x M1 Abrams
1x AH-1Z Viper
1x F/A-18E Super Hornet
1x Centurion C-RAM
2x M220 TOW Launcher

US

CHECKPOINT

2x Growler ITV
2x M1 Abrams
1x M220 TOW Launcher

A

FOREST

B

HILLTOP

1x 9M133 Kornet Launcher

C

GAS STATION

1x VDV Buggy
1x T-90A
1x M220 TOW Launcher

D

RU

RU BASE

2x VDV Buggy
2x T-90A
1x Mi-28 Havoc
1x SU-35BM Flanker-E
1x Pantsir-S1
2x 9M133 Kornet Launcher

N

In this head-on Conquest match, the US and RU teams fight for domination of a tightly contested border crossing area. There are four control points, meaning each team must strive to capture and hold at least three flags to initiate a ticket drain on the opposing team. For the US team, the Checkpoint (A), Forest (B), and Hilltop (C) are the best options. When playing as the RU team, attempt to take and hold the Gas Station (D), Hilltop (B), and Forest (B). As in any conquest match, don't stretch your team too thin, especially if playing with fewer than 32 players. Capture each point, then immediately dig in to prepare for the inevitable enemy counterattack. This is a very large map and there's a lot of terrain to cover on foot. So don't forget to make use of the vehicles that spawn at your team's base. The control points in the center of the map provide very few vehicles, so the team that consistently fields vehicles produced from their bases will have the upper hand in this conflict.

US BASE

Base Assets	NAME	Growler ITV	M1 Abrams	AH-1Z Viper	F/A-18E Super Hornet	Centurion C-RAM	M220 TOW Launcher
	QUANTITY	2*	2*	1	2	1	2
	RESPAWN TIME	5 sec.	20 sec.	60 sec.	40 sec.	—	30 sec.

* = only 1 when Checkpoint (A) is controlled by US

Positioned on the north edge of the map, the US Base is a long hike from even the nearest control points, so make sure you hitch a ride if you choose to spawn here. By taking the highway to the west, you can quickly race to the Checkpoint (A) and secure a couple more vehicles. However, when the Checkpoint (A) is captured by the US team, the US Base spawns only one Growler ITV and one M1 Abrams. To the east of the US Base is a dirt road leading toward the Forest (B) and Gas Station (D). The Growler ITVs are well suited for traveling this road, particularly at the start of a round. While the US Base is off-limits to RU troops, be ready for aerial harassment. If aerial assaults become a problem, man the Centurion C-RAM air defense system to fend off the attacking jets and choppers.

RU BASE

Base Assets	NAME	VDV Buggy	T-90A	Mi-28 Havoc	SU-35BM Flanker-E	Pantsir-S1	9M133 Kornet Launcher
	QUANTITY	2*	2*	1	2	1	2
	RESPAWN TIME	5 sec.	20 sec.	60 sec.	40 sec.	—	30 sec.

* = only 1 when Gas Station (D) is controlled by RU

The RU team has setup camp in the large base to the south. Like all bases in Conquest, this one is off-limits to US troops and ground vehicles. However, be prepared to fend off frequent strafing runs by US jets and attack helicopters, particularly early during the round. The Pantsir-S1 air defense system should be manned early on to deter such aerial attacks. The dirt road to the east is the major artery leading out of the RU Base and directly to the Gas Station (D) and Hilltop (C)—use the VDV Buggies to capture these points early in the round. If the RU team manages to capture the Gas Station (D), only one VDV Buggy and one T-90A spawn back at the RU Base instead of the default number of two each—think of it as these assets moving to the forward staging area.

A CHECKPOINT

Control Point Assets		
US CONTROL	**RU CONTROL**	**RESPAWN TIME**
Growler ITV (1)	—	25 sec.
M1 Abrams (1)	—	40 sec.
M220 TOW Launcher	M220 TOW Launcher	30 sec.

This control point (A) sits on the major highway on the west side of the map. Although it is centrally positioned, the US team has a slight edge when it comes to capturing this point early during a round. Utilizing the smooth, paved highway, the US team can capture this area early on using their fast-moving Growler ITVs. By capturing this point, the US gains access to one Growler ITV and one M1 Abrams. However, these assets are simply moved forward from the US Base and do not add to the total count of US vehicles. The flag here is situated within the Checkpoint facility, along the east side of the highway. Given the open nature of the area, this spot is best captured by tanks. However, infantry can capture and contest the flag from within the concrete structure to the north of the flagpole. This structure can be completely demolished, denying infantry suitable cover and concealment. Still, there are plenty of hiding spots outside, though none of them offer the protection of the concrete building.

B FOREST

The Forest control point (B) provides no vehicles to either team. But don't let that deter your team from capturing and defending this critical central location. Holding this area gives your team a spawn point in the middle of the map, which is ideal for launching raids on the Checkpoint (A), Hilltop (C), or Gas Station (D). Given the uneven terrain and lack of road access, this control point is best attacked and defended by infantry. Tanks are particularly vulnerable to ambush here, so try to move in on foot when possible. The trees (while still standing) offer decent concealment from air attacks and the massive boulders offer great cover. When defending, attacks mostly come from the west, originating from the other control points. So constantly watch for infantry and vehicles crossing the shallow stream to the west. Controlling the Hilltop (C) makes it much easier to hold this position. There, your team can use the high elevation to cover the approach to the flag.

Control Point Assets

US CONTROL	RU CONTROL	RESPAWN TIME
9M133 Kornet Launcher (1)	9M133 Kornet Launcher (1)	30 sec.

Regardless of which team you're on, taking the high ground of the Hilltop (C) should always be a priority. The RU team has the best chance of reaching this location early due to its relative close proximity to their base. However, US troops can make a claim here, too, by bailing out of jets or helicopters in the early moments of a match. While the control point offers very little in the way of assets, it has a great view of the surrounding terrain, making it a popular sniping perch for recon soldiers. If it's well defended, the Hilltop is also a tough nut to crack. The rocky cliff side to the east is completely impassable, which forces attacking units to approach the flag from the two dirt roads to the east. Both of these roads can be mined or booby-trapped with C4 to deter attacks by enemy vehicles. The flag itself sits atop the hill and can be captured or contested within the garage-like structure to the east. However, this concrete building will not last long under a sustained attack by tanks, jets, and helicopters. So be prepared to create your own concealment by deploying smoke.

Control Point Assets

US CONTROL	RU CONTROL	RESPAWN TIME
—	VDV Buggy (1)	25 sec.
—	T-90A (1)	40 sec.
M220 TOW Launcher	M220 TOW Launcher	30 sec.

The Gas Station (D) serves as the RU team's forward base, providing them with a VDV Buggy and T-90A closer to the map's central control points. However, these vehicles do not add to the RU team's total vehicle count. When the Gas Station is controlled by the RU team, the RU Base produces one fewer VDV Buggy and T-90A—these vehicles have not disappeared, they've just moved closer to the action. Given its close proximity to the RU Base, the RU team has the best chance of maintaining control of this location throughout the match. Still, the US team should attempt to capture the Gas Station to deny the RU team these vehicles. The flag is located near the roadway, not far from the flaming wreck of a truck. The fiery wreck emits a black cloud of smoke that helps conceal ground units from air attack. The gas pumps here are explosive, so keep your distance during firefights. If you're defending here, consider destroying all the pumps to make your job a little safer—or wait until attackers get near the pumps, then detonate them. Refuge can be sought in the Gas Station building, where you can either capture or contest the flag.

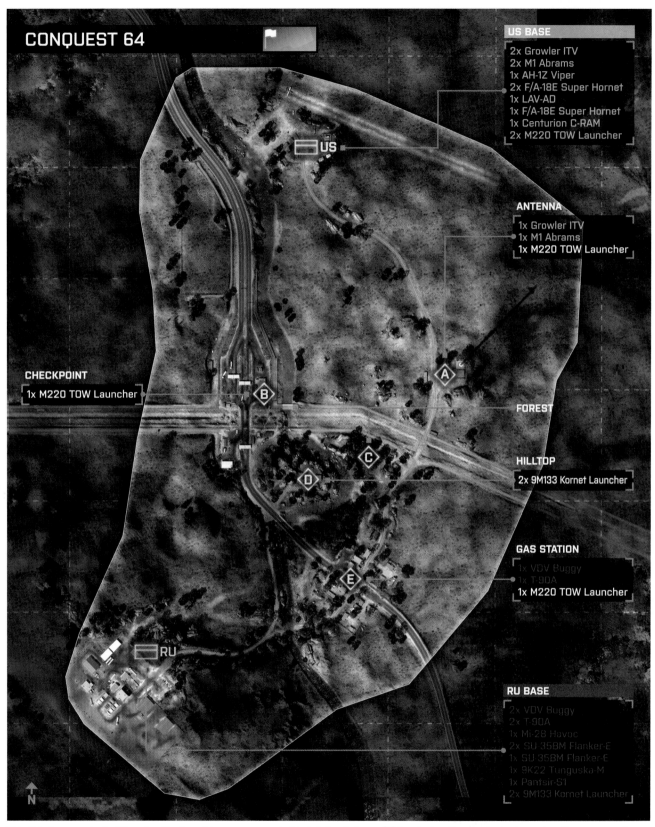

US BASE
2x Growler ITV
2x M1 Abrams
1x AH-1Z Viper
2x F/A-18E Super Hornet
1x LAV-AD
1x F/A-18E Super Hornet
1x Centurion C-RAM
2x M220 TOW Launcher

ANTENNA
1x Growler ITV
1x M1 Abrams
1x M220 TOW Launcher

CHECKPOINT
1x M220 TOW Launcher

FOREST

HILLTOP
2x 9M133 Kornet Launcher

GAS STATION
1x VDV Buggy
1x T-90A
1x M220 TOW Launcher

RU BASE
2x VDV Buggy
2x T-90A
1x Mi-28 Havoc
2x SU 35BM Flanker-E
1x SU 35BM Flanker-E
1x 9K22 Tunguska-M
1x Pantsir-S1
2x 9M133 Kornet Launcher

This 64-player variant of Caspian Border adds one new control point: the Antenna (A) located on the map's eastern edge. To compensate for the larger number of players, the map has also been loaded with vehicles, which mostly spawn at the US and RU Bases. Now with five control points in play, team strategies should adjust accordingly. Your team must hold at least three of the control points to drain the opposing team's ticket count. For the US team, this means focusing primarily on the Antenna (A), Checkpoint (B), and Hilltop (D). The RU team should try to capture an hold the Gas Station (E), the Hilltop (D), and the Forest (C). Even with a full complement of 64 players, it's important not to spread your resources too thin. Decide which three control points you must hold early on, then constantly reinforce each point with vehicles spawned at your team's base. The logistics of moving vehicles from your base to the front line control points is extremely important and should not be overlooked.

US BASE

Base Assets	NAME	Growler ITV	M1 Abrams	AH-1Z Viper	F/A-18E Super Hornet	LAV-AD	Centurion C-RAM	M220 TOW Launcher
	QUANTITY	5	2	1	2	1	1	2
	RESPAWN TIME	5 sec.	30 sec.	60 sec.	40 sec.	120 sec.	—	30 sec.

Positioned on the north edge of the map, the US Base is a long hike from even the nearest control points, so make sure you hitch a ride if you choose to spawn here—likewise, make sure you offer rides to teammates before taking off. By taking the highway to the west, you can quickly race to the Checkpoint (B). To the east of the US Base is a dirt road leading toward the Antenna (A), Forest (C), and Gas Station (E). The Growler ITVs are well suited for traveling this road, particularly at the start of a round. Capturing the Antenna (A) is critical for the US team, as it provides them with a couple of extra vehicles. While the US Base is off-limits to RU troops, be ready for aerial harassment. If aerial assaults become a problem, man the Centurion C-RAM air defense system to fend off the attacking jets and choppers. The LAV-AD is also well suited for countering air strikes at the US Base, but is best deployed at nearby control points.

RU BASE

Base Assets	NAME	VDV Buggy	T-90A	Mi-28 Havoc	SU-35BM Flanker-E	9K22 Tunguska-M	Pantsir-S1	9M133 Kornet Launcher
	QUANTITY	5	2	1	2	1	1	2
	RESPAWN TIME	5 sec.	20 sec.	60 sec.	40 sec.	120 sec.	—	30 sec.

The RU team has set up camp in the large base to the south. Like all bases in Conquest, this one is off-limits to US troops and ground vehicles. However, be prepared to fend-off frequent strafing runs by US jets and attack helicopters, particularly early in the round. The Pantsir-S1 air defense system and 9K22 Tunguska-M should be manned early on to deter such aerial attacks. The dirt road to the east is the major artery leading out of the RU Base, leading directly to the Gas Station (E) and Hilltop (D)—use the VDV Buggies to capture these points early during the round. Also, make a play to capture the Forest (C) and Antenna (A). Although distant, taking control of the Antenna will deny the US team a couple of vehicles, making it a worthwhile venture.

Control Point Assets

US CONTROL	RU CONTROL	RESPAWN TIME
Growler ITV (1)	—	40 sec.
M1 Abrams (1)	—	60 sec.
M220 TOW Launcher	M220 TOW Launcher	30 sec.

This control point (A) is exclusive to Conquest 64 and serves as a forward base for the US team, providing them with a Growler ITV and an M1 Abrams. While these vehicles may not seem like much, they can make a big difference when attacking the nearby Forest (C), Gas Station (E), or Checkpoint (B). Located along the dirt road on the east side of the map, the Antenna is easily accessible from the US Base, Forest (C), or Gas Station (E). As a result, defenders should monitor the control of the nearby flags and prepare for attacks originating from these directions. The control point's flag is located only a few meters from the base of the massive Antenna. Infantry can capture or contest the flag from within the nearby concrete structure. This small building provides adequate protection while it remains standing. Otherwise, seek cover among the rocks or within the hollow Antenna itself. Pilots should note that colliding with the Antenna's various support cables does not damage their aircraft or helicopter—you simply pass right through them. But colliding with the Antenna is a different story, so be sure to steer clear of the massive red and white structure.

B CHECKPOINT

Control Point Assets

US CONTROL	RU CONTROL	RESPAWN TIME
M220 TOW Launcher	M220 TOW Launcher	30 sec.

This control point (B) sits on the major highway on the west side of the map. Although it is centrally positioned, the US team has a slight edge when it comes to capturing this point early in a round. Utilizing the smooth, paved highway, the US team can capture this area early on using their fast-moving Growler ITVs. In this game mode, the Checkpoint produces no vehicles for either team. So it's important that defenders move vehicles to this position from their base or nearby control points. The flag here is situated within the Checkpoint facility, along the east side of the highway. Given the open nature of the area, this spot is best captured by tanks. However, infantry can capture and contest the flag from within the concrete structure to the north of the flagpole. But this structure can be completely demolished, denying infantry suitable cover and concealment. Still, there are plenty of hiding spots outside, though none of them offer the protection of the concrete building.

The Forest (C) control point provides no vehicles to either team. But don't let that deter your team from capturing and defending this critical central location. Holding this area gives your team a spawn point in the middle of the map, which is ideal for launching raids on the Antenna (A), Checkpoint (B), Hilltop (D), or Gas Station (E). Given the uneven terrain and lack of road access, this control point is best attacked and defended by infantry. Tanks are particularly vulnerable to ambush here, so try to move in on foot when possible. The trees (while still standing) offer decent concealment from air attacks and the massive boulders offer great cover. When defending, attacks can come from any direction, originating from the surrounding control points. So constantly monitor the status of the surrounding control points and watch for attackers approaching from the enemy-held points, particularly from the nearby Hilltop (D) or Antenna (A). There is very little cover near the flag, so watch the control point from a distance, using the surrounding foliage to conceal your position. Defenders here can easily pick off attackers loitering near the flag.

◇ HILLTOP

Control Point Assets		
US CONTROL	RU CONTROL	RESPAWN TIME
9M133 Kornet Launcher (2)	9M133 Kornet Launcher (2)	30 sec.

Regardless of which team you're on, taking the high ground of the Hilltop (D) should always be a priority. The RU team has the best chance of reaching this location early due to its relative close proximity to their base. However, US troops can make a claim here, too, by bailing out of jets or helicopters in the early moments of a match. While the control point offers very little in the way of assets, it has a great view of the surrounding terrain, making it a popular sniping perch for recon soldiers. If it's well defended, the Hilltop is also a tough nut to crack. The rocky cliff side to the east is completely impassable, which forces attacking units to approach the flag from the two dirt roads to the east. Both of these roads can be mined or booby-trapped with C4 to deter attacks by enemy vehicles. The flag itself sits atop the hill and can be captured or contested within the garage-like structure to the east. However, this concrete building will not last long under a sustained attack by tanks, jets, and helicopters. So be prepared to create your own concealment by deploying smoke. Due to its central location, defending this control point is a full-time job. So make sure at least one squad stays here and actively defends at all times.

Control Point Assets

US CONTROL	RU CONTROL	RESPAWN TIME
—	VDV Buggy (1)	40 sec.
—	T-90A (1)	60 sec.
M220 TOW Launcher	M220 TOW Launcher	30 sec.

The Gas Station (E) serves as the RU team's forward base, providing them with a VDV Buggy and T-90A closer to the map's central control points. Given its close proximity to the RU Base, the RU team has the best chance of maintaining control of this location throughout the match. Still, the US team should attempt to capture the Gas Station to deny the RU team these vehicles. The flag is located near the roadway, not far from the flaming wreck of a truck. The fiery wreck emits a black cloud of smoke that helps conceal ground units from air attack. The gas pumps here are explosive, so keep your distance during firefights. If you're defending here, consider destroying all the pumps to make your job a little safer—or wait until attackers get near the pumps, then detonate them. Refuge can be sought in the Gas Station building, where you can either capture or contest the flag.

RUSH

ZONE 1

ZONE 2

ZONE 3

US DEPLOYMENT
RU DEPLOYMENT

N

In this Rush battle, the US attackers strive to push back the RU defenders through three zones, destroying two M-COM stations at each location. If you like Rush matches with a variety of vehicles, this is the map for you. Both teams have a variety of air and ground units at their disposal, making each match a chaotic scramble for domination. The RU team starts by defending the Checkpoint area before eventually falling back to the Gas Station and Depot to the south. With only three areas to defend, winning as the RU team requires teamwork and a mastery of the few vehicles offered to hold each zone.

RU DEPLOYMENT
2x T-90A
1x SU-25TM Frogfoot
1x 9M133 Kornet Launcher

N

A M-COM STATION A

M-COM Station A is located in a small building in the southeast corner of the Checkpoint facility. Initially there are two entrances into the building, but more can be made by blasting holes in the walls with explosive munitions. Destroying the walls of the building may actually benefit the RU defenders most, as it opens new sight lines so the M-COM Station can be covered from the south and east. The M-COM Station A is not far from the RU Deployment area so US attackers should establish a defensive perimeter around the building before attempting to arm the station.

B M-COM STATION B

This M-COM station is safely nestled among a cluster of shipping containers in the southwest corner of the checkpoint facility. The shipping containers cannot be destroyed, thereby offering excellent cover for those attempting to arm or disarm the charge on the M-COM station. The area to the west offers the best distant sight line on the objective. Both the attackers and defenders can use this area to cover the objective from long range. However, defenders will want to keep some troops loitering among the shipping containers, greeting attackers with deadly shotgun blasts as they attempt to set their charge.

US DEPLOYMENT

Deployment Area Assets	NAME	M1114 HMMWV	M1 Abrams	UH-1Y Venom	A-10 Thunderbolt
	QUANTITY	2	3	1	1
	RESPAWN TIME	20 sec.	30 sec.	90 sec.	40 sec.

The US team begins with plenty of vehicles useful for traveling the distance to the Checkpoint area, where the first two M-COM stations are located. While the M1114 HMMWV are great for transporting teammates, consider bailing out before you get too close to the Checkpoint, where you're likely to face incoming fire from RU tanks and AT missile launchers. The M1 Abrams tanks and aircraft are ideal for distracting the RU defenders while infantry assault at close range in an attempt to arm the M-COM stations. The deployment area lacks AA defense, so engineers armed with Stingers are your best chance at downing the RU team's pesky SU-25TM.

RU DEPLOYMENT

Deployment Area Assets	NAME	T-90A	SU-25TM Frogfoot	9M133 Kornet Launcher
	QUANTITY	2	1	2
	RESPAWN TIME	60 sec.	40 sec.	30 sec.

The RU team deploys just south of the Checkpoint, which allows them to quickly establish rudimentary defensive positions before the US team attacks. The US team attacks with three tanks versus the two T-90As supplied by the RU deployment area. Outgunned, the RU team must rely on engineers armed with anti-tank weapons in addition to their tanks to help even the odds. While the SU-25TM is primarily a ground attack aircraft, it is more effective here by attacking the US aircraft. Shooting down the A-10 and UH-1Y is key to holding out here. When not suppressing the US team's air power, the SU-25TM should make frequent strafing runs on the US tanks.

ZONE 2: GAS STATION

US DEPLOYMENT
2x M114 HMMWV
3x M1 Abrams
1x UH-1Y Venom
1x A-10 Thunderbolt

RU DEPLOYMENT
2x T-90A
1x SU-25TM Frogfoot
1x 9M133 Kornet Launcher

Ⓐ M-COM STATION A

This M-COM station is located to the east of the Gas Station and housed within a metal shed. The shed opens onto a small courtyard flanked by a few other structures. The RU defenders can cover the M-COM station from within these nearby buildings, stealthily picking off any US attackers who get close. Therefore, the US team may want to deploy at least one M1 Abrams to this location when attacking. The nearby buildings can be demolished with explosive munitions, thereby denying the defenders a suitable hiding spot. The shed itself provides very little cover or protection for those arming or disarming the charge. So smoke is vital when loitering near the M-COM station.

Ⓑ M-COM STATION B

M-COM Station B is located within the Gas Station's garage, sitting along the eastern exterior wall. The US attackers will most likely attack this location first, as it's closer to their deployment area. While it's important for the RU defenders to cover the road to prevent vehicle attacks, it's equally important to establish security along the northern side of the Gas Station to prevent US infantry from sneaking into the garage through the back door. But once rockets, tank shells, and other explosive ordnance start flying, doorways become irrelevant as the Gas Station walls crumble. In such instances, the attackers need to rely on smoke to reach the M-COM station without being cut down by the RU team. Close support from tanks and aircraft is essential when planting the charge here.

US DEPLOYMENT

Deployment Area Assets				
NAME	M1114 HMMWV	M1 Abrams	UH-1Y Venom	A-10 Thunderbolt
QUANTITY	2	3	1	1
RESPAWN TIME	20 sec.	30 sec.	90 sec.	40 sec.

After eliminating the first two M-COM stations, the US ground forces deploy from the Checkpoint. The A-10 and UH-1Y still deploy at the previous base. While the RU team has been pushed back to the Gas Station, always be prepared for residual pockets of resistance. There may be RU troops hiding in the building or among the shipping containers, waiting to score easy kills or steal freshly spawned US vehicles to claim for their own team. When moving out, utilize the main highway to reach the Gas Station quickly. However, be prepared for ambushes and watch for mines and other booby traps waiting for you along the road.

RU DEPLOYMENT

Deployment Area Assets			
NAME	T-90A	SU-25TM Frogfoot	9M133 Kornet Launcher
QUANTITY	2	1	2
RESPAWN TIME	60 sec.	40 sec.	30 sec.

While the RU team deploys in this area just south of the Gas Station, it's important to spread out early and form a defensive barrier to the west. Most attacks come along the highway, making it a critical choke point the RU team can utilize to score some easy kills. Place mines and C4 along the roadway while troops assume the high ground on the Hilltop to the north. In addition to the two 9M133 Kornet Launchers near the Gas Station, there are also a couple near the Hilltop, which are ideal for taking out US vehicles. However, don't focus your entire defensive effort on the highway. US troops can sneak in through a variety of directions, as well as parachute down from their UH-1Y, so be sure to keep some troops within close proximity to each M-COM station.

ZONE 3: DEPOT

RU DEPLOYMENT

1x SU-25TM Frogfoot
1x 9M133 Kornet Launcher

US DEPLOYMENT

2x M114 HMMWV
3x M1 Abrams
1x UH-1Y Venom
1x A-10 Thunderbolt

N

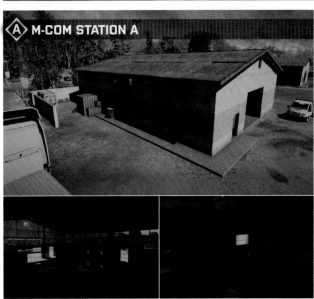

A M-COM STATION A

B M-COM STATION B

Located in a warehouse just south of the Depot's main gate, this M-COM station is farthest from the RU deployment area, making it somewhat vulnerable to US attack. By deploying Radio Beacons around the warehouse, the US team can apply consistent pressure against this M-COM station. But the RU defenders can play the same game, placing their own Radio Beacons nearby to avoid the long hike from the RU deployment area to the northwest. There are multiple entry points into the warehouse, so the RU defenders are best off hiding inside and ambushing the US troops as they try to plant the charge. When playing as the US, it's highly advisable to sweep the warehouse interior before even thinking about planting a charge.

This M-COM station is housed in a small building on the northeastern edge of the Depot, not far from the RU deployment area. The US team is advised to attack this location first. Otherwise it's tough to approach if the entire RU team is spawning nearby and focused on defending this last M-COM station. The walls of the structure provide cover and concealment for the attackers so the RU team is well served by knocking out the walls with explosive munitions. Without the walls and ceiling to protect them, the attackers are completely exposed while setting the charge and must rely on smoke for concealment. But if they do manage to set the charge, it is the RU team who must approach the M-COM station and disarm it. So think carefully before taking out the walls—it cuts both ways.

US DEPLOYMENT

Deployment Area Assets					
		M1114 HMMWV	M1 Abrams	UH-1Y Venom	A-10 Thunderbolt
	NAME	M1114 HMMWV	M1 Abrams	UH-1Y Venom	A-10 Thunderbolt
	QUANTITY	2	3	1	1
	RESPAWN TIME	20 sec.	30 sec.	90 sec.	40 sec.

This is the final deployment area for the US team located only a few hundred meters from the Depot where the RU team makes their last stand. As at the Checkpoint, US ground vehicles now appear at the Gas Station, primed for the final assault. The UH-1Y and A-10 still spawn at the first US base far to the north. The narrow dirt road to the west leads directly to the depot and is the main path available to ground vehicles. However, this route is most likely defended by RU troops eager to stage ambushes. While vehicles are still important during this assault, approaching the Depot on foot is far less treacherous, allowing for greater concealment among the trees. Plant some Radio Beacons around the Depot and spawn continuously to apply pressure on the final M-COM stations.

RU DEPLOYMENT

Deployment Area Assets			
		SU-25TM Frogfoot	9M133 Kornet Launcher
	NAME	SU-25TM Frogfoot	9M133 Kornet Launcher
	QUANTITY	1	2
	RESPAWN TIME	40 sec.	30 sec.

This is the final base for the RU team. To make matters worse, no tanks are available for the final defense. So the RU team must rely heavily on engineers to mine the dirt road to the east to halt incoming US vehicles. RU ground units spawn in the northwest corner of the Depot, which puts them only a few meters away from the final M-COM stations. It's important to establish a solid line of defense on the northeast side of the facility. The dirt road leading to the depot is a critical choke point the defenders should take advantage of. However, make sure at least one squad stays behind and watches over the two M-COM stations, as US troops will eventually look for ways to avoid the traversing the dirt road. Get the SU-25TM in the air and use it to shoot down the US UH-1Y—this helicopter poses a serious threat, potentially dropping US troops into the Depot via parachute.

SQUAD RUSH

ZONE 1

ZONE 2

US DEPLOYMENT

RU DEPLOYMENT

This Squad Rush match centers around the Hilltop and Gas Station as the US attackers attempt to knock out two M-COM stations. With no vehicles to use, the US attackers have far to travel in each engagement. Radio Beacons and squad spawning are essential for maintaining a presence close to each M-COM station. The RU defenders definitely have the upper hand in this match, holding the hard-to-climb Hilltop zone at the outset. The surrounding trees and rocks provide plenty of cover and concealment that is ideal for staging ambushes on unsuspecting attackers.

ZONE 1: HILLTOP

In this first round of the match, the US attackers deploy near the Checkpoint and must attack an M-COM station on the Hilltop. It's literally an uphill climb for the US team in this zone, so the RU defenders should try to take advantage of the height offered by the Hilltop. The M-COM station is located in a tiny concrete structure next to the large com tower. Initially there is only one narrow entrance into this small structure, but by using explosive weapons you can create your own doorway. However, completely demolishing the structure isn't a wise move for the attackers as this leaves them totally exposed while attempting to set a charge. If the structure is completely destroyed, make sure to deploy smoke before attempting to set or disarm the charge.

The second and final M-COM station is located in the Gas Station's garage, next to the staircase leading up to the roof. The rooftop is a good cover point for at least one of the defenders and is ideal for spotting distant attackers. However, most of the defending team should stay on the ground and cover the western and eastern entrances into the garage. The US attackers have a decent hike from their deployment area at the Hilltop. Placing a Radio Beacon somewhere near the Gas Station significantly cuts down the commute time. However, a coordinated squad attack is required to make a move on the final M-COM station. Don't get suckered into using the eastern and western entrances. Use rockets or grenades to make your own entry points and plant the charge.

SQUAD DEATHMATCH

The action in this game mode centers around the Forest and Gas Station areas for a mix of urban and woodland combat. There are four potential spawn areas for the IFV, all located near the roads around the Gas Station. If your squad is fortunate enough to take control of a IFV, drive it far away from the Forest and Gas Station. There are far too many hiding places for engineers in these places, making your ride a rocket and C4 magnet. Instead, drive it to the open terrain to the south or northeast and back it up against the map's border while firing toward the center of the map. This is a great way to score some easy kills and help your squad secure the lead. But anytime you're in the vehicle, you're going to get attention from the other squads. So make sure you have at least one engineer on your squad to conduct repairs.

TEAM DEATHMATCH

In the Team Deathmatch variant, controlling the structures around the Gas Station is a good strategy for dominating a round. The Gas Station is at the very center of this map, along with several other small structures to its south and east. While the buildings may seem like safe positions from which to defend, keep in mind that almost every wall is destructible. The crossroads at the center of the map is a good place to avoid. Both the paved and dirt roads offer long sightlines and are frequently watched by recon and support players looking for easy kills. If you want to avoid getting sniped, head for the woods north of the Gas Station. Here, you can find decent concealment that is ideal for launching ambushes. However, as in any Team Deathmatch, never wander off on your own. Stay with at least one other teammate, or form a small posse of teammates and orbit around the perimeter of the map looking for easy prey. Being constantly moving is preferable to defending one static position unless you have the dedicated manpower to make a stand.

DAMAVAND PEAK

A rugged, mountainous area around Damavand Peak will play a major role in deciding whether Russian or American troops are successful in combat operations throughout the sector, as the area is home to key radar installations.

On orders from CentCom, a specially trained unit of US Marines is leading a mountain assault on a uranium mine in North Khorassan Province. The once-abandoned area is now heavily defended by Russian forces stretching from the processing area through access tunnels that run up to a network of radar control stations used to warn the garrison of attacks.

RU BASE
1x GAZ-3937 Vodnik
1x T-90A
1x Z-11W

NORTH ENTRANCE
1x GAZ-3937 Vodnik

TUNNEL

SOTH ENTRANCE
1x M1114 HMMWV

US BASE
1x M1114 HMMWV
1x M1 Abrams
1x AH-6J Little Bird

N

With only three control points up for grabs, this is a relatively small-scale Conquest match, where defense is often more important than offense. The US team starts in the south while the RU team starts in the north. Between these two bases are three control points. The US team should focus on capturing and maintaining control of the South Entrance (A) and Tunnel (B) to initiate a ticket drain on the RU team. The RU team is best served by controlling the North Entrance (C) and Tunnel (B) to begin bleeding the US team's ticket count. Unless the opportunity arises, there's no need for either team to try to capture all three flags. It's much better to consolidate your forces around two control points and set up a solid line of defense within the Tunnel. The team that manages to hold the two control points nearest their base for the duration of the match stands the best chance of winning.

US BASE

Base Assets			
NAME	M1114 HMMWV	M1 Abrams	AH-6J Little Bird
QUANTITY	1	1	1
RESPAWN TIME	15 sec.	30 sec.	90 sec.

In this Conquest match, the US team starts out on the south end of the map, spawning at the Factory Valley. This puts the US team within a few meters of the South Entrance (A) control point, making it relatively easy for them to hold for the duration of the match. Use the M114 HMMWV to get to the nearby control point as quickly as possible at the start of the match, and reinforce the position with an M1 Abrams tank. The US Base is off-limits to RU ground units, but be prepared to defend against attacks by their Z-11W scout helicopter. It's easiest to shoot this chopper down with the engineer's FIM-92 Stinger. The US team's own scout helicopter, the AH-6J Little Bird, spawns on the helipad to the east. Spawn directly into the helicopter when it's available.

RU BASE

Base Assets			
NAME	GAZ-3937 Vodnik	T-90A	Z-11W
QUANTITY	1	1	1
RESPAWN TIME	15 sec.	30 sec.	90 sec.

The RU Base is located at the opposite end of the map, within the Mining Area to the north, spawning only a few meters away from the North Entrance (C) control point. Using a GAZ-3937 Vodnik, the RU team has no problem capturing this nearby control point early on before advancing toward the Tunnel (B). While the two ground vehicles spawn around the Mining Area, the RU team's Z-11W scout helicopter appears to the northwest and benefits from its own on-board spawn point. So if you want to take a ride in the helicopter, spawn directly into it instead of hiking to where it appears. Be prepared to confront the US team's own scout helicopter buzzing over the RU Base and shoot it down with the engineer's SA-18 IGLA. In a pinch, the machine gun turrets on the Vodnik and T-90A serve as good deterrents to air attacks.

Ⓐ SOUTH ENTRANCE

Control Point Assets		
US CONTROL	**RU CONTROL**	**RESPAWN TIME**
M1114 HMMWV [1]	—	20 sec.

The South Entrance [A] is definitely within the US team's sphere of influence given its proximity to the US Base. The US team should use this control point as a first line of defense in the event the RU team takes the Tunnel [B] control point. From this location, it's easy to pick off enemy troops and vehicles emerging from the dark Tunnel cutting through the large mountain to the north. Use the turret on an HMMWV to suppress and cut down an RU troops that come rushing out of the Tunnel. The flag here is located near a fork in the road by the Tunnel's entrance, making it easy for both infantry and vehicles to capture. The chain-link fence surrounding the flag can be easily cut with a knife. So if you find yourself standing on the road, slice your way through the fence and seek cover near one of the shipping containers south of the flagpole while capturing or contesting this point.

Ⓑ TUNNEL

The Tunnel control point [B] supplies no vehicles to either team, but it remains the most crucial point on the map. Since there's only three control points on this map, whichever team controls the Tunnel has a good chance of bleeding the opposing team's ticket count, which all but guarantees a victory. The flag here is located along a side road on the east side of the Tunnel, and can be captured or contested from within the nearby buildings. While the main Tunnel entrances to the south and north are the only approaches for vehicles, infantry can utilize the narrow side passages on the eastern edge of the Tunnel to access this area directly. This is the preferred method of advancing on this area while on foot because it allows infantry to detour heated vehicle battles on the main road. This area is very dark, so make use of Tactical Lights and Laser Sights to blind your opponents. The IRNV [IR 1x] scope and Flash Suppressor are also useful here if you wish to avoid detection. This is particularly useful for defenders—find a nice corner with a good view of the flag, and pick off any attackers that move into view.

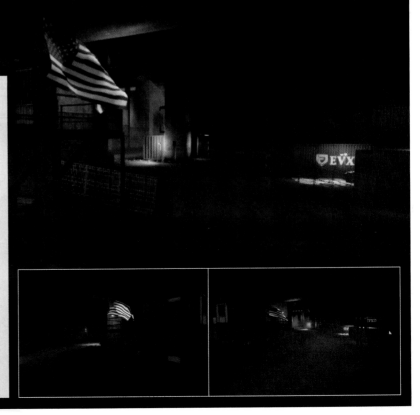

⊂ NORTH ENTRANCE

Control Point Assets

US CONTROL	RU CONTROL	RESPAWN TIME
—	GAZ-3937 Vodnik (1)	20 sec.

The North Entrance (C) serves as a forward base for the RU team, providing a spawn point near the Tunnel (B). Located only a few meters from the RU Base, the RU team should have little problem maintaining control of this location throughout the duration of the match. But if the US team holds the South Entrance (A) and Tunnel (B), RU troops should be prepared to fend off attackers here. Like at the South Entrance (A), the North Entrance flag is located right next to the road outside the Tunnel, and can be captured by either vehicles or infantry. The lack of cover along the road makes it safer for infantry to slice through the nearby fence and seek cover among the rusty metal retaining walls to the north. However, there are plenty of hiding spots for attackers and defenders alike, so it may require a thorough patrol of the area before you can eliminate opposing forces within the flag's capture radius.

CONQUEST 64

RU BASE
2x GAZ-3937 Vodnik
1x T-90A
1x Z-11W

MINING AREA
1x GAZ-3937 Vodnik

RU

E

NORTH ENTRANCE

D

TUNNEL

C

SOUTH ENTRANCE

B

FACTORY VALLEY
1x M1114 HMMWV

US BASE
2x M1114 HMMWV
1x M1 Abrams
1x AH-6J Little Bird

A

US

N

Unlike most Conquest maps, this one is completely linear, with all five control points neatly aligned from north to south. Although a linear plan of attack is not mandatory, it makes the battle much easier if your team can control at least three adjoining control points. The US team should focus on capturing and controlling the Factory Valley (A), South Entrance (B), and Tunnel (C) in an attempt to drain the RU team's ticket count. On the opposite side of the map, the RU team should hold the Mining Area (E), North Entrance (D), and Tunnel (C) to bleed the US tickets. While these plans of attack are the easiest, they aren't the only way to capture and hold three control points. If your team gets bogged down in the Tunnel, bypass this choke point using your team's helicopter and open up new fronts by capturing the control points close to your opponent's base. Even if you can capture one of these control points temporarily, it may be enough to divert enemy resources away from the Tunnel, giving teammates a chance to capture that central critical point.

US BASE

Base Assets				
NAME		M1114 HMMWV	M1 Abrams	AH-6J Little Bird
QUANTITY		2	1	1
RESPAWN TIME		20 sec.	60 sec.	90 sec.

The US Base is nestled against the cliff side, just below Damavand Peak on the map's southern edge. There aren't many vehicles spawned here, so most of the US team must advance to the nearby control points on foot. Players that manage to get in a HMMWV at the start of a match should pass on capturing the Factory Valley (A) and South Entrance (B) control points and make a move for the Tunnel (C) before the RU team can do the same. US infantry and the M1 Abrams can handle taking the nearby points, but the speed of the HMMWV is essential for capturing the Tunnel (C) early on. The AH-6J Little Bird is spawned on the helipad to the east and is great for harassing RU ground units to the north. You can also use this scout helicopter to covertly drop troops at the distance North Entrance (D) and Mining Area (E) control points.

RU BASE

Base Assets				
NAME		GAZ-3937 Vodnik	T-90A	Z-11W
QUANTITY		2	1	1
RESPAWN TIME		20 sec.	60 sec.	90 sec.

Like the US team, the RU team only has a few vehicles that spawn at their base, which require careful deployment during the early moments of a match. Vodnik drivers should wait until every seat is filled, then head directly for the Tunnel (C) control point. Capturing this central control point early on and reinforcing it is extremely important. The nearby Mining Area (E) and North Entrance (D) control points can be captured by infantry and the T-90A. The Z-11W scout helicopter spawns on the helipad to the west of the RU Base. While the helicopter is useless for attacking or defending the Tunnel (C) it comes in handy for launching raids on distant control points like the South Entrance (B) and Factory Valley (A). However, the RU team is strongest when consolidating their forces at the three control points closest to their base.

⟨A⟩ FACTORY VALLEY

Control Point Assets

US CONTROL	RU CONTROL	RESPAWN TIME
M1114 HMMWV (1)	—	20 sec.

The Factory Valley (A) control point is centered around a massive industrial complex surrounded by chain-link fences and several large warehouses. The flag is located in an open area in the complex, near a forklift and some shipping containers. Despite the area's open nature, there are still plenty of places to hide while capturing or contesting the flag. However, given the control point's close proximity to the US Base, the Factory Valley is likely to stay in US control for the duration of the match. Outside of their base, this is the only control point that supplies the US team with an extra vehicle, which makes it a location worth defending. The HMMWV deployed here can play a vital role in defending the nearby South Entrance (B) control point from RU attacks originating from the Tunnel (C).

⟨B⟩ SOUTH ENTRANCE

The South Entrance (B) is definitely within the US team's sphere of influence given its proximity to the Factory Valley (A). The US team should use this control point as a first line of defense in the event the RU team takes the Tunnel (C) control point. From this location, it's easy to pick off enemy troops and vehicles emerging from the dark Tunnel cutting through the large mountain to the north. Use the turret on an HMMWV to suppress and cut down an RU troops that come rushing out of the Tunnel. The flag here is located near a fork in the road by the Tunnel's entrance, making it easy for both infantry and vehicles to capture. The chain-link fence surrounding the flag can be easily cut with a knife. So if you find yourself standing on the road, slice your way through the fence and seek cover near one of the shipping containers south of the flagpole while capturing or contesting this point. When playing as the US, make sure at least one squad defends this point at all times to prevent the RU team from gaining a foothold on the south side of the map.

◈ C TUNNEL

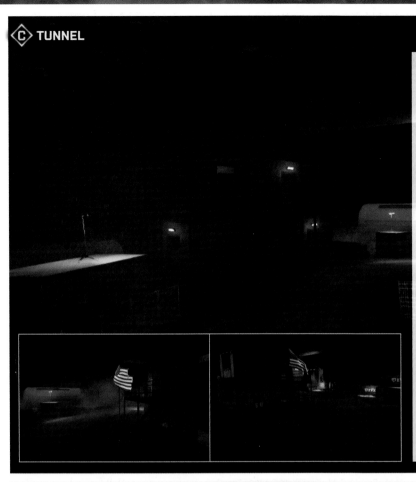

The Tunnel (C) control point supplies no vehicles to either team, but it remains the most crucial point on the map. With five control points on this map, whichever team controls the Tunnel has a good chance of bleeding the opposing team's ticket count and all but guarantee a victory. The flag is located along a side road on the east side of the Tunnel and can be captured or contested from within the nearby buildings. While the main Tunnel entrances to the south and north are the only approaches for vehicles, infantry can utilize the narrow side passages on the eastern edge of the Tunnel to access this area directly. This is the preferred method of advancing on this area while on foot, allowing infantry to detour heated vehicle battles on the main road. However, these narrow passages can be deadly if properly defended by opposing forces. The Tunnel is very dark, so make use of Tactical Lights and Laser Sights to blind your opponents. The IRNV (IR 1x) scope and Flash Suppressor are also useful here if you wish to avoid detection. This is particularly useful for defenders—find a nice corner with a good view of the flag, and pick off any attackers that move into view. If necessary, don't forget to move vehicles from your base to this point to better defend it against enemy attack.

◈ D NORTH ENTRANCE

The North Entrance (D) serves as a forward base for the RU team, providing a spawn point near the Tunnel. Because the North Entrance is located on the north side of the map, the RU team should have little problem maintaining control of this location throughout the duration of the match. But if the US team holds the Tunnel (C), RU troops should be prepared to fend off attackers here. Like at the South Entrance (B), the flag here is located right next to the road outside the Tunnel and can be captured by either vehicles or infantry. The lack of cover along the road makes it safer for infantry to slice through the nearby fence and seek cover among the rusty metal retaining walls to the north. However, there are plenty of hiding spots for attackers and defenders alike, so it may require a thorough patrol of the area before you can eliminate opposing forces within the flag's capture radius. The RU team should always post a squad of defenders here in an effort to prevent US troops from advancing through the Tunnel and gaining a foothold on the north side of the map. If the North Entrance falls to the US, they'll have an easier time taking the nearby Mining Area (E), thereby securing a near rout of the RU team.

E⟩ MINING AREA

Control Point Assets

US CONTROL	RU CONTROL	RESPAWN TIME
—	GAZ-3937 Vodnik (1)	20 sec.

Located a short hike south of the RU Base, the Mining Area (E) is likely to stay under the RU team's control for most of the match. This control point supplies the RU team with an extra Vodnik, which is ideal for launching fast attacks on the Tunnel (C) or defending the nearby North Entrance (D). The flag here is located within the small office-like structure. However, the flag can be converted or contested from outside the building as well. However, the surrounding objects make it difficult (and potentially dangerous) to maneuver large vehicles like tanks in this area. So this area is best attacked and defended by infantry. There are plenty of hiding spots surrounding the control point, making it relatively easy to defend. However, once secured, the RU team is best served by focusing most defensive efforts around the North Entrance (D) and Tunnel (C). Still, don't neglect this control point entirely as it may still be captured by US aerial attacks staged with their scout helicopter.

RUSH

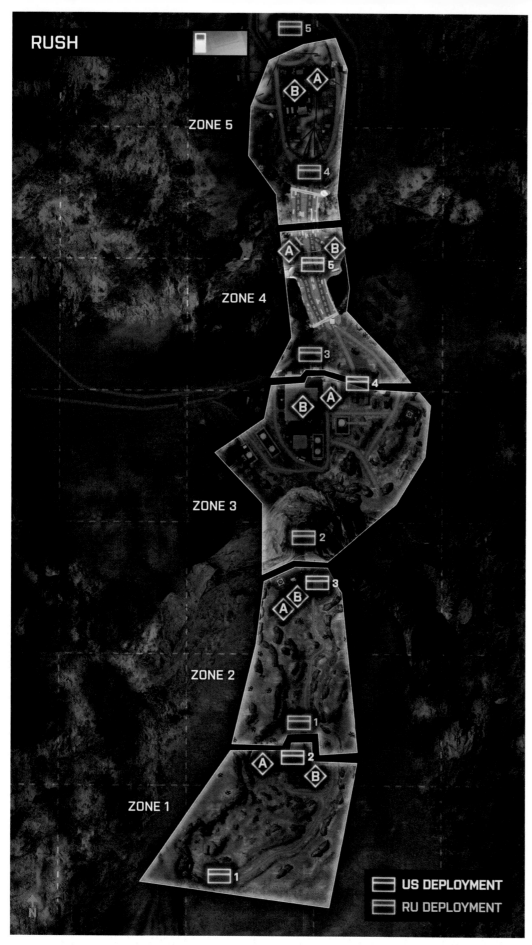

ZONE 5

ZONE 4

ZONE 3

ZONE 2

ZONE 1

US DEPLOYMENT
RU DEPLOYMENT

This is a truly epic Rush battle, requiring the US team to take out ten M-COM stations spread across five separate zones. Helicopters play a large role in this battle. Good chopper pilots can be a complete game changer, so both teams should prepare for ways to counter these aerial threats. While helicopters can support the fight from the air, its still up to infantry to do the dirty work. US attackers must still manually plant charges on each station, requiring teamwork and constant situational awareness. The RU team doesn't gain any ground vehicles until the very end, so stopping the US advance early on falls largely to infantry. The RU team starts by defending two sites on Damavand Peak before being pushed back to the valley floor, where they attempt to hold out at the Factory Valley, Tunnel, and finally the Mining Area.

ZONE 1: COMMUNICATIONS FACILITY

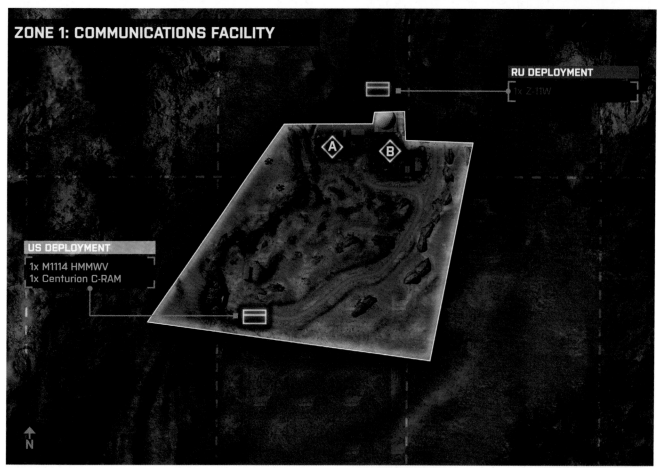

RU DEPLOYMENT
1x Z-11W

US DEPLOYMENT
1x M1114 HMMWV
1x Centurion C-RAM

N

A M-COM STATION A

This M-COM Station A is located on the western side of the facility, placed against the exterior wall of a moderately sized building. The area around the M-COM station is well within view of US recon troops posted on the hillside to the south, presenting a threat to RU defenders. Seek cover in nearby buildings or among the shipping containers. However, the adjacent building blocks the view of snipers, preventing them from hitting anyone standing directly next to the M-COM station. Of course, new sight lines can be attained by blowing holes through walls with explosive weapons. The facility's wall directly to the south is one advisable breach point for US attackers approaching this location. The M-COM station is completely exposed to the north and east, so deploying smoke is highly recommended before attempting to set or disarm a charge here. Both teams can benefit from Radio Beacons planted within the nearby building, as they allow for quicker response.

B M-COM STATION B

M-COM Station B is located inside the small trailer-like structure directly south of the massive communications tower. The walls of the structure make it difficult for attackers and defenders to cover the M-COM station directly from long range. Defenders may wish to take out the walls to take out the structure's northern and western walls, thereby allowing them to better see attackers sneaking into the building. The attackers can benefit by demolishing the structure's southern wall to allow recon troops to cover the M-COM station from long range and pick off RU defenders as they attempt to disarm the charge. Ultimately, destroying the structure's walls benefits the defenders most, denying the attackers cover as they approach the M-COM station. Still, defenders need to seek suitable cover themselves to avoid getting hit by attacking snipers.

Deployment Area Assets		M114 HMMWV	Centurion C-RAM
	NAME	M114 HMMWV	Centurion C-RAM
	QUANTITY	1	1
	RESPAWN TIME	30 sec.	—

The US team starts on the very southern tip of the map with only a few assets at their disposal. While the HMMWV is great for rushing the Communications Facility to the north, it's usually much safer to approach on foot. During the advance on the Communications Facility, make sure the Centurion C-RAM is manned to counter the RU team's Z-11W. Otherwise a skilled pilot can wreck havoc on your team's advance. The engineer's FIM-92 Stinger is also well suited for countering this serious threat. While moving to the Communications Facility, avoid the dirt road to the east and use the rocks on the north side of the facility for cover. Planting a Radio Beacon in a covered position can greatly reduce your squad's commute, allowing you to apply consistent pressure against the M-COM stations below. The US team attacks downhill, so take advantage of the high ground by posting recon troops along the hillside and fire down on the RU defenders to the north.

Deployment Area Assets		Z-11W
	NAME	Z-11W
	QUANTITY	1
	RESPAWN TIME	90 sec.

The RU team's ground forces deploy near a guard tower just north of the Communications Facility. It's a short hike up the hill to reach the M-COM stations to the south. However, the US troops may rush the facility in their HMMWV, so speed is essential at the start of a match. Sprint up the hill and immediately take up positions around both M-COM stations. Seek out cover to prevent getting sniped from the hill above the facility. The RU team's Z-11W helicopter spawns at Peak Facility's helipad to the north. While this area is off-limits, you can spawn directly into the helicopter when it's available. But don't take the pilot's seat unless you have some experience. A skilled pilot is required to strafe the US attackers while avoiding the incoming fire of the Centurion C-RAM located at their deployment area.

ZONE 2: PEAK FACILITY

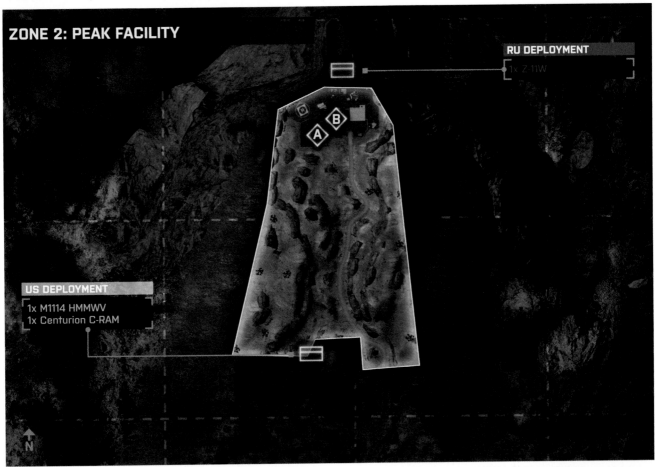

RU DEPLOYMENT
1x Z-11W

US DEPLOYMENT
1x M1114 HMMWV
1x Centurion C-RAM

A M-COM STATION A

M-COM Station A is located in the southwest corner of the Peak Facility and is likely to be the first objective attacked by the US team due to its close proximity to the southern exterior wall. The M-COM Station sits on the bottom floor of the small gray two-story structure next to the concrete perimeter wall. Instead of circling around the wall, US troops should simply blast their way through to easily access this M-COM station. RU defenders should hold to the north and take out the walls on the bottom floor of the structure. This allows them to engage attackers attempting to set a charge. Denying the attackers this cover can go a long way in holding out here.

B M-COM STATION B

While this M-COM Station B is partially fenced in by concrete walls, these walls can be destroyed with explosive weapons, allowing the US team to stage their attack from practically any direction. The M-COM station is flanked by two shipping containers that cannot be destroyed, providing excellent cover for troops attempting to set or disarm a charge. However, anyone standing in front of the M-COM station is completely exposed from the east. So whether you're attacking or defending, the east side offers the best cover point. The wall directly behind the M-COM station can also be destroyed for those who wish to cover the station from the west. However, the station must still be armed or disarmed from the east side.

Deployment Area Assets	NAME	M114 HMMWV	Centurion C-RAM
	QUANTITY	1	1
	RESPAWN TIME	30 sec.	—

After destroying the first two M-COM stations, the RU team is pushed farther to the north while the US team claims the Communications Facility for their base. The US team is granted the same assets as before: one HMMWV and a Centurion C-RAM for air defense. The US team still holds the high ground at this location, but it's still a long hike to the Peak Facility down the slope to the north. Fortunately there's plenty of large rocks that US troops can use for cover on the way down. The road to the east offers the quickest access into the Peak Facility, but it's likely to be mined or booby-trapped. Still, rushing the Peak Facility along this road in a HMMWV is by far the quickest way to gain a foothold near the M-COM stations. Once in or near the facility, utilize Radio Beacons to allow squad mates to spawn closer to the action.

Deployment Area Assets	NAME	Z-11W
	QUANTITY	1
	RESPAWN TIME	90 sec.

After losing their first base, the RU team is pushed back to the very edge of Damavand Peak, deploying near the helipad perched on the northernmost tip of the mountain. The M-COM stations are located within the facility to the south, only a few meters away. However, RU defenders should prepare for early rush attacks by the US HMMWV. If the US team acts quickly, they can gain a foothold in the facility before the RU team has a chance to establish a defensive perimeter. Barring early rush attacks, the RU defenders have a solid chance of holding out here. US recon troops sniping from the hillside to the south are still a problem here for defenders, so avoid silhouetting yourself in windows or on rooftops. Stay low and focus you attention on the two M-COM stations. Perform routine security sweeps of the facilities perimeter and destroy any US Radio Beacons placed near the facility. Keep the Z-11W in the air at all times to strafe the advancing US troops.

ZONE 3: FACTORY VALLEY

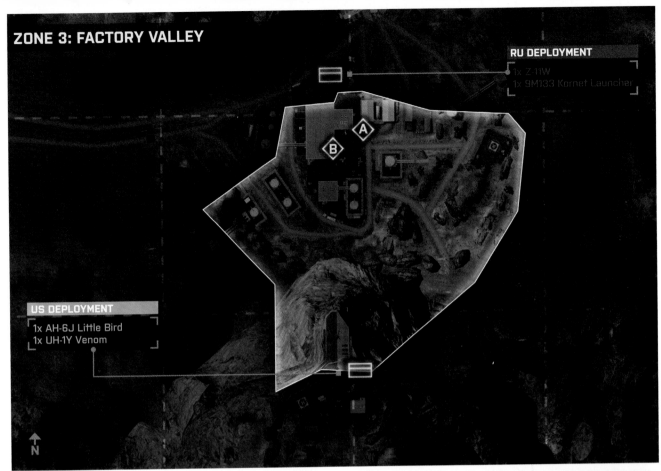

RU DEPLOYMENT
1x Z-11W
1x 9M133 Kornet Launcher

US DEPLOYMENT
1x AH-6J Little Bird
1x UH-1Y Venom

N

Ⓐ M-COM STATION A

Ⓑ M-COM STATION B

This M-COM Station A is positioned in a yellow shipping container alongside the road outside the large warehouse facility. Both the northern and southern ends of the shipping container are open, allowing access to the M-COM station from either side. Once inside the cramped shipping container, it's relatively safe to set or disarm a charge. However, getting inside can be tough, especially if both entrances are watched by the opposing team. The shipping container is surrounded by multiple elevated positions, offering both attacking and defending recon troops a clear view of anyone entering or exiting. Therefore smoke is essential in concealing advances toward the shipping container's entrances. For the US attackers, it's best to get inside, set the charge, and then exit, covering shipping container from a distance as the defenders rush to disarm the charge. Loitering inside the shipping container only makes you vulnerable to incoming grenades and close-quarters assaults.

While attacking the shipping container can be challenging, it's nothing compared to approaching this M-COM Station B located on the ground floor of the large warehouse. If well defended, the RU team can hold out here indefinitely, stealthily picking off US attackers from the catwalks and other elevated positions. Attackers must embrace the element of surprise by punching holes through the warehouse's exterior walls and creating their own entry points. This helps keep the RU defenders on their toes, constantly guessing where the next infiltration will come from. Both teams can also benefit from Radio Beacons placed in and around the warehouse, which is ideal for maintaining a constant presence in this area. Attacking and defending this location requires a concerted team effort. Failing to coordinate will most certainly lead to defeat.

US DEPLOYMENT

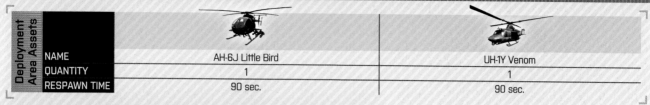

Deployment Area Assets	NAME	AH-6J Little Bird	UH-1Y Venom
	QUANTITY	1	1
	RESPAWN TIME	90 sec.	90 sec.

The fight is long from over after the US team knocks out the latest M-COM stations at the Peak Facility. Next comes one of the most unique and exciting advances in any Rush map: It requires the US team to drop off the edge of the mountain and secure a foothold in the valley below. There are a couple of ways to safely reach the valley floor. The most obvious is by helicopter transport. This base now spawns an AH-6J and UH-1Y for the US team. If you can't hitch a ride on a chopper, the only other way down is by base jumping off the northern edge of the mountain. This is far less dangerous than it looks, but you must be careful when deploying your parachute. If you deploy your parachute too early, the RU defenders will have any easy time spotting you, making you vulnerable to incoming fire as you slowly drift to the ground. The key is opening your parachute when you're only a few meters from the ground. Not only is this the fastest way down, but you're also less likely to get shot during the descent. Once safely on the ground, make sure your squad deploys a Radio Beacon in a safe spot to secure a spawn point in the valley.

RU DEPLOYMENT

Deployment Area Assets	NAME	Z-11W	9M133 Kornet Launcher
	QUANTITY	1	1
	RESPAWN TIME	90 sec.	60 sec.

After losing the Peak Facility, the RU team deploys near the South Entrance by the Tunnel. The M-COM stations are only a few meters south of the deployment area, but the US helicopters give the attackers increased mobility to quickly secure spawn points on the valley floor. RU engineers armed with SA-18 IGLA launchers are needed to combat the threat posed by the US choppers. But RU troops should also watch for attackers base jumping off Damavand Peak. Base jumpers are particularly vulnerable if they deploy their parachutes too early. So spot them for your teammates, then open fire. Hitting a slowly descending opponent with a parachute isn't easy, but if multiple teammates concentrate their fire on one target, chances are the base jumper won't survive. Still, don't get distracted by shooting down choppers and base jumpers. Sprint to each M-COM station and establish a defensive perimeter ASAP.

ZONE 4: TUNNEL

RU DEPLOYMENT
1x T-90A
1x Z-11W
1x 9M133 Kornet Launcher

US DEPLOYMENT
1x M114 HMMWV
1x M1 Abrams
1x AH-6J Little Bird
1x UH-1Y Venom

N

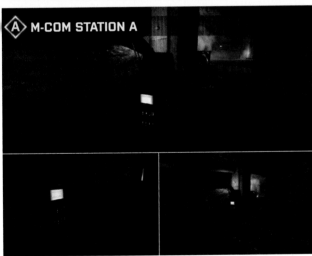

Ⓐ M-COM STATION A

This M-COM Station A is located in a construction zone on the western side of the Tunnel. The objective is surrounded by piles of rock and debris, preventing both attackers and defenders from covering this area from long range. So prepare for some close-quarters firefights around this objective. Utilize Tactical Lights and Laser Sights to cut through the darkness and blind your opponents. If you want to avoid giving away your position, equip the IRNV (IR 1x) scope and a Flash Suppressor to spot enemies while remaining undetected. Given the uneven terrain, vehicle attacks on this position aren't easy. Infantry are best suited for attacking and defending this M-COM station. RU defenders should cover the narrow passage directly south of the objective. This is a popular avenue of attack and should be locked down by support troops.

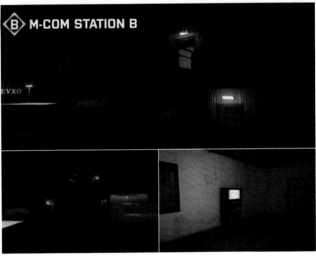

Ⓑ M-COM STATION B

M-COM Station B is located on the opposite side of the Tunnel, in the turn-out area to the east. The construction on this side of the Tunnel is more complete, including a smooth U-shaped road connecting to the main road on the north and south ends. This makes approaches by vehicles much easier, both for the attackers and the defenders. The M-COM station itself is located on the bottom floor of the small trailer-like structure to the east. A similar trailer is located across the road to the west and provides a good cover point of the objective. RU defenders should mine the road to the south to prevent US vehicles from getting too close for comfort. But the bulk of the US attack is likely to come from the narrow passage to the south. This avenue of attack can also be booby-trapped with Claymores and C4. But dedicated defenders covering this passage are necessary, too. Focusing light machine gun fire down this narrow passage is a great way to score some easy kills.

Deployment Area Assets		M114 HMMWV	M1 Abrams	AH-6J Little Bird	UH-1Y Venom
	NAME	M114 HMMWV	M1 Abrams	AH-6J Little Bird	UH-1Y Venom
	QUANTITY	1	1	1	1
	RESPAWN TIME	30 sec.	60 sec.	90 sec.	90 sec.

Once the US team has secured a presence in the valley, they must press forward into the Tunnel. Fortunately they gain some ground vehicles for this task, while still maintaining their helicopters spawned at the Peak Facility. Both the HMMWV and M1 Abrams are helpful for attacking the two M-COM Stations nestled deep inside the Tunnel. While the Tunnel entrance directly to the north is the only entry point for vehicles, infantry should utilize the narrow side passages on the east and west. If the RU team hasn't defended these passages, these are by far the best way to get inside the Tunnel and plant charges on each M-COM station. The helicopters aren't very effective during this stage of the battle, but they can harass RU units spawned near the Tunnel's North Entrance—taking out their T-90A is very helpful.

RU DEPLOYMENT

Deployment Area Assets		T-90A	Z-11W	9M133 Kornet Launcher
	NAME	T-90A	Z-11W	9M133 Kornet Launcher
	QUANTITY	1	1	1
	RESPAWN TIME	60 sec.	90 sec.	60 sec.

In this zone, the RU team deploys outside the Tunnel, near the North Entrance. But finally, they have some serious firepower in the form of a T-90A. This tank is crucial for countering the US M1 Abrams, which spawns at the US deployment area at the South Entrance. Park the tank in the Tunnel, facing toward the south, and blast any attackers that move into view. Placing the tank in the Tunnel protects it from the US choppers, but it will still draw plenty of fire from the US ground forces. However, a dedicated team of engineers can keep the T-90A in the fight. RU infantry should gather around the two M-COM stations on the east and west sides of the Tunnel. Pay particular attention to the two narrow side passages leading in from the South Entrance. Support troops training light machine guns down these narrow passages is an effective way to halt US advance.

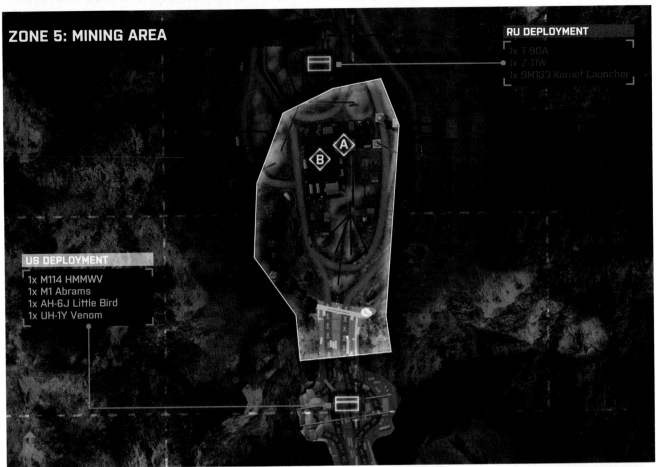

RU DEPLOYMENT
1x T-90A
1x Z-11W
1x 9M133 Kornet Launcher

US DEPLOYMENT
1x M114 HMMWV
1x M1 Abrams
1x AH-6J Little Bird
1x UH-1Y Venom

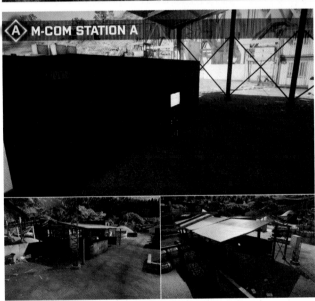

⬧A M-COM STATION A

This M-COM Station A is nestled up against a shipping container beneath a large steel equipment shelter on the east side of the Mining Area. The eastern side of the shipping container is open, making it an awesome hiding spot for both attackers and defenders. Consider placing a Radio Beacon inside the shipping container to maintain a presence next to the M-COM station. Defenders should note that the concrete wall to the south and west can be breached with explosives, thereby opening new avenues of attack for the US team. The red-and-white trailer to the east serves as a great cover point, regardless of which direction the attackers come from. Drop prone atop the stairs here and pick off anyone tampering with the objective.

⬧B M-COM STATION B

M-COM Station B is on the ground floor of the gray two-story office trailer at the center of the Mining Area. The walls of this structure can be completely destroyed but the structure will remain standing. Peeling away the walls allows a better view of the objective for defenders. Still, it's better to simply cover the two entry points on the west and north sides. Tanks are likely to play a role in the fight for this M-COM station, so engineers on both sides should come prepared with anti-tank weaponry, including mines and C4. If the M-COM station becomes completely exposed through the destruction of the surrounding walls, be prepared to deploy smoke on the objective prior to setting or disarming the charge.

Deployment Area Assets		M114 HMMWV	M1 Abrams	AH-6J Little Bird	UH-1Y Venom
	NAME	M114 HMMWV	M1 Abrams	AH-6J Little Bird	UH-1Y Venom
	QUANTITY	1	1	1	1
	RESPAWN TIME	30 sec.	60 sec.	90 sec.	90 sec.

This is the US team's final deployment area, located inside the Tunnel. The Tunnel's exit to the north is a deadly choke point that is easily defended by the RU team and their two T-90A tanks. Therefore, look for other ways to advance on the final M-COM stations. The helicopters offer the best method of moving troops to the north end of the valley. Once on the ground, Radio Beacons can be deployed near the M-COM stations, allowing teammates spawn close to the action without rushing through the carnage near the Tunnel's exit. Beyond transporting troops, the AH-6J plays a pivotal role in attacking the RU team's tanks by helping the M1 Abrams advance to support assault operations on the M-COM stations.

RU DEPLOYMENT

Deployment Area Assets		T-90A	Z-11W	9M133 Kornet Launcher
	NAME	T-90A	Z-11W	9M133 Kornet Launcher
	QUANTITY	2	1	2
	RESPAWN TIME	60 sec.	90 sec.	60 sec.

Although this is the final zone for the RU defenders, they have a good chance of holding out here. There's only one way through the mountain and that's the Tunnel to the south. The Tunnel's exit is a perfect choke point and should be taken advantage of. Deploy the two T-90A tanks so they can cover the exit, picking off US infantry and vehicles that emerge. The biggest threat comes in the form of an aerial assault staged by the US helicopters. If the RU team isn't paying close attention, the choppers can drop troops directly onto the M-COM stations. The best defense against such attacks are engineers armed with SA-18 IGLA missile launchers—just be sure to take out any survivors that manage to bail out. Also, perform periodic sweeps of the area to locate and destroy US Radio Beacons. If the RU team can force the US team to spawn in the Tunnel, they'll have a much easier time holding out long enough to achieve a victory.

SQUAD RUSH

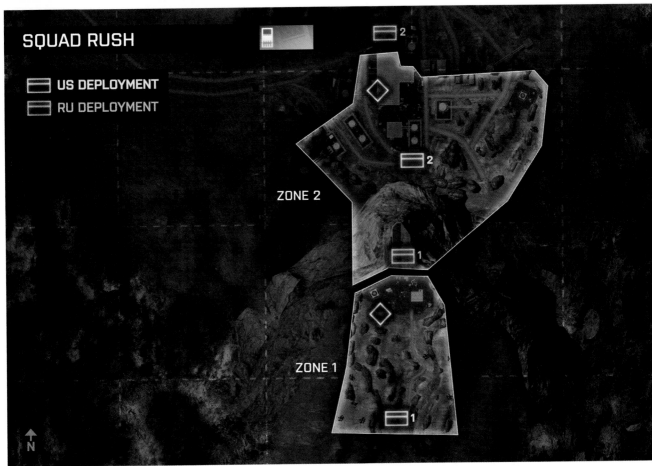

☐ **US DEPLOYMENT**

☐ **RU DEPLOYMENT**

ZONE 2

ZONE 1

This small-scale Rush battle centers around the Peak Facility and the Factory Valley, as the US team is tasked with taking out two M-COM stations. While both teams start on relatively even footing at the start, the RU defenders have the upper hand when it comes to defending the final M-COM station inside the warehouse. An effective RU squad can turn the warehouse interior into a treacherous kill zone, thus requiring the US team to quickly adapt and experiment with different plans of attack.

ZONE 1: PEAK FACILITY

In the first round, the RU team defend an M-COM station at the Peak Facility, on the northern edge of Damavand Peak. The M-COM station is on the south side of the facility on the bottom floor of the small gray structure. The RU defenders may wish to knock out the walls of the lower floor so they have a better view of the M-COM station at long range. Taking out the walls denies the US attackers cover while they're planting the charge. But the US team has the high ground here and they should take full advantage of it. A skilled US recon player can provide sniping cover from the hillside to the south while squad mates rush in and set the charge. While attacking, use explosive weapons to bring down perimeter wall sections. This will keep the defenders on their toes, never knowing where the attackers will infiltrate.

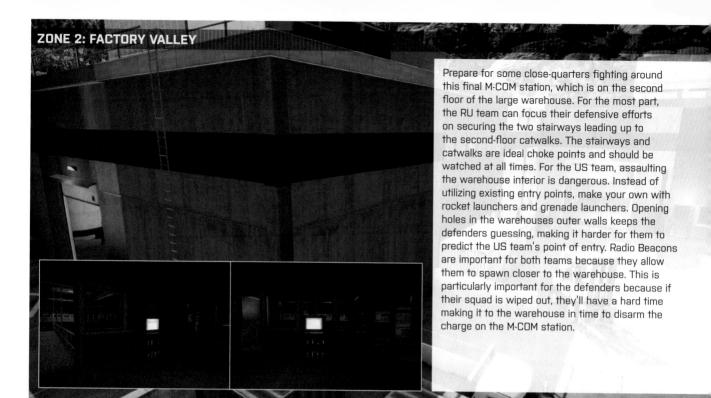

Prepare for some close-quarters fighting around this final M-COM station, which is on the second floor of the large warehouse. For the most part, the RU team can focus their defensive efforts on securing the two stairways leading up to the second-floor catwalks. The stairways and catwalks are ideal choke points and should be watched at all times. For the US team, assaulting the warehouse interior is dangerous. Instead of utilizing existing entry points, make your own with rocket launchers and grenade launchers. Opening holes in the warehouses outer walls keeps the defenders guessing, making it harder for them to predict the US team's point of entry. Radio Beacons are important for both teams because they allow them to spawn closer to the warehouse. This is particularly important for the defenders because if their squad is wiped out, they'll have a hard time making it to the warehouse in time to disarm the charge on the M-COM station.

SQUAD DEATHMATCH

The Factory Valley is the location of this battle, as you and your squad fight for dominance. This sprawling industrial area offers plenty of cover and concealment, particularly around the massive warehouse. Fights in this area often take place at close to intermediate range, so choose your kit loadout accordingly. For those who prefer putting a bit more distance between themselves and their enemies, the high ground on the east side of the map offers long sight lines that are ideal for recon troops looking for long-range kills. The IFV spawns in one of four locations surrounding the warehouse. If your squad gets access to one of these IFVs, don't linger around the map's core. You'll only be a magnet for incoming rockets and C4 attacks. Instead, race to the perimeter of the map where there's less cover for enemy squads. Also, make sure you have at least one engineer on your squad to perform repairs. Make the most of your time in the IFV, scoring as many kills as possible to give your squad the lead.

TEAM DEATHMATCH

When playing on a full server, the fight in and around this Mining Area can get extremely intense. If you find yourself on the valley floor, immediately seek cover among the small buildings or mining equipment. The hillside to the east is a popular sniping spot for recon players. From this high vantage point, they have a relatively clear view of the map. However, the hillside offers very little cover, making it fairly easy to counter-snipe these opponents. Or look for opportunities to flank squads camping the high ground by attacking from the north or south and claiming the high ground for your own team. Instead of trying to occupy the center of the map, work the perimeter. Otherwise, enemy attacks can come from any direction. Still, an organized team can make a solid defensive effort by claiming a fixed position and holding it. Just make sure you have plenty of teammates around to cover all angles.

GRAND BAZAAR

The battle for central Teheran has reached its second week; what was expected to be over within days continues as Russian and US forces clash for the control over this ancient city. No one knows how this will end, but military experts claims that risks are high as the soldiers fight, street by street, in the now deserted city.

US infantry supported by armored vehicles is trying to find a way out of downtown Teheran. A collapsed building is blocking the closest route, so they have to go through the central districts, securing each sector as they advance. Russian infantry is hiding everywhere in the alleys and buildings. The American contingent is attempting to secure the two main squares and the surrounding area.

CONQUEST

SQUARE

US

US BASE
1x M1114 HMMWV
1x LAV-25
1x M220 TOW Launcher

A

B

C

ALLEYWAY

MARKET

RU BASE
1x GAZ-3937 Vodnik
1x BMP-2M
1x 9M133 Kornet Launcher

RU

N

Ready for some urban combat? This head-on Conquest match is an intense conflict centered around a hotly contested city block in the center of the map. Only three control points are up for grabs, which means each team must hold at least two to initiate a drain on the opposing team's tickets. For the US team, it makes the most sense to capture and lock down the Square (A) and Alleyway (B) while the RU team strives to hold the Market (C) and Alleyway (B). The fight for the central Alleyway (B) can be costly, and may ultimately not be worth the large number of tickets it takes to capture and hold. Therefore both team's should consider possible flanking maneuvers in an attempt to hold the nonadjacent Square (A) and Market (C) instead of grinding against the Alleyway (B). In any case, holding the control points to the north and south makes it much easier to apply pressure on the Alleyway.

US BASE

Base Assets		M1114 HMMWV	LAV-25	M220 TOW Launcher
	NAME	M1114 HMMWV	LAV-25	M220 TOW Launcher
	QUANTITY	1	1	1
	RESPAWN TIME	30 sec.	60 sec.	30 sec.

The US Base is located in the northwest corner of the map. This dead-end street is more of a deployment area than a base, as it spawns only a HMMWV and an LAV-25. The lack of vehicles at this base should prepare you for what is mostly a infantry battle in this urban center. Early on, US troops should make a push for the nearby Square (A) control point while the HMMWV and LAV-25 assault the Market (C) far to the south. While the adjacent streets are safe to cross at the beginning of a match, it's best to deploy from one of the central control points later on. The streets offer long sight lines for enemy snipers and they may be waiting for you to enter the intersection just east of the base. So unless there are vehicles available, avoid spawning at the US Base once a match gets underway.

RU BASE

Base Assets		GAZ-3937 Vodnik	BMP-2M	9M133 Kornet Launcher
	NAME	GAZ-3937 Vodnik	BMP-2M	9M133 Kornet Launcher
	QUANTITY	1	1	1
	RESPAWN TIME	30 sec.	60 sec.	30 sec.

The RU team starts in the southeast corner of the map. Like the US Base, the RU Base spawns only a couple of vehicles. Both the Vodnik and BMP-2M should be used early on to rush the Square (A) control point to the north while the RU infantry secure the nearby Market (C). The eastern street, running north and south, provides a clear sight line into the RU Base. So infantry spawning here should be prepared for taking fire from long range while exiting the base. It's much safer to utilize the alleyway to the west of the base when attempting to reach the Market (C) control point on foot. However, once a control point is held by the RU team, it's best to spawn away from the base. This will put you (and your squad) closer to the action while keeping you safe from enemy snipers scanning for prey on the city streets.

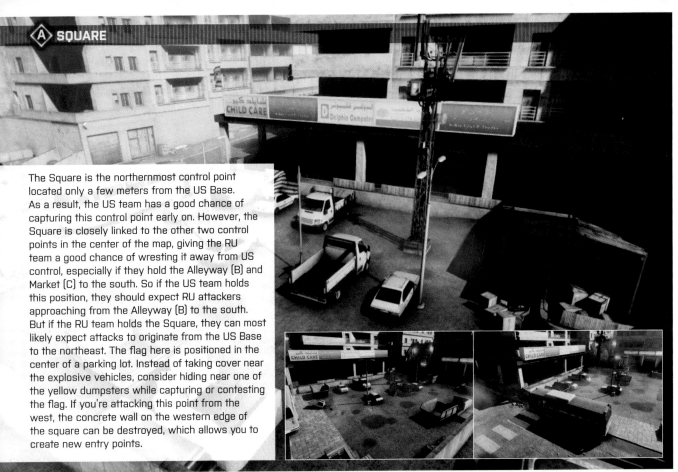

A SQUARE

The Square is the northernmost control point located only a few meters from the US Base. As a result, the US team has a good chance of capturing this control point early on. However, the Square is closely linked to the other two control points in the center of the map, giving the RU team a good chance of wresting it away from US control, especially if they hold the Alleyway (B) and Market (C) to the south. So if the US team holds this position, they should expect RU attackers approaching from the Alleyway (B) to the south. But if the RU team holds the Square, they can most likely expect attacks to originate from the US Base to the northeast. The flag here is positioned in the center of a parking lot. Instead of taking cover near the explosive vehicles, consider hiding near one of the yellow dumpsters while capturing or contesting the flag. If you're attacking this point from the west, the concrete wall on the western edge of the square can be destroyed, which allows you to create new entry points.

B ALLEYWAY

Sitting at the dead center of the city block, the Alleyway (B) is the most contentious control point on the map. Flanked by the Square (A) to the north and the Market (C) to the south, it will see heavy action throughout the duration of the match. The Alleyway is too narrow for vehicles to enter, so this is a control point that must be completely captured or contested by infantry. The flag sits at the center of this narrow passage, making it a dangerous location for attackers and defenders alike. When attempting to capture or contest the flag, always seek cover in one of the stalls to the east or west. This allows you to stay within the flag's capture radius without exposing yourself to fire from the north or south ends of the Alleyway. These alcoves also come in handy when defending the control point; use them to ambush attackers. With little cover, attackers must largely rely on smoke to conceal their advance on this position. Otherwise they're open to both long- and close-range attacks. It's usually safer to secure both the Square (A) and Market (C) before closing in on this control point.

C MARKET

The Market (C) is the southernmost control point, and is therefore within the RU team's sphere of influence. Although the Market spawns no vehicles, it gives the RU team a foothold on the central city block, allowing them to stage attacks on the nearby Alleyway (B) and Square (A). The flag here sits in the center of an abandoned marketplace. The stalls offer decent cover and concealment for infantry attempting to capture or contest the flag. The Market sits on a raised platform, which prevents vehicles from entering. However, vehicles can provide fire support from the streets to the south and east. Heavy machine gun fire can tear through the light cover of the fruit stalls, so never assume you're safe. If it's held by the RU team, most attacks originate from the Alleyway (B) to the north. But if the US team manages to hold this control point, they can expect stiff resistance coming from the RU Base to the southeast. A couple of balconies on the north side of the Market are ideal for defending this location from above. However, attackers that manage to sneak in and take cover among the fruit stands may be hard to spot from a distance, which requires a more close-quarters approach to defense—use a shotgun!

CONQUEST 64

SQUARE
1x M1114 HMMWV

JUNCTION

US

D

A

US BASE
1x M1114 HMMWV
1x LAV-25
1x M220 TOW Launcher

B

HIGHWAY

E

C

ALLEYWAY

MARKET
1x GAZ-3937 Vodnik

RU BASE
1x GAZ-3937 Vodnik
1x BMP-2M
1x 9M133 Kornet Launcher

RU

N

Given the large number of players, this is a relatively compact map. So prepare to rub elbows with plenty of teammates and enemies. This is largely an infantry battle, but don't neglect the firepower offered by the few vehicles available. The machine gun turrets mounted on each vehicle have a zoom option so gunners can accurately engage targets at long range. This allows the vehicles to completely dominate the city streets—zones infantry should avoid completely or cross while at running at a full sprint. With five control points on the map, your team needs to hold at least three flags to initiate a drain on the opposing team's ticket count. When possible, avoid the meat grinder Alleyway (C) control point in the center of the map and try to control those on the perimeter of the map like the Junction (D) and Highway (E) control points. With some dedicated defenders, the Square (A) and Market (C) can be locked rather easily, too. But the tactical situation is always fluid on this map, so constantly monitor the control of the flags and look for opportunities to capture those points left unguarded by the opposing team.

US BASE

Base Assets	NAME	M1114 HMMWV	LAV-25	M220 TOW Launcher
	QUANTITY	1	1	1
	RESPAWN TIME	30 sec.	60 sec.	30 sec.

The US Base is located in the northwest corner of the map. This dead-end street is more of a deployment area than a base, as it spawns only a HMMWV and an LAV-25. The lack of vehicles at this base should prepare you for what is mostly a infantry battle in this urban center. Early on US troops should make a push for the nearby Square (A) control point while the HMMWV and LAV-25 assault the Highway (E) and Junction (D) control points. While the adjacent streets are safe to cross at the beginning of a match, it's best to deploy from one of the central control points later on. The streets offer long sight lines for enemy snipers, and they may be waiting for you to enter the intersection just east of the base. So unless there are vehicles available, avoid spawning at the US Base once a match gets underway. There is an alley just south of the deployment area that offers a relatively safe way to travel south on foot. This is a good way to make the approach to the Highway (E) control point.

RU BASE

Base Assets	NAME	GAZ-3937 Vodnik	BMP-2M	9M133 Kornet Launcher
	QUANTITY	1	1	1
	RESPAWN TIME	30 sec.	60 sec.	30 sec.

The RU team starts in the southeast corner of the map. Like the US Base, the RU Base only spawns a couple of vehicles. Both the Vodnik and BMP-2M should be used early on to rush the Highway (E) and Junction (D) control points while RU infantry secure the nearby Market (C). The eastern street, running north and south, provides a clear sight line into the RU Base. So infantry spawning here should be prepared to take fire from long range while exiting the base. It's much safer to utilize the alleyway to the west of the base when attempting to reach the Market (C) or Highway (E) control points on foot. However, once a control point is held by the RU team, it's best to spawn away from the base. This will put you (and your squad) closer to the action while keeping you safe from enemy snipers scanning for prey on the city streets.

Ⓐ SQUARE

Control Point Assets		
US CONTROL	RU CONTROL	RESPAWN TIME
M1114 HMMWV (1)	—	30 sec.

The Square (A) is located only a few meters from the US Base and is the northernmost point in the central city block. As a result, the US team has a good chance of capturing this control point early on. However, the Square is closely linked to the other two control points in the center of the map, which gives the RU team a good chance of wresting it away from US control, especially if they hold the Alleyway (B) and Market (C) to the south. So if the US team holds this position, they should expect RU attackers to approach from the Alleyway (B) to the south. But if the RU team holds the Square, they can most likely expect attacks to originate from the US Base to the northeast. The Junction (D) control point is also another possible staging area for attacks. So constantly monitor the ever-changing battlefield situation and adjust your defensive tactics accordingly. The HMMWV spawned here is a huge defensive asset—use its machine gun turret to cut down enemy troops advancing along the northern street. The flag here is positioned in the center of a parking lot. Instead of taking cover near the explosive vehicles, consider hiding near one of the yellow dumpsters while capturing or contesting the flag. If you're attacking this point from the west, the concrete wall on the western edge of the square can be destroyed and you can create new entry points.

Ⓑ ALLEYWAY

Sitting at the dead center of the city block, the Alleyway (B) is the most contentious control point on the map. Flanked by the Square (A) to the north and the Market (C) to the south, expect heavy action here throughout the duration of the match. The Alleyway is too narrow for vehicles to enter, so this is a control point that must be completely captured or contested by infantry. The flag sits at the center of this narrow passage, which makes it a dangerous location for attackers and defenders alike. When attempting to capture or contest the flag, always seek cover in one of the stalls to the east or west. This allows you to stay within the flag's capture radius without exposing yourself to fire from the north or south ends of the Alleyway. These alcoves also come in handy when defending the control point because you can ambush attackers. With little cover, attackers must largely rely on smoke to conceal their advance on this position. Otherwise they're open to both long- and close-range attacks. It's usually safer to secure both the Square (A) and Market (C) before closing in on this control point.

Control Point Assets

US CONTROL	RU CONTROL	RESPAWN TIME
—	GAZ-3937 Vodnik (1)	30 sec.

The Market (C) is the southernmost control point in the central city block, and that puts it within the RU team's sphere of influence. Capturing it gives the RU team a foothold in the map's center, allowing them to stage attacks on the nearby Alleyway (B) and Square (A). The flag here sits in the center of an abandoned marketplace. The stalls offer decent cover and concealment for infantry attempting to capture or contest the flag. The Market sits on a raised platform, which prevents vehicles from entering. However, vehicles can provide fire support from the streets to the south and east. The Vodnik spawning here for the RU team is great for covering the nearby streets as well as pinning down attackers attempting to convert the flag. Heavy machine gun fire can tear through the light cover of the fruit stalls, so never assume you're safe. If held by the RU team, most attacks originate from the Alleyway (B) to the north or the Highway (E) control point to the west. But if the US team manages to hold this control point, they can expect stiff resistance coming from the RU Base to the southeast. There are a couple of balconies on the north side of the Market that are ideal for defending this location from above. However, attackers that manage to sneak in and take cover among the fruit stands may be hard to spot from a distance. It requires a more close-quarters approach to defense—use a shotgun!

Ⓓ JUNCTION

Located in the northeast corner of the map, the Junction (D) control point is somewhat isolated from the heated action found in the central city block. Don't forget about this control point. Located approximately equidistant from the bases, both teams have a good chance of taking this flag early on. Once captured, don't neglect to defend it. Tucked in the northeast corner, it's relatively easy to lock down. The flag sits in a small courtyard exposed only to the street to the west and a covered alleyway to the south. Attacks advancing along the two nearby streets are easy to spot and counter. So if you're looking to sneak into this control point, take the alley to the south. The alley is covered and parallels the easternmost street, so you can avoid getting picked off by snipers searching the streets for easy targets. However, defenders can booby-trap this narrow passage with Claymores or C4, so watch your step!

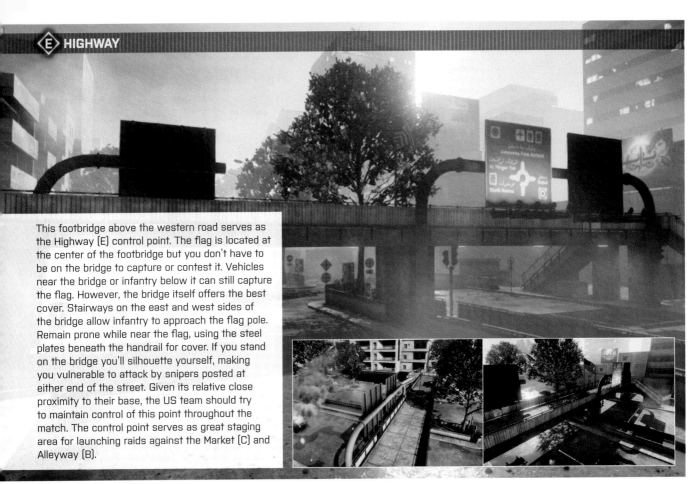

This footbridge above the western road serves as the Highway (E) control point. The flag is located at the center of the footbridge but you don't have to be on the bridge to capture or contest it. Vehicles near the bridge or infantry below it can still capture the flag. However, the bridge itself offers the best cover. Stairways on the east and west sides of the bridge allow infantry to approach the flag pole. Remain prone while near the flag, using the steel plates beneath the handrail for cover. If you stand on the bridge you'll silhouette yourself, making you vulnerable to attack by snipers posted at either end of the street. Given its relative close proximity to their base, the US team should try to maintain control of this point throughout the match. The control point serves as great staging area for launching raids against the Market (C) and Alleyway (B).

RUSH

US DEPLOYMENT

RU DEPLOYMENT

ZONE 1

ZONE 4

ZONE 3

ZONE 2

N

As in the Conquest modes, this is primarily an infantry fight as the US conducts raid after raid on the RU team's M-COM stations. There are four zones on this map, beginning in the northeast corner and proceeding around the edge of the map in a clockwise fashion. The action starts in the Eastern Street, then transitions to the Market, Junction, and Square. While the streets provide the most obvious way to get around, the map is filled with narrow alleyways that offer safe shortcuts for infantry to advance through. This mostly works in the US team's favor, allowing them to sneak up on objectives from various directions. However, this is one map where the shortest path from one area to the next is not always the safest path. So constantly experiment with different routes instead of grinding against areas that are well defended.

ZONE 1: EASTERN STREET

A M-COM STATION A

B M-COM STATION B

M-COM Station A sits on the east side of the street in a small, shaded courtyard. There are only two approaches to this objective: from the street and from the narrow alley to the north. This makes the location relatively easy for RU defenders to lock down, assuming they can reach the area before the attackers do. The street is best covered by recon and support troops positioned to the south. A squad of defenders posted near the M-COM station can ambush enemy troops rushing through the alley. For the US team, it's vital to reach this objective before the defenders can lock it down. An early rush utilizing the alley is the best option. Set the charge while teammates pick off defenders sprinting up the street.

This objective, M-COM Station B, is slightly more secure, as it is located within a storeroom on the west side of the street. This storeroom can be entered from the street or from an alley to the west. Therefore defenders need to prepare for attacks coming from each direction. Covering the entry points is preferable to defending the room where the M-COM station is located. The storeroom is relatively small and make defenders vulnerable to grenade attacks. The US team should utilize the western alley when attacking this objective, avoiding the high potential for carnage in the street. However, always be prepared to battle defenders at close range. Always toss grenades into the room before entering, then rush the room, blasting any survivors prior to setting the charge.

The US team begins this fight with no vehicles. So it's purely up to infantry to secure the area around each M-COM station and set the charges. The US deployment area is located in the northeastern corner of the map, a few meters north of the first set of objectives. The street directly to the south is likely to be watched by RU defenders, so avoid the street entirely. There are side alleys on the east and west sides of the street that allow a more covert approach to each M-COM station. Smoke is also effective for limiting the RU team's line of sight. However, if the US team moves out quickly at the start of the round, they have a good chance of reaching the objectives before the RU defenders have a chance to establish a perimeter. After all, there is a reason why this game mode is called Rush!

Like the US attackers, the RU team gets no vehicles during this first stage of the match. So instead of searching the deployment area for vehicles that don't exist, run (don't walk) toward the objectives to the north. The street is the most obvious avenue of attack and is likely to be used by the majority of US attackers, especially early in the match. Recon sharpshooters and support troops armed with light machine guns can effectively shut down the street, But the street isn't the only approach that must be covered. Be sure to focus defensive efforts around each objective. Each M-COM station can be attacked from alleys running parallel to the street, so make sure these narrow passages are covered as well. Speed is essential early on, so get into position before the attackers can set charges on the objectives.

ZONE 2: MARKET

A M-COM STATION A

B M-COM STATION B

This objective is located in a souk on the south side of the map. The M-COM station is nestled amongst abandoned stalls near the souk's T-intersection. The main entrance to the souk is accessible from the southern street. However, there are two side entrances located to the east and west. Defenders positioned at the western entrance can cover the M-COM station as well as the eastern approach, a path commonly used by attackers. Since the defenders have plenty of time to set up ambushes here, the US attackers should use smoke to conceal their entry while preparing for some close-quarters firefights around the objective. Defender counterattacks from the northern and western souk entrances are all but guaranteed, so position your team accordingly.

M-COM Station B is on the northern side of the Market, directly across the street from the souk. US attackers usually approach this objective from the adjacent alley to the north. If left undefended, this alleyway is by far the quickest path to the objective. However, only a handful of defenders can effectively lock down this passage and pepper attackers with automatic fire and hand grenades. Attacks from the Market or nearby street are a possibility as well, particularly if the alleyway has been shut down. The Market offers plenty of cover and hiding spots that are ideal for both attackers and defenders. Due to the close quarters, neither side gets a distinct advantage here, so it often comes down to the team with the most skilled players in the fight. However, the balcony overlooking the Market to the north can be a handy cover point and a great place to deploy a Radio Beacon.

Despite taking out both objectives in the previous zone, the US team still deploys in approximately the same area located in the northeastern corner of the map. This puts them a great distance from the next set of M-COM stations centered around the Market to the south. The US still has no vehicles, so prepare for another advance on foot. To avoid getting gunned down in the street, use the alleyways to the west and east while pressing toward the Market. Use the western alleys when attacking M-COM Station B and the eastern alleys when advancing on M-COM Station A. However, be prepared for dug-in defenders around each objective.

RU DEPLOYMENT

In the second phase of this conflict, the RU team deploys near the southwestern intersection, by the Junction footbridge. This puts them within relatively close proximity to both objectives, particularly M-COM Station B. The RU team still has no vehicles, so it's solely up to infantry to stop the latest wave of US attackers. Some attacks are likely to come from the street to the east, so don't forget to post sharpshooters here to counter this threat. But expect most attackers to utilize the alleys flanking the street. Post defenders in and around these alleyways and ambush the US team as they attempt to reach the objectives.

ZONE 3: HIGHWAY

US DEPLOYMENT
1x M1 Abrams

RU DEPLOYMENT
1x 9M133 Kornet Launcher

Ⓐ M-COM STATION A

Ⓑ M-COM STATION B

This objective is located in a small alcove on the east side the street. While the street offers the most direct access to this M-COM station, it's not the only way to approach it. The corridor to the east connects to the street to the south as well as the central alley to the west. With so many possible approaches, the defenders are best served by keeping an eye on the M-COM station itself. Defenders positioned to the west, on the opposite side of the street, have a relatively clear view of the objective and can fire through the gate to hit anyone tampering with the M-COM station. Booby traps like C4 and Claymores also work well here. The US team can benefit from their tank by having it clear out nearby defenders and provide security while infantry set the charge. If the tank isn't available, obscure the objective in smoke before attempting to set the charge. Also, consider planting a Radio Beacon in the alley to the west to maintain a nearby spawn point.

M-COM station B is directly across the street from the other objective, which makes it relatively easy for defenders posted on the nearby footbridge to keep an eye on both. This objective is relatively exposed so it is difficult for infantry from both teams to arm or disarm a charge without getting shot in the back. The US M1 Abrams can be used to partially shield the objective, thereby allowing friendly infantry to set a charge. If the US team is successful in setting the charge, the RU team will have a difficult time reaching it from their distant deployment area. Therefore, the RU team should strongly consider placing Radio Beacons in the intersection to the south. This gives them a much better chance to respond to charges being set on either objective. Spawning in the southwest corner of the map is also likely to catch the attackers off-guard.

US DEPLOYMENT

Deployment Area Assets		
NAME		M1 Abrams
QUANTITY		1
RESPAWN TIME		60 sec.

The US team finally gets a tank in this stage of the battle; it spawns in the eastern street, not far from the destroyed objectives of the first stage. As in the previous stage, the US team spawns far away from the next set of objectives to the west. Once again, this gives the defenders a chance to establish a perimeter around the two objectives to the southwest. US infantry should head directly west from the deployment area, cutting through the nearby alleys in an effort to reach the objectives. Meanwhile, the M1 Abrams can provide fire support from a distance. Position the M1 near the southwest intersection and use its weapons to suppress the defenders in the western street. Shutting down the street to enemy foot traffic goes a long way in hampering the RU team's defensive efforts around the objectives.

RU DEPLOYMENT

Deployment Area Assets		
NAME		9M133 Kornet Launcher
QUANTITY		2
RESPAWN TIME		30 sec.

The RU team deploys in the western street, by the Square, just north of the latest set of objectives. While the US team gains a tank in this stage, the RU team must do their best to counter this threat using two Kornet launchers and any anti-tank weapons deployed by the team's engineers. Attack the US tank aggressively and knock it out of commission as quickly as possible—mines are very effective. If allowed to survive, the M1 Abrams can pose a serious threat to the RU team's defense of the M-COM stations. Recon and support troops are very effective at suppressing US infantry advances along the street. However, position more troops in the alleys to the east to prevent the attackers from sneaking up on M-COM Station A.

ZONE 4: SQUARE

RU DEPLOYMENT
1x 9M133 Kornet Launcher

US DEPLOYMENT
1x M1 Abrams

N

A M-COM STATION A

B M-COM STATION B

This objective sits in a relatively isolated storefront on the west side of the street near the northwestern footbridge. Two entry points lead to this M-COM station. The most common approach is from the street through the storefront's main entrance. There's also a back entrance that connects to the alley running behind the store to the west. The alley approach is the safest option, especially if there's heavy fighting going on in the street. Once inside, the store is cramped, which means it's ideal for shotguns, PDWs, and grenades. The M-COM station itself sits in a corner of the store so it is tough to cover from the exterior. So defenders may want to find a hiding spot inside the store to cover the objective directly. Otherwise, both entry points must be covered, a task that may require a full squad. US attackers should expect to face stiff resistance inside the store—always begin entry by tossing in a few grenades.

M-COM Station B is beneath the eastern staircase of the footbridge near the Square. This objective is much more exposed than M-COM Station A, and therefore it requires a cautious approach by attackers. This is one instance where having the M1 Abrams nearby to suppress and distract defenders can make a big difference. Otherwise the attackers must rely on smoke and careful covering tactics to set a charge on the objective. When possible, attack from the Square to the east, eliminating defenders hiding among the nearby produce stalls before moving in on the objective. For the defenders, securing the street and central alley are the keys to locking down this position. In addition to covering the most likely avenues of attack, it's also important to keep defenders next to the M-COM station. There are plenty of sneaky hiding spots next to the objective that are ideal for ambushing the attackers when they are at close to intermediate range.

Deployment Area Assets	NAME	M1 Abrams
	QUANTITY	1
	RESPAWN TIME	60 sec.

In the final stage, the US deployment area finally moves up a significant distance to the Market. However, it's still far from the new objectives located near the Square in the northwest corner of the map. The US team maintains their M1 Abrams, an asset essential for dominating the western street. While the M1 must stick to the streets to reach the objectives, infantry can snake through the nearby alleys to attack the objectives from the east. Although the RU defenders still lack vehicles, US infantry should still avoid the city streets to avoid falling victim to sniper fire. Advance through the alley to the north of the Market and establish a foothold in the Square, deploying Radio Beacons to keep you team close to the action.

RU DEPLOYMENT

Deployment Area Assets	NAME	9M133 Kornet Launcher
	QUANTITY	2
	RESPAWN TIME	30 sec.

Still lacking vehicle support, the RU defenders must make their stand near the Square and prevent the US from destroying the final two objectives. During this stage, the RU team deploys near the large hotel north of the Square. From here the defenders can easily branch out and establish perimeters around the two M-COM stations to the south. Of the two objectives, focus early efforts on covering M-COM Station B located near the footbridge just west of the Square. The US team is likely to attack this objective first, as it's closest to their deployment area and can be reached quickly through the central alleyway. As in the last stage, deny the attackers their tank as quickly as possible by slamming it with the Kornet Launchers and engineer anti-tank weaponry. Knocking out the US tank evens the playing field, making it much easier to hold out here.

SQUAD RUSH

| US DEPLOYMENT |
| RU DEPLOYMENT |

ZONE 1

ZONE 2

Prepare for some intense close-quarters firefights in this compact Rush battle set around the Market. Both objectives are located in small, cramped interiors, so choose your weapons accordingly. Shotguns, carbines, PDWs, and grenades are all very effective in this fight. The RU team starts out defending an objective in the Market before being pushed back to the second objective located in a small storeroom across the street. While there's plenty of hiding spots ideal for ambushing opponents, don't stay put in one location too long unless you want to donate your dog tags.

ZONE 1: MARKET

Early on, it's a foot race to reach this objective located in the small building on the southwest corner of the Market. The US team spawns at a deployment area to the northeast while the RU team spawns near the souk, across the street to the south. While the US team is most likely going to approach from the north, the RU defenders should prepare for anything. The building can be entered from the northern doorway or the wide opening on the south side that faces the street. However, attackers can make their own entry points by blasting holes in the concrete walls surrounding the objective. For this reason, the defenders shouldn't guard the objective from within. Instead, it's best to scatter around the Market, using the various stalls for cover and concealment. Both teams should expect close-quarters fighting, so consider bringing along a shotgun or PDW.

The last objective is located in a storeroom east of the souk. After the destruction of the previous M-COM station, the RU defenders are given a few seconds to establish a defensive perimeter here before the US team can attack. The storeroom is easily accessed from the alley to the west of the objective. But it can also be approached from the street to the east. Most US attacks come down the alleyway to the west, as it's the most direct route from their deployment area in the Market. This makes defending the alley extremely important. Still, it's a good idea to post at least one defender (or a Claymore) near the eastern entrance. When playing as the US, make an effort to always enter from the east side, as it's less likely to be defended. Distractions may be necessary to catch the defenders off guard. So consider having a couple of squad mates feint an attack from the west while the rest of the squad sneaks in from the east to set the charge on the M-COM station. However, whenever attacking from the east, beware of defenders spawning at the end of the street to the south—don't let them see you.

SQUAD DEATHMATCH

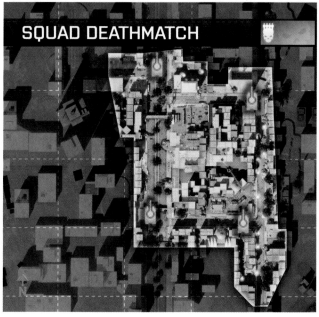

In Grand Bazaar's Squad Deathmatch, the entire map is open, which makes for a chaotic and epic urban battle with no sense of a front line. The streets flanking the central city block are often patrolled by the IFV, spawned at one of four locations near the intersections. If you want to avoid confronting the IFV, stick to the alleys in the middle of the map or on the perimeter. Unless you're packing long-range and anti-tank weapons, the streets are a good place to avoid at all times. But the cramped alleyways cutting through the central city block aren't much safer. Equip close-range weapons like shotguns and PDWs to gain the upper hand in firefights here. Also, never wander too far from your squad. Given the tight confines and twisting pathways, its easy to get separated. So keep an eye on the HUD's green squad icons as well as the minimap to keep up with your squad mates. This is definitely a map where you'll want friends around to watch your back.

TEAM DEATHMATCH

In Team Deathmatch the combat zone is limited to the southeast corner around the Market. This is a very small area even if played with only a dozen players. Instead of constantly running around the map and getting killed, work out a plan with your team to hold a specific area. The area around the Market is an ideal defensive position, assuming your team has enough players to lock it down. Camp the alleys to the north and utilize the balconies on the north side of the Market to fire down on opponents in the street to the south. When possible, avoid the street to the east, as it's a natural kill zone for recon troops camped on the north or south ends. If snipers become a problem here, flank them from the alleys to the west and steal their dog tags. But always keep close tabs on your squad and teammates. Otherwise this battle quickly becomes a chaotic deathmatch with no real sense of teamwork.

KHARG ISLAND

Kharg Island is Iran's biggest oil export terminal. If the US can stake control over this island, it will deny the Russians critical access to Iranian oil reserves. A Marine Expeditionary Force is on the way to the island as part of a major push by US Forces to secure local resources for operations in the region.

Reports also refer to recent shipments of arms and equipment to the Kharg harbor. A preemptive assault has been initiated to stop the Russians from further mobilizing the weaponry. Locking down the harbor is the overall goal of the mission, but establishing a beachhead will be the primary objective if the operation is to succeed.

RU BASE
2x VDV Buggy
2x T-90A
1x Mi-28 Havoc
1x SU-35BM Flanker-E
1x RHIB
1x Pantsir S-1

DOCKS
1x VDV Buggy

CONSTRUCTION SITE

OFFICES

GAS STATION
1x Growler ITV

US BASE
1x Growler ITV
2x M1 Abrams
1x AH-1Z Viper
1x F/A-18E Super Hornet
2x RHIB
1x Centurion C-RAM

All modes of transportation are represented in this battle: Air, land, and sea vehicles are provided for both teams. While vehicles play in significant role in this fight, it's important not to lose sight of the victory conditions. There are four control points on this map; your team needs to hold at least three to begin draining the opposing team's ticket count. While any three control points will work, it's best to hold the three flags closest to your base. For instance, the US team should hold the Gas Station (A), Offices (B), and Construction Site (C). Meanwhile the RU team should forces on the Docks (D), Construction Site (C), and Offices (B). This is a very large map so it's important not to spread your forces too thin. The division of labor works best when assigning each squad a specific control point to attack and defend throughout the match. This allows squads to remain focused on one area (preferably with the use of Radio Beacons) instead of constantly racing all over the map.

US BASE

Base Assets	Growler ITV	M1 Abrams	AH-1Z Viper	F/A-18E Super Hornet	RHIB	Centurion C-RAM
NAME	Growler ITV	M1 Abrams	AH-1Z Viper	F/A-18E Super Hornet	RHIB	Centurion C-RAM
QUANTITY	1	2	1	1	2	1
RESPAWN TIME	10 sec.	20 sec.	90 sec.	40 sec.	10 sec.	—

The US Base is spread across two locations, so be careful where you choose to spawn. All of the ground vehicles spawn on the beach, which is located on the southern shoreline of the island. The US team also gets an RHIB at the beach and it allows for sneaky ocean attacks on the coastal control points to the north. All the air assets, an RHIB and the Centurion C-RAM, spawn on the aircraft carrier south of the beach. If you want to fly, spawn directly into the Super Hornet or Viper. Otherwise, you'll appear belowdecks and have to take the second RHIB to shore. At the start of a round, make a quick move to capture the Gas Station (A) with the ground vehicles. Pilots may want to ditch their aircraft to capture the Offices (B) or Construction Site (C), too. Capturing three control points early on can pay off in the long run.

RU BASE

Base Assets	VDV Buggy	T-90A	Mi-28 Havoc	SU-35BM Flanker-E	RHIB	Pantsir S-1
NAME	VDV Buggy	T-90A	Mi-28 Havoc	SU-35BM Flanker-E	RHIB	Pantsir S-1
QUANTITY	2	2	1	1	1	1
RESPAWN TIME	10 sec.	20 sec.	90 sec.	40 sec.	10 sec.	—

Like the US Base, there are two different spawn locations for the RU team. The bulk of their ground vehicles (and one RHIB) are located on a dock on the northeastern coast of the island. Even infantry spawning here will have no problem reaching the nearby Docks (D) control point. The RU team's air assets (and one VDV Buggy) spawn along the main coastal highway to the northeast. Spawn directly into the Havoc or Flanker-E for guaranteed access. If you don't get in the chopper or jet, you can always take the VDV Buggy to the front lines. The RU team is well-positioned to take at least three control points early on. But speed is essential, so communicate with teammates to ensure that the vehicles are utilized to their full potential to reach the Docks (D), Construction Site (C) and Offices (B) control points early on.

A GAS STATION

Control Point Assets

US CONTROL	RU CONTROL	RESPAWN TIME
Growler ITV (1)	—	10 sec.

Located only a few hundred meters north of the US Base, the Gas Station (A) is likely to stay under US control for the duration of the match. While the control point supplies the US only an extra Growler ITV, simply having a spawn point within striking distance of the nearby Offices (B) and Construction Site (C) is well worth the effort it takes to hold on to this flag. However, all the explosive gas pumps, fuel tanks, and vehicles make it a relatively dangerous place to loiter. When capturing or contesting the flag, always seek cover in the concrete building just east of the flagpole. This will keep you relatively safe from strafing runs by enemy aircraft as well as any secondary explosions. While the road to the west is the most obvious route to this control point, it can also be accessed from the sea to the east. Use a RHIB to sneak in from the coast and establish a foothold on the east side of the Gas Station.

B OFFICES

Although the Offices (B) spawn no vehicles for either team, they are, as a central control point, likely to see plenty of action throughout the course of the battle. Given its location near the center of the map, this control point is really up for grabs at the start of a round. Both teams should consider rushing this location early on with their fastest vehicles. Capturing it first may mean ditching a jet or chopper. The flag sits out in the open, not far from the road to the west. While capturing or contesting this point, scatter around the flag's capture radius, preferably taking cover in the nearby buildings. Like the Gas Station (A), this control point sits on the coast, which makes it a good candidate for amphibious assaults. The road access also makes it easy to capture in any ground vehicle. Defenders here have a relatively easy time watching the flag from a distance. The partially constructed three-story buildings across the street to the west offer excellent views of the flag. But defenders posted here might not be able to spot infantry hiding in the nearby buildings. So regular sweeps of the buildings are necessary to prevent covert captures. Or simply level the buildings and surrounding concrete walls to deny attackers any hiding spot within the flag's capture radius.

C CONSTRUCTION SITE

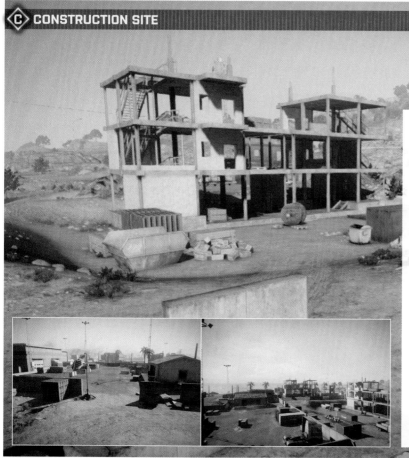

Like the Offices (B), the Construction Site (C) is another central control point that's likely to see heavy action. If captured and properly defended, this flag can be a tough one to wrestle away from a determined team. Surrounded by tall buildings and other structures, defenders here have an easy time watching the flag from a distance. Therefore, always approach this flag with caution and be ready to take cover. Tanks have a relatively easy time rushing the flag's capture radius and converting the flag. However, tanks (and any other vehicles) should be prepared for the presence of mines and C4 placed near the flagpole. Defenders determined to hold on to this position should place a Radio Beacon in or near the large warehouse to the west. Therefore, even if the opposing team converts the flag, your squad will still have a spawn point at the Construction Site, which allows for a quick counteroffensive. The Construction Site spawns no vehicles for either team. So be sure to reinforce it with ground assets brought up from your team's base. This is often a front line control point, so the more firepower you can bring here, the more likely your team is to hold this flag.

D DOCKS

Control Point Assets

US CONTROL	RU CONTROL	RESPAWN TIME
—	VDV Buggy (1)	10 sec.

The Docks (D) are a short distance from the RU Base, which gives the RU team the best chance of capturing this control point and holding it for the duration of the match. The Docks spawn one VDV Buggy for the RU team; it's ideal for launching high-speed raids on the nearby Construction Site (C) and Offices (B) control points. The flag is located on the west side of a large warehouse. Vehicles parked near the flag or infantry hiding in the warehouse can capture or contest this point. So instead of simply watching the flag from one angle, defenders must rely on regular patrols to counter potential sneak attacks. One popular avenue of attack is from the ocean to the east. Attackers can dock RHIBs near one of the ladders to the north or east and rush into the warehouse to covertly convert the flag. Defenders posted on the warehouse roof have a good view of the surrounding area, so they can spot attacks coming from the sea. However, the large collection of shipping containers to the west offers plenty of hiding spots. This is a good place for both attackers and defenders to place Radio Beacons, which help guarantee a spawn point at this location regardless of which team holds the flag.

CONQUEST 64

RU BASE
3x VDV Buggy
2x T-90A
1x 9K22 Tunguska-M
1x Z-11W
1x Mi-28 Havoc
2x SU-35BM Flanker-E
1x RHIB
1x Pantsir S-1

DOCKS
1x VDV Buggy

CONSTRUCTION SITE

OFFICES

ARMY OUTPOST
1x Growler ITV
1x VDV Buggy

GAS STATION
1x Growler ITV

US BASE
2x Growler ITV
2x M1 Abrams
1x LAV-AD
1x AH-6J Little Bird
1x AH-1Z Viper
2x F/A-18E Super Hornet
2x RHIB
1x Centurion C-RAM

With 64 players and over a dozen vehicles on the map at any given time, this battle is downright chaotic. So do your best to stay focused on the big picture as tanks rumble across the landscape and jets streak overhead. There are five control points on this map. Your team must hold at least three flags to begin bleeding the opposing team's ticket count. The action here is extremely fluid and requires careful team coordination. The best way to go about this is by assigning each squad a single control point to attack and defend throughout the duration of the match. This helps ensure that captured control points are defended at all times. So before the match starts, call out which control point your squad will cover to help guarantee that each squad covers a different flag. The central control points like the Offices (C) and Construction Site (D) may require the full-time attention of two squads each. In a full 64-player match, you have the manpower to defend each control point with at least one squad, so don't let the enemy score easy captures. Rid your team of the bad habits and defend each control point. To maintain a constant presence at their assigned control point, squads should deploy a Radio Beacon nearby so they have a spawn point whether they hold the flag or not.

Base Assets	Growler ITV	M1 Abrams	LAV-AD	AH-6J Little Bird	AH-1Z Viper	F/A-18E Super Hornet	RHIB	Centurion C-RAM
NAME								
QUANTITY	2	2	1	1	1	2	2	1
RESPAWN TIME	10 sec.	20 sec.	60 sec.	90 sec.	90 sec.	40 sec.	10 sec.	—

The US Base is spread across two locations, so be careful where you choose to spawn. All of the ground vehicles spawn on the beach, which is on the southern shoreline of the island. The US team also gets an RHIB at the beach; it can make sneaky ocean attacks on the coastal control points to the north. All the air assets, a RHIB, and the Centurion C-RAM spawn on the aircraft carrier south of the beach. If you want to fly, spawn directly into the Super Hornets, Viper, or Little Bird. Otherwise you'll appear belowdecks and have to take the second RHIB to shore. At the start of a round, make a quick move to capture the Gas Station (A) and Army Outpost (B) with the ground vehicles. Pilots may want to ditch their aircraft to capture the Offices (C) or Construction Site (D), too. Capturing four control points early on can pay off in the long run. However, getting teammates to the map's center takes communication and coordination, so don't leave the base in an empty vehicle—always offer squad and teammates a ride. Otherwise, it's a very long hike to the nearest control point.

RU BASE

Base Assets	VDV Buggy	T-90A	9K22 Tunguska-M	Z-11W	Mi-28 Havoc	SU-35BM Flanker-E	RHIB	Pantsir S-1
NAME								
QUANTITY	3	2	1	1	1	2	1	1
RESPAWN TIME	10 sec.	20 sec.	40 sec.	90 sec.	90 sec.	40 sec.	10 sec.	—

Like the US Base, there are two different spawn locations for the RU team. The bulk of their ground vehicles (and one RHIB) are located on a dock on the northeastern coast of the island. Even infantry spawning here will have no problem reaching the nearby Docks (E) control point. The RU team's air assets (and one VDV Buggy) spawn along the main coastal highway to the northeast. Spawn directly into the helicopters or jets for guaranteed access. If you don't get in the choppers or jets, you can always take the VDV Buggy to the front lines. The RU team is well positioned to take at least three control points early on. But speed is essential, so communicate with teammates to ensure that the vehicles are utilized to their full potential to reach the Docks (E), Construction Site (D) and Offices (C) control points early on. Work together to capture and secure these points early to initiate a drain on the US team's ticket count. From that point, the RU team can go on defense. But very few vehicles are produced by the control points so don't forget to move ground vehicles forward to aid the defensive efforts around each control point.

Control Point Assets

US CONTROL	RU CONTROL	RESPAWN TIME
Growler ITV (1)	—	10 sec.

Located only a few hundred meters north of the US Base, the Gas Station (A) is likely to stay under US control for the duration of the match. While the control point supplies the US with only an extra Growler ITV, simply having a spawn point within striking distance of the nearby Army Outpost (B) and Offices (C) is well worth the effort it takes to hold this flag. Otherwise, US troops spawning back at the US Base have a long journey ahead of them. However, all the explosive gas pumps, fuel tanks, and vehicles make it a relatively dangerous place to loiter. When capturing or contesting the flag, always seek cover in the concrete building just east of the flagpole. This will keep you relatively safe from strafing runs by enemy aircraft as well as any secondary explosions. While the road to the west is the most obvious route to this control point, it can also be accessed from the sea to the east. Use a RHIB to sneak in from the coast and establish a foothold on the east side of the Gas Station.

Control Point Assets

US CONTROL	RU CONTROL	RESPAWN TIME
Growler ITV (1)	VDV Buggy (1)	10 sec.

As the most inland control point, it's easy to forget about the Army Outpost (B) in the hills to the west. Despite it's relatively remote location, this control point is just as crucial as any other on the map because it provides a spawn point as well as a Growler ITV for the US team and a VDV Buggy for the RU team. This semi-fortified outpost is easily accessed via the two dirt roads branching off the main highway. The flag is located right next to the dirt road, making it easy for vehicles to capture. But take a more cautious approach if the flag is held by the opposing team. The surrounding buildings, guard towers, and elevated rocks to the west provide excellent overwatch positions, allowing defenders to covertly pick-off attackers from long range. There isn't much cover near the flagpole, so utilize smoke to conceal your position while attempting to convert the flag. Once held, the Army Outpost serves as a great staging area for attacks on the central control points like the Construction Site (D) Offices (C).

Although the Offices spawn no vehicles for either team, as a central control point it's likely to see plenty of action throughout the battle. Given its location near the center of the map, this control point is really up for grabs at the start of a round. Both teams should consider rushing this location early on with their fastest vehicles. Capturing it first may mean ditching a jet or chopper. The flag sits out in the open, not far from the road to the west. While capturing or contesting this point, scatter around the flag's capture radius, preferably taking cover in the nearby buildings. Like the Gas Station (A), this control point sits on the coast, so it is good candidate for amphibious assaults. The road access also makes it easy to capture in any ground vehicle. Defenders here have a relatively easy time watching the flag from a distance. The partially constructed three-story buildings across the street to the west offer excellent views of the flag. But defenders posted here might not be able to spot infantry hiding in the nearby buildings. So regular sweeps of the buildings are necessary to prevent covert captures. Or simply level the buildings and surrounding concrete walls to deny attackers a hiding spot within the flag's capture radius. If playing a match with a full complement of 64 players, don't leave this flag undefended. Defending here is a full-time job that never gets dull, especially when playing on a full server.

Like the Offices (C), the Construction Site (D) is another central control point likely to see heavy action. If captured and properly defended, this flag can be a tough one to wrestle away from a determined team. Because it is surrounded by tall buildings and other structures, defenders here have an easy time watching the flag from a distance. Therefore, always approach this flag with caution and be ready to take cover. Tanks have a relatively easy time rushing the flag's capture radius and converting the flag. However, tanks (and any other vehicles) should be prepared for the presence of mines and C4 placed near the flagpole. Defenders determined to hold on to this position should place a Radio Beacon in or near the large warehouse to the west. Therefore, even if the opposing team converts the flag, your squad will still have a spawn point at the Construction Site, which allows for a quick counteroffensive. The Construction Site spawns no vehicles for either team so be sure to reinforce it with ground assets brought up from your team's base. This is often a frontline control point, so the more firepower you can bring here, the more likely your team is to hold this flag. Constantly monitor the ever-changing tactical situation. Be ready to defend attacks coming from the nearby Offices (C) to the west, the Docks (E) to the north, and the Army Outpost (B) to the south. In a large match, it may take two squads to adequately lock down this flag.

⟨E⟩ DOCKS

Control Point Assets

US CONTROL	RU CONTROL	RESPAWN TIME
—	VDV Buggy (1)	10 sec.

The Docks (E) are a short distance from the RU Base, which gives the RU team the best chance of capturing this control point and holding it for the duration of the match. The Docks spawn one VDV Buggy for the RU team and it is ideal for launching high-speed raids on the nearby Construction Site (D) and Offices (C) control points. The flag is located on the west side of a large warehouse. Vehicles parked near the flag or infantry hiding in the warehouse can capture or contest this point. So instead of simply watching the flag from one angle, defenders must rely on regular patrols to counter potential sneak attacks coming from the warehouse. One popular avenue of attack is from the ocean to the east. Attackers can dock RHIBs near one of the ladders to the north or east and infiltrate the warehouse to covertly convert the flag. Defenders posted on the warehouse roof have a good view of the surrounding area and can spot attacks coming from the sea—but always stay prone to avoid silhouetting yourself. The large collection of shipping containers to the west offers plenty of hiding spots. This is a good place for both attackers and defenders to place Radio Beacons, which help guarantee a spawn point at this location regardless of which team holds the flag.

RUSH

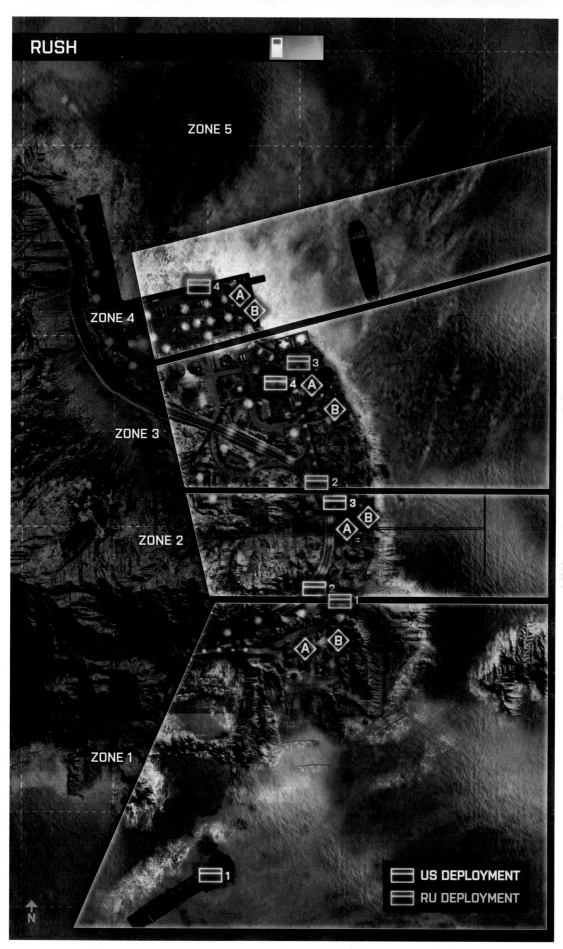

Like the Conquest maps, this Rush map also features a wide assortment of vehicles that give the US attackers the chance to advance by ground, air, or sea. At the start, the US must push their way ashore by staging an amphibious assault on the island's southern beach. From there, it's a steady push through the Gas Station, Offices, and Docks. Throughout the battle, the RU defenders are short-handed on the vehicle front. This requires expert deployment of the few resources available as well as a heavy reliance on engineers to deal with the onslaught of US vehicles. An RU team comprised largely of engineers (and support troops to resupply them) will have the best chance of halting the US advance.

ZONE 5

ZONE 4

ZONE 3

ZONE 2

ZONE 1

US DEPLOYMENT

RU DEPLOYMENT

N

ZONE 1: BEACH

RU DEPLOYMENT
1x T-90A
1x SU-25TM Frogfoot

US DEPLOYMENT
- 3x LAV-25
- 1x AAV-7A1 AMTRAC
- 1x AH-1Z Viper
- 1x A-10 Thunderbolt
- 2x RHIB
- 1x Centurion C-RAM

N

Ⓐ M-COM STATION A

M-COM station A is completely exposed and flanked by two missile batteries on the northwest edge of the beach—the missile batteries don't function. With no cover around the objective itself, defenders are best served by covering this position from a distance, using the nearby rocks for cover and concealment. Planting mines and C4 around the objective isn't a bad idea either. The attackers must use the support of vehicles to get close enough to plant a charge on this M-COM station. Otherwise, obscuring the objective in smoke is the next best option. The LAV-25s are great for suppressing nearby infantry, providing enough of a distraction for one brave attacker to plant a charge on the objective. Once a charge is placed, attackers should form a defensive perimeter around the objective while continuing to use the vehicles to suppress defenders attempting to disarm the charge.

Ⓑ M-COM STATION B

This objective is located within the mobile communications trailer on the northeast side of the beach. The trailer can be entered from the north and south. But instead of defending the objective from within the cramped space, it's best for the RU team to cover the two entry points. Hiding inside only makes you vulnerable to grenades tossed in through the doorways. Still, booby-rapping the interior with C4 and Claymores can be very effective. Like M-COM Station A, the US team is best served by using their LAV-25s to secure the area around the communications trailer before sending infantry inside to plant the charge. Once again, covering the two entry points is key to preventing the defenders from disarming the charge, so make sure both doorways are covered, especially the northern one nearest the RU deployment area.

Base Assets	NAME	LAV-25	AAV-7A1 AMTRAC	AH-1Z Viper	A-10 Thunderbolt	RHIB	Centurion C-RAM
	QUANTITY	3	1	1	1	2	1
	RESPAWN TIME	60 sec.	60 sec.	90 sec.	40 sec.	30 sec.	—

The US team starts on the aircraft carrier southwest of the beach. There are plenty of vehicles available with which US troops can make an amphibious landing and establish a beachhead. The two RHIBs are the fastest of way to get troops onto the beach, but they also offer the least protection. So use these only early in the round before the RU defenders have a chance to reach the beach. The LAV-25s and AMTRAC are slower, but they offer much more protection. Regardless of how they get ashore, the US team should promptly deploy Radio Beacons in isolated, well-covered areas of the beach. The AMTRAC also serves as a mobile spawn point, so consider parking it on the beach in an area where it can't be easily spotted by the enemy. This lets teammates spawn directly on the beach instead of on the aircraft carrier. Air power is critical for securing a beachhead so get the Viper and A-10 up in the air as soon as possible to perform strafing runs on the defenders. The aircraft are also essential for countering the RU team's SU-25TM during the amphibious landing.

Base Assets	NAME	T-90A	SU-25TM Frogfoot
	QUANTITY	1	1
	RESPAWN TIME	120 sec.	40 sec.

Given the flood of US vehicles coming ashore, the RU team has a tough fight ahead of them at the beach. Engineers are critical in fending off the waves of vehicles pushing ashore as well as shooting down the US aircraft—anti-tank weapons and the SA-18 IGLA anti-air missile launcher are essential. A good SU-25TM pilot can make all the difference, so don't spawn in the jet unless you're up to the task and have the necessary unlocks to shoot down aircraft or deploy devastating air-to-ground munitions. The RU team has only one tank, so it must be kept healthy by a team of dedicated engineers while accurately targeting the incoming LAV-25s and AMTRAC. The tank's Guided Shell weapon unlock, when used in conjunction with a recon soldier's SOFLAM laser target designator, can be a game changer, allowing for pinpoint accuracy even if the T-90A does not have line of sight. So use recon troops to lase targets while the T-90A holds back and fires from a safe location. Meanwhile, infantry should perform routine patrols of the beach, killing any hiding enemies while destroying US Radio Beacons. The longer you can keep the US team spawning on their carrier, the better your chances of holding out here.

ZONE 2: GAS STATION

US DEPLOYMENT

2x M1114 HMMWV
2x M1 Abrams
1x AAV-7A1 AMTRAC
1x AH-1Z Viper
1x A-10 Thunderbolt
2x RHIB
1x Centurion C-RAM

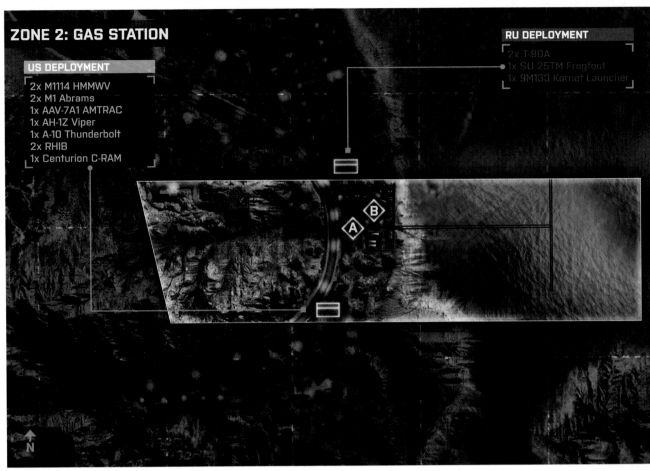

N

A M-COM STATION A

This objective is located in a unique position, flanked by the two pipelines on the south side of the Gas Station. The area between the pipelines forms a narrow trench that makes it relatively easy for attackers to sneak up on the M-COM station without being spotted. Therefore, defenders need to find elevated positions around the objective so they can see down into this trench and counter sneaky advances by the US team. Booby-trapping the area around the objective with C4 or Claymores is a very effective defensive tactic. Avoid defending from within the trench area as it leaves you open to attacks from above. Although it's possible to sneak up on this objective, attackers should still rely on their vehicles to provide fire support before attempting to set a charge on the objective.

B M-COM STATION B

M-COM station B is on the east side of the 's concrete building at the Gas Station, partially concealed by some shipping containers and metal crates. While the concrete building can be completely demolished, the shipping containers and crates can't be destroyed. This limits the sight lines to the objective, requiring both attackers and defenders to get up-close to the M-COM station to cover it. Both teams can seek cover in the nearby building (while it's still standing) and cover the objective from the windows. Attacks can come from any direction, so the defenders may wish to plant a T-UGS motion sensor near the objective to monitor enemy movement around it. This can serve as an early warning so defenders can respond before a charge is set.

Base Assets	NAME	M1114 HMMWV	M1 Abrams	AAV-7A1 AMTRAC	AH-1Z Viper	A-10 Thunderbolt	RHIB	Centurion C-RAM
	QUANTITY	2	2	1	1	1	2	1
	RESPAWN TIME	40 sec.	25 sec.	60 sec.	90 sec.	40 sec.	30 sec.	—

Shortly after the first two M-COM stations are destroyed, two large hovercraft arrive on the beach loaded with a fresh batch of ground vehicles, including two M1 Abrams tanks and a couple of HMMWVs. The US team also retains the AMTRAC, AH-1Z, A-10, and two RHIBs, which are spawned back at the carrier. Before racing for the Gas Station to the north, make sure you don't leave any teammates stranded on the beach or carrier. It's important to consolidate your forces and coordinate a simultaneous attack on the objectives at the Gas Station in an attempt to overwhelm the defenders. This time the defenders have two T90A tanks, so failing to coordinate attacks can lead to disaster. Use the aircraft to distract and suppress enemy ground units while your vehicles roll in to assault the objectives.

Base Assets	NAME	T-90A	SU-25TM Frogfoot	9M133 Kornet Launcher
	QUANTITY	2	1	1
	RESPAWN TIME	180 sec.	40 sec.	30 sec.

The RU team deploys on the hill just north of the Gas Station. This gives them adequate time to move into position and establish a perimeter around the objectives before the US team arrives. The two T-90A tanks are crucial to defending this location, so don't let them get destroyed. It takes a whopping three minutes for each tank to respawn, so do your best to keep each tank healthy by surrounding it with a team of engineers. The tanks are crucial for countering the two M1 Abrams. Position the T-90As so they can support each other while covering the main road to the south. The SU-25TM also plays a big role in stopping the US assault. While it's a useful ground attack asset, the SU-25TM is best deployed here as a fighter. So load it out with heat-seeking missiles and use them to shoot down the US team's AH-1Z and A-10. Engineers can support the SU-25TM by firing their own IGLA missiles at enemy aircraft.

ZONE 3: OFFICES

RU DEPLOYMENT
1x T-90A
1x SU-25TM Frogfoot
4x 9M133 Kornet Launcher

US DEPLOYMENT
1x M1114 HMMWV
1x M1 Abrams
1x AAV-7A1 AMTRAC
1x AH-1Z Viper
1x A-10 Thunderbolt
2x RHIB
1x Centurion C-RAM

A M-COM STATION A

B M-COM STATION B

This is one of the most defensible M-COM stations on the map, and the RU team has a strong chance of holding off the US attack here. Located on the second floor of a partially constructed building, this objective can be accessed only by infantry climbing staircases on the structure's northern and southern sides. Barring parachute assaults from above, the defenders can effectively block access to the objective by covering these staircases. While the concrete exterior walls of the building can be destroyed, the building itself will not collapse, even under the most intense bombardment. So it's up to the attackers to infiltrate the second floor and plant a charge. Both teams can benefit from Radio Beacons placed on the rooftop or third floor of the building to guarantee a nearby spawn point. Although it's farther from their deployment area, the US team should attack this M-COM station first to prevent the entire RU team from rallying around this location.

M-COM Station B is located along the west side of a building near the coast. The building is surrounded by a low concrete wall with entrances to the east and west. However, attackers shouldn't bother entering through these choke points. Instead, breach the exterior wall with explosives of any kind to make your own entrance. Meanwhile, defenders should cover the objective directly by hiding in the nearby building and firing at attackers through the west-facing windows. However, defenders should also prepare for the possibility of attackers arriving in RHIBs and attacking from the sea to the east. With some many potential directions of attack, a T-UGS motion sensor comes in handy for monitoring enemy movement around the objective.

US DEPLOYMENT

Base Assets	NAME	M1114 HMMWV	M1 Abrams	AAV-7A1 AMTRAC	AH-1Z Viper	A-10 Thunderbolt	RHIB	Centurion C-RAM
	QUANTITY	1	1	1	1	1	2	1
	RESPAWN TIME	30 sec.	120 sec.	60 sec.	90 sec.	40 sec.	30 sec.	—

In this stage of the battle, the US team deploys near the Gas Station. Although the US maintains a large number of vehicles, they are spread out between this location and the aircraft carrier. So don't forget about the AH-1Z, A-10, AMTRAC, and RHIBs back at the carrier. The AMTRAC is slow but serves as a mobile spawn point. Consider parking it in an isolated area to the north to provide teammates a forward spawn point near the Offices. The RHIBs offer a quick way to flank the defenders from the sea and avoiding the carnage along the highway. With fewer tanks at your disposal, the aircraft must play a bigger role in the ground attack, constantly strafing the RU team's positions to the north.

RU DEPLOYMENT

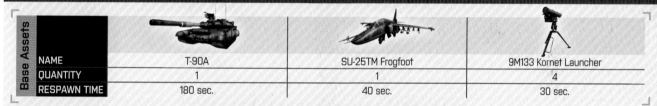

Base Assets	NAME	T-90A	SU-25TM Frogfoot	9M133 Kornet Launcher
	QUANTITY	1	1	4
	RESPAWN TIME	180 sec.	40 sec.	30 sec.

Having been pushed back to the Offices, the RU team now deploys near the coastal road north of the new objectives. The RU team only has one tank this time, so make the most of it. Consider using the Guided Shell weapon to lock on to distant targets spotted by friendly recon troops using the SOFLAM. You can deploy the tank's main cannon without exposing the tank to frontline combat. The Kornet launchers can also make an impact on the US advance, so look for opportunities to fire these powerful manually guided missiles at incoming ground vehicles. However, the US aircraft still pose a significant threat, so be prepared to counter them with the SU-25TM as well as shoulder-fired IGLA missiles carried by engineers.

ZONE 4: DOCKS

RU DEPLOYMENT
1x T-90A
1x SU-25TM Frogfoot
3x 9M133 Kornet Launcher

US DEPLOYMENT
1x M1 Abrams
1x AAV-7A1 AMTRAC
1x AH-1Z Viper
1x A-10 Thunderbolt
2x RHIB
1x Centurion C-RAM

A M-COM STATION A

B M-COM STATION B

Located on the second floor of the warehouse, this M-COM station is tough to reach if it is well defended. The upper-floor platform on which the objective sits is accessible via the surrounding catwalk system. This upper level can be reached by three staircases inside the warehouse. The staircases are pure choke points and the RU defenders should take advantage of them. The interior of the warehouse is rather dark, making Tactical Lights and Laser Sights very effective for both teams. When attacking, expect stiff resistance inside the warehouse. Instead of entering through one of the existing doorways, blow a hole in one of the exterior walls to make your own entrance, then rush the objective before the defenders realize what's happening.

This M-COM station is barricaded in a eastern office on the ground floor of the warehouse. For the attackers, reaching this objective can be deadly unless you think outside the box. The wall directly behind the M-COM station can be destroyed, allowing for easy access from the warehouse's western exterior. So simply blow a hole in the wall with a rocket or grenade launcher, hop inside the office and plant the charge. Defenders must prepare for such unorthodox attacks by defending the western exterior of the warehouse. But not all attackers think alike, so defenders must also cover the interior approach. Since both objectives are in the same building, defenders posted inside the warehouse should be prepared to respond to attacks on either M-COM station.

Base Assets	M1 Abrams	AAV-7A1 AMTRAC	AH-1Z Viper	A-10 Thunderbolt	RHIB	Centurion C-RAM
NAME	M1 Abrams	AAV-7A1 AMTRAC	AH-1Z Viper	A-10 Thunderbolt	RHIB	Centurion C-RAM
QUANTITY	1	1	1	1	2	1
RESPAWN TIME	25 sec.	60 sec.	90 sec.	40 sec.	30 sec.	—

Six M-COM stations down, two more to go. For the final stage of this battle, the US team deploys near the Offices. The objectives in the large warehouse at the docs require a greater focus on close-quarters infantry tactics, but vehicles still play a role in transporting troops and securing entry. While the warehouse can't be destroyed, the exterior walls can be blasted open with explosive munitions. Use the M1 Abrams to punch holes in the warehouse walls so teammates can enter. Meanwhile, use the A-10 and AH-1Z to provide close air support by strafing enemy units outside the warehouse, including the RU team's T-90A. The RHIBs spawned at the carrier offer one of the best methods of assaulting the Docks, so don't forget to utilize these boats.

Base Assets	T-90A	SU-25TM Frogfoot	9M133 Kornet Launcher
NAME	T-90A	SU-25TM Frogfoot	9M133 Kornet Launcher
QUANTITY	1	1	3
RESPAWN TIME	90 sec.	40 sec.	30 sec.

Despite previous defeats, the RU team has a good chance of making a final stand here at the Docks. Both M-COM stations here are located within the warehouse. Therefore, the lack of vehicles isn't as much of a factor here as it was in the previous zones. Still, the RU team should make an effort to stop US troops from reaching the warehouse. Using the shipping containers for cover and concealment, the T-90A is great for defending the warehouse's western side, a popular entry point for attackers. The US aircraft are more of a nuisance than a threat here, so don't expend too many resources on shooting them down. Load out the SU-25TM for ground attack and use it to knock out US vehicles approaching from the south. But the bulk of the team should focus their efforts on defending the warehouse exterior and interior from US infantry attacks. Spawning only a few meters from the warehouse, the defenders have a relatively easy time locking down this location.

SQUAD RUSH

ZONE 2

ZONE 2

2

1

ZONE 1

1

N

In this scaled-down variant of Rush, both teams face off near the Offices and Docks as the US team attempts to knock out M-COM stations located within buildings. The buildings are large and have multiple entry points that require the defenders to focus their efforts around the objectives instead of trying to lock down each structure. Unlike some of the smaller buildings, these large structures cannot be destroyed. So instead of trying to topple each building, focus on finding a way in. Prepare for a mix of intermediate- and close-range combat, so choose your weapons accordingly. When operating in the dark warehouse at the Docks, consider deploying Tactical Lights and Laser Sights to temporarily blind your opponents.

ZONE 1: OFFICES

This is definitely not the way the US team wanted to start this match. The M-COM station is on the second floor of a partially constructed building. The staircases on the north and south ends of the building are the only way to access the second floor. Defenders only need to cover these two staircases to lock down the second floor. However, it is a large building, which makes it difficult for only four players to adequately cover them at all times. Attackers should post a fire team in the gray trailer to the south and have them provide fire support while the rest of the squad assaults the building. If the attackers can manage to wipe out the defenders, it gives them just enough time to set the charge and establish a perimeter of their own.

The last objective is in an office on the ground floor of the warehouse. Attacking through the warehouse is dangerous and unnecessary. Instead, blow a hole in the western wall of the warehouse's exterior to access the office where the objective is sitting. Make sure your squad brings along C4, a rocket launcher, or a grenade launcher to blast a hole in the wall. Hop through the hole and plant a charge on the M-COM station. This is the preferred method of attack for this objective, so defenders should be prepared to guard the warehouse's western exterior as well as the interior.

SQUAD DEATHMATCH

This game mode is centered around the Construction Site, which provides a frantic taste of urban combat as each squad fights for dominance. There are plenty of two- and three-story buildings in this area that make it easy for squads to take the high ground and pick off opponents running around this relatively compact combat zone. There are four possible IFV spawn points, mostly positioned along the road that cuts down the center of the map. If your squad gets access to an IFV, use it to counter foot traffic along the roads. While the IFV's auto-cannon is nice for punching holes through walls, it's the machine gun turret that can really drive up your squad's score by zooming in on distant opponents and pumping them full of lead. Whether you are driving around in the IFV or moving on foot, stay together and cautiously work the perimeter of the map and constantly scour the center for enemies.

TEAM DEATHMATCH

Located on the Docks portion of the map, there are two key areas in this match and each requires completely different weapons and tactics. The west side of the docks is littered with stacks of shipping containers. The rows between each stack of shipping containers create long sight lines that are ideal for recon and support troops. So expect long-range combat to dominate in this area of the map. On the east side of the Docks is the large warehouse. Work together with your team to claim warehouse early and use it as a fort throughout the match. This makes it easy to ambush opponents that wander into the massive structure. The warehouse also has second-floor windows facing west that are ideal for firing down on enemies hiding among the shipping containers. While most combat within the warehouse occurs at close range, choose a weapon that also allows you to score kills at a distance—carbines and assault rifles are well suited for this fight. The team that manages to hold on to the warehouse has the best chance of coming out on top.

NOSHAHR CANALS

US Marines are launching a strike upon a major harbor by the Noshahr Canals on the Iranian coast. The strategically important port allows for deep-water vessels to off-load cargo and essential materials.

The key objective for the Americans will be capturing an inland airfield currently occupied by Russian forces. However, the success of the mission will depend entirely on how quickly Marines can establish a foothold on the harbor itself.

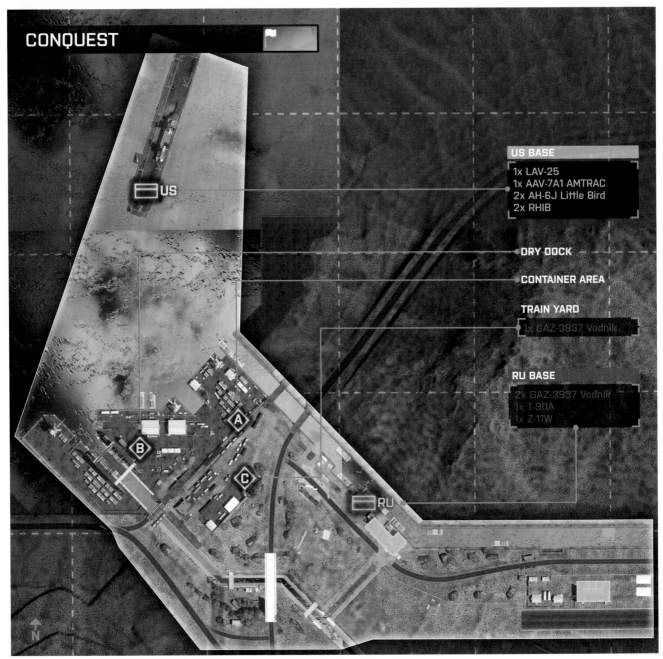

US BASE
1x LAV-25
1x AAV-7A1 AMTRAC
2x AH-6J Little Bird
2x RHIB

DRY DOCK

CONTAINER AREA

TRAIN YARD
1x GAZ-3937 Vodnik

RU BASE
2x GAZ-3937 Vodnik
1x T-90A
1x Z-11W

On this map, US forces launch an amphibious assault on an industrial dock facility. Initially, simply gaining a foothold on shore is the US team's primary goal. But if the RU team can make a strong showing, they can push the US back into the ocean. At the start of the round, the US team should make an effort to capture the Dry Dock (B) and Container Area (A). By using the speed and passenger capacity of the Little Birds, the US can drop troops at each location within the first minute of the match. Since there are only three control points on the map, each team only needs to hold at least two flags to drain the opposing team's ticket count. For the US, holding the Dry Dock (B) and Container Area (A) make the most sense. As for the RU team, they're better off controlling all three flags, thereby denying the US team a solid spawn point on land. If the RU team can push the US back to their carrier, then they must establish a line of defense on the northern coast to prevent US amphibious and air assets from regaining a foothold. RU vehicles and engineers armed with anti-tank and SA-18 IGLA missile launchers all play a big role in confining the US team to their carrier.

US BASE

Base Assets		LAV-25	AAV-7A1 AMTRAC	AH-6J Little Bird	RHIB
	NAME	LAV-25	AAV-7A1 AMTRAC	AH-6J Little Bird	RHIB
	QUANTITY	1	1	2	2
	RESPAWN TIME	30 sec.	60 sec.	90 sec.	15 sec.

The US team begins the match on an aircraft carrier on the north side of the map. With no presence on shore, the early moments of the match are critical as US troops attempt to secure a foothold to the south. The AH-6J Little Birds offer the quickest way to get troops on land. So if you're piloting one of these helicopters, don't take off until it's fully loaded—your passengers can jump out of the chopper and secure control points by parachuting down to the ground. But the RU team is likely to use similar tactics with their Z-11W helicopter, so speed is essential. US troops spawning belowdecks in the carrier can utilize the slower LAV-25, AMTRAC, and RHIBs to make amphibious landing near the Dry Dock (B). In this match, the carrier is the US team's only source of vehicles. So even after your team has secured control points, don't forget to spawn back at the carrier to occasionally bring the LAV-25 and AMTRAC ashore.

RU BASE

Base Assets		GAZ-3937 Vodnik	T-90A	Z-11W
	NAME	GAZ-3937 Vodnik	T-90A	Z-11W
	QUANTITY	2	1	1
	RESPAWN TIME	15 sec.	30 sec.	90 sec.

The RU team deploys from their base near a warehouse along the northern canal on the south side of the map. Given its distance from the nearest control points, it's nearly impossible to prevent the US team from taking at least one flag, especially if they use their speedy Little Bird helicopters to drop troops from the air. The RU team's Z-11W can attempt similar tactics, but it requires speed. Spawn directly into the Z-11W at the start of the match, then have your squad mates spawn on you as you're flying toward the control points. Drop one squad member at each flag in an attempt to capture all three points before the US team can. Capturing all three flags at the start of the match is a long shot, but it's always worth the effort. Reinforce the captured flags with the T-90A and Vodniks spawned at the RU base. The US team has no tanks in this battle, so the T-90A can be a game changer if deployed wisely and serviced by engineers. Even if the T-90A is destroyed, it respawns relatively fast back at the RU base. So don't forget to retrieve the tank and bring it up to the front lines, where it can make a big difference.

This flag (A) is positioned along a narrow roadway flanked by dozens of shipping containers to the north and elevated train tracks to the south. Both infantry and vehicles can capture this flag. However, infantry have a slight advantage here since they can convert and contest the flag by hiding in the nearby shipping containers. The elevated railway tracks provide an excellent overwatch position, allowing well-concealed defenders to pick off enemies approaching or gathering near the flag. Mines and C4 are the best defense against vehicle attacks. Scatter mines along the road to the east and west of the flag to prevent captures by enemy vehicles. Although this control point spawns no vehicles, it serves as a central spawn point that is ideal for staging attacks on the nearby Dry Dock (B) and Train Yard (C). So race to capture this one early and don't forget to leave a few defenders behind to secure it.

B DRY DOCK

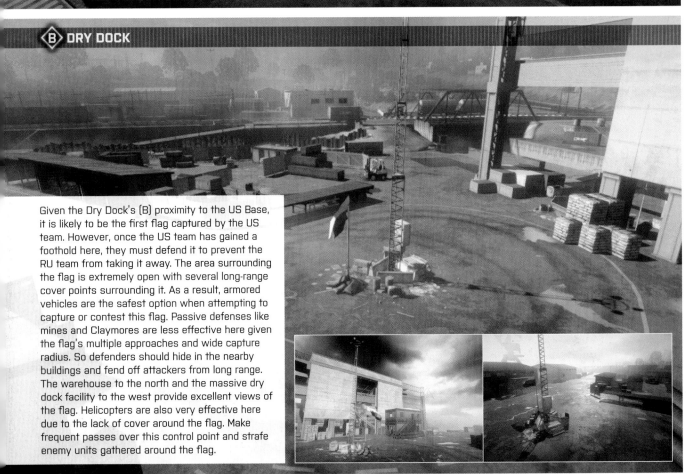

Given the Dry Dock's (B) proximity to the US Base, it is likely to be the first flag captured by the US team. However, once the US team has gained a foothold here, they must defend it to prevent the RU team from taking it away. The area surrounding the flag is extremely open with several long-range cover points surrounding it. As a result, armored vehicles are the safest option when attempting to capture or contest this flag. Passive defenses like mines and Claymores are less effective here given the flag's multiple approaches and wide capture radius. So defenders should hide in the nearby buildings and fend off attackers from long range. The warehouse to the north and the massive dry dock facility to the west provide excellent views of the flag. Helicopters are also very effective here due to the lack of cover around the flag. Make frequent passes over this control point and strafe enemy units gathered around the flag.

Control Point Assets

US CONTROL	RU CONTROL	RESPAWN TIME
—	GAZ-3937 Vodnik (1)	15 sec.

Located a short distance from the RU Base, the RU team has the best chance of capturing this Train Yard (C) flag early during a match. When playing as the RU team, rush this locations with a Vodnik or the Z-11W to take control of it before the US team can. The Train Yard is unique because it's the only control point that produces a vehicle, awarding the RU team with an extra Vodnik—the US team gets nothing. But instead of driving the Vodnik to another location, the RU team may want to keep it around for defense, using its powerful machine gun turret (with zoom functionality) to pepper attackers approaching from the control points to the north. Infantry attacks originating from the Container Area (A) are very common, and so the Vodnik is a valuable defensive asset. But even without vehicle support, defenders have plenty of hiding spots from which to contest flag captures. So attackers should carefully sweep the nearby sheds and shipping containers before approaching the flag. Close-quarters encounters are likely, so begin any assault by tossing grenades into potential hiding spots.

CONQUEST 64

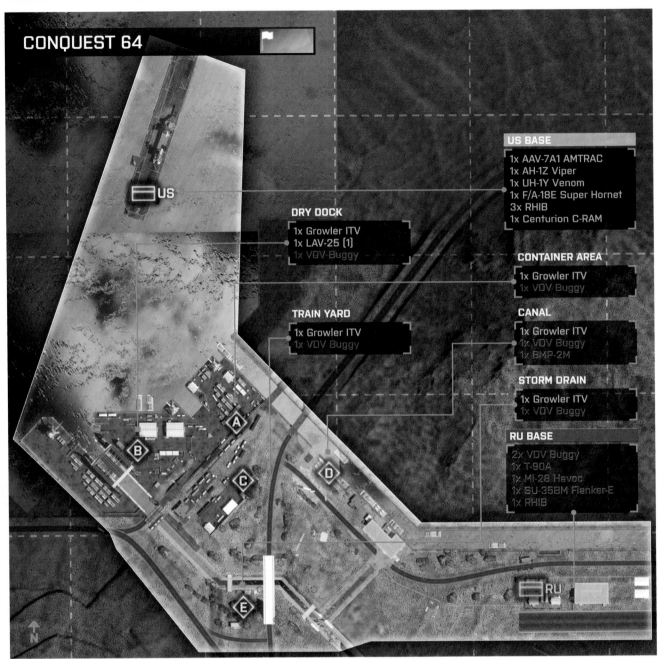

US BASE
- 1x AAV-7A1 AMTRAC
- 1x AH-1Z Viper
- 1x UH-1Y Venom
- 1x F/A-18E Super Hornet
- 3x RHIB
- 1x Centurion C-RAM

DRY DOCK
- 1x Growler ITV
- 1x LAV-25 (1)
- 1x VDV Buggy

CONTAINER AREA
- 1x Growler ITV
- 1x VDV Buggy

TRAIN YARD
- 1x Growler ITV
- 1x VDV Buggy

CANAL
- 1x Growler ITV
- 1x VDV Buggy
- 1x BMP-2M

STORM DRAIN
- 1x Growler ITV
- 1x VDV Buggy

RU BASE
- 2x VDV Buggy
- 1x T-90A
- 1x Mi-28 Havoc
- 1x SU-35BM Flanker-E
- 1x RHIB

At the start of the match, the US team is isolated on their aircraft carrier to the north. With only one transport helicopter, the rest of the team must rely on amphibious vehicles to reach the shore. Given the shortage of vehicles on the carrier, some teammates may wish to hold in the spawn screen until a control point has been captured—it beats twiddling your thumbs on the carrier waiting for a vehicle to spawn. Meanwhile, the RU team starts out at an airbase to the south, relying primarily on ground vehicles to reach the control points. With five control points up for grabs, each team must hold at least three flags to bleed the opposing team's ticket count. The US team should focus their efforts around the Container Area (A), Dry Dock (B), and Canal (D). The RU team is best served by capturing and defending the Train Yard (C), Canal (D), and Storm Drain (E). However, if the RU team can capture all the control points, they can deny the US team a spawn point on the land, forcing them to spawn on their aircraft carrier. In a full 64-player match, it's possible for either team to capture and defend all five flags. So look for opportunities to contain the opposing team within their base, then lay siege for the rest of the match as the enemy ticket count dwindles away.

US BASE

Base Assets	NAME	AAV-7A1 AMTRAC	AH-1Z Viper	UH-1Y Venom	F/A-18E Super Hornet	RHIB	Centurion C-RAM
	QUANTITY	1	1	1	1	3	1
	RESPAWN TIME	30 sec.	90 sec.	90 sec.	40 sec.	5 sec.	—

Once again, the aircraft carrier off the coast serves as the base for the US team, requiring them to launch a successful amphibious assault on the dock facility to the south. With no presence on shore, the early moments of the match are critical as US troops attempt to secure a foothold on land. The UH-1Y offers the quickest way to get troops to the control points. So if you're piloting this helicopter, don't take off until it's fully loaded—your passengers can jump out of the chopper and secure control points by parachuting down to the ground. US troops spawning belowdecks in the carrier can utilize the slower AMTRAC and RHIBs to make amphibious landing near the Dry Dock (B). The F/A-18E should be deployed primarily as a fighter, so arm it with heat-seeking missiles and use it to counter the RU team's SU-35BM and Havoc attack chopper. Maintaining air superiority over the carrier is critical during the opening moments of the match as your teammates struggle to push ashore. So when piloting this jet, constantly patrol the area between the carrier and Dry Dock (B) until teammates have secured a flag.

RU BASE

Base Assets	NAME	VDV Buggy	T-90A	Mi-28 Havoc	SU-35BM Flanker-E	RHIB
	QUANTITY	2	1	1	1	1
	RESPAWN TIME	R15 sec.	30 sec.	90 sec.	40 sec.	5 sec.

The RU team deploys from the airfield in the southeast corner of the map. The VDV Buggies that spawn here provide the best way for the RU team to capture the nearby flags at the Train Yard (C) and Storm Drain (E). The RHIB, spawned in the canal to the north is well positioned to raid the Canal (C) control point to the west. However, don't take off until you have some passengers in your vehicle. This is a very large map and the RU team has few vehicles. So it's important to transport as many troops to the center of the map as quickly as possible. Bailing out of a Mi-28 or SU-35BM to capture more distant control points isn't a bad idea either. When playing with a full complement of 64 players, some teammates may wish to avoid spawning into the game until a control point has been captured. At that point they can spawn and enter the game closer to the action. Otherwise spawning at the RU Base after all the vehicles have left could lead to a very long hike. The RU Base supplies the only tank on the map in the form of the T-90A. So even once the action has shifted to the middle of the map, don't forget to bring this tank up to the front lines so it can lay waste to the lighter US vehicles.

Control Point Assets

US CONTROL	RU CONTROL	RESPAWN TIME
Growler ITV (1)	VDV Buggy (1)	15 sec.

This flag (A) is positioned along a narrow roadway flanked by dozens of shipping containers to the north and elevated train tracks to the south. Both infantry and vehicles can capture this flag. However, infantry have a slight advantage here since they can convert and contest the flag by hiding in the nearby shipping containers. The elevated railway tracks provide an excellent overwatch position, allowing well-concealed defenders to pick off enemies approaching or gathering near the flag. Mines and C4 are the best defense against vehicle attacks. Scatter mines along the road to the east and west of the flag to prevent captures by enemy vehicles. The Container Area spawns vehicles for both teams: a Growler ITV for the US team and a VDV Buggy for the RU team. Use these fast-moving vehicles to launch high-speed raids on the nearby control points like the Dry Dock (B) and the Train Yard (C). But in your haste to move on, don't forget to leave some teammates behind to secure this flag.

Control Point Assets

US CONTROL	RU CONTROL	RESPAWN TIME
Growler ITV (1)	VDV Buggy (1)	15 sec.
LAV-25 (1)	—	30 sec.

Given the Dry Dock's (B) proximity to the US Base, it is likely to be the first flag captured by the US team. However, once the US team has gained a foothold here, they must defend it to prevent the RU team from taking it away. And this is a flag well worth defending because it supplies the US team with their only LAV-25 as well as a Growler ITV. (The RU team gains a VDV Buggy when they hold this flag.) The area surrounding the flag is extremely open with several long-range cover points surrounding it. As a result, armored vehicles are the safest option when attempting to capture or contest this flag. Passive defenses like mines and Claymores are less effective here given the flag's multiple approaches and wide capture radius. So defenders should hide in the nearby buildings and fend off attackers from long range. The warehouse to the north and the massive Dry Dock facility to the west provide excellent views of the flag. Jets and helicopters are also very effective here due to the lack of cover around the flag. Make frequent passes over this control point and strafe enemy units gathered around the flag.

Control Point Assets

US CONTROL	RU CONTROL	RESPAWN TIME
Growler ITV (1)	VDV Buggy (1)	15 sec.

Because it is located near the center of the map, both teams have a good chance of capturing this Train Yard (C) flag at the start of the match, with a slight edge given to the RU team. When playing as the RU team, rush this location with a VDV Buggy or the Havoc to take control of it before the US team can. The Train Yard provides an extra vehicle to each team: a Growler ITV to the US team and a VDV Buggy to the RU team. Although they lack armor and firepower, these fast-moving vehicles are great for getting around the map quickly and for staging raids on the surrounding control points. Defenders have plenty of hiding spots from which to contest flag captures at the Train Yard. So attackers should carefully sweep the nearby sheds and shipping containers before approaching the flag. Close-quarters encounters are likely so begin any assault by tossing grenades into potential hiding spots. Given the numerous hiding spots near the flag, avoid attacking this location in vehicles. You're better off moving in on foot where you have the opportunity to maneuver and counter potential ambushes.

◇ CANAL

Control Point Assets

US CONTROL	RU CONTROL	RESPAWN TIME
Growler ITV (1)	VDV Buggy (1)	15 sec.
—	BMP-2M (1)	30 sec.

This Canal (D) flag is located on the western bank of the northern canal, not far from the RU Base. As a result, the RU team has the best chance of capturing this control point early on. But that doesn't mean they'll be able to hold onto it. The canal itself makes this control point vulnerable to US amphibious attacks by RHIBs, the LAV-25, or AMTRAC. While the road to the west is the most common avenue of attack, defenders should be prepared for assaults from the canal. The flag is located near a small concrete building. This structure is a great place to hide while capturing or contesting the flag. Vehicle access is rather cramped here, making it tough to maneuver. So use vehicles to provide fire support from a distance while infantry move in to capture. The RU team should make an effort to hold on to this control point because it spawns the only BMP-2M as well as an extra VDV Buggy—the US team only gets a Growler ITV. Use the BMP-2M and T-90A (spawned at the RU Base) to gang up on US vehicles. Both vehicles function best around the Dry Dock (B), where there's plenty of room to maneuver.

Control Point Assets

US CONTROL	RU CONTROL	RESPAWN TIME
Growler ITV (1)	VDV Buggy (1)	15 sec.

The Storm Drain control point (E) is located on the southern edge of the map, flanked by a rocky cliff to the south and a narrow drainage canal to the north. Unlike the northern Canal, this nearby canal is narrow, best suited for RHIBs. US troops spawning back at their carrier can stage amphibious assaults on this flag by entering the canal south of the Dry Dock (B) and following it all the way to this control point. However, the dirt road is the most common avenue of attack. When defending here, place mines on the road to prevent vehicle attacks and take up overwatch positions on the tall bridge to the east. The small buildings and sheds surrounding the flagpole also provide good hiding spots for anyone capturing or contesting this control point. The Storm Drain's remote location makes it one of the least contested control points on the map. However, don't leave this flag undefended, particularly during tight matches. Just one squad of dedicated defenders should have no problem locking down this location.

RUSH

US DEPLOYMENT
RU DEPLOYMENT

ZONE 1

ZONE 2

ZONE 3

ZONE 4

ZONE 5

N

In this epic Rush match, the US team begins on an aircraft carrier to the north. It's up to the RU team to stop the US amphibious assault, preventing them from gaining a foothold and pushing their way inland. But the US have a serious advantage when it comes to vehicles. So the RU team must improvise and make the most of the vehicles they have, especially when it comes to countering the US helicopters. All together, the US must conquer five separate zones, beginning with the Dry Dock. From there the advance stretches from the Train Yard all the way to the airfield on the east side of the map. Along the way, the US attackers must destroy ten M-COM stations. If each zone is well defended, the RU team has a good chance of halting the US advance. However, the fight for the first zone is critical. If the RU team can deny the US access to the Dry Dock objective, they force the US to spawn on their carrier. As a result, locking down the first zone is the RU team's best chance of securing a victory.

ZONE 1: DRY DOCK

US DEPLOYMENT
1x AAV-7A1 AMTRAC
1x AH-6J Little Bird
1x UH-1Y Venom
3x RHIB

RU DEPLOYMENT
1x GAZ-3937 Vodnik
1x 9K22 Tunguska-M

A M-COM STATION A

This M-COM Station A is tucked away in the southwest corner of a dark warehouse near the coast. The large warehouse has multiple entry points, but more can be made by blowing holes in the exterior walls. But no matter how much damage is dealt to this structure, it won't collapse. Since there's no way to predict which direction the attackers will enter from, it's best to defend the objective from within the warehouse. There are plenty of hiding spots inside, so try to find a location that conceals you and offers a view of the M-COM station. Regardless of whether you're attacking or defending, using Tactical Lights and Laser Sights can be effective for blinding opponents in this dark setting. But they can also give away your position, so be sure you're the one who pulls the trigger first.

B M-COM STATION B

This objective, M-COM Station B, is housed within a steel shelter, just south of the warehouse where M-COM station A is located. The shelter does little more than protect the objective from rain, with a wide opening to the north and a narrow doorway to the south. This can be a tricky spot for defenders to watch as the only decent cover point is located to the north—the same direction from which the attackers are advancing. So if you hide in one of the warehouses to the north while watching M-COM Station B, you're likely to get a knife in the back. Instead, try to watch the steel shelter from the east or west and engage the cross traffic as attackers dart out of the warehouse and make a move for the objective. Parking the Vodnik to the east or west works well; you can gun down attackers with the machine gun turret. To prevent such ambushes, attackers should always deploy smoke when advancing toward the objective and setting the charge. The AMTRAC can also serves as a mobile shield by protecting infantry as they advance on the objective.

Base Assets		AAV-7A1 AMTRAC	AH-6J Little Bird	UH-1Y Venom	RHIB
	NAME	AAV-7A1 AMTRAC	AH-6J Little Bird	UH-1Y Venom	RHIB
	QUANTITY	1	1	1	3
	RESPAWN TIME	60 sec.	90 sec.	90 sec.	15 sec.

As in the Conquest game modes, the US team begins this Rush match on the aircraft carrier to the north. Utilizing a couple of helicopters, an AMTRAC, and a few RHIBs, the US must race toward the shore and establish a foothold near the objectives. The Little Bird and Venom offer the quickest way to get troops on the ground, so take off with a full load and have your passengers parachute down to the Dry Dock area. Once on the ground, recon troops should deploy Radio Beacons so their squad doesn't have to spawn on the carrier. Remember, the AMTRAC is also a spawn point and should be deployed near the Dry Dock, preferably out of view from the RU defenders. With spawn points at or near the Dry Dock, the US team will have a much easier time applying consistent pressure against each objective.

Base Assets		GAZ-3937 Vodnik	9K22 Tunguska-M
	NAME	GAZ-3937 Vodnik	9K22 Tunguska-M
	QUANTITY	1	1
	RESPAWN TIME	15 sec.	30 sec.

The RU team deploys near the Train Yard, just south of the objectives. Given the US air assets spawned at the carrier, the RU troops need to move out fast if they hope to secure the M-COM stations before the attackers arrive. The Vodnik is the quickest way to move troops to the Dry Dock area. Consider holding off on spawning into the game until one of your squad members has reached the objectives. This frees up seats in the Vodnik for other teammates. Initially, the US helicopters pose the biggest threat. So move the Tunguska-M forward to deal with these choppers. Engineers armed with SA-18 IGLA surface-to-air missiles can also put a damper on the US team's air assault. Since the deployment area is so far from the objectives, have recon troops deploy Radio Beacons around the Dry Dock area to secure spawn points near the M-COM stations.

ZONE 2: TRAIN YARD

US DEPLOYMENT
1x M1114 HMMWV
1x AAV-7A1 AMTRAC
1x AH-6J Little Bird
1x UH-1Y Venom

RU DEPLOYMENT
1x GAZ-3937 Vodnik
1x 9K22 Tunguska-M

N

A · M-COM STATION A

B · M-COM STATION B

As the northernmost objective, M-COM Station A is likely to be the first to come under attack by the US team. The objective is flanked by a concrete building to the west and a green shipping container to the east. It's important for both teams to secure the nearby building, as it serves as the best position from which to defend or attack the M-COM station. Once inside, deploy a Radio Beacon so your squad has a spawn point near the objective. The rooftop of the building is accessible and offers a sweeping view of the Dry Dock and Train Yard. But avoid standing on the rooftop, as it makes you an easy target for snipers and strafing helicopters. If you must get on the roof, remain prone to avoid silhouetting yourself. For the US team, even after destroying M-COM Station A, this building serves as a good forward base for launching attacks on M-COM Station B to the south.

This objective, M-COM Station B, is located inside a light blue shipping container on the Train Yard's loading platform to the south. Both ends of the container are open, allowing entry from the east or west. This can be a tricky objective to attack and defend, given the container's cramped space. Instead of hiding inside the shipping container, the RU defenders should focus on covering the two entry points from long range. There are plenty of hiding spots in the Train Yard to the east and west where you can watch this container—just make sure nobody can sneak up behind you and steal your dog tags. Parking the Tunguska-M nearby can also be an effective deterrent. The US team really needs the support of their vehicles and the concealment of smoke to safely reach this M-COM station and plant the charge. Also, toss a grenade in the shipping container before entering to detonate any booby traps such as C4 or Claymores.

US DEPLOYMENT

Base Assets	M1114 HMMWV	AAV-7A1 AMTRAC	AH-6J Little Bird	UH-1Y Venom
NAME				
QUANTITY	1	1	1	1
RESPAWN TIME	15 sec.	60 sec.	90 sec.	90 sec.

With the first set of M-COM stations destroyed, the US team's deployment area moves up to the Dry Dock. This is where the US team's new ground vehicles spawn, including an HMMWV as well as an AMTRAC. The US team also retains the same air assets from the previous stage that are still spawned at the aircraft carrier. So if you want to fly, spawn directly into the Little Bird or Venom on the carrier's flight deck. Use the helicopters to harass and distract the RU team while your ground units move in to assault the objectives. The AMTRAC is very effective here as a mobile spawn point that allows you to deploy freshly spawned players close to the action. However, keep it out of view of defending engineers as well as the RU team's Tunguska-M. Likewise, avoid driving the HMMWV directly into the heated action—it won't last long. Instead, position it to the east or west side of the Train Yard and use its machine gun turret to provide fire support.

RU DEPLOYMENT

Base Assets	GAZ-3937 Vodnik	9K22 Tunguska-M
NAME		
QUANTITY	1	1
RESPAWN TIME	15 sec.	30 sec.

The RU team deploys along a dirt road south of the Train Yard. Following the destruction of the M-COM stations at the Dry Dock, the RU team has a few precious seconds to get into position around the new objectives before the US team can attack. Use this time wisely to establish a perimeter around the Train Yard. Move the newly spawned Vodnik and Tunguska-M forward to defend the new objectives. Both vehicles have enough firepower to counter attacks by the US helicopters and ground vehicles. But engineers are necessary to keep both vehicles healthy. And if the vehicles are destroyed, don't forget to retrieve new ones from their spawn points to the south. In addition to repairing the vehicles, engineers can also assist them by shooting down the US helicopters with SA-18 IGLA missiles. But don't let the helicopters distract you too much. Deploy infantry (and Radio Beacons) near each objective to defend them from US troops infiltrating the Train Yard from the north.

ZONE 3: RUNWAY APPROACH

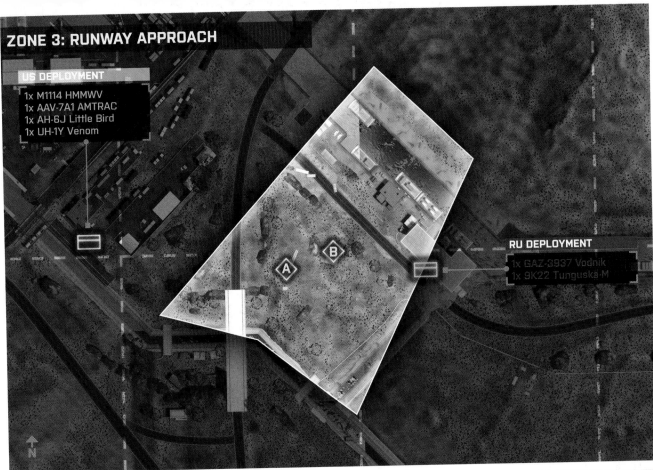

US DEPLOYMENT

1x M1114 HMMWV
1x AAV-7A1 AMTRAC
1x AH-6J Little Bird
1x UH-1Y Venom

RU DEPLOYMENT

1x GAZ-3937 Vodnik
1x 9K22 Tunguska-M

N

A M-COM STATION A

B M-COM STATION B

M-COM Station A sits at the crest of the hill, just beneath an array of runway approach lights. With the exception of the small trailer and light towers, there's very little cover here. This means it is a particularly challenging objective to approach when the hilltop is well defended. The slopes of the hill are covered in trees and shrubs that provide plenty of concealment for defenders camped around the objective. Attackers or defenders posted on the large bridge to the southwest have a relatively clear view of the hilltop, making it an ideal cover point for snipers. Defenders should primarily cover the western slope to engage infantry approaching from the Train Yard. But it's also important to defend against potential flanking attacks, including US infantry dropping onto the hilltop via parachute.

This objective is located in a dark, bunkerlike building on the eastern slope of the hill. Initially the south-facing doorway is the only entrance into this concrete building. However, each wall of the building can be completely destroyed, allowing attackers to approach the M-COM station from any direction. So instead of covering the doorway or interior, defenders are better off surrounding the building and locking down the nearby hilltop. Attackers should come armed with rocket launchers, grenade launchers, or C4 so they can breach the walls of the structure and create doorways of their own. However, if all the walls are destroyed, the M-COM station will not be crushed by falling debris. Instead, the objective remains standing, exposed in all directions. So don't blow too many holes in the structure or else you'll have a difficult time approaching the M-COM station—those walls provide excellent cover when setting or disarming a charge.

Base Assets				
	M1114 HMMWV	AAV-7A1 AMTRAC	AH-6J Little Bird	UH-1Y Venom
NAME	M1114 HMMWV	AAV-7A1 AMTRAC	AH-6J Little Bird	UH-1Y Venom
QUANTITY	1	1	1	1
RESPAWN TIME	15 sec.	60 sec.	90 sec.	90 sec.

As the battle continues, the US team moves up to the Train Yard in preparation for their assault on the hill to the southeast. The Train Yard deployment area spawns a HMMWV and an AMTRAC while the aircraft carrier continues to produce the same Little Bird and Venom helicopters. In this stage, the RU defenders hold the high ground, so look for opportunities to stage flanking attacks instead of charging straight up the hill. The paved road to the north of the objectives is a good route for the HMMWV and AMTRAC to take; they can hook around the hill and flank the defenders. Parking the AMTRAC somewhere near the canal is also a good way to provide the team with a forward spawn point. As vehicles and infantry advance, air support is essential. Even if they don't inflict much damage, the helicopters provide a useful distraction.

Base Assets		
	GAZ-3937 Vodnik	9K22 Tunguska-M
NAME	GAZ-3937 Vodnik	9K22 Tunguska-M
QUANTITY	1	1
RESPAWN TIME	15 sec.	30 sec.

The RU team deploys along the paved road on the north side of the hill, next to the large warehouse. Following the loss of the objectives at the Train Yard, immediately rush toward the new objectives and establish a perimeter. Rush attacks by the US helicopters are likely, so be prepared to shoot them down. Engineers armed with SA-18 IGLA missile launchers are very effective, as is the Tunguska-M, which is spawned within the warehouse. If troops bail out of the choppers, immediately spot them and gun them down before they can parachute to the ground. While engineers and the Tunguska-M focus on the helicopters, the rest of the team should prepare for infantry assaults originating from the Train Yard. The hill gives the defenders a decent height advantage, so it's easy for recon troops to snipe approaching infantry.

ZONE 4: AIRFIELD OUTSKIRTS

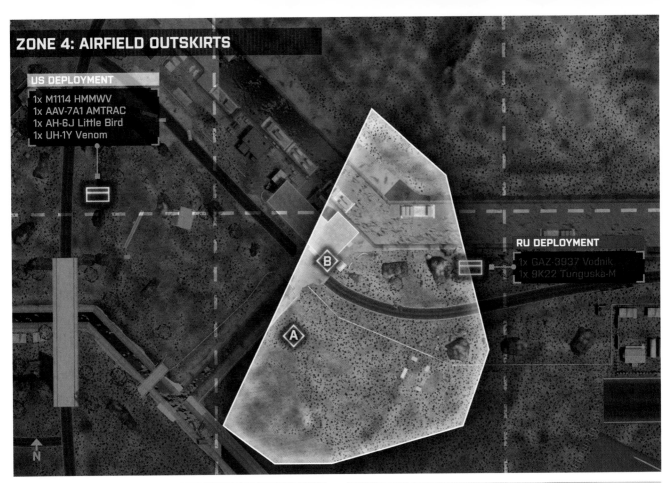

US DEPLOYMENT

- 1x M1114 HMMWV
- 1x AAV-7A1 AMTRAC
- 1x AH-6J Little Bird
- 1x UH-1Y Venom

RU DEPLOYMENT

- 1x GAZ-3937 Vodnik
- 1x 9K22 Tunguska-M

A M-COM STATION A

B M-COM STATION B

Located in a small red-and-white trailer south of the large warehouse, M-COM station A is relatively vulnerable to attack, despite the fences surrounding it. Attackers can easily slice through the chain-link fences with their knives or simply knock them over with vehicles like the HMMWV or AMTRAC. However, entering the trailer itself can be dangerous, especially if the interior is booby-trapped with C4 or Claymores. So always toss a grenade through the doorway before entering to trigger any explosives or kill any defenders hiding inside. While the walls of the trailer can be destroyed, it's best to keep them in place to offer cover while planting or disarming the charge. The canal to the northwest serves as a natural barrier. Therefore most US attackers approach from the road by the warehouse. Parking the Vodnik or Tunguska-M on the road can serve as a deterrent, prompting attackers to swim across the canal. Defenders should prepare for attacks from either direction as well as watch for enemy troops dropped from helicopters.

M-COM Station B is located on the ground floor of the large warehouse, situated in an office on the southern corner by the road. By blasting holes in the warehouses exterior walls, US attackers can easily access the M-COM station without worrying about infiltrating the warehouse. However, defenders posted inside the warehouse can still cover the objective regardless of which direction the attackers approach from. If the US team wants a little extra firepower inside the warehouse, they can drive the AMTRAC directly inside via the ramp on the north side adjacent to the canal. Of course, driving an armored vehicle into a building is never safe, but it may provide enough of a distraction to allow friendly troops enough time to plant the charge. If the AMTRAC survives, its machine gun turret is awesome for targeting defenders attempting to disarm the charge on the objective.

US DEPLOYMENT

Base Assets	NAME	M1114 HMMWV	AAV-7A1 AMTRAC	AH-6J Little Bird	UH-1Y Venom
	QUANTITY	1	1	1	1
	RESPAWN TIME	15 sec.	60 sec.	90 sec.	90 sec.

In this stage of the battle, the US team deploys on the hilltop, beneath the runway approach lights. While this location is where the HMMWV and AMTRAC appear, the helicopters are still available back at the aircraft carrier. So don't forget to spawn directly into the helicopters to provide air support for the next attack. The hilltop provides a great view of the next objective area to the east. Recon troops posted on the hill can score some long range kills here. Just make sure the entire team doesn't hold back and admire the view. While sniper support is welcome, the bulk of the team should make an aggressive push for the objectives.

RU DEPLOYMENT

Base Assets	NAME	GAZ-3937 Vodnik	9K22 Tunguska-M
	QUANTITY	1	1
	RESPAWN TIME	15 sec.	30 sec.

The RU team deploys along the paved road, east of the objectives. Infantry and vehicles spawning here are vulnerable to strafing runs by the US helicopters, so don't loiter here long. Spread out among the objectives and consider placing Radio Beacons in the warehouse where M-COM Station B is located. Move the Vodnik to a position along the road between both objectives. From this vantage point the Vodnik's machine gun turret can engage infantry and vehicles approaching from the US deployment area to the northwest. The US helicopters remain a nuisance in this fight, so be prepared to shoot them down with the Tunguska-M as well as IGLA missiles fired by defending engineers.

ZONE 5: AIRFIELD

US DEPLOYMENT
- 1x M1114 HMMWV
- 1x AAV-7A1 AMTRAC
- 1x AH-6J Little Bird
- 1x UH-1Y Venom
- 1x RHIB

RU DEPLOYMENT
- 1x GAZ-3937 Vodnik
- 1x 9K22 Tunguska-M

A M-COM STATION A

This objective is located in a small concrete structure within the airfield's perimeter wall. Of the two objectives at the airfield, M-COM Station A is the easiest for the RU team to defend. Located only a few meters from their deployment area, the RU team has no problem reaching this location throughout this phase of the battle. Due to the barricades surrounding the structure, the US team can only access this objective by ground from the north or east. Of course, there's always the possibility of parachuting down from a helicopter. But such attempts are dangerous given the objective's close proximity to the RU deployment area. When US troops do manage to get into the airfield, they should blow a hole in the structure's southern wall to enter. The north-facing entrance is most likely being watched by defenders, so sneaking in from the back is advised. Since gaining access is so difficult, the US may want to attack this objective first while the defenders are still spread out, covering both M-COM stations. It's much tougher to plant a charge here when the entire RU team is defending this location.

B M-COM STATION B

Flanked by a the road to the south and the canal to the north, the location of this M-COM station favors the US attackers. The objective is located in a gray trailer outside the airfield's perimeter wall. The concrete slabs on the west and south sides of the trailer partially protect the trailer from heavy attack. However, the north side of the trailer is completely open, giving attackers advancing from the canal easy access. As a result, the RU defenders must completely envelop this trailer while watching for attacks approaching from the road and canal. By knocking out the trailer's east-facing walls, defenders can gain a long sight line into the trailer; Therefore, they can engage anyone who enters and tampers with the M-COM station. However, there's very little cover or concealment to the east, so remain prone to avoid giving away your position.

US DEPLOYMENT

Base Assets	NAME	M1114 HMMWV	AAV-7A1 AMTRAC	AH-6J Little Bird	UH-1Y Venom	RHIB
	QUANTITY	1	1	1	1	1
	RESPAWN TIME	15 sec.	60 sec.	90 sec.	90 sec.	15 sec.

For the final phase of this battle, the US team deploys near the warehouse with nearly the same vehicle assets they've had since securing the Dry Dock. In addition to the HMMWV, AMTRAC, and helicopters, the US team also has access to an RHIB. Use this boat or the AMTRAC to sneak up on M-COM Station B by racing along the canal to the east. However, the helicopters (spawned back at the aircraft carrier) remain the most valuable assets for the US team. Use them to strafe and harass the defenders while dropping troops behind enemy lines. This is the quickest way to gain access to the airfield. The road leading into the airfield is most likely defended with mines, so look for other ways in when driving one of the ground vehicles. Consider crashing through the fence by the runway and attacking M-COM Station A from the south. Radio Beacons placed in and around the airfield are also a great way to apply pressure on the objectives by spawning teammates close to the action.

RU DEPLOYMENT

Base Assets	NAME	GAZ-3937 Vodnik	9K22 Tunguska-M
	QUANTITY	1	1
	RESPAWN TIME	15 sec.	30 sec.

Despite deploying from an airfield, the RU team still has no helicopters or jets to help fend off the US attack. While the Vodnik and Tunguska-M are decent for dealing damage to the US helicopters, it's largely up to the RU engineers to lock down the objectives. Engineers deploying here should carry a mix of mines, anti-tank rockets, and surface-to-air missiles in an effort to immobilize and destroy the incoming US vehicles. While the road is the airfield's most popular access point, prepare for flanking attacks to originate from the canal to the north and runway to the south. Also, make periodic sweeps around the airfield's perimeter to search for US Radio Beacons. Denying the US team spawn points near the objectives is critical if the RU team hopes to hold out here for a victory.

SQUAD RUSH

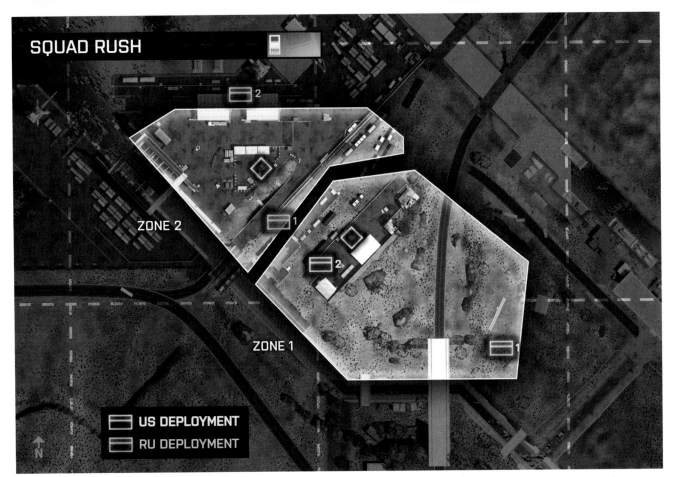

ZONE 2

ZONE 1

US DEPLOYMENT
RU DEPLOYMENT

N

In this Squad Rush variant, the direction of attack is reversed as the US team approaches from the east, hitting the Train Yard before moving onto the Dry Dock. In this small-scale battle, prepare for a mix of intermediate- and close-range combat. Assault troops are very effective here, thanks to their ability to revive squad mates as well as deploy smoke. Each squad should consider bringing along a recon soldier to deploy a Radio Beacon near each objective to guarantee a nearby spawn point. Attacking recon troops can also benefit from a MAV to spot the locations of defenders hiding around each objective.

ZONE 1: TRAIN YARD

The first objective is located beneath this steel equipment shelter on the Train Yard loading platform. Barricades restrict access to this shed only allowing for access from the east and west. When defending this location as the RU team, it's a good idea to split up and have a couple of squad mates defend the shelter from the exterior with sniper or assault riles, while the rest of the squad camps the objective with shotguns and submachine guns. When playing as the attackers, assume the objective is well covered by the defenders. Instead of rushing the M-COM station, carefully sweep the Train Yard, picking off as many defenders as possible. After killing two or three opponents in quick succession, make an aggressive push for the M-COM station, plant the charge, and then go on defense until the objective is destroyed.

This final objective is crammed between several crates in a storage area of the Dry Dock. The configuration of the crates allows access only from the southwest. While the crates provide some excellent cover for anyone arming or disarming a charge on the M-COM station, it leaves their back completely exposed. So before even approaching the objective, scour the area to the southwest for well-hidden defenders. Consider circling around the entire storage area to hunt for defenders hiding along the perimeter. Even then, deploying smoke on the objective is strongly advised, whether you're attempting to arm or disarm a charge on the M-COM station.

SQUAD DEATHMATCH

Squad Deathmatch on this map encompasses the Dry Dock, Container Area, and Train Yard. While on foot, avoid the Dry Dock as there's minimal cover and the tall buildings are popular perches for snipers. The Container Area and the Train Yard offer more protection, and fewer long sight lines means fewer deaths by snipers. The Train Yard sits on higher ground, too, which is ideal for firing down on enemies racing around the area to the north. The IFV spawn points are all located around the Dry Dock and Container Area. But if you manage to snag one of these vehicles, keep it near the Dry Dock area, where there's plenty of room to maneuver and spot enemy infantry. If necessary, you can drive into one of the warehouses to conduct repairs, away from the chaotic action outside. Once fully repaired, get the IFV back into the fight to give your squad a lead in total kills.

TEAM DEATHMATCH

In Team Deathmatch, the action is centered around the Container Area, making for a frantic fight among the maze of shipping containers. Before spawning into this match, carefully consider where you want to go on the map. This will help determine what class and weapons are best to use. If you prefer close-quarters combat, choose a shotgun or submachine gun and head for the containers in the center of the map. This is a good spot to ambush opponents at point-blank range. Recon soldiers equipped with sniper rifles are best deployed on the southeast side of the map to use the elevated terrain of the Train Yard to pick off enemies on the east and west flanks of the Container Area. While the high ground offers a great view, there's very little cover, so stay on your belly to avoid silhouetting yourself. If your prefer to stay on the move, equip an assault rifle or carbine and work your way around the perimeter of the map, hunting for prey.

OPERATION FIRESTORM

The oil fields outside of Tehran are poised to be the scene of what some experts are calling the biggest engagement of the war. Both the American and Russian armies are trying to exert control over Iran's biggest source of oil in the Northern provinces. Securing the outskirts of this area will offer full control of the sector and its key facilities. However, crossing the open ground and main road may prove more difficult than expected, as Russian troops will undoubtedly attempt to hold the refinery as the first line of defence against any large-scale assault.

CONQUEST

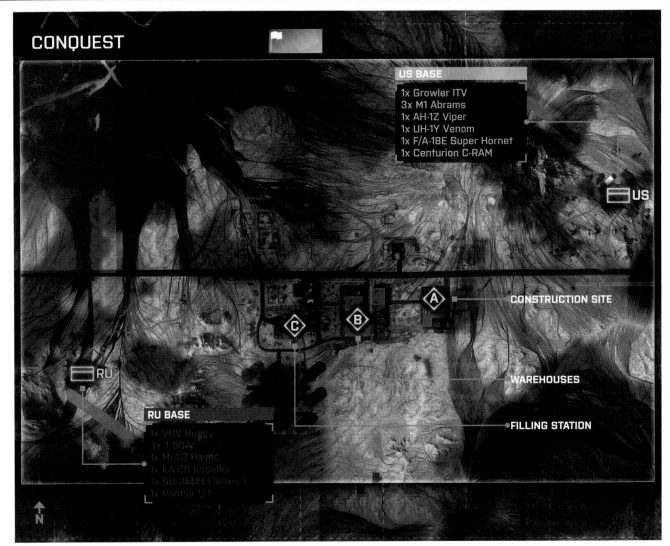

US BASE
1x Growler ITV
3x M1 Abrams
1x AH-1Z Viper
1x UH-1Y Venom
1x F/A-18E Super Hornet
1x Centurion C-RAM

US

A — CONSTRUCTION SITE

B

C

WAREHOUSES

RU

RU BASE
1x VDV Buggy
3x T-90A
1x Mi-28 Havoc
1x KA-60 Kasatka
1x SU-35BM Flanker-E
1x Pantsir S1

FILLING STATION

N

This is a very linear, head-on Conquest map with all three control points situated along the central highway slicing through the center of the map from east to west. While it's possible to capture and defend all three control points, it's better to consolidate your team's forces around two flags. Therefore, the US team should try to hold the Construction Site (A) and Warehouses (B) while the RU team focuses on the Filling Station (C) and Warehouses (B). Your team must hold a minimum of two control points to initiate the drain on the opposing team's ticket count, so dig in and don't let the enemy wrestle a flag away from you. Tanks are necessary for punching through enemy defenses and capturing flags. But tanks (and all other vehicles) are spawned only at the bases. So it's critical to constantly transport these assets to the center of the map, where they can make a big difference. Even if you draw a line in the sand at Warehouses, flanking attacks are common. The transport helicopters make it possible to drop troops at any point on the map, so make sure every flag your team holds is well defended against both ground and airborne assaults.

US BASE

Base Assets	NAME	Growler ITV	M1 Abrams	AH-1Z Viper	UH-1Y Venom	F/A-18E Super Hornet	Centurion C-RAM
	QUANTITY	1	3	1	1	1	1
	RESPAWN TIME	5 sec.	20 sec.	60 sec.	90 sec.	40 sec.	—

The US team starts this battle at their base on the east side of the map, far from the nearest control point. Fortunately, there are plenty of vehicles available to transport the team to the map's center. So if you're driving or flying, make sure your vehicle is filled to capacity before leaving the base—otherwise it's a long, dusty hike for any teammates left behind. The UH-1Y Venom is the best way to quickly move troops to the control points. Fly it over the Construction Site [A] and Warehouses [B], dropping two troops at each location in an attempt to beat the RU team to these two critical flags. Once captured, reinforce these control points (particularly the Warehouses) with the M1 Abrams tanks. Use the tanks and AH-1Z Viper to counter the RU team's T-90As while the F/A-18E provides air cover, attacking the enemy jet and helicopters with heat-seeking missiles. In this match, no vehicles are spawned by the control points in the center of the map. So as the round commences, don't forget to spawn back at the base to bring tanks and other vehicles to the front lines.

RU BASE

Base Assets	NAME	VDV Buggy	T-90A	Mi-28 Havoc	KA-60 Kasatka	SU-35BM Flanker-E	Pantsir-S1
	QUANTITY	1	3	1	1	1	1
	RESPAWN TIME	5 sec.	20 sec.	60 sec.	90 sec.	40 sec.	—

The RU Base is on the far west side of the map, several hundred meters from the nearest control point. So it's important to make the most out of the vehicles provided to transport the team to the control points. If you find yourself without a vehicle, immediately ask teammates for a ride before they leave the base. The KA-60 Kasatka transport helicopter is the best way to move multiple troops to the map's center. Use this helicopter to drop troops (by parachute) at the Filling Station [C] and Warehouses [B] control points. But a few infantry won't last long against the onslaught of US tanks, so act quickly to reinforce the control points with the T-90A tanks while the Mi-28 Havoc provides close air support. The SU-35BM is best deployed as a fighter, so choose heat-seeking missiles for your loadout when piloting this jet and use them to shoot down the US team's air assets. During the course of the battle, spawn back at the RU base periodically to bring ground vehicles forward to help attack and defend the central control points. The control points provide no vehicles, so the team that masters of the logistics of moving tanks forward has the upper hand in this battle.

Ⓐ CONSTRUCTION SITE

The Construction Site (A) is the easternmost control point, well within easy striking distance of the US Base. As a result, the US team is likely to capture this flag first. But after the early moments of the round, this control point is very much up for grabs. While it's the closest control point to the US Base, it's by no means adjacent. So unless the US team is constantly defending this location and reinforcing it with vehicles, it's relatively easy for the RU team to steal it. The flag is in a parking lot outside an office building. Once captured, the Construction Site is relatively easy to lock down by any squad willing to stay put. Defenders can deter vehicle attacks by placing mines and C4 around the flagpole. The nearby two-story office and partially constructed buildings across the road to the east provide excellent views of the flag and allow defenders to pick off attackers. However, the office building can be destroyed, so you may want to seek better cover if you come under heavy bombardment. Although the Construction Site doesn't produce any vehicles, in a match with only three flags, defending this site is critical for either team.

Ⓑ WAREHOUSES

As the central control point, the Warehouses (B) are the most contentious site on the map. At the start of the round, both teams should attempt to capture this flag early. The transport helicopters spawned at each base are the best way to take control of this site quickly. Load a chopper with troops, then fly low and fast, dropping troops on the rooftop of the large warehouse near the flag. While infantry can capture this flag, it takes tanks and close air support provided by helicopters and jets to defend it. The flagpole is located outside the large warehouse; tanks and other ground vehicles can camp its capture radius. So if you're attacking on foot, always approach from the warehouse interior. It's possible to capture and contest this flag from inside the warehouse. This beats lying prone next to the flagpole. With so many possible approaches, it takes a dedicated squad of defenders to patrol the warehouse and ferret out any opponents attempting to convert the flag from within. A T-UGS motion sensor planted near the flag is a great way to monitor enemy traffic. Infantry are also effective outside; they utilize the surrounding rooftops and catwalks to spot incoming vehicles and troops. Spotting enemies can be a full-time job here, so find a good elevated spot and simply call out the locations of hostile forces to help direct attacks by your team's air units. Or better yet, use a SOFLAM to paint enemy vehicles for guided munitions fired by friendly tanks, helicopters, and jets.

Ⓒ FILLING STATION

This sprawling industrial facility serves as the westernmost control point in this match, closest to the RU Base. While the RU team has the best chance of capturing the Filling Station (C) early, there's no guarantee they'll be able to hold onto it, especially if it's left undefended. The flagpole here is located on an open piece of asphalt surrounded by three explosive tanker trucks. It's a good idea to destroy the tanker trucks upon arrival because you don't want them to explode while you're attempting to capture the flag, especially if you're on foot. With minimal cover nearby, this is a control point best captured and contested by tanks. However, infantry can play a large role in defending this flag. Given the likelihood of heavy vehicle traffic around the flag, mines and C4 are very effective. The surrounding structures and catwalks also offer great elevated vantage points of the flag that are ideal for scoring hits on attacking infantry and vehicles. Regardless of which team you're playing on, make an effort to reinforce this control point with tanks spawned at your team's base.

CONQUEST 64

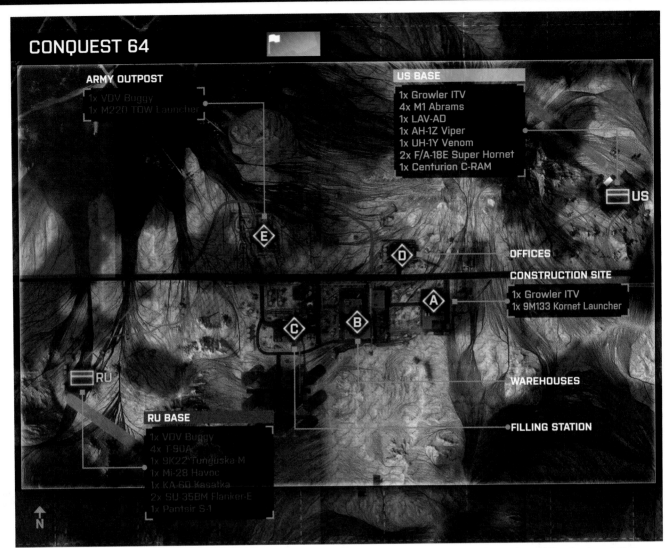

ARMY OUTPOST
1x VDV Buggy
1x M220 TOW Launcher

US BASE
1x Growler ITV
4x M1 Abrams
1x LAV-AD
1x AH-1Z Viper
1x UH-1Y Venom
2x F/A-18E Super Hornet
1x Centurion C-RAM

US

E

D

OFFICES

CONSTRUCTION SITE
1x Growler ITV
1x 9M133 Kornet Launcher

A

C   B

RU

RU BASE
1x VDV Buggy
4x T-90A
1x 9K22 Tunguska-M
1x Mi-28 Havoc
1x KA-60 Kasatka
2x SU-35BM Flanker-E
1x Pantsir S-1

WAREHOUSES

FILLING STATION

N

Prepare for an epic clash of armor on this massive map centered around a sprawling oil refinery complex in the middle of a desert. Both sides maintain four tanks throughout the match that are spawned at the bases. So don't forget to move these tanks to the center of the map to take advantage of their devastating firepower. Air power also plays a large role in this battle, with each team possessing two jets, an attack helicopter, and a transport helicopter. So choose the loadouts of the aircraft carefully and determine whether to fill a ground or air attack role. With all of the tanks rumbling about and jets screaming overhead, it's easy to lose sight of the objective. There are five control points on this map, meaning your team needs to hold at least three to bleed the opposing team's ticket count. The area between the Warehouses (B) and Refilling Station (C) is always a deadly kill zone. So instead of grinding against these two control points, consider working the perimeter of the map by capturing the Construction Site (A), Offices, (D), and Army Outpost (E). Capturing and defending these flags is much easier, and results in fewer casualties, which helps to ensure that your team has the most tickets at the end of the round. But like any 64-player match, the battle is very fluid, so be ready to alter your game plan accordingly. The key is capturing and defending control points the opposing team has inexplicably abandoned.

US BASE

Base Assets	NAME	Growler ITV	M1 Abrams	LAV-AD	AH-1Z Viper	UH-1Y Venom	F/A-18E Super Hornet	Centurion C-RAM
	QUANTITY	1	4	1	1	1	2	1
	RESPAWN TIME	5 sec.	20 sec.	20 sec.	60 sec.	90 sec.	40 sec.	—

The US team starts this battle at their base on the east side of the map, far from the nearest control point. Fortunately, there are plenty of vehicles available to transport the team to the map's center. So if you're driving or flying, make sure your vehicle is filled to capacity before leaving the base—otherwise it's a long, dusty hike for any teammates left behind. The UH-1Y Venom is the best way to quickly move troops to the control points. Fly it over the Construction Site (A), Warehouses (B) and Offices (D), and drop one soldier at each location in an attempt to beat the RU team to these critical flags. Once captured, reinforce these control points (particularly the Warehouses) with the M1 Abrams tanks. Use the tanks and AH-1Z Viper to counter the RU team's T-90As, while the Super Hornets provide air cover and attack the enemy jet and helicopters with heat-seeking missiles. The vehicles spawning at this base make tempting targets for the RU team's jets and helicopters. So utilize the provided LAV-AD and Centurion C-RAM to deter such attacks, particularly at the start of the round. Later, the LAV-AD is best deployed with the tanks, helping to provide air defenses near the central control points. In this match, no tanks are spawned by the control points in the center of the map. So as the round commences, don't forget to spawn back at the base to bring tanks and other vehicles to the front lines.

RU BASE

Base Assets	NAME	VDV Buggy	T-90A	9K22 Tunguska-M	Mi-28 Havoc	KA-60 Kasatka	SU-35BM Flanker-E	Pantsir-S1
	QUANTITY	1	4	1	1	1	2	1
	RESPAWN TIME	5 sec.	20 sec.	20 sec.	60 sec.	90 sec.	40 sec.	—

The RU Base is located on the far west side of the map, several hundred meters from the nearest control point. So it's important to make the most out of the vehicles provided to transport the team to the control points. If you find yourself without a vehicle, immediately ask teammates for a ride before they leave the base. The KA-60 Kasatka transport helicopter is the best way to move multiple troops to the map's center. Use this helicopter to drop troops (by parachute) at the Filling Station (C), Warehouses (B), and Army Outpost (E) control points. But a few infantry won't last long against the onslaught of US tanks, so act quickly to reinforce the control points with the T-90A tanks while the Mi-28 Havoc provides close air support. At least one of the SU-35BM jets should assume the role of a fighter and shoot down the US jets and helicopters. Air cover is particularly important during the opening moments of the match, so get fighters in the air and man the Pantsir-S1 and Tunguska-M to counter attacks by the US jets. During the course of the battle, spawn back at the RU base periodically to bring ground vehicles forward to help attack and defend the central control points. The control points provide no tanks, so the team that masters of the logistics of moving tanks forward has the upper hand in this battle.

◆Ⓐ CONSTRUCTION SITE

Control Point Assets		
US CONTROL	RU CONTROL	RESPAWN TIME
Growler ITV (1)	—	20 sec.
9M133 Komet Launcher	—	30 sec.

The Construction Site (A) is the easternmost control point, well within easy striking distance of the US Base. As a result, the US team is likely to capture this flag first. But after the early moments of the round, this control point is very much up for grabs. While it's the closest control point to the US Base, it's by no means adjacent. So unless the US team is constantly defending this location and reinforcing it with vehicles, it's relatively easy for the RU team to steal it. The flag is located in a parking lot outside an office building. Once captured, the Construction Site is relatively easy to lock down by any squad willing to stay put. Defenders can deter vehicle attacks by placing mines and C4 around the flagpole. The nearby two-story office and partially constructed buildings across the road to the east provide excellent views of the flag so defenders can pick off attackers. However, the office building can be destroyed, so you may want to seek better cover if you come under heavy bombardment. Outside their base, the Construction Site is the only control point that spawns a vehicle for the US team—the RU team gets nothing here. While the Growler ITV spawned here isn't a game changer, it's useful for launching raids on distant control points—try stealing the Offices (D) or Army Outpost (E).

◆Ⓑ WAREHOUSES

As the central control point, the Warehouses (B) are the most contentious site on the map. At the start of the round, both teams should attempt to capture this flag early. The transport helicopters spawned at each base are the best way to take control of this site quickly. Load a chopper with troops, then fly low and fast, dropping troops on the rooftop of the large warehouse near the flag. While infantry can capture this flag, it takes tanks and close air support provided by helicopters and jets to defend it. The flagpole is located outside the large warehouse; tanks and other ground vehicles can camp in it's capture radius. So if you're attacking on foot, always approach from the warehouse interior. It's possible to capture and contest this flag from inside the warehouse. This beats lying prone next to the flagpole. With so many possible approaches, it takes a dedicated squad of defenders to patrol the warehouse and ferret out any opponents attempting to convert the flag from within. Infantry are also effective outside. They can utilize the surrounding rooftops and catwalks to spot incoming vehicles and troops. A T-UGS motion sensor planted near the flag is a great way to monitor enemy traffic. Spotting enemies can be a full-time job here, so find a good elevated spot and simply call out the locations of hostile forces to help direct attacks by your team's air units. Or better yet, use a SOFLAM to paint enemy vehicles for guided munitions fired by friendly tanks, helicopters, and jets.

Ⓒ FILLING STATION

Located on the west side of the map, this massive industrial facility is closest to the RU Base. While the RU team has the best chance of capturing the Filling Station (C) early, there's no guarantee they'll be able to hold onto it, especially if it's left undefended. The flagpole here is located on an open piece of asphalt surrounded by three explosive tanker trucks. It's a good idea to destroy the tanker trucks upon arrival because you don't want them to explode while you're attempting to capture the flag, especially if you're on foot. With minimal cover nearby, this is a control point best captured and contested by tanks. However, infantry can play a large role in defending this flag. Given the likelihood of heavy vehicle traffic around the flag, mines and C4 are very effective. The surrounding structures and catwalks also offer great elevated vantage points of the flag that are ideal for scoring hits on attacking infantry and vehicles. Regardless of which team you're playing on, make an effort to reinforce this control point with tanks spawned at your team's base.

Ⓓ OFFICES

Located just north of the Construction Site (A), this control point at the Offices (D) shares a very similar configuration as its neighbor. The flag here is posted just outside the front door of an office building. This allows infantry to hide inside the building while capturing and contesting the flag. But the concrete office building will not hold up to heavy bombardment. The tall, partially constructed buildings to the west offer a great view of the flag as well as the surrounding control points. Recon troops posted here can snipe and spot targets as far away as the Army Outpost (E) to the far west. So if you want to be a forward spotter for aircraft, this is an excellent position from which to use the SOFLAM. However, infantry in these tall buildings cannot prevent the capture of the flag at the Offices and must leave their perch if they wish to contest the flag, particularly if enemy troops are hiding in the office building. A T-UGS motion sensor planted near the flag can serve as a great early warning system to alert you when enemy troops are in the area. Despite the close proximity to the US Base, the Offices control point is likely to change hands frequently during the course of the battle unless it's properly defended. In a 64-player game, there's no reason why any captured flag should be abandoned. So convert this flag and dig in!

◆ E ◆ ARMY OUTPOST

Control Point Assets

US CONTROL	RU CONTROL	RESPAWN TIME
—	VDV Buggy (1)	20 sec.
—	r	30 sec.

The Army Outpost (E) is the closest control point to the RU Base, and it is relatively easy for the RU team to capture it in the early moments of the match. Use a VDV Buggy spawned at the RU Base to rush to this control point and secure it before the US team can. The Army Outpost serves as a good forward base for the RU team because it provides them with an extra VDV Buggy that is ideal for raiding the other flags. Simply having a spawn point near the heart of the battle is a huge benefit. But don't expect enemy troops to be intimidated by the Army Outpost's guard towers and perimeter fence. Make sure at least one squad holds back and defends the flag. The flagpole is located near the center of the outpost and can be accessed from any direction by vehicles and infantry. When attacking, instead of huddling near the flag, hide in the nearby trailer to the south. Instead of guarding the perimeter, defenders here should center their efforts around the flag itself, planting mines and C4 around the flag while performing routine patrols of the capture radius. But make sure you find adequate cover, as this control point is a popular strafing target for jets and helicopters. Engineers armed with IGLA or Stinger anti-aircraft missiles have plenty of air targets to choose from, with few line-of-sight obstructions.

RUSH

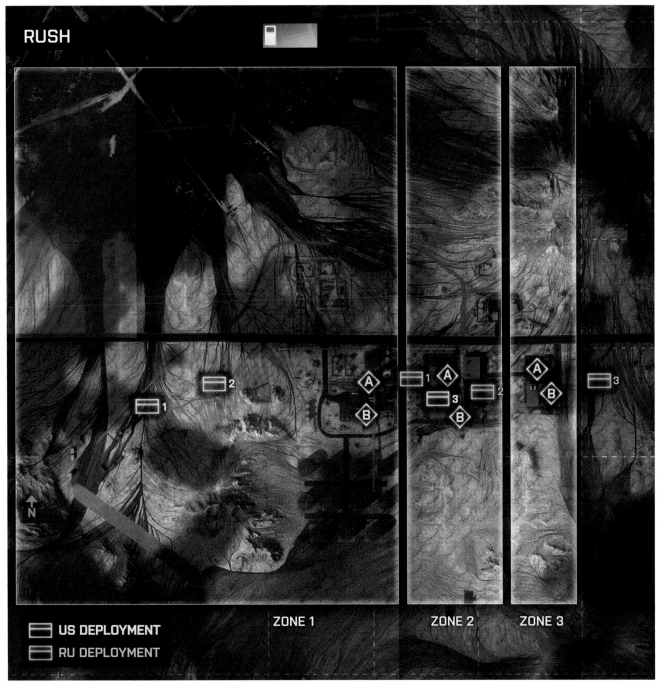

US DEPLOYMENT
RU DEPLOYMENT

ZONE 1   ZONE 2   ZONE 3

The Operation Firestorm Rush map offers a variety of action, including heated tank duels, tense dogfights, and frantic close-quarters infantry engagements. With only three zones to defend, the RU team has their work cut out for them. Their best chance is to deny the US team entry into the refinery facility by blocking them at the Filling Station. The desert to the west is the perfect kill zone for tanks and jets loaded with air-to-ground ordnance. Therefore the US must rely on speed and flanking maneuvers to establish a presence near the first two objectives. As the action moves to the Warehouses and Construction Site, both teams must adapt their tactics, relying more on infantry than vehicles to attack and defend the remaining M-COM stations.

ZONE 1: FILLING STATION

US DEPLOYMENT
- 2x Growler ITV
- 2x M1 Abrams
- 1x A-10 Thunderbolt

RU DEPLOYMENT
- 2x T-90A
- 1x SU-25TM Frogfoot
- 2x M220 TOW Launcher

A M-COM STATION A

M-COM Station A is located beneath the large refinery structure and can only be accessed by infantry. The tight quarters and multiple entry points make this a tough objective to attack and defend. In addition to defending the perimeter of the structure, the RU team must constantly post troops down here to fend off sneaky attacks. Unless defenders keep eyes on the objective, the US has a relatively easy time sneaking in here and planting a charge. But a dedicated squad of defenders scattered around the objective has an easy time ambushing attackers—consider placing a Radio Beacon here to maintain a constant presence. Regardless of which team you're on, prepare for close-quarters combat. Shotguns, submachine guns, grenades, Claymores, and C4 are very effective here. The attacking team may also want to deploy smoke around the objective before attempting to the plant the charge. The nearby staircase is a popular overwatch position, so be sure to sweep it for enemies before approaching the objective.

B M-COM STATION B

This objective sits out in the open on the south side of the Filling Station and it is surrounded by catwalks and other elevated vantage points that defenders can utilize to spot and engage attackers. Of the two objectives, the RU team has the easiest time locking down M-COM Station B. If well defended, the RU team can hold out here indefinitely. In addition to posting infantry around the Filling Station's upper levels, defenders should also rely on their tanks to lend their devastating firepower to this defensive effort. As a result, the US attackers should prepare for an absolute war. Vehicle support is essential here, so get the M1 Abrams tanks near the objective in an effort suppress the RU tanks and infantry. Meanwhile, move troops into the concrete building west of the objective. This structure serves as a great staging area for attacks on the M-COM station. But the building can be destroyed, so be ready to find a new staging area if the structure collapses. While the tanks suppress and distract enemy units, pop smoke on the objective and plant a charge.

US DEPLOYMENT

Base Assets	NAME	Growler ITV	M1 Abrams	A-10 Thunderbolt
	QUANTITY	2	2	1
	RESPAWN TIME	20 sec.	30 sec.	40 sec.

The US ground forces start their assault from the desert on the west side of the map. This is where the Growler ITVs and M1 Abrams tanks spawn, along with infantry. The A-10 Thunderbolt spawns on the runway to the south. So if you want to fly the Thunderbolt, spawn directly into the pilot's seat from the spawn screen instead wasting a vehicle by driving south to the runway. Given the open terrain, the US deployment area is vulnerable to strafing attacks by the RU team's SU-25TM. So either post engineers armed with Stinger missiles nearby or use the A-10 (armed with heat-seeking missiles) to counter attacks on the team's ground units. The A-10 is also needed to target the RU team's T-90A tanks at the Filling Station. But the M1 Abrams tanks remain the spearhead of this assault, so keep them healthy by repairing them frequently, even if it means temporarily halting the advance. The fast-moving Growler ITVs are great for flanking attacks approaching from the north or south of the Filling Station—this is the fastest way to sneak troops inside the facility. Once at the Filling Station, deploy a Radio Beacon to give your squad a spawn point near the objectives.

RU DEPLOYMENT

Base Assets	NAME	T-90A	SU-25TM Frogfoot	M220 TOW Launcher
	QUANTITY	2	1	2
	RESPAWN TIME	90 sec.	40 sec.	30 sec.

The RU team deploys on the east side of the Filling Station, near the Warehouses. But there's little time to spare at the start of the round, so move the T-90A tanks toward the objectives. The SU-25TM spawns at the airstrip to the far east, so get it in the air and commence strafing runs on the approaching US tanks. The US usually attacks from the open desert to the west. This allows for some long-range tank duels. So keep your tanks healthy by surrounding them with engineers. The spawn time on the US tanks is considerably less than the spawn time for RU tanks, so it's extremely important to keep the T-90As fully repaired. But tanks alone cannot defend the objectives. So scatter troops around the Filling Station, making use of the various catwalks and other elevated positions to gain vantage points on the M-COM stations. Watch out for US troops performing quick raids on the objectives using their Growler ITVs. Be sure to spot incoming vehicles and do your best to hunt down the occupants before they can establish a presence at the Filling Station.

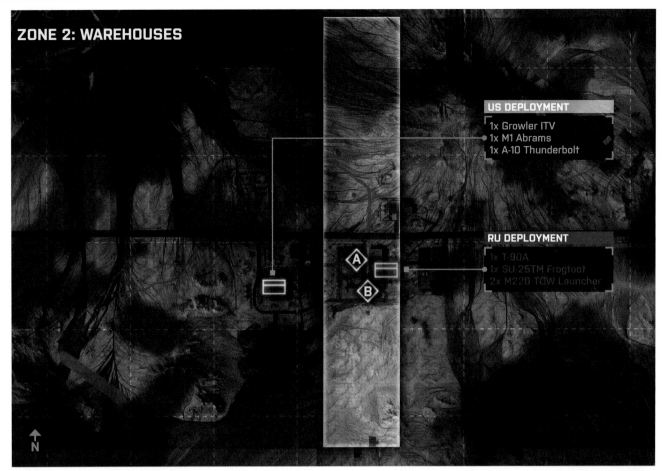

ZONE 2: WAREHOUSES

US DEPLOYMENT
- 1x Growler ITV
- 1x M1 Abrams
- 1x A-10 Thunderbolt

RU DEPLOYMENT
- 1x T-90A
- 1x SU-25TM Frogfoot
- 2x M220 TOW Launcher

N

Ⓐ M-COM STATION A

Ⓑ M-COM STATION B

M-COM Station A is located on the floor of the northwestern warehouse. The surrounding offices, stairways, and catwalks offer excellent cover positions for defenders and attackers alike. However, it's the RU defenders who stand the best chance of reaching this location first and securing it. Given the large size of this building, it takes at least two full squads to defend the interior. This is preferable to guarding the exterior, as it allows more cover and concealment while offering a clear view of the objective. This is a tough nut to crack for the US attackers, who must rely on the element of surprise and brute force to destroy this M-COM station. Blast holes in the warehouse's exterior walls to make your own entrances in an attempt to catch the defenders off guard. If manpower allows, perform a thorough sweep of the warehouse before planting the charge. In any case, always deploy smoke on the M-COM station to conceal the assault.

This objective is located on the ground floor of the southern warehouse and it provides the RU team with a second chance to halt the US attack. However, due to the M-COM station's position near the southern exterior wall, the US team has a slightly easier time of reaching this objective. Instead of attacking through the warehouse, the US team should approach from the south and blast holes in exterior walls near the objective. This allows them to gain quick access to the M-COM station and plant a charge. For this reason, defenders should cover the interior as well as the exterior. If this is the last objective standing, the RU team should park the T-90A on the south side of the warehouse to deter such flanking attacks. This also allows the tank to cover the M-COM station directly by firing through the warehouse windows or existing holes in the exterior wall.

US DEPLOYMENT

Base Assets	NAME	Growler ITV	M1 Abrams	A-10 Thunderbolt
	QUANTITY	1	1	1
	RESPAWN TIME	20 sec.	30 sec.	40 sec.

Having established a foothold on the refinery facility, the US team deploys from the Filling Station in this phase of the battle. The attack on the objectives at the Warehouses to the west requires a greater reliance on infantry tactics since the M-COM stations are located inside buildings. However, the vehicles still play a supporting role, particularly during the advance. Use the M1 and A-10 to attack the RU team's T-90A, while infantry rush west to infiltrate the two Warehouses. When advancing toward the objectives, look for opportunities to flank and enter the Warehouses from the north and south instead of performing a predictable frontal assault from the west. The Growler ITV is great for launching quick flanking attacks that allow you to evade the RU team's tank and secure a foothold near or inside one of the warehouses.

RU DEPLOYMENT

Base Assets	NAME	T-90A	SU-25TM Frogfoot	9M133 Kornet Launcher
	QUANTITY	1	1	2
	RESPAWN TIME	60 sec.	40 sec.	30 sec.

The objectives here are located inside the large warehouses, giving the RU team a significant advantage. However, it takes at least two squads to secure the interiors of these massive structures. While a majority of the team should focus on defending the Warehouse interiors, the rest of the team should cover the approach from the Filling Station. Given the large number of buildings and structures, performing ground attacks here is difficult for the SU-25TM. So in this stage, use the jet to primarily counter the US A-10, shooting it down with heat-seeking missiles. Meanwhile, use the T-90A to halt advances by the M1 and Growler ITV. While the M1 poses the most direct threat, the Growler ITV serves as an effective transport for the US team. Fortunately it can't sustain much damage, so blast it as soon as you see it racing toward the Warehouses.

ZONE 3: CONSTRUCTION SITE

US DEPLOYMENT
1x Growler ITV
1x M1 Abrams
1x A-10 Thunderbolt

RU DEPLOYMENT
1x T-90A
1x SU-25TM Frogfoot
2x M220 TOW Launcher

N

A M-COM STATION A

B M-COM STATION B

M-COM Station A is likely the first objective to come under attack. However, the US team is better off attacking this objective after M-COM Station B has been destroyed. Located farthest from the RU deployment area, it's much tougher for the defenders to reinforce this location than it is the warehouse to the south. Surrounded by stacks of shipping containers, this objective offers plenty of cover for attackers and defenders. Therefore, the RU team should work hard to prevent the attackers from infiltrating this area. Establish a perimeter covering the western, northern, and southern approaches, even if it means hiding among the containers. The two-story building to the east offers a great view of the M-COM station; sharpshooters can pick-off attackers from long range. Since the objective is completely exposed from the east and west, attackers should always deploy smoke before attempting to plant a charge. Each team's tanks can play a big supporting role in securing this location, so don't forget to move your team's tank forward to assist in this battle.

Housed within the large warehouse to the south, M-COM Station B offers the RU team one last chance to improve their close-quarters combat skills. Spawning only meters away, the RU team should have no problem securing this warehouse for the duration of the match. Two squads posted inside the warehouse should have little problem dealing with attackers. Fortify the exterior of the warehouse, too. Consider parking the T-90A on the north side of the warehouse so it can adequately cover both objectives. While the M-COM station is easily accessible through the large doorway on the north side, attackers are better off infiltrating the warehouse from the south, hopefully catching the defenders by surprise. With infantry pushing from the south and the M1 attacking from the north, the US team has a good chance of locking down the warehouse and planting the charge on the objective. But reinforcements from the nearby RU deployment area always pose a threat, so move quickly to prevent the RU team from retaking the warehouse.

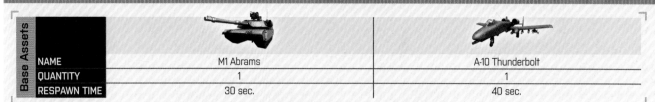

US DEPLOYMENT

Base Assets	NAME	M1 Abrams	A-10 Thunderbolt
	QUANTITY	1	1
	RESPAWN TIME	30 sec.	40 sec.

The Warehouses serve as the final deployment area for the US team. With only one tank and an A-10, the US team must advance on the Construction Site and destroy the last two M-COM stations. As in the previous stage, the vehicles play more of a supporting role in this zone; they help secure the area around each objective so infantry can plant charges. Unfortunately, no transportation vehicles are provided, so US infantry must cross the sparse no-man's-land between the Warehouses and the Construction Site. During this advance, the M1 and A-10 serve as excellent distractions that help pin and draw fire from the defenders while the infantry inch their way toward the Construction Site. Once a secure position near the objectives has been established, immediately deploy Radio Beacons to provide nearby spawn points for squad members.

RU DEPLOYMENT

Base Assets	NAME	T-90A	SU-25TM Frogfoot	9M133 Kornet Launcher
	QUANTITY	1	1	2
	RESPAWN TIME	60 sec.	40 sec.	30 sec.

This is the end of the line for the RU team. They must defend at least one of these two M-COM stations or face defeat. Immediately following the destruction of the objectives at the Warehouses, move into action to defend the final M-COM stations. Post at least one squad around each objective while the rest of the team forms a defensive line to the west. The undeveloped area to the west is a great spot to ambush advancing US troops. Position troops along the northern and southern sides of this strip of land and flank the attackers as they sprint toward the objectives. Thanks to the lack of nearby buildings, a good SU-25TM pilot can score some easy kills here by strafing with the cannon and rockets. Denying the attackers a foothold at the Construction Site is the best way to wear down their advance and give the RU team a better chance of holding out long enough for a victory.

SQUAD RUSH

US DEPLOYMENT
RU DEPLOYMENT

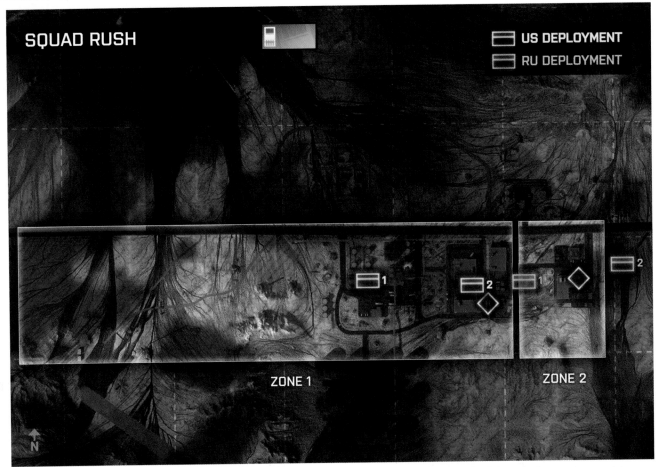

ZONE 1

ZONE 2

In Squad Rush the action is centered around more objectives located in warehouses. While most of the fighting in the warehouses takes place at close to intermediate ranges ideal for shotguns and submachine guns, the outdoor approaches feature long sight lines best suited for assault and sniper rifles. So when attacking, discuss loadouts with your team and mix things up—you can't go wrong with carbines and assault rifles. The defending squad should primarily focus their efforts around the objectives, making close-range firearms, Claymores, and C4 the weapons of choice.

ZONE 1: WAREHOUSES

This objective is in the same location as M-COM Station B from Rush mode. But with only one squad and no vehicle support, attacking and defending this objective is a little different. The defenders shouldn't bother trying to cover all the warehouse entry points. The structure is simply too large for four players to adequately cover it. Instead, hide inside the warehouse and take up elevated positions where possible to camp the M-COM station. When playing as the US, always attack from the south side of the warehouse. Consider taking up positions in the office behind the objective and picking off defenders hiding inside the warehouse. At the earliest opportunity, deploy smoke on the objective and plant the charge while preparing for the inevitable RU counterattack.

ZONE 2: CONSTRUCTION SITE

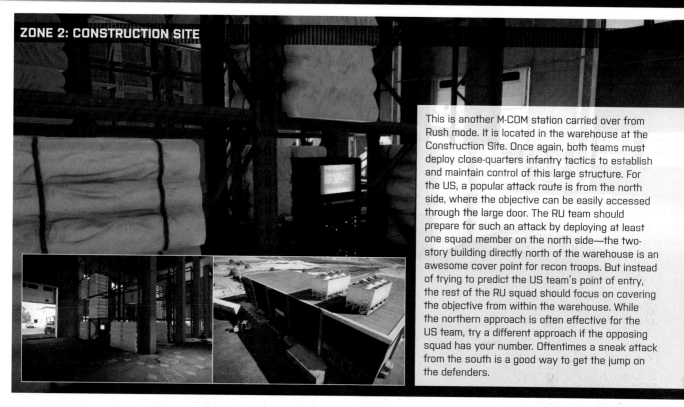

This is another M-COM station carried over from Rush mode. It is located in the warehouse at the Construction Site. Once again, both teams must deploy close-quarters infantry tactics to establish and maintain control of this large structure. For the US, a popular attack route is from the north side, where the objective can be easily accessed through the large door. The RU team should prepare for such an attack by deploying at least one squad member on the north side—the two-story building directly north of the warehouse is an awesome cover point for recon troops. But instead of trying to predict the US team's point of entry, the rest of the RU squad should focus on covering the objective from within the warehouse. While the northern approach is often effective for the US team, try a different approach if the opposing squad has your number. Oftentimes a sneak attack from the south is a good way to get the jump on the defenders.

SQUAD DEATHMATCH

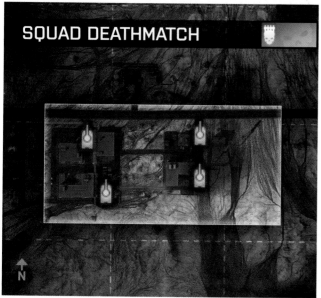

The map in Squad Deathmatch is restricted to the areas around the Warehouses and Construction Site. There are four large warehouses in this area, which make for some chaotic interior fightfights. With the IFV spawning at one of four spots on the perimeter, squads often seek shelter in the warehouses to avoid getting wiped out. But this often puts them in close contact with opposing squads. So come prepared to do battle at close range. Engineers armed with carbines and rocket launchers are well suited for countering most threats on this map. Unless your squad occupies the IFV, avoid moving through the undeveloped area between the Warehouses and the Construction Site. With little cover to hide behind, this area is often camped by snipers firing from warehouse windows and rooftops to the east and west. While it may seem like a good idea to stay put inside a warehouse and blast any opponents who enter, chances are your squad won't score enough kills to maintain the lead. So if this safe tactic doesn't work in your favor, begin moving around to seek out new prey.

TEAM DEATHMATCH

Looking for more warehouse combat? In Team Deathmatch, the action is centered around the three warehouses in the center of the map. In this case, pre-round communication is essential to determine where your team will hold out. It's strongly advised to pick a warehouse or two and use them as forts. This allows your team to stay put and go on the defensive, picking off any opponents unlucky enough to wander into your team's zone of control. But such a game plan requires discipline and teamwork. In such a transient game mode, convincing teammates to stay put is difficult. But if your team is more interested in winning than accruing personal stats, a defensive strategy is the best way to come out on top. It certainly beats wandering around the map hoping the individual skills of your teammates are enough to achieve a victory.

OPERATION MÉTRO

As part of a bigger US invasion force, your mission is to help the French to retake Paris. Your attacking platoon is supporting a French paratrooper force that will try to surprise the Russians by air-dropping behind enemy lines. Reports indicate the French Air Force is suffering heavy casualties due to a series of anti-air batteries around Chardonnay Park. With limited air support, the French are having a hard time mobilizing enough forces into the central districts of Paris.

Heavy fighting is expected as US forces push to secure the financial district in central Paris. Russian anti-air emplacements in the outskirts of the park are likely to be the first target as US Marines attempt to gain control of the airspace ahead of the main ground assault.

CONQUEST AND CONQUEST 64 ⚑

US BASE

US

CAFE

TICKET HALL

PLATFORM

RU BASE

A

B

C

RU

N

The Conquest and Conquest 64 maps are identical in Operation Métro, with the same control point layout. The only difference between these game modes is the number of players allowed on the map.

This is a linear tug-of-war style Conquest match, with three control points lined up from north to south. With only three flags up for grabs, your team must capture and hold at least two control points to drain the opposing team's ticket count. The US team should try to hold the Platform (C) and Ticket Hall (B). By building up a line of defense at the Ticket Hall (B), the US team can lock down the entire métro station by covering the three entry points to the south, all while bleeding the RU team's tickets. The RU team is best served by capturing all three control points, and forming their line of defense at the Platform (C). This allows them to ambush US troops in the dark tunnels north of the Platform (C). But even if the Platform (C) falls to the US, the RU team can establish a solid defense at the Ticket Hall (B) to hold out for the win. Regardless of which team you're on, prepare for a mix of close-quarters and intermediate-range infantry combat. So make sure your squad has a wide mix of weapons to engage opponents in a variety of environments. As in any Conquest match, your team's ticket count is crucial, and in a tight match, assault troops equipped with defibrillators can make all the difference.

In both variants of Conquest, the US team starts the match in the tunnels near the park. There are two tunnels running parallel to each other, both leading toward the nearby Platform (C) control point. The eastern tunnel is the widest, offering quick, direct access to the Platform (C). There are plywood barriers on the southern end of the eastern tunnel that can be destroyed. However, it's best to keep these sheets of plywood in place to deny the RU team long sight lines down this tunnel. The western tunnel is a narrow maintenance shaft that drops down onto the western subway tracks. This is offers a sneakier way to reach the Platform (C), but it can also be a popular spot for opponents looking for an easy ambush. So always proceed with caution when dropping down onto the tracks—smoke can help conceal your squad's descent from the maintenance shaft. Within each tunnel are a variety of side passages that are useful for avoiding snipers and other opponents posted to the south. Despite the multiple paths, the US team should work hard to avoid spawning here. If the RU team takes control of all three control points, they have an easy time locking down both tunnels, denying the US access to other spawn points. Therefore it's extremely important that US team captures and holds the Platform (C) throughout the course of the match. Otherwise the advance through the tunnels can turn into a bloodbath favoring the RU team.

The RU team deploys from their base in the Finance Ministry building on the south end of the map. If you spawn inside the building, don't feel bad about shooting out the windows to escape. With the Cafe (A) control point located directly across the street to the north, the RU team has no problem securing their first control point. But capturing one control point isn't enough. The RU team must continue pushing north into the métro station to secure the Ticket Hall (B) before they can go on the defensive. If the Ticket Hall (B) falls to the US, they'll have an easy time locking down the entire station by covering the three entry points. In addition to the Ticket Hall (B), the Cafe (A) should always be defended, too. If the US manages to capture all three control points, the RU team will have a tough time simply getting out of the Finance Ministry building without getting gunned down by US troops positioned in the buildings to the north surrounding the Cafe (A). If your team does find itself under siege by the US at the RU Base, instead of grinding against the Cafe (A), sneak around the streets to the east or west to try to secure a control point in the métro station. Although the layout of this map is rather linear, there are always flanking paths available that are less likely to be covered by opponents.

Ⓐ CAFE

The Cafe (A) control point is sandwiched between the RU Base and the métro station's southern entrance. This becomes a high-traffic area whenever the US team holds the Ticket Hall (B) and the RU team holds the Cafe (A). Given the close proximity to their base, the RU team stands the best chance of holding onto this control point throughout the battle. But the chance to lay siege to the RU Base may prove tempting to the US team, so the RU team should never take this control point for granted. The flagpole is relatively unprotected, standing as it does between two large buildings to the east and west. But the flag's capture radius is very large, so it can be captured and contested from within the surrounding buildings. As a result, the buildings are a great place for attackers and defenders to hide. Consider deploying a Radio Beacon in one of these buildings to give your squad a spawn point near the flag, regardless of which team controls the Cafe (A). Both buildings offer access to multiple floors. So use the upper floor windows to keep an eye on the flag as well as the approaches from the RU Base and métro station.

Ⓑ TICKET HALL

In the center of the map, the Ticket Hall (B) is the most hotly contested control point in this battle, requiring constant attention by both teams. In the footrace to reach the flag at the start of the match, the RU team has a slight advantage. But players on both teams should perform a continuous sprint to reach this location before the opposing team takes control. Even if you reach this spot first, your opponents won't be far behind, so drop prone and find a good cover position within the flag's wide capture radius. Regardless of which team captures the flag first, it's likely to change hands several times. When defending here, seek cover along the perimeter, preferably on the eastern and western sides of the flag. If the opposing team is advancing from the north, it's strongly advised to defend all the escalators and the stairway to the northwest—these are the only access points to the station's upper level and serve as great choke points. When defending attacks from the south, utilize the métro station entry points. There are three entrances into the station to the south, east, and west. By locking down each of these entrances, you can prevent the opposing team from even gaining a foothold within the station, effectively blocking access to the Ticket Hall (B) and Platform (C).

Ⓒ PLATFORM

Although the Platform (C) is relatively close to the US Base, it's not necessarily safe from capture by the RU team. By holding this flag, the RU team not only blocks access to the other control points, but they can also lay siege to the US Base and ambush advancing troops as they move through the dark tunnels to the north. For this reason alone, the US team must work to capture and secure this control point throughout the match. The flag here is positioned in the middle of the station platform. When attempting to capture or contest the flag, instead of gathering at the base of the flagpole, spread out and hide in the nearby maintenance passage to the north or within the subway cars to the east and west. Given the flag's wide capture radius, there are plenty of hiding spots for both attackers and defenders. So pay close attention to the circular flag status icon on the HUD to determine whether enemy troops are present.

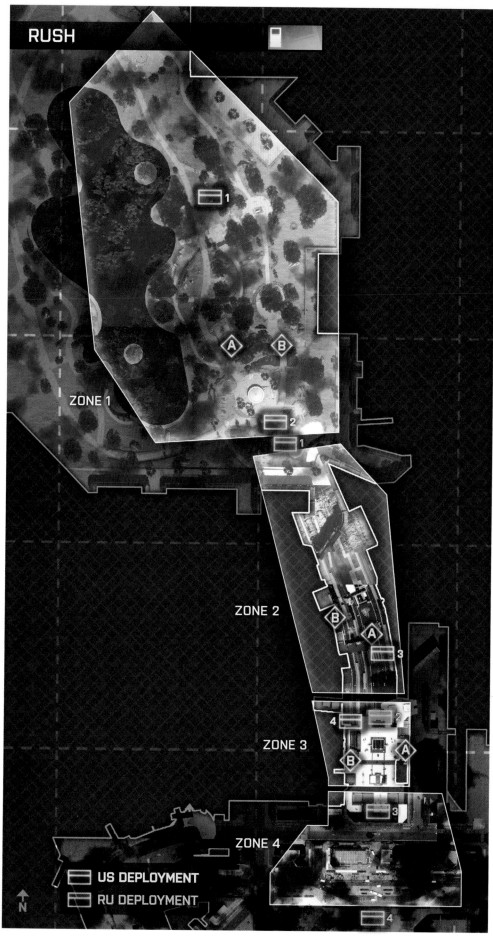

RUSH

ZONE 1

ZONE 2

ZONE 3

ZONE 4

US DEPLOYMENT
RU DEPLOYMENT

Prepare yourself for a frantic fight through four distinct zones centered around a métro station in the heart of Paris. Like the other game modes for this map, there are no vehicles available in Rush mode, so it's up to infantry to attack and defend the objectives on their own. Starting in the park to the north, the battle continues through the métro station before the RU defenders make their last stand in the city streets to the south. The combat in each zone differs drastically, so prepare to alter your classes, loadouts, and tactics based on the environment. For example, engagements in the park tend to take place at intermediate to long range, making recon and assault soldiers quite effective. Meanwhile, support and engineer troops armed with light machine guns and carbines are successful during the firefights in the métro station. The team that manages to adapt to each unique environment stands the best chance of achieving a victory here. So if things aren't going your team's way, perhaps it's time to switch weapons and tactics.

ZONE 1: PARK

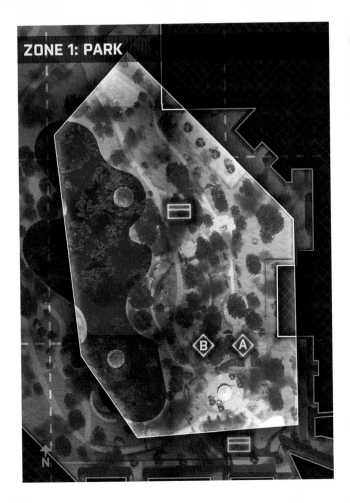

A M-COM STATION A

M-COM Station A is located on the east side of the park, in a small plaza near a mobile radar dish. With the exception of some small concrete blocks on the north side, there is very little cover around the objective. Therefore, both teams must work hard to secure the area around the M-COM station before attempting to arm or disarm a charge. When attacking as the US team, try sneaking around the east side and huddling near the radar dish before moving in on the objective. The RU team usually reinforces this position from the nearby footbridge to the south. Hiding near the radar dish allows you to flank these reinforcements. The RU team has the easiest time defending here if they maintain a solid presence on the north side of the objective. If the US team secures the plaza north of the footbridge, always flank from the east to catch them by surprise—avoid crossing the bridge. Regardless of which side you're playing on, always deploy smoke on this objective and remain prone while attempting to set or disarm a charge. Otherwise you'll be an easy target to pick off.

B M-COM STATION B

This objective is located within a playground on the west side of the park. Compared to M-COM Station A, there is quite a bit of cover surrounding this objective, including a high metal wall to the west, a radar dish to the east, and a low sandbag wall to the north. Once the area surrounding the playground has been secured, US troops have little trouble planting a charge on the objective. The RU defenders should position themselves along the rocks to the south and east to get a good vantage point on the northern approaches to the playground as well as the objective. The trees and rocks to the north of the playground also provide a good defensive position, allowing the RU team to cover the western footpaths. For the US team, it's best to avoid a frontal assault here, especially once the defenders have had time to get settled. So look for flanking opportunities from the east, a maneuver that is best accomplished once M-COM Station A has been destroyed. But if you can rout the defenders around the objective, rush toward the objective and plant a charge while preparing for counterattacks from the south.

US DEPLOYMENT

At the start of the battle, US troops deploy on the north end of the park. There are no vehicles at this deployment area or any other locations in this Rush match. The RU team doesn't have any vehicles either, so both teams are on an even footing. However, the RU team has the benefit of defending static locations; they can take cover and hide around each objective. With the exception of some trees and large boulders, the park is relatively open, with long sight lines stretching from north to south. So stay low as you advance from one piece of cover to the next, slowly working your way toward the objectives. Running flat out toward an objective is suicide here, so calm down and take it one meter at a time. If you come under fire, immediately drop prone and crawl to the nearest piece of cover. Don't attempt to retaliate—you'll be dead before you locate your attacker. Also, try to avoid the paved footpaths, as they offer little cover. Given the tough advance in the park, you should deploy Radio Beacons to the south to give your team's squads spawn points closer to the objectives. At the very least, use squad spawning to stay close to the action.

RU DEPLOYMENT

The RU team deploys on the south side of the park within a few meters of the objectives. Despite starting close to the objectives, the RU team must act quickly to establish a defensive perimeter. It's an absolute footrace at the beginning of the round as both teams rush toward the M-COM stations, so make sure your team spreads out and covers both objectives. It's important that squads cover the low area on the west side of the park to defend M-COM Station B as well as the high ground to the east to cover M-COM Station A. Although the objectives are relatively close to one another, the elevation differences in terrain make it difficult to cover both from any one position. So when playing as squad leader, pick an objective for your team to defend and stick with it. Recon troops are ideal here, as they are capable of scoring long-range kills. Support troops, armed with light machine guns, are also very effective at suppressing and ultimately slowing the US advance. This is crucial at the start of a match, so lay down some heavy fire to send the US troops scrambling for cover while your team moves into defensive positions around each objective. Remember, when firing sniper rifles or light machine guns, always drop prone and use a bipod for increased stability.

ZONE 2: PLATFORM

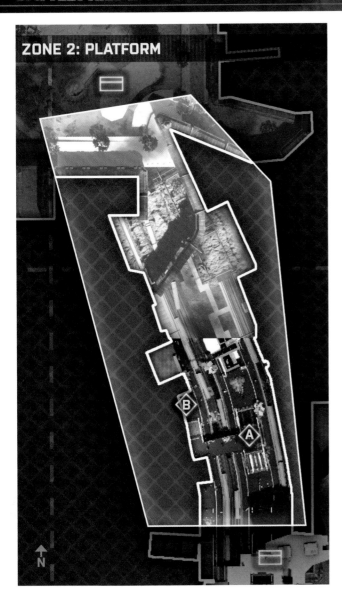

A M-COM STATION A

Of the two objectives in this zone, M-COM station A is the most defensible. Located in a restroom on the Platform, the objective can only be approached from two narrow doorways on the east and west sides. There are a couple of ways to defend this location. If manpower allows, it's best to cover both doorways from outside the restroom. But this requires careful coordination. The most direct option is to cover the M-COM station from within the restroom—post defenders in each corner to constantly watch both doorways. The pillar opposite the objective is also a good hiding spot; it helps absorb shrapnel from incoming grenades. In any case, US attackers should always expect to find at least a few defenders clustered around the objective. For this reason, always toss grenades (or C4) through the doorway before entering, and always enter with at least one other teammate. A simultaneous assault through both doorways is most effective.

B M-COM STATION B

M-COM Station B is nestled in a cramped storage area along the western wall of the métro station. It can only be approached from the narrow opening to the east and the stairway to the south. When defending this location, consider taking up position along the stairs. This allows you to keep an eye on the M-COM station and flank anyone approaching it from the east. Hiding near the objective is less effective and makes you vulnerable to grenades. While attacking through the narrow opening to the east is the most direct path, it's safest to head up the escalators on the central platform and loop around to attack from the stairs south of the objective. This allows you to flank any defenders posted on the steps as well as spot anyone hiding near the objective. Securing this southern approach is vital when playing against a well organized team of defenders.

Immediately following the destruction of the previous M-COM stations, a massive explosion rocks the south side of the park, leaving behind two massive holes in the ground. Each hole in the ground leads into a separate tunnel of the subway system. The US team deploys outside, just north of these tunnel entrances. The tunnels are parallel to each other and ultimately lead to the Platform area of the métro station. However, those wishing to attack M-COM Station A should use the eastern tunnel, while those attacking M-COM Station B should travel through the western tunnel. Both tunnels are very dark and filled with smoke, making the advance extremely dangerous especially if well-defended. To gain the upper hand, consider equipping a Tactical Light or Laser Sight to blind your opponents. If unlocked, the IRNV IR 1x scope is also very effective; with it you can spot the infrared signatures of enemies hiding in the tunnels without giving away your position.

RU DEPLOYMENT

The RU team deploys from the station's upper level, south of the objectives. After losing the objectives at the park, the RU team has a few seconds to establish their defensive perimeters around each objective. Division of labor is extremely important in this phase of the battle as the US advances down two separate tunnels. So make sure at least two squads cover each tunnel, while the remaining squads focus on covering the objectives. Ambushing the US troops in the tunnels is very effective and can completely halt the enemy advance, but only if your squads maintain a constant presence in each tunnel. Radio Beacons and squad spawning are essential for maintaining forward positions in each tunnel.

Hide among the rubble and within the subway cars to catch the attackers by surprise. Destroy the plywood barriers in the eastern tunnel to open a longer sight line for defenders positioned to the south. In addition to the tunnels, don't forget to cover the maintenance passage in the middle—this is a popular flanking path and should be patrolled or monitored with a T-UGS motion sensor.

ZONE 3: TICKET HALL

A M-COM STATION A

M-COM Station A is positioned behind a counter in a small office on the east side of the Ticket Hall. While the counter provides excellent cover for players attempting to arm or disarm a charge on the objective, simply getting to this location can be dangerous. There's a long north-south sight line just outside the office to the west, where both teams score long-range kills. Anyone entering the office must cross this sight line. So if you need to get to the objective, deploy smoke outside the office to break this sight line and give yourself just enough time to race into the office. The office is surrounded by large windows and can also be watched from the alcoves directly to the north and south. These flanking positions are great for keeping an eye on the objective without exposing yourself to the chaotic firefights in the middle of the Ticket Hall.

B M-COM STATION B

Because it is sandwiched between the turnstiles and maintenance corridor, the fight for M-COM Station B is always intense, dominated by close-quarters combat. To reach this objective, the US attackers must pass through one of two deadly choke points. The turnstiles to the east of the objective are always a good area to avoid since they're easily covered by defenders posted anywhere in the Ticket Hall. That leaves the maintenance corridor as the safest route. This passage can be accessed after climbing the western steps, and it provides a direct path to M-COM Station B. For this reason, it's essential that the RU team defend this passage as well as the adjacent western steps. Shotguns, submachine guns, and grenades are ideal for both attacking and defending this tight corridor. The team that manages to control this corridor determines the fate of M-COM Station B.

Now that the US team has secured a foothold within the métro station, they deploy from the Platform area, poised for the attack on the Ticket Hall. Advancing from the lower level of the tunnels to the upper level where the next objectives are located can be dangerous. Avoid the escalators at all costs. These narrow stairways are deadly choke points that are likely to be camped and booby-trapped by the RU defenders. The stairway to the west offers safest route to reach the upper level, but it is probably defended, too. Therefore, only attempt the ascent when accompanied by a full squad or two. Once on the upper floor, immediately seek cover in the maintenance corridor on the west side. Deploy Radio Beacons here and use the corridor as a staging area for attacks on the objectives.

In this stage of the battle, the RU team spawns at the station's entrance, just south of the Ticket Hall. This gives them just enough time to get into position before the US team rushes toward the objectives. The RU team holds the high ground here and should take advantage by covering the two sets of escalators and the western stairway. By locking down these choke points, the RU team can prevent the US from even reaching the upper floor. However, breaches in the forward line are likely, so form a second defensive line near the two objectives in the Ticket Hall. The western maintenance corridor is a popular hiding spot for attackers, so be sure to actively defend or at least patrol this area. Defenders posted near the turn styles have a clear view of the Ticket Hall—shoot out the glass between the turnstiles for a better view and easier north-south movement. The central ticket booth in the center of the Ticket Hall is also a good defensive position with a good vantage point on the areas around both objectives.

ZONE 4: RUE CATHARINE

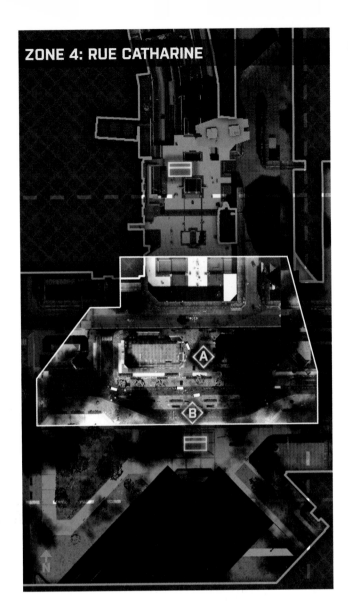

This objective is housed within the Cafe directly south of the métro station. Initially the Cafe's windows are boarded up with large sheets of plywood. So attackers must destroy these barriers before hopping through a window—sustained small arms fire is enough to break the plywood sheets. The M-COM station is behind the Cafe's display case. While the upper floor windows of the building to the west offer great elevated views of the Cafe, defenders should also be posted closer to the objective to fend off flanking attacks from the east. With so many potential hiding spots, it may be necessary to perform floor-by-floor sweeps of each building to root out attackers. Consider placing a T-UGS motion sensor near the objective to locate enemy troops. When playing as the US, try to sneak into the cafe from the south side, as it's less likely to be defended. Once inside, the display case provides adequate cover while you set the charge. Once the charge is set, defend the Cafe from within, blasting any defenders that rush inside.

B M-COM STATION B

M-COM Station B is in the street directly north of the Finance Ministry building where the RU team spawns. Although it's the objective farthest from their deployment area, the US team should try to take out M-COM Station B first. If this is the last standing objective, the RU team has an easy time defending it, thanks to their nearby deployment area. So early on, the US team should try to sneak up on this objective by flanking from the east or west while the bulk of the RU forces are gathered around the métro station and Cafe. The objective is located next to a white van in the middle of the street, which blocks views from RU defenders spawning at the Finance Ministry building. The nearby bus offers excellent cover from snipers posted in the buildings to the north. However, defenders posted along the street to the east and west have clear views of the approaches to this objective. Ultimately, it may require defenders posted near the objective to stop the US team from planting a charge—consider hiding in the bus to surprise attackers.

For the final stage of the battle, the US team deploys from the Ticket Hall. Before advancing on the last two objectives, the US team's first goal is to simply exit the métro station. There are three exits to choose from to the east, south, and west. The southern exit is the most heavily traveled and defended. Stepping out here leaves you open to attacks from all directions. The eastern exit is a little better, and you can sneak along the eastern edge of the map for stealthy, flanking attacks on M-COM Station B. The western exit offers the most cover and is less likely to be watched by RU defenders. When exiting here, race across the street and take up positions in the upper floors above the Cafe where M-COM Station A is located. Deploy Radio Beacons inside this building and use it as a forward staging area for attacks on the final objectives.

The RU team deploys from the Finance Ministry building, only a few meters from M-COM Station B. Despite losing control of the park and métro station, the RU team has a good chance of holding off the US advance here. After losing the objectives in the Ticket Hall, quickly gather around the métro station's three exits in an attempt to contain the US attack. These three narrow exits serve as excellent choke points. Posting at least one squad at each exit is a great way to prevent the attackers from even leaving the métro station. In preparation for break-out attacks, post a squad at each of objective as well. There are many defensive cover positions in the streets and buildings that are ideal for containing the US attack. But securing a victory here largely hinges on wearing down the US at the métro station exits.

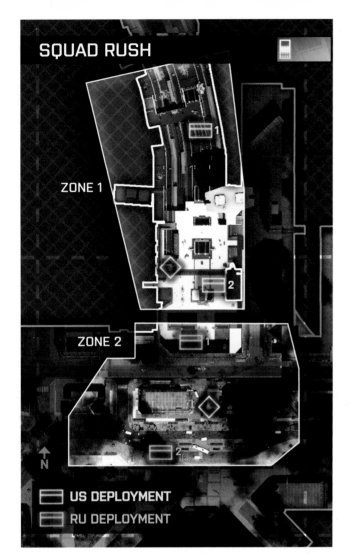

SQUAD RUSH

ZONE 1

ZONE 2

N

US DEPLOYMENT

RU DEPLOYMENT

The Squad Rush variant of this map revisits some locations and objectives from the standard Rush mode, centered around the Ticket Hall and Cafe. Experience on Rush mode greatly aids you squad's performance here as it allows you to become familiar with the different approaches to each objective. Prepare for a mix of close-to-intermediate range engagements here. While there are long sight lines around the Ticket Hall and Cafe, the action around each objective takes place at close range. So choose a versatile weapon like a carbine or assault rifle when selecting your class and load-out.

ZONE 1: TICKET HALL

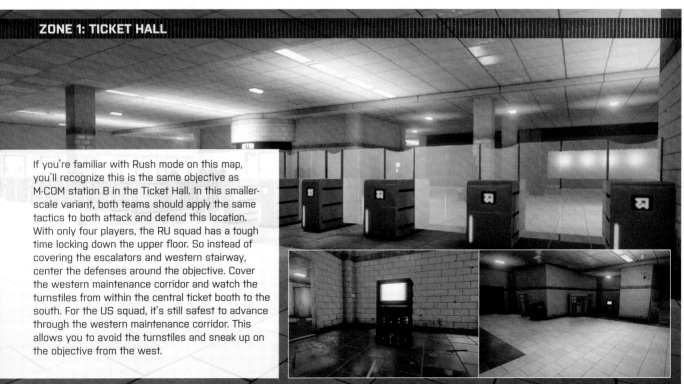

If you're familiar with Rush mode on this map, you'll recognize this is the same objective as M-COM station B in the Ticket Hall. In this smaller-scale variant, both teams should apply the same tactics to both attack and defend this location. With only four players, the RU squad has a tough time locking down the upper floor. So instead of covering the escalators and western stairway, center the defenses around the objective. Cover the western maintenance corridor and watch the turnstiles from within the central ticket booth to the south. For the US squad, it's still safest to advance through the western maintenance corridor. This allows you to avoid the turnstiles and sneak up on the objective from the west.

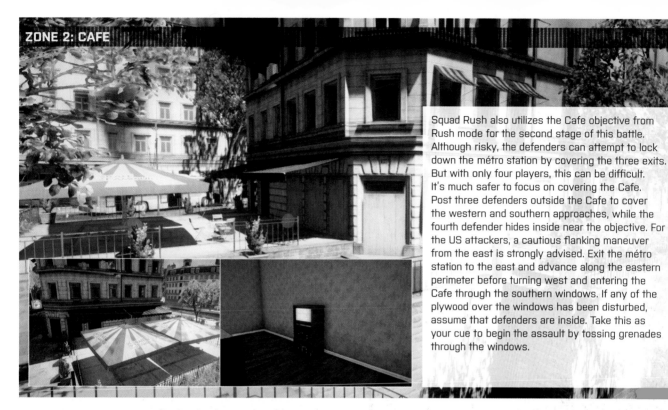

Squad Rush also utilizes the Cafe objective from Rush mode for the second stage of this battle. Although risky, the defenders can attempt to lock down the métro station by covering the three exits. But with only four players, this can be difficult. It's much safer to focus on covering the Cafe. Post three defenders outside the Cafe to cover the western and southern approaches, while the fourth defender hides inside near the objective. For the US attackers, a cautious flanking maneuver from the east is strongly advised. Exit the métro station to the east and advance along the eastern perimeter before turning west and entering the Cafe through the southern windows. If any of the plywood over the windows has been disturbed, assume that defenders are inside. Take this as your cue to begin the assault by tossing grenades through the windows.

SQUAD DEATHMATCH

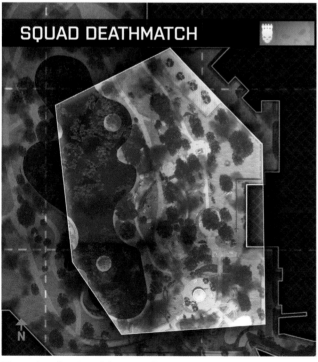

The park is the site of this Squad Deathmatch, providing a mix of lush terrain to carve up with your squad's weapons. There are no IFV spawn points on this map, so it's purely an infantry battle, with the most skilled squad claiming victory. Given the open terrain of the park, there are not many advantageous locations from which to defend. But that won't stop recon troops from setting up camp and sniping opponents. As usual, avoid the paved footpaths and other open areas that lack cover, such as the pond to the west. Instead, methodically creep along the map's east side, using the trees and boulders for cover while training your weapons on opponents in the center of the map. By keeping your backs against the eastern boundary, you can avoid being attacked from behind.

TEAM DEATHMATCH

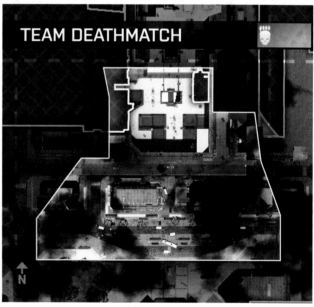

In Team Deathmatch the action is restricted to the métro station exit and Paris street on the southern end of the map. With no front line or objectives to rally around, the fight here can become frantic as players from both teams aimlessly wander around the map looking for opponents to shoot. Although it's impossible to tell where your opponents will spawn, controlling the streets is a good way to give your team the upper hand. And the best way to control the streets is by occupying the two buildings south of the métro station. The upper floor windows offer great views of the streets to the north and south, as well as the plaza between the two buildings. Still, it takes teamwork to properly occupy and hold these two buildings. So don't leave the entrances undefended or else a single opponent can sneak up behind teammates posted at the windows and steal their dog tags. If you want to avoid the streets, consider hiding out in the métro station; gun down any opponents who come charging through the entrances. In any case, try to find a defensible position and lock it down with the help of your teammates.

SEINE CROSSING

The American invasion of Russian occupied Paris is in full motion. The upscale area in the 7th District of Paris serves as the battleground as the US attempts a bold advance across the Seine River.

With what can be described as a total disregard for collateral damage, US Forces are leading their attack on the Seine River area with the largest bombardment thus far witnessed in Paris.

Although the objective is to push Russian forces out of the district and back beyond the historic corporate headquarters of a major French bank, US Marines will first have to navigate and control the urban areas and main roads in and around two key bridges over the Seine.

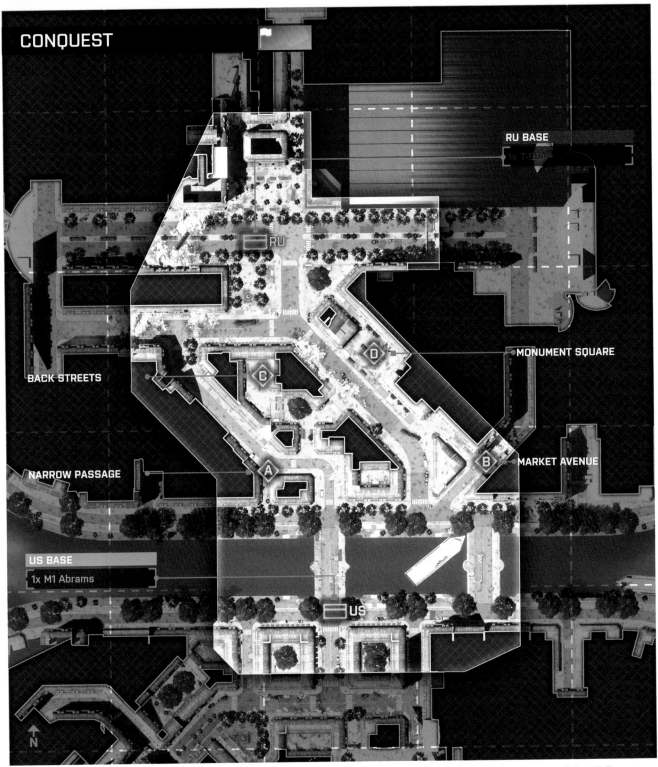

RU BASE
1x T-90

RU

MONUMENT SQUARE

D

BACK STREETS

C

NARROW PASSAGE

A

B

MARKET AVENUE

US BASE
1x M1 Abrams

US

N

The streets of Paris are the site of this intense urban battle as the US and RU team's fight for dominance. The position of the US Base on the south side of the Seine puts them at a potentially dangerous disadvantage. In a lopsided match, the RU team can secure all the flags and contain the US team to the south side of the river by controlling the two bridges. Therefore the US team must constantly struggle to maintain a presence on the north side of the river. With four control points up for grabs, each team must hold at least three flags to begin draining the opposing team's ticket count. The US team should try to capture the Narrow Passage (A) and Market Avenue (B) control points early on followed by a push to secure the Back Streets (C). Meanwhile, the RU team should capture the Back Streets (C), Monument Square (D), and Market Avenue (B) control points. None of the control points spawn vehicles on this map, but both bases provide their team with a tank. The tanks are best deployed as supporting vehicles and should never be driven headlong into a crowd of enemy infantry. Instead, hold back and attack from a distance where you're less likely to be flanked by enemy troops.

Base Assets	NAME	M1 Abrams
	QUANTITY	1
	RESPAWN TIME	90 sec.

The US team deploys on the south side of Seine, not far from the two bridges that serve as the only access points the city's center. All of the control points are located on the north side of the bridges, meaning the US team must secure at least one flag to establish a spawn point on the opposite side of the river. If the RU team manages to hold all the flags, they can lay siege to the US Base by locking down the two bridges—the US team can't afford to let this happen. Use infantry to capture the nearby Narrow Passage (A) while the M1 Abrams races to secure the Market Avenue (B) control point. Once a flag is held, make sure at least one squad stays back to defend it. While the M1 Abrams is great for deterring attacks on control points, it's better deployed on offense because it's perfect for countering the RU team's T-90A. Keep the tank healthy by surrounding it with engineers. If the tank is destroyed, it eventually respawns back at the US Base, so don't forget to bring it forward to assist in the fight.

RU BASE

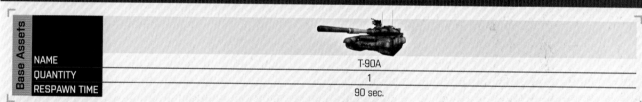

Base Assets	NAME	T-90A
	QUANTITY	1
	RESPAWN TIME	90 sec.

The RU team starts off on the north side of the map, near the large bank building. Like the US team, the RU team only has one tank in this battle leaving it up to infantry to handle most of the heavy lifting, including the capturing of control points. Early on, RU troops should rush toward the Back Street (C) and Monument Square (D). The T-90A should join the assault on Monument Square (D) to help secure the wide eastern street nearby. Urban environments are not ideal for tank warfare, so never rush off in the T-90A on your own. Make sure you're always surrounded by friendly engineers to conduct repairs. Although the RU team has only one tank, make an effort to keep it in the battle, even if it means spawning back at the RU Base to drive it to the front lines. In a tight match, the tank's awesome firepower can make all the difference by depleting the US team's ticket count with its main cannon and machine gun turret. The T-90A is also the best option for defeating the US team's M1 Abrams.

◈ A NARROW PASSAGE

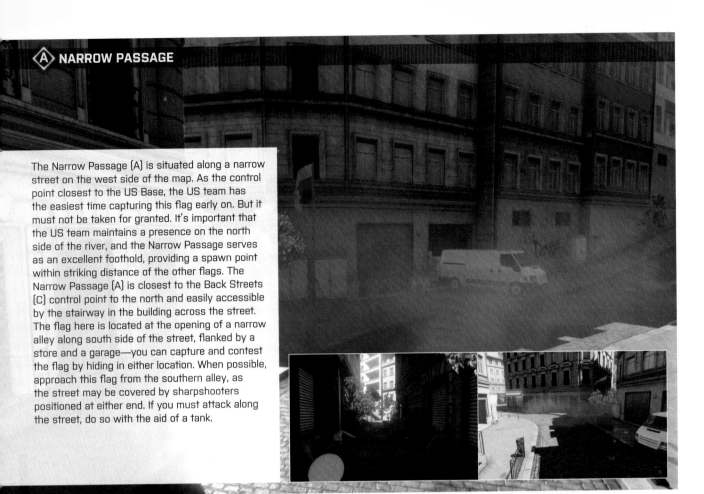

The Narrow Passage (A) is situated along a narrow street on the west side of the map. As the control point closest to the US Base, the US team has the easiest time capturing this flag early on. But it must not be taken for granted. It's important that the US team maintains a presence on the north side of the river, and the Narrow Passage serves as an excellent foothold, providing a spawn point within striking distance of the other flags. The Narrow Passage (A) is closest to the Back Streets (C) control point to the north and easily accessible by the stairway in the building across the street. The flag here is located at the opening of a narrow alley along south side of the street, flanked by a store and a garage—you can capture and contest the flag by hiding in either location. When possible, approach this flag from the southern alley, as the street may be covered by sharpshooters positioned at either end. If you must attack along the street, do so with the aid of a tank.

◈ B MARKET AVENUE

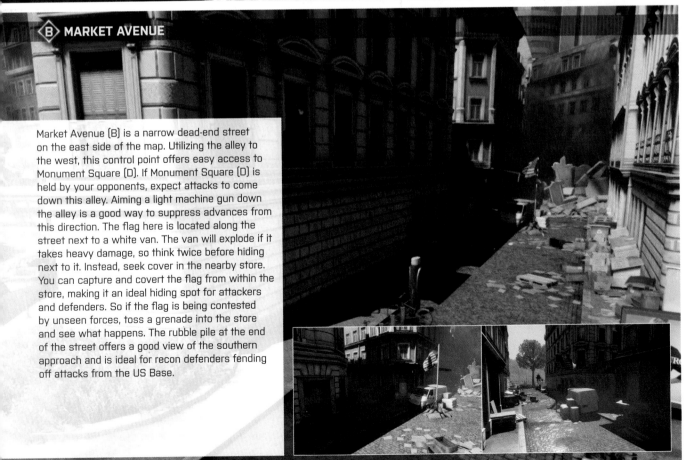

Market Avenue (B) is a narrow dead-end street on the east side of the map. Utilizing the alley to the west, this control point offers easy access to Monument Square (D). If Monument Square (D) is held by your opponents, expect attacks to come down this alley. Aiming a light machine gun down the alley is a good way to suppress advances from this direction. The flag here is located along the street next to a white van. The van will explode if it takes heavy damage, so think twice before hiding next to it. Instead, seek cover in the nearby store. You can capture and covert the flag from within the store, making it an ideal hiding spot for attackers and defenders. So if the flag is being contested by unseen forces, toss a grenade into the store and see what happens. The rubble pile at the end of the street offers a good view of the southern approach and is ideal for recon defenders fending off attacks from the US Base.

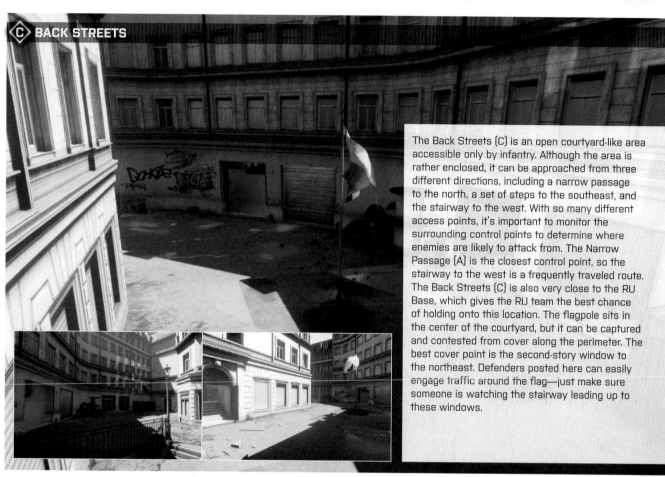

The Back Streets (C) is an open courtyard-like area accessible only by infantry. Although the area is rather enclosed, it can be approached from three different directions, including a narrow passage to the north, a set of steps to the southeast, and the stairway to the west. With so many different access points, it's important to monitor the surrounding control points to determine where enemies are likely to attack from. The Narrow Passage (A) is the closest control point, so the stairway to the west is a frequently traveled route. The Back Streets (C) is also very close to the RU Base, which gives the RU team the best chance of holding onto this location. The flagpole sits in the center of the courtyard, but it can be captured and contested from cover along the perimeter. The best cover point is the second-story window to the northeast. Defenders posted here can easily engage traffic around the flag—just make sure someone is watching the stairway leading up to these windows.

D MONUMENT SQUARE

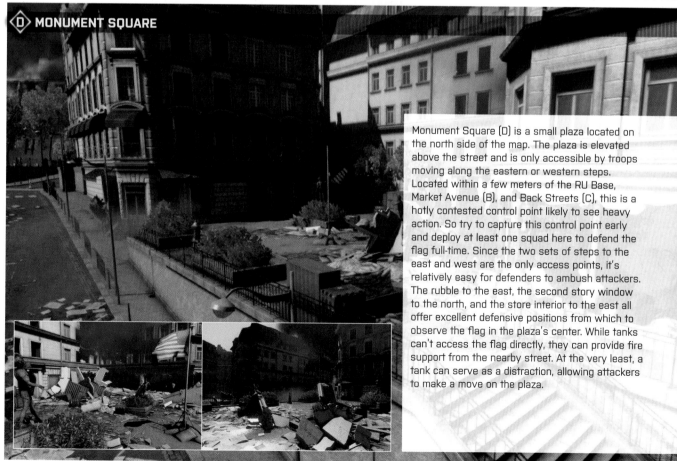

Monument Square (D) is a small plaza located on the north side of the map. The plaza is elevated above the street and is only accessible by troops moving along the eastern or western steps. Located within a few meters of the RU Base, Market Avenue (B), and Back Streets (C), this is a hotly contested control point likely to see heavy action. So try to capture this control point early and deploy at least one squad here to defend the flag full-time. Since the two sets of steps to the east and west are the only access points, it's relatively easy for defenders to ambush attackers. The rubble to the east, the second story window to the north, and the store interior to the east all offer excellent defensive positions from which to observe the flag in the plaza's center. While tanks can't access the flag directly, they can provide fire support from the nearby street. At the very least, a tank can serve as a distraction, allowing attackers to make a move on the plaza.

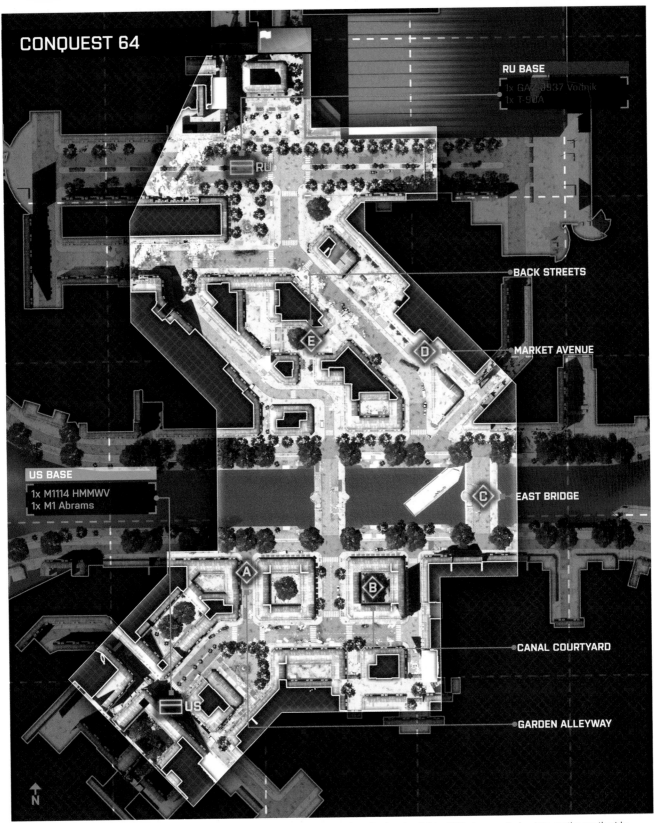

In this epic urban combat brawl, controlling the flow of traffic at the river is often the key to victory. With two control points on the north side of the river and two control points on the south side, the East Bridge (C) is the prize for both teams. This means the US team should attempt to control the Garden Alleyway (A), Canal Courtyard (B), and East Bridge (C) to give them a lock on the map's south side. Meanwhile, the RU team should try holding the Back Streets (E), Market Avenue (D), and East Bridge (C) to lock down the north side. Consolidating your team's forces around three control points is much better than spreading your team thin at four or five flags. In addition to holding the East Bridge (C), each team should attempt to lock down the western bridge to prevent flanking attacks on their rear control points. If defenses at the East Bridge (C) fail or prove too costly to hold, look for other control points to snatch up. With five control points on the map, your team must hold at least three to begin bleeding the opposing team's ticket count. Or, if you're team is feeling confident, grab all five flags and lay siege to the opposing team's base.

US BASE

Base Assets	NAME	M1114 HMMWV	M1 Abrams
	QUANTITY	1	1
	RESPAWN TIME	45 sec.	90 sec.

Located on the south side of the map, the US Base supplies the US team with only a couple of vehicles. Therefore, it's important to put these vehicles to good use, particularly in the opening moments of a round. While infantry sprint toward the Garden Alleyway (A) and Canal Courtyard (B) control points, the HMMWV and M1 should make a beeline for the critical East Bridge (C) control point. Securing these three control points early on can make a huge difference in the battle and allow the US to initiate a drain on the RU team's ticket count. If the US team successfully holds these three flags, there's no need to advance to the north side of the map. So instead of spreading your team thin, focus on defending the three southernmost control points and hold out for a victory. The M1 Abrams is critical for fending off attacks at the two bridges, so surround it with engineers to keep it repaired.

RU BASE

Base Assets	NAME	GAZ-3937 Vodnik	T-90A
	QUANTITY	1	1
	RESPAWN TIME	45 sec.	90 sec.

The RU team deploys from their base on the north side of the map, near the large bank building. The opening moments of the battle are extremely critical when it comes to securing control points so don't waste a second. The first priority is to get the Vodnik and T-90 to the East Bridge (C). While the vehicles attempt to capture the East Bridge (C), RU troops should race for the nearby Back Streets (D) and Market Avenue (E) control points. Leave one squad behind to cover both of the two northern control points while the rest of the team (and vehicles) focus on holding the East Bridge (C) as well as the bridge to the west. These two bridges serve as critical choke points, allowing the RU team to contain the US to the south banks of the Seine. However, breakout attacks by the US are likely, so never leave the Back Streets (D) and Market Avenue (E) control points undefended. If the US gains a foothold on the north side of the river, the strategy falls to pieces quickly. However, instead of pushing to the south side of the river, keep your forces consolidated around the East Bridge (C) and the two northern control points.

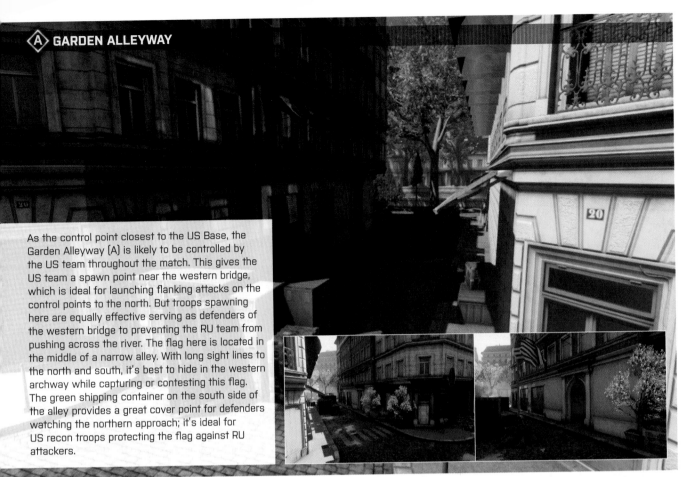

A GARDEN ALLEYWAY

As the control point closest to the US Base, the Garden Alleyway (A) is likely to be controlled by the US team throughout the match. This gives the US team a spawn point near the western bridge, which is ideal for launching flanking attacks on the control points to the north. But troops spawning here are equally effective serving as defenders of the western bridge to preventing the RU team from pushing across the river. The flag here is located in the middle of a narrow alley. With long sight lines to the north and south, it's best to hide in the western archway while capturing or contesting this flag. The green shipping container on the south side of the alley provides a great cover point for defenders watching the northern approach; it's ideal for US recon troops protecting the flag against RU attackers.

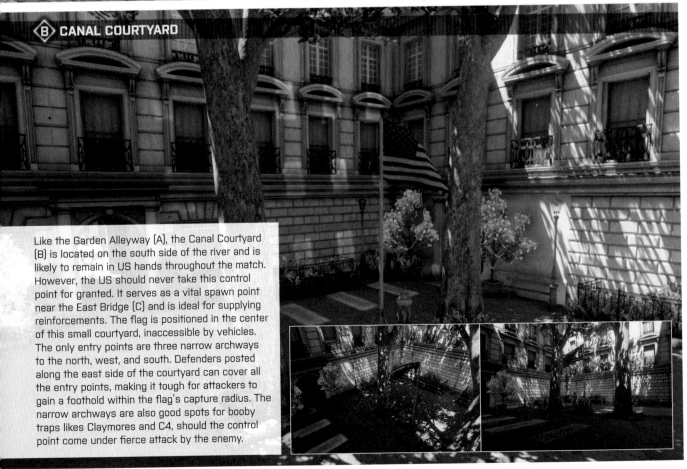

B CANAL COURTYARD

Like the Garden Alleyway (A), the Canal Courtyard (B) is located on the south side of the river and is likely to remain in US hands throughout the match. However, the US should never take this control point for granted. It serves as a vital spawn point near the East Bridge (C) and is ideal for supplying reinforcements. The flag is positioned in the center of this small courtyard, inaccessible by vehicles. The only entry points are three narrow archways to the north, west, and south. Defenders posted along the east side of the courtyard can cover all the entry points, making it tough for attackers to gain a foothold within the flag's capture radius. The narrow archways are also good spots for booby traps likes Claymores and C4, should the control point come under fierce attack by the enemy.

The East Bridge (C) is the most hotly contested flag on the map; it's likely to be the focal point the heaviest action. Strategically, the flag here is of vital importance to both teams, often giving them the majority of the control points necessary to bleed the opposing team's ticket count. At the start of the round, each team should race to this location with their vehicles in an attempt to gain control. But an early capture is the easy part. Defending the bridge from constant attack is a challenge. The flag is located on the west side of the bridge, surrounded by a low sandbag wall. The sandbags provide great protection while capturing or converting the flag, as long as you remain prone. Vehicles parked nearby can also enter the flag's capture radius. But vehicles are likely to take heavy fire when positioned here. Consider parking your vehicles on the north or south side of the river and provide fire support while infantry move in to perform the capture. There is a guard tower next to the flag, but don't bother getting inside—you'll only silhouette yourself and be an easy target for snipers. It's much better to stay low, using the sandbags and bridge's stone guardrails for cover. Smoke is also a huge asset here, particularly when attacking. So use mortars or grenade launchers to saturate the bridge with smoke before attempting to rush the flag.

◇D◇ MARKET AVENUE

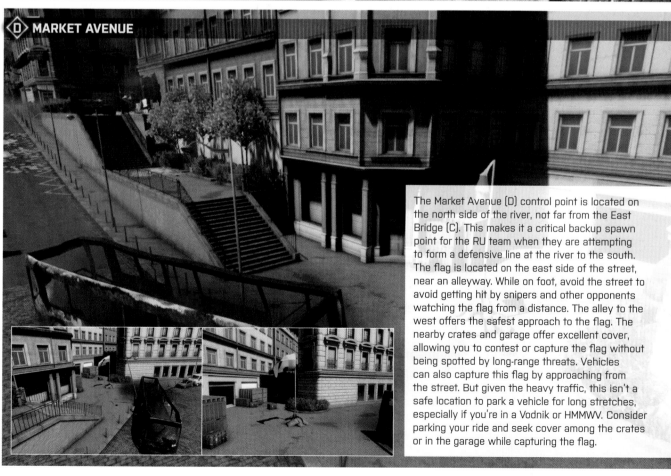

The Market Avenue (D) control point is located on the north side of the river, not far from the East Bridge (C). This makes it a critical backup spawn point for the RU team when they are attempting to form a defensive line at the river to the south. The flag is located on the east side of the street, near an alleyway. While on foot, avoid the street to avoid getting hit by snipers and other opponents watching the flag from a distance. The alley to the west offers the safest approach to the flag. The nearby crates and garage offer excellent cover, allowing you to contest or capture the flag without being spotted by long-range threats. Vehicles can also capture this flag by approaching from the street. But given the heavy traffic, this isn't a safe location to park a vehicle for long stretches, especially if you're in a Vodnik or HMMWV. Consider parking your ride and seek cover among the crates or in the garage while capturing the flag.

⬡Ε BACK STREETS

This control point is closest to the RU Base and thus is likely to remain under the RU team's control throughout the match, especially if they lock down the bridges to the south and prevent the US team from accessing the north side of the map. However, breakouts are likely to occur, meaning the RU team should prepare for attacks on the Back Streets (E). Located in a wide alley, the flag can be approached from multiple directions, but only on foot—vehicles cannot access this area. The red shipping container north of the flag is a popular hiding spot for attackers attempting to convert the flag. So if the flag is being contested, fire a rocket or toss a grenade into the shipping container to root out attackers. The steps to the west provide an elevated view of the flag, ideal for RU defenders approaching from the RU Base. Hold here to gun down enemies approaching from the river or the Market Avenue (D) control point.

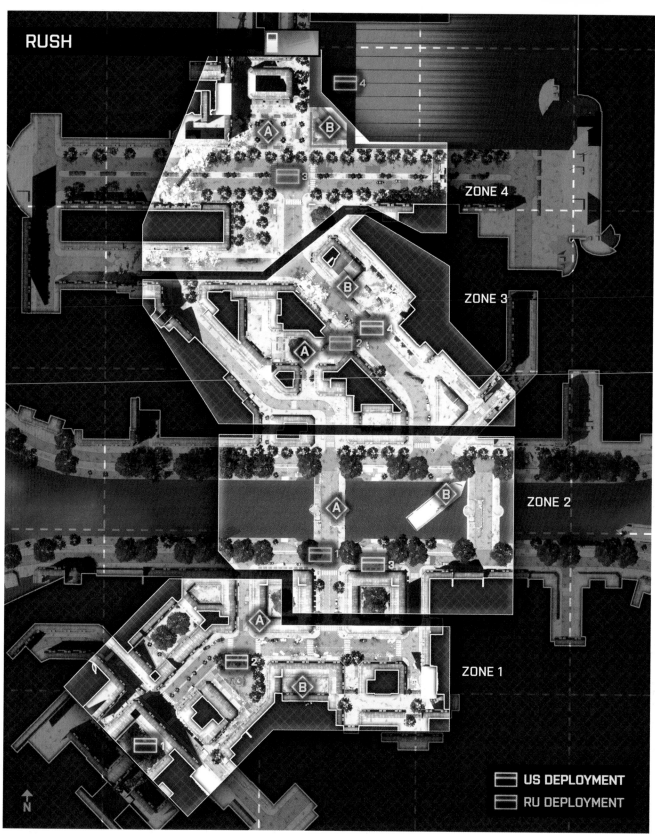

RUSH

ZONE 4

ZONE 3

ZONE 2

ZONE 1

US DEPLOYMENT

RU DEPLOYMENT

In this Rush battle, the US team advances through the streets of Paris in a drive to destroy eight M-COM stations scattered across four zones. The assault starts in the south and eventually crosses the Seine before heading north toward the bank plaza. The US team has access to an LAV-25 throughout the duration of the match, which gives them a slight advantage. But the LAV-25 must be deployed wisely to prevent it from becoming nothing more than a flaming wreck. In each zone, there is one objective where the LAV-25 can't support the US advance directly, leaving it up to infantry to fight it out. It's in these areas where the RU team has the best chance of holding out for a victory. Regardless of whether you're attacking or defending, prepare for some intense urban combat. As usual, make an effort to avoid the streets. Instead, utilize the less traveled side alleyways to approach the objectives from unpredictable directions.

ZONE 1: SOUTHERN STREETS

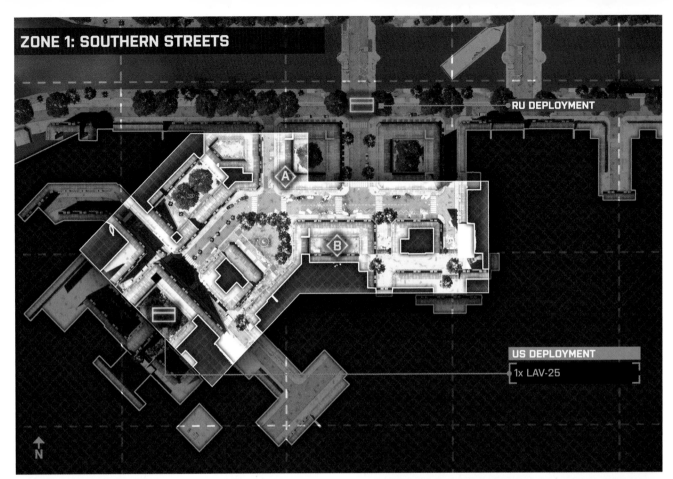

RU DEPLOYMENT

US DEPLOYMENT

1x LAV-25

N

A M-COM STATION A

B M-COM STATION B

M-COM Station A is housed within a corner store on the west side of the street. RU defenders posted here should expect heavy action as the LAV-25 attacks from the south end of the street. While the LAV-25 can blow holes in the walls of the store, it can't damage the M-COM station. But in terms of providing fire support, the LAV-25 is absolutely deadly. So RU defenders posted here must take out the LAV-25 as quickly as possible. After destroying the LAV-25, the RU team must secure the area around the store, while being sure to watch the street to the south as well as the adjacent narrow street to the west. When playing as the US, the LAV-25 is key to securing the area around the store. Park the LAV-25 to the south and use it to bombard the RU team's positions while infantry advance along the street toward the store. Always toss grenades into the store before entering to kill any defenders hiding near the M-COM station. Once a charge has been set, prepare for the RU counterattack approaching from the north.

This objective is situated in an enclosed alley on the opposite side of the street from M-COM Station A. There is no vehicle access here, so the RU defenders don't have to worry about the LAV-25 providing direct fire support for the attackers. The narrow passages leading into this alley serve the defenders well, allowing them to focus their fire on these choke points to gun down their opponents. The southwestern passage is the most common entry point for the attackers and should be covered at all times. The objective can also be watched from the small garage on the south side of the alley. This is a good hiding spot for attackers and defenders alike. But gaining access to this alley proves the most difficult part for the US team. While it's possible to push through the southwestern passage, look for flanking opportunities and try to attack from the north or west to catch the defenders off guard.

Base Assets		
NAME		LAV-25
QUANTITY		1
RESPAWN TIME		120 sec.

The US team begins the battle in the narrow streets and alleys on the southern tip of the map. The LAV-25 spawned here is extremely useful in supporting the advance toward the objectives to the north. Instead of using it to charge headlong into throngs of RU troops, position it on the street south of the objectives and provide fire support from a distance. The LAV-25's auto-cannon and machine gun turret are great for suppressed defenders positioned around M-COM Station A. But the IFV is likely to take a lot of fire, so make sure some engineers are nearby to constantly repair it. Even if the LAV-25 doesn't score many kills, it serves as a useful enemy distraction, allowing friendly troops to approach the objectives. If the LAV-25 is destroyed, it takes a full two minutes for it to respawn. So use this vehicle wisely to give your team the upper hand during this advance.

RU DEPLOYMENT

The RU team spawns near the western bridge spanning the Seine, just north of the objectives. This doesn't give them much time to reach the objectives before the US troops do. And with no vehicles at their disposal, the RU defenders must sprint toward the objectives in an effort to form a defensive line. Division of labor is very important in this first stage, as the objectives must be covered by two distinct groups. Those defending M-COM Station A should prepare to deal with the US team's LAV-25; engineers armed with anti-tank weapons are essential. M-COM Station B is more isolated and is best defended by infantry armed with close-quarters weapons like carbines and shotguns. So before the round begins, decide which objective your squad will defend and choose your class and weapons accordingly.

ZONE 2: RIVER

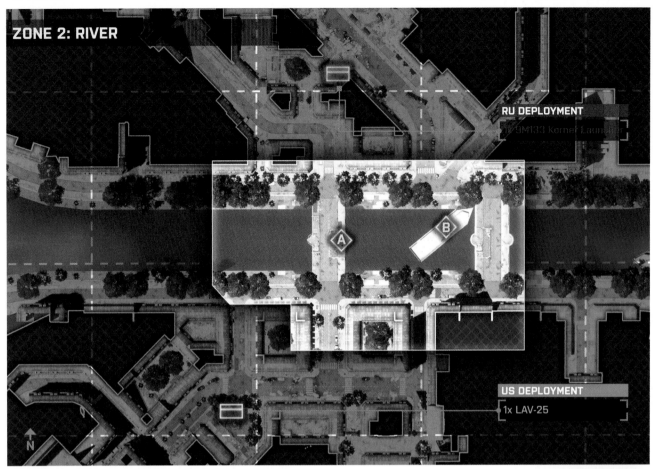

RU DEPLOYMENT

9M133 Kornet Launcher

US DEPLOYMENT

1x LAV-25

N

A M-COM STATION A

B M-COM STATION B

M-COM Station A is located on the heavily fortified west bridge, surrounded by a low sandbag wall and several crates. If the US team rushes this objective early, they have a chance of securing the bridge before the RU team can get into position. So load up some troops in the LAV-25 and assault this objective aggressively. However, if the RU team reaches this position first, they have a good chance of holding back the US assault. Defenders should quickly mine the south side of the bridge to prevent rushes by the LAV-25. Meanwhile, defenders hiding among the crates and sandbags can easily take attackers by surprise as they race toward the M-COM station. Consider placing a Radio Beacon within the green shipping container by the objective to give your squad a presence on this bridge. Once the bridge is locked down by the RU defenders, the US team's best chance is to wear them down by attacking with the LAV-25 from a safe distance. Suppressing the RU troops at the bridgecan give infantry the opening they need to reach the objective and plant a charge.

This objective is located within the listing ferry near the East Bridge. While the US team's LAV-25 can't approach or even fire at the ferry, it can help the attackers by securing the area around the East Bridge. There are only a few ways to access the ferry. For the attackers, the easiest way to hop onboard is by jumping off the west side of the East Bridge and landing on top of the ferry. Whenever possible, avoid swimming to the ferry, as it leaves you open to attack with no way to defend yourself. If you want to keep your feet dry, the northern riverbank offers the easiest way to hop onboard. While simply reaching the ferry presents challenges for the US team, defending this objective isn't much easier. Obviously, holding the East Bridge is the best way to control traffic in this area as well as in the river below. But the RU team must also post defenders along the riverbanks as well as within the ferry itself to sufficiently lock down M-COM Station B. If you find yourself stuck in the river, use the ladders along the riverbanks to climb out of the water.

	Base Assets	
NAME		LAV-25
QUANTITY		1
RESPAWN TIME		120 sec.

Having destroyed the first two objectives, the US now deploys from the small plaza across the street from the store. Once again, the LAV-25 is the most valuable asset in the next advance toward the objectives at the river. As in the previous stage, use the LAV-25 as a stand-off weapons platform to hammer the defenders posted around M-COM Station A on the west bridge. But avoid driving onto the bridge itself, as it may be mined or booby-trapped with C4. It's best to hold on the south side of the riverbank and provide fire support from a safe distance. Make an effort to destroy M-COM Station A before going after M-COM Station B in the ferry to the east. This allows your team to use the west bridge as an overwatch position that is ideal for covering the advance on the second objective.

RU DEPLOYMENT

	Base Assets	
NAME		9M133 Kornet Launcher
QUANTITY		1
RESPAWN TIME		45 sec.

After losing their foothold on the south side of the river, the RU team deploys from an alley to the north. This time the defenders have a few extra seconds to reach the objectives along the river before the US team can advance. Reinforcing M-COM Station A on the west bridge is the most critical, as it's likely to come under attack first. So move engineers to the west bridge to prepare for the impending US attack, which most likely will be led by their LAV-25. Defending M-COM Station B is equally important, so get troops near the ferry by the East Bridge. Controlling traffic along both bridges is critical to securing these objectives. So position troops on the north side of the river and focus your fire on these narrow choke points to halt the US team's advance. Booby-trapping the bridges with mines, C4, and Claymores is also very effective.

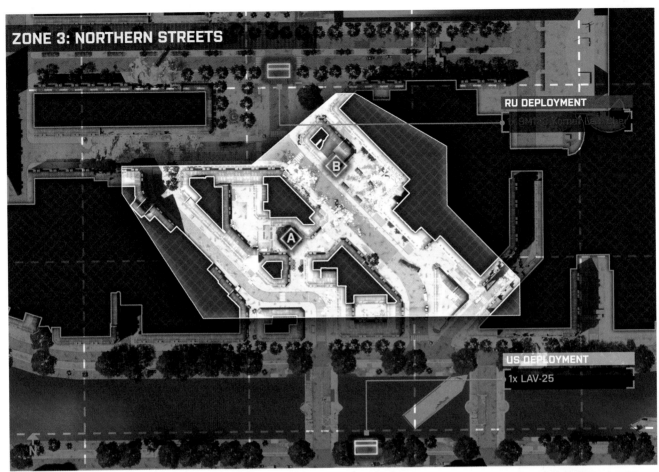

RU DEPLOYMENT

US DEPLOYMENT
1x LAV-25

A M-COM STATION A

M-COM Station A is located in the Back Streets area, housed within the red shipping container. When spawning at their deployment area, the RU defenders can reach this area quickly by rushing through the alley to the north. This gives them an elevated view of the shipping container and they can easily pick off attackers approaching from the south. Both ends of the shipping container are open, but attackers are most likely to enter from the east. So consider placing C4 or Claymores near this entry point. When attacking this location, try to approach from the alleys to the south and east, preferably after M-COM Station B has been destroyed. RU defenders and reinforcements are most likely to hold the high ground to the west. Securing the northern alley is the only way to effectively secure the Back Streets, so consider staging a flanking attack from this direction. When approaching the shipping container, always toss grenades inside before entering to detonate booby traps and eliminate any defenders waiting inside. Once the charge is set, prepare to fend off counterattacks in the northern alley.

B M-COM STATION B

This objective is located inside the small corner store on the northwest end of Monument Square. The wide street to the south allows the US team's LAV-25 to approach and bombard the area around the objective, so defenders must find suitable cover. The Kornet launcher on the south side of the square has a great view of the street, so don't forget to use it to destroy the approaching LAV-25. There are plenty of good hiding spots around Monument Square that are useful for both attackers and defenders. On the northeast side of the square is a second-story window that is ideal for covering the southern side of the store. There are also upper-story windows across the street to the southwest, where sharpshooters can cover the street approach—this is an excellent overwatch position for US troops, so consider planting a Radio Beacon here. Given the numerous hiding spots, attacking this objective is always dangerous. So utilize smoke and covering fire from the LAV-25 to safely reach the store and plant the charge. Defenders may be hiding inside, so always toss a grenade through a window before rushing to the M-COM station.

Base Assets

NAME	LAV-25
QUANTITY	1
RESPAWN TIME	120 sec.

Although the US team has destroyed the objectives at the river, they still deploy on the south side. They are forced to cross one of the two bridges to reach the objectives to the north. At the start of this stage, prepare to deal with a few RU stragglers loitering around the bridges. Quickly sweep the area for any surviving defenders before advancing toward the objectives. The LAV-25 deploys near the west bridge, but is best used by advancing across the East Bridge and making a push toward M-COM Station B. As in the previous zones, use the LAV-25 to pound Monument Square from a distance while infantry move in to plant the charge on the objective. But the LAV-25 is of little use against M-COM Station A—infantry alone must enter the Back Streets where this objective is located.

RU DEPLOYMENT

Base Assets

NAME	9M133 Kornet Launcher
QUANTITY	1
RESPAWN TIME	45 sec.

In the third stage of the battle, the RU team deploys near the intersection south of the bank. Get engineers to M-COM station B by Monument square as quickly as possible—this is the site most likely to come under attack by the US team's LAV-25. But don't neglect M-COM Station A in the Back Streets. This objective is closest to the US deployment area and likely to be rushed by infantry. As in the previous zones, the environments surrounding each objective are different and require different tactics. While defenders in Monument Square are best served by assault rifles, sniper rifles, and anti-tank weapons, the troops in the Back Streets are most effective when armed with close-quarters weapons like carbines, submachine guns, and shotguns. So figure out where you're going to defend before choosing your gear.

ZONE 4: BANK PLAZA

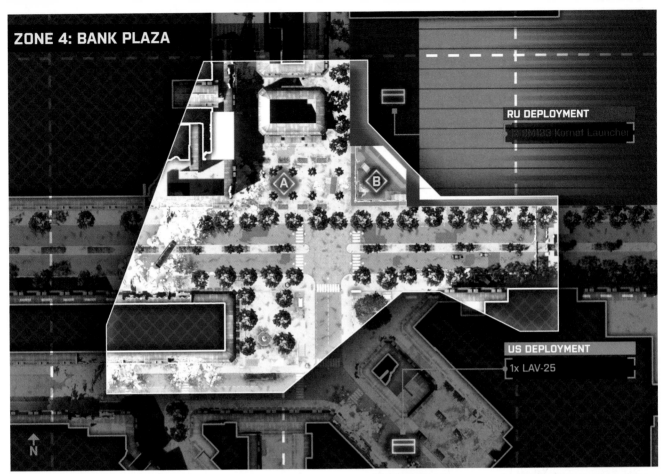

RU DEPLOYMENT

1x M133 Kornet Launcher

US DEPLOYMENT

1x LAV-25

N

A M-COM STATION A

B M-COM STATION B

Located in the plaza outside the bank, M-COM Station A offers little cover for attackers attempting to set a charge. Once again, the attackers must rely on their LAV-25 to distract and suppress the RU defenders posted around this objective. With some careful maneuvering, it's possible to drive the LAV-25 onto the plaza and park it right next to the M-COM station. Then, infantry can use the vehicle as a shield while setting the charge. The LAV-25 may not last long in such attacks, but at least its wreckage stays behind to serve as cover. If the LAV-25 isn't available or can't move into position, always deploy smoke on the objective before attempting to set the charge. The RU defenders can effectively lock down this location by hiding along the perimeter of the plaza. If manpower allows, a forward defensive line to the south can also hamper the US advance as they rush along the street from their deployment area. Patrol the square across the street to the southwest, too, as this is a popular staging area for US troops.

Because it is located only a few meters from the RU deployment area at the back of the bank, the RU team has a good chance of holding out by defending this objective. M-COM Station B sits on the floor of the bank's lobby, surrounded by crates and large stone planters. The objects around the objective make it difficult for defenders to gain a long sight line here, so they should prepare to deal with attacking troops at close range. There are two entry points into the bank. The most obvious is the main entrance. The steps leading up to the main entrance are lined with sandbags, which offer decent cover for defenders posted here. There is also a side entrance on the west side of the bank that is accessible from the plaza. This narrow entrance is less likely to be guarded and provides easy access onto the lobby floor via a short flight of steps. Always toss grenades around the objective to eliminate defenders hiding nearby before attempting to set a charge. Once a charge is set, ambush defenders rushing out of the corridor to the north while waiting for the M-COM station to explode.

US DEPLOYMENT

Victory is close, but the US team still has two more objectives to destroy before they can celebrate. During this final stage of the battle, the US attackers deploy from Monument Square. The streets and intersection south of the bank plaza are wide open, offering very little cover for US troops. Once again, rely on the LAV-25 to serve as a distraction while troops infiltrate the plaza from the west. The small square across the street from the plaza serves as a good staging area for the US team, so consider placing Radio Beacons here to give your squads a spawn point near the action. While the LAV-25 can help suppress defenders posted around M-COM Station A in the plaza, US infantry must enter the bank building on their own to knock out M-COM Station B. If possible, try to take out M-COM Station B first. Otherwise the RU team will have an easy time defending it, given its close proximity to their deployment area inside the bank.

RU DEPLOYMENT

For the final stage of the battle, the RU team must hold out at the bank plaza. Deploying from within a rear corridor in the bank, the RU team has just enough time to prepare for the US team's assault. Get troops out of the bank and around the plaza to the west to defend M-COM Station A. But don't leave the bank's interior undefended either, as this is where M-COM Station B is located. Engineers and troops armed with intermediate- to long-range weapons are best posted in the plaza to deal with the LAV-25 and the US infantry advancing along the street to the south. Close-quarters weapons are ideal for defenders posted inside the bank. Attacks may come from the main entrance as well as from the side entrance to the west, so be sure to cover each entry point. Holding the plaza is tricky, but the RU team has a good chance of staging an upset by locking down the bank, thereby protecting M-COM Station B and securing a victory.

SQUAD RUSH

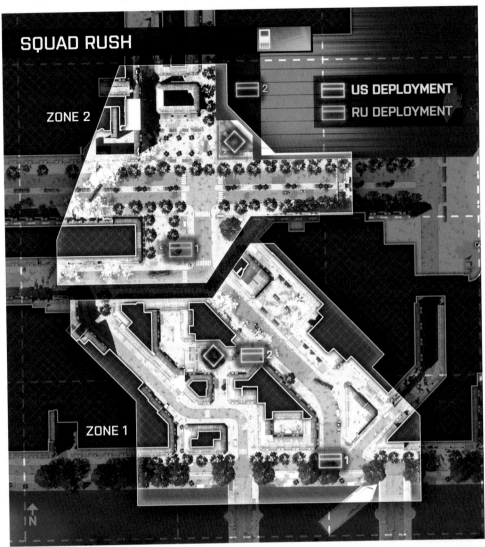

ZONE 2

ZONE 1

US DEPLOYMENT
RU DEPLOYMENT

N

Even in this condensed variant, this is a very large map for only eight players. So it's important that both teams remain focused on the objectives. Each M-COM station is located in a relatively cramped area that is ideal for small-scale firefights. So instead of equipping sniper rifles and assault rifles with high-powered scopes, consider bringing along carbines, shotguns, and submachine guns. These close-quarters weapons are best suited for the engagements surrounding each M-COM station. Defenders can add to the intensity by placing C4 and Claymores near the objectives.

ZONE 1: BACK STREETS

If you've played Rush mode, this Back Streets objective should look familiar. It's inside the red shipping container on the north side of this wide alley. Deploying from the street to the southeast, the US attackers are likely to enter this area from the east. As a result, defenders should watch the shipping container from the steps to the west. From this elevated position they can view attackers rushing in from the south or east. Instead of scattering about the nearby streets and alleys, the defenders are better off focusing their efforts around the objective. There is no easy way for the attackers to sneak in unseen, so either pick off all the defenders or deploy smoke to conceal your entry into the shipping container. But always toss a grenade into the container before entering to detonate any booby trap and eliminate any defenders hiding next to the objective.

ZONE 2: BANK

This objective is also carried over from the Rush mode; it is located within the bank. This is a relatively large building for a squad of four players to defend. Fortunately, there are only two entry points that, if properly defended, can prevent the US attackers from even stepping foot inside the bank. Post a couple of defenders near the main entrance, using the sandbags for cover. Also, make sure to have at least one defender cover the steps connected to the side entrance to the west. Finally, post one defender near the objective as a fail-safe. The US squad's best chance is sneaking in through the western side entrance. If the defenders leave this entry point unguarded, you can sneak up behind the defenders and steal their dog tags before setting a charge on the objective. The RU team deploys from the hall to the north, so expect a counterattack from this direction.

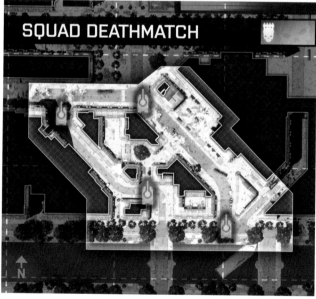

SQUAD DEATHMATCH

In this Squad Deathmatch, the map is restricted to the area around the Back Streets, Monument Square, and Market Avenue on the north side of the river. There are four possible IFV spawn points located along the perimeter streets. However, this is a dangerous map for vehicles given the numerous hiding spots for enemy engineers and support troops armed with C4. So if your squad gains access to an IFV, move to the northern street, turning your rear armor to the north and your front armor to the south. This allows you to fire down the western and eastern streets from an elevated position while protecting the vehicle's weak rear armor from flanking attacks. If your squad doesn't have the IFV, avoid the streets at all costs. Even if the IFV isn't present, the streets are likely to be covered by enemy sharpshooters. Instead, patrol the narrow streets and alleys on the perimeter. The Back Streets area in the center of the map acts as a hub that is frequently traveled by all squads. If your squad can hide here, you're bound to score dozens of kills that help to secure the lead.

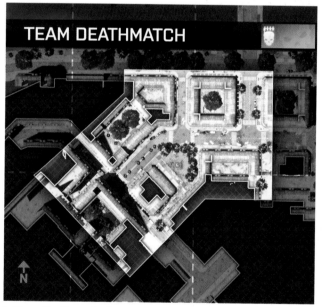

TEAM DEATHMATCH

In Team Deathmatch, the action takes place in the streets and alleyways on the south side of the river. Although there are no vehicles in this match, it's still a good idea to avoid the wide central street. The alleys and courtyards flanking the street offer a much safer route to move east and west. But don't expect these areas to be clear of threats. Opponents will likely use these perimeter paths to move around, too. So avoid sprinting and keep your weapon raised and ready to fire at all times. When working together with a small group of teammates, it's possible to defend some of the small alleys and courtyards on the perimeter of the map. These are high-traffic areas ideal for staging ambushes. Look for good hiding spots along the perimeter and engage the cross traffic to score some easy kills. Whether moving about or ambushing opponents from a fixed position, always stay within sight of at least one teammate so you can offer each other support. If you try to win this battle on your own, your frequent deaths will only aid the opposing team's score.

TEHRAN HIGHWAY

The battle for Iran's capital city is a complicated and bloody affair, often involving attacking forces overextending into enemy-held territory to achieve an important objective. This engagement along one of Tehran's major highways is no exception as the two armies vie for control over major access routes crossing the metropolitan area.

USMC forces are using the cover of darkness to make a push from the hills to attack the outskirts of the city. Farther ahead lies a disruptive MLRS site situated past the downtown area. The Russian forces are well prepared and have set up defensive positions along the main entrance points to the Capital. The ensuing clash will likely involve fierce, close-range street fighting where no position is safe from counterattack.

CONQUEST

US BASE
1x LAV-25
1x M1 Abrams

BACK YARD
1x M1114 HMMWV

TRUCK
1x M1114 HMMWV
1x GAZ-3937 Vodnik

GAS STATION
1x GAZ-3937 Vodnik

RU BASE
1x BMP-2M
1x T-90A

N

In this conquest battle, there are only three control points up for grabs, which makes defensive efforts around captured flags essential to securing a victory. Each team most hold at least two flags to initiate the drain on the opposing team's ticket counts. So instead of spreading your team thin, capture two flags and hold on to them. Deploying from the north, the US team should capture the Back Yard (A) and Truck (B). Meanwhile, the RU team should focus on holding the Gas Station (C) and Truck (B). Expect heavy fighting around the Truck (B) control point in the center of the map. If capturing or holding this flag becomes too costly, consider holding the two perimeter control points instead. Since the battle takes place at night, this is a very dark map. Vehicles equipped with the Thermal Optics upgrade have a huge advantage here, as this makes it easy to spot the heat signatures of enemy vehicles and troops. The IRNV (IR 1x) scope is also helpful for cutting through the darkness without giving away your position.

US BASE

Base Assets		LAV-25	M1 Abrams
	NAME	LAV-25	M1 Abrams
	QUANTITY	1	1
	RESPAWN TIME	30 sec.	60 sec.

The US team deploys from the base on the north side of the map, on the outskirts of the city. Although they're not the fastest vehicles, the M1 Abrams and LAV-25 spawned here are essential for securing the nearby Back Yard (A) and the more distant Truck (B) control points to the south. So as soon as the match begins, load the LAV-25 with troops and make a beeline for the Truck (B). The RU team may attempt the same maneuver, arriving in their BMP-2M, so be prepared for a fight while capturing the flag. The M1 Abrams and infantry spawned at the US Base have no problem reaching and securing the Back Yard (A) before the RU team can reach it. Leave at least one squad behind to watch the Back Yard (A) and move the rest of the team (including the M1 Abrams) toward the Truck (B) in an attempt to reinforce the LAV-25. If the M1 tank and LAV-25 are destroyed, don't forget to spawn back at the US Base to bring fresh vehicles to the front lines. Keeping the LAV-25 and M1 in the fight gives your team a huge advantage, especially if the RU team fails to bring their heavy hitters forward.

RU BASE

Base Assets		BMP-2M	T-90A
	NAME	BMP-2M	T-90A
	QUANTITY	1	1
	RESPAWN TIME	30 sec.	60 sec.

The bus depot on the south side of the map serves as the RU Base. The opening moments of the match are critical, with all three flags up for grabs. The BMP-2M and T-90A are your best chances for securing at least two of these flags. Quickly load the BMP-2M with infantry and race toward the Truck (B) control point in the center of the map. Troops deployed to the Truck (B) are likely to encounter the first resistance, so come prepared for a fight. Meanwhile, use infantry and the T-90A to secure the Gas Station (C) just north of the RU Base. But once the flag is captured, get the T-90A to the Truck (B) to help hold the control point from inevitable attacks by the US team. If the RU team can hold on to the Gas Station (C) and Truck (B), there is no need to advance on the Back Yard (A). Simply consolidate your forces around the two southern control points and don't forget to reinforce them with fresh vehicles spawned at the RU Base. The BMP-2M and T-90A provide a lot of firepower, so don't leave them sitting on the sidelines.

Control Point Assets

US CONTROL	RU CONTROL	RESPAWN TIME
M1114 HMMWV (1)	—	20 sec.

The Back Yard (A) control point is closest to the US Base, making it relatively easy for the US team to capture early on during the match. However, with only three control points on the map, the US team should never take this flag for granted. Once it's captured, at least one full-time squad should hold here and defend. A HMMWV is spawned here when the Back Yard is controlled by the US. Instead of using this vehicle to transport troops, consider using its machine gun turret to defend the road to the east—this is the most popular route for approaching vehicles. The road to the west is only accessible via a set of steps, which makes it the preferred approach by infantry attacking from the Truck (B). While the flagpole sits in the middle of an open area much like a parking lot, the flag has a large capture radius that allows it to be captured or contested from pieces of cover along the perimeter. So take cover behind the crates to the northeast or inside the garage to the south while attempting to capture the flag.

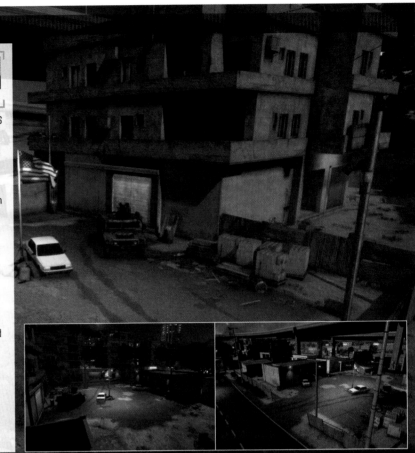

Control Point Assets

US CONTROL	RU CONTROL	RESPAWN TIME
M1114 HMMWV (1)	GAZ-3937 Vodnik (1)	20 sec.

As the central control point, the Truck (B) sees a lot of action throughout the course of the battle. Both teams should use the IFVs spawned at their bases to rush to this flag early during the match in an attempt to secure it. The flag is located on a road next to the flaming wreckage of a truck and overturned flatbed trailer. The truck, trailer, and spilled cargo all provide excellent cover for infantry within the flag's capture radius. But given the likelihood of vehicle traffic here, hiding near the flag isn't the safest defensive position. Almost all vehicles utilize the north/south approach of the road, while infantry are likely to filter in from the east and west, attacking from the Back Yard (A) and Gas Station (C). So instead of constantly spinning in circles, consider defending this flag from a distance. Elevated positions are available along both sides of the street to the east and west. The footbridge to the south provides an even better view of the control point . Vehicles defending here are best parked on the north or south sides of the flag, where they're less likely to be flanked by infantry approaching from the surrounding control points. Both the US and RU teams gain a light vehicle here, so put the machine gun turrets to use by targeting enemy infantry moving along the perimeter.

Control Point Assets

US CONTROL	RU CONTROL	RESPAWN TIME
—	GAZ-3937 Vodnik (1)	20 sec.

Located only a few meters north of the RU Base, the Gas Station (C) sits firmly within the RU team's zone of control. But in this chaotic fight, anything can happen. So after the RU team captures this flag early during the round, they should leave at least one squad behind to defend it. The Gas Station (C) is easily accessible by traveling along the road on the map's western edge—this is the only route vehicles can take to reach the flag. However, infantry attacks often come from the eastern steps, usually by infantry approaching from the Truck (B). Therefore, defenders here must prepare for attacks from both sides. The machine gun turret on the Vodnik, spawned here for the RU team, is great for covering both approaches. Consider parking it on the western road to deter vehicle attacks, or park it on the road to the east to counter infantry attacks. When capturing or contesting the flag here, stay far away from the explosive gas pumps. Instead, seek cover in or near the service station to the south. The interior of this small building offers a good view of the flag, making it a great defensive cover point.

CONQUEST 64

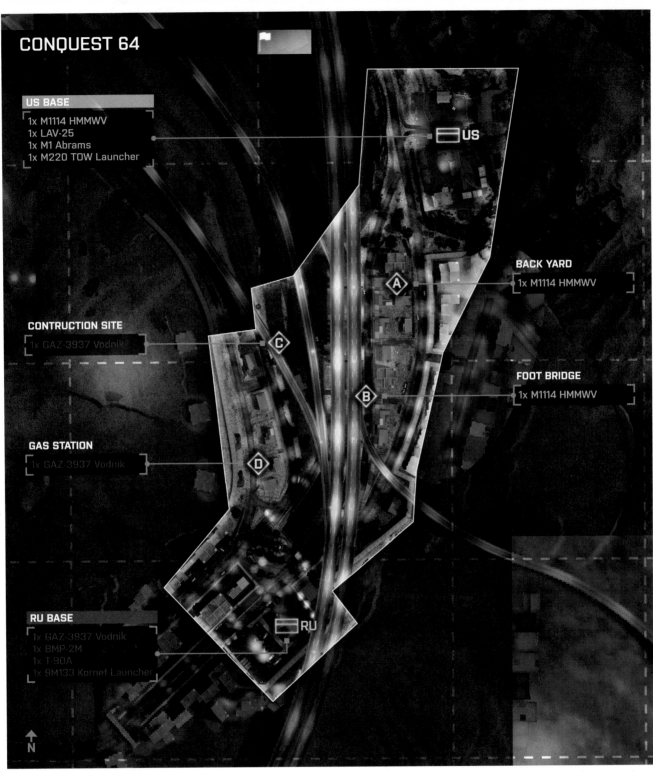

US BASE
1x M1114 HMMWV
1x LAV-25
1x M1 Abrams
1x M220 TOW Launcher

US

BACK YARD
1x M1114 HMMWV

Ⓐ

CONTRUCTION SITE
1x GAZ-3937 Vodnik

Ⓒ

FOOT BRIDGE
1x M1114 HMMWV

Ⓑ

GAS STATION
1x GAZ-3937 Vodnik

Ⓓ

RU BASE
1x GAZ-3937 Vodnik
1x BMP-2M
1x T-90A
1x 9M133 Kornet Launcher

RU

N

The Conquest 64 variant of Tehran Highway is exactly the same size as the standard Conquest version. However, there are four control points instead of three, offering more flags to fight over. With four flags up for grabs, each team must try to hold at least three to begin bleeding the opposing team's ticket count. The US team should focus their efforts around the Back Yard (A), Foot Bridge (B), and Construction Site (C). Meanwhile, the RU team should try to capture the Gas Station (D), Construction Site (C), and Foot Bridge (B). The centrally located Construction Site (C) and Foot Bridge (B) are likely to see the heaviest action. So move your team's tank and IFV (spawned back at your base) to these spots to help defend these flags. If the fight in the center of the map becomes too heated, consider flanking attacks against the Back Yard (A) or Gas Station (D). Just because these flags are near bases doesn't mean they're hard to capture. Despite the swarms of infantry racing around this map, it can still be tough to spot enemies due to the low light conditions. So consider choosing the Thermal Optics upgrade when selecting loadouts for your vehicles. When on foot, the IRNV (IR 1x) scope is a great way to zero in on the heat signatures of enemy troops and vehicles.

US BASE

Base Assets		M1114 HMMWV	LAV-25	M1 Abrams	M220 TOW Launcher
	NAME	M1114 HMMWV	LAV-25	M1 Abrams	M220 TOW Launcher
	QUANTITY	1	1	1	1
	RESPAWN TIME	20 sec.	60 sec.	90 sec.	60 sec.

As in the standard Conquest mode, the US team deploys from this base on the north side of the map. Considering the number of players in this battle, the three vehicles provided disappear fast. But instead of hopping in a vehicle and driving to some random control point, it's best to determine your destination based on the speed of the vehicle and distance to the flags. The HMMWV is the fastest vehicle and should race toward the distant Foot Bridge (B) at the start of the match. Send the LAV-25 to the Construction Site (C) while the M1 Abrams and infantry secure the nearby Back Yard (A). By deploying the vehicles in this fashion, your team has a good chance of snatching three flags at the start of the battle. But it takes reinforcements to hold these positions, especially the front line flags at the Foot Bridge (B) and Construction Site (C). So move troops and vehicles to these areas to support defensive efforts. The US Base supplies the only LAV-25 and M1 Abrams on this map, so don't forget to transport these valuable assets to the front line positions where they can make a difference.

RU BASE

Base Assets		GAZ-3937 Vodnik	BMP-2M	T-90A	9M133 Kornet Launcher
	NAME	GAZ-3937 Vodnik	BMP-2M	T-90A	9M133 Kornet Launcher
	QUANTITY	1	1	1	1
	RESPAWN TIME	20 sec.	60 sec.	90 sec.	60 sec.

Once again, the bus depot on the south side of the map serves as the RU Base, providing them with just enough vehicles to make a move on three of the four flags. Forget about trying to secure the Back Yard (A)—it's too far away and too close to the US Base. Instead, focus on the other three control points. But it takes speed and coordination to secure these control points before the US team can. Send the speedy Vodnik (filled with troops) to the Construction Site (C) while the BMP-2M advances on the Foot Bridge (B). The T-90A and troops spawned at the RU Base can secure the nearby Gas Station (D), but don't leave the tank there—it's needed to attack and defend the forward positions of the Construction Site (C) or Foot Bridge (B). With the exception of one or two squads left behind at the Gas Station (C) to defend, the rest of the team should focus on attacking and defending the two central flags throughout the duration of the match. The RU Base is the team's only source for a T-90A and a BMP-2M, so don't forget to bring these armored assets forward to counter the US team's vehicles.

◇A◇ BACK YARD

Control Point Assets

US CONTROL	RU CONTROL	RESPAWN TIME
M1114 HMMWV (1)	—	20 sec.

The Back Yard (A) control point is closest to the US Base so it is relatively easy for the US team to capture early on during the match. However, in a battle this crazy, the US team should never take this flag for granted. Once captured, at least one full-time squad should hold here and defend. A HMMWV is spawned here when controlled by the US. Instead of using this vehicle to transport troops, consider using its machine gun turret to defend the road to the east—this is the most popular route for approaching vehicles. The road to the west is accessible only via a set of steps, making it the preferred approach by infantry attacking from the Foot Bridge (B) or Construction Site (C). While the flagpole sits in the middle of an open area much like a parking lot, the flag has a large capture radius that allows it to be captured or contested from pieces of cover along the perimeter. So take cover behind the crates to the northeast or inside the garage to the south while attempting to capture the flag.

◇B◇ FOOT BRIDGE

Control Point Assets

US CONTROL	RU CONTROL	RESPAWN TIME
M1114 HMMWV (1)	—	20 sec.

Surrounded by the Gas Station (E) to the southwest, the Construction Site (C) to the northwest, and the Back Yard (A) to the northeast, the Foot Bridge (B) is a high-traffic area likely to change hands several times during the match. The flag here is located on the east side of the narrow bridge crossing over the nearby highway. With the flag so close to the road, this control point is best captured by tanks and IFVs capable of withstanding small arms fire. If you're on foot, don't huddle near the flag. Instead, get to the top of the bridge and drop prone on its eastern side. You can capture or contest the flag without exposing yourself to incoming fire. The street spanning the north/south approach has a long sight line that makes it a popular kill zone for snipers. Vehicles (like the HMMWV spawned here for the US) positioned at the northern and southern ends of this street can also score some long-range kills by using the zoom function on their machine gun turrets. This is a great way to cover the flag from a distance, but it might not be possible to see attackers on the bridge itself. Therefore it takes a squad to keep a close eye on the flag and the nearby bridge to deter sneaky infantry attacks. If attacks along the bridge persist, consider deploying Claymores or C4 within the capture radius.

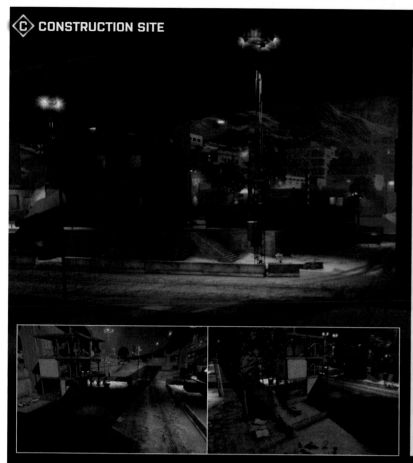

Control Point Assets

US CONTROL	RU CONTROL	RESPAWN TIME
—	GAZ-3937 Vodnik (1)	20 sec.

Like the Foot Bridge (B) to the west, the Construction Site (C) is another high-traffic central location likely to see plenty of action. If rushed early with a Vodnik, the RU team has a slight edge when it comes to capturing this flag first. Regardless of which team secures this control point first, don't leave it undefended. The flag is flanked by two large, partially constructed buildings to the north and south. Both buildings provide excellent overwatch positions. Recon troops posted on the upper floors or rooftops of these structures also have clear views of the areas around the Foot Bridge (B) to the east. So holding the Construction Site (C) only strengthens defenses around the Foot Bridge (B). While there are plenty of hiding spots around the flag for infantry, vehicles can also easily access the capture radius by entering the site from the roads to the east and west. But vehicles parked near the flag are vulnerable to attacks from the upper floors of the surrounding building, not to mention mines or C4 planted near the flagpole. So unless the enemy team has completely abandoned this flag, consider attacking on foot and start by sweeping the nearby buildings. The RU team gains an extra Vodnik here, which is useful for defense or launching speedy raids on the Gas Station (C) or Back Yard (A)—don't attack the Foot Bridge (B) with such a lightly armored vehicle.

Control Point Assets

US CONTROL	RU CONTROL	RESPAWN TIME
—	GAZ-3937 Vodnik (1)	20 sec.

Located only a few meters north of the RU Base, the Gas Station (D) sits firmly within the RU team's zone of control. But in this chaotic fight, anything can happen. So after the RU team captures this flag early during the round, they should leave at least one squad behind to defend it. The Gas Station (D) is easily accessible by traveling along the road on the map's western edge—this is the only route vehicles can take to reach the flag. However, infantry attacks often come from the eastern steps, usually by infantry approaching from the Foot Bridge (B) or Construction Site (C). Therefore, defenders here must prepare for attacks from both sides. The machine gun turret on the Vodnik, spawned here for the RU team, is great for covering both approaches. Consider parking it on the western road to deter vehicle attacks, or park it on the road to the east to counter infantry attacks. When capturing or contesting the flag here, stay far away from the explosive gas pumps. Instead, seek cover in or near the service station to the south. The interior of this small building offers a good view of the flag, so it is a great defensive cover point.

RUSH

ZONE 1

ZONE 2

ZONE 3

ZONE 4

US DEPLOYMENT

RU DEPLOYMENT

N

Set on the outskirts of Tehran, this conflict requires the US team to push through four urban zones during a night assault. The fight starts out on the north end of the map before trickling down through the city streets to the south. Although the US team has the most vehicles in each stage, these assets must be deployed wisely to avoid falling victim to ambushes staged by RU tanks and engineers. Despite the risks, a timid approach never fares well here for the US team. With some careful coordination, the US team must use the provided speed and firepower of these vehicles to overwhelm the defenders at each location. Meanwhile, the RU team must make the most of the limited resources provided. This means keeping their tanks fielded and constantly repaired. A RU team consisting largely of engineers has the best chance of stopping the US advance. Both teams can benefit from infrared technology in this night battle, so choose the Thermal Optics upgrade for vehicles and consider attaching a IRNV (IR 1x) scope to your weapon.

ZONE 1: HILLTOP BASE

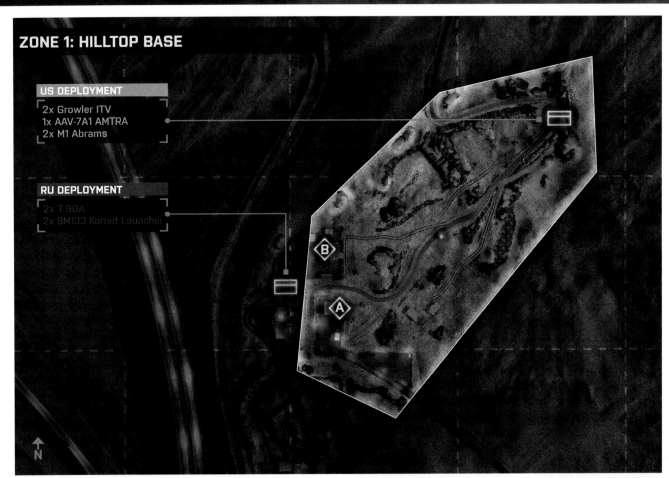

US DEPLOYMENT
2x Growler ITV
1x AAV-7A1 AMTRA
2x M1 Abrams

RU DEPLOYMENT
2x T-90A
2x 9M133 Kornet Launcher

N

Ⓐ **M-COM STATION A**

Ⓑ **M-COM STATION B**

M-COM Station A is located on the south side of the base, placed outside the northeast corner of a two-story concrete building. RU recon troops posted on the second floor of the building have a great view of the eastern approach; it is ideal for spotting and engaging incoming troops and vehicles. But the building can be completely leveled with sustained shelling by the US tanks. Attackers should not be deterred by the slabs of concrete, chain-link fence, and sandbags placed around this objective. The concrete can be destroyed with explosive munitions, the fence can be sliced open with a knife, and the sandbags can be jumped. In many respects, an attack from the east is the safest way to access this objective—it beats circling around the fence and attacking from the west. However, attackers should prepare to face defenders in the nearby building and narrow alleys adjacent to the M-COM station. So if the building is still standing, consider securing it before attempting to plant the charge.

This objective is positioned on the north side of the base, behind a small single-floor concrete building. Defenders have the best time watching this M-COM station from the north, as the building to the east and flatbed trailer to the west form a narrow alley that makes it difficult to spot the objective from any other angle. Given the tight confines around the objective, this narrow alley behind the building is a great spot for Claymores. To avoid exposing themselves to RU defenders approaching from their deployment area to the west, US attackers should advance through the building, infiltrating it from the east side. Consider dropping a Radio Beacon inside this structure to secure a spawn point for your squad before attempting to plant a charge on the objective. By blowing a hole in the west side of the building, from the interior, you can gain easy access to the objective without exposing yourself to fire from the south or west. Still, it's a good idea to deploy smoke on the objective to conceal yourself against attacks from the north.

US DEPLOYMENT

Base Assets	NAME	Growler ITV	AAV-7A1 AMTRAC	M1 Abrams
	QUANTITY	2	1	2
	RESPAWN TIME	5 sec.	30 sec.	60 sec.

The US team starts this battle by deploying on an arid hillside northeast of the objectives. The advance across the sparse landscape is extremely dangerous, so utilize the provided vehicles to transport troops into the base held by the RU team. The Growler ITVs are the fastest vehicles available, great for staging early raids on the objectives. However, these light vehicles are vulnerable to attacks by RU engineers and the two T-90As, so limit their use if the RU team forms a solid defensive line along the east side of the base. The two M1 Abrams are your team's best bet for punching through RU team's defensive line. So hold them to the east and engage the T-90As from long range, preferably with the Guided Shell upgrade. Although slow, the AMTRAC is great for moving infantry near the base. Park it behind some large rocks on the east side of the base and use it as a forward spawn point. The AMTRAC's machine gun turret is also great for suppressing RU infantry to the west.

RU DEPLOYMENT

Base Assets	NAME	T-90A	9M133 Kornet Launcher
	QUANTITY	2	2
	RESPAWN TIME	60 sec.	60 sec.

At the start of the match, the RU team has only a few seconds to spare before the US team comes rolling into the base. So don't waste anytime moving troops and the two T-90As to the east side of the base to counter the US assault. The dusty approach to the east provides little cover for the attackers, so try to confront the US team here before they can infiltrate the base. Initially, the speedy Growler ITVs pose the biggest threat because they are capable of transporting troops within the base. So be ready to blast these light vehicles with rockets and tank rounds. Carefully hunt down any survivors that escape. The T-90As and Kornet launchers are essential for knocking out the incoming M1 tanks and AMTRAC. Engineers can assist by firing rockets or by dropping mines along the base's eastern entry points. While forming a defensive line to the east is important, don't push too far away from the objectives. Keep at least two squads back inside the base to watch the objectives, defending them from sneaky flanking attacks by US infantry.

ZONE 2: DEPOT

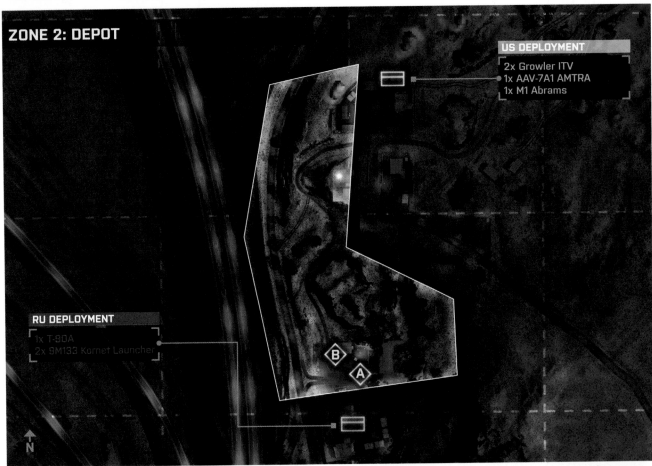

⟨A⟩ M-COM STATION A

⟨B⟩ M-COM STATION B

M-COM Station A is located in the depot's northeast corner. If properly defended, this can be a tough objective for the attackers to destroy given the lack of cover and numerous hiding spots around the perimeter. Defenders should prepare for US troops rushing down the hill to the north. A forward line of defenders posted along the hill can slow such attacks. But it's important to post defenders around the objective, too. The truck and trailer on the south side of the objective provides great cover and concealment for defenders. Consider lying prone beneath the trailer to pick off attackers dropping down into the depot. Hiding on the north side of the depot is also effective; you can hit attackers from behind as they drop down into the depot and rush toward the M-COM station. If infantry attacks from the hill are unsuccessful, the US team must rely on their vehicles to help secure the area around the objective. Both the M1 and AMTRAC can make a serious dent in the defensive efforts here, buying infantry enough time to set a charge on the M-COM station.

This objective is located on the depot's northwest corner within a small concrete building. The dirt road to the west is a popular avenue of attack for the US team, they deploy troops and heavy firepower here. Therefore the RU defenders must counter by positioning their T-90A within view of this road. RU engineers can also assist by attacking incoming vehicles with rockets and mines at this northwestern choke point. But the defenders must also prepare for infantry rushing down the hillside to the north. Initially, there are only two entrances into the building housing the M-COM station. But instead of using these entrances, attackers should blow a hole in the northern wall of the structure to get easy access to the objective. This way, the US troops can infiltrate the building without exposing themselves to defenders (and the T-90A) posted near the center of the depot. The RU team should constantly watch the north side of this building to prevent such sneak attacks.

US DEPLOYMENT

Base Assets	NAME	Growler ITV	AAV-7A1 AMTRAC	M1 Abrams
	QUANTITY	2	1	1
	RESPAWN TIME	20 sec.	30 sec.	60 sec.

With the first set of the M-COM stations destroyed, the US team now deploys from the hilltop base in preparation for their assault on the depot to the south. There are two main approaches to the depot. Infantry moving directly south can sneak into the depot's north side by attacking from the hilltop. However, by moving along the high ground, you may silhouette yourself and make it easy for RU defenders below to spot you. So stay low and utilize the large rocks for cover. Vehicles spawned here should use the road to the west to attack the depot. There is a sharp turn in the road as you descend the hill, so watch your speed. The M1 Abrams and AMTRAC attacking along this road serve as a welcome distraction to troops descending the hill. So use the vehicles to attack from the west side of the depot while troops push in from the north. If possible, park the AMTRAC near the northwest corner of the depot and use it to spawn troops near M-COM Station B.

RU DEPLOYMENT

Base Assets	NAME	T-90A	9M133 Kornet Launcher
	QUANTITY	1	2
	RESPAWN TIME	60 sec.	60 sec.

After being pushed off their hilltop base, the RU team deploys on the south side of this depot. There are only a few seconds to spare before the US team comes racing down the hill, so it's important to secure the objectives on the north side of the depot. Deploy the T-90A so it can counter vehicles approaching along the roads to the north and west. This is the only tank provided to the RU team here, so keep it repaired with a team of engineers. Engineers can assist the tank by targeting incoming vehicles with rockets or by placing mines along the depot's northwestern entry points. While the T-90A covers the roads, position infantry on the hillside to the north and east to ambush US troops rushing toward the objectives. Expect large waves of US attackers to come charging down the hill, dropping down into the depot from the north. Constantly patrol the north side of the depot to search for attackers.

ZONE 3: HIGHWAY

US DEPLOYMENT
1x Growler ITV
1x AAV-7A1 AMTRA
1x M1 Abrams

RU DEPLOYMENT
1x T-90A
2x 9M133 Kornet Launcher

N

A) M-COM STATION A

M-COM Station A is located in the neighborhood on the east side of the highway, sitting outside a small concrete building. The street to the east of the objective is directly connected to the depot to the north, giving US attackers easy access to this location from their deployment area. Therefore, the RU defenders must gather around this objective to prevent rush attacks. The Kornet launcher here has a clear view of the northern approach and is ideal for targeting incoming vehicles. But attacking infantry may push through the neighboring buildings to the north as well, avoiding the long sight lines of the eastern street. This is the preferred method of attack when approaching this objective on foot. When possible, try to occupy the building directly west of the objective. From inside, you can blow a hole in the wall just behind the objective and access the M-COM station from the rear to plant a charge. This is a great way to avoid exposing yourself to defenders positioned in the courtyard and street to the east.

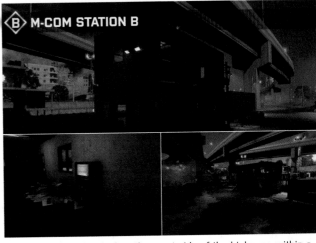

B) M-COM STATION B

This objective is located on the west side of the highway, within a trailer by the Construction Site. The street to the east is the most popular avenue of attack, so defenders should watch this approach at all times. The Kornet launcher here is well positioned to target vehicles approaching from the north. The RU team may also want to consider parking their T-90A along this street to counter vehicle and infantry attacks. While the eastern street offers the quickest path to the objective for the attackers, it is not the safest. Instead, try to flank the objective from the west. There's a short flight of steps on this side of the trailer that infantry can use to sneak up on the objective. If you prefer a more direct assault, use the M1 Abrams and AMTRAC to aggressively attack the area around the trailer. This is a great way to distract the surrounding defenders, allowing infantry to infiltrate the trailer and set a charge on the M-COM station.

US DEPLOYMENT

Base Assets	NAME	Growler ITV	AAV-7A1 AMTRAC	M1 Abrams
	QUANTITY	1	1	1
	RESPAWN TIME	20 sec.	30 sec.	60 sec.

In this stage of the battle, the US team deploys from the depot. Before moving out, work to secure the depot and hunt down any RU stragglers hiding in this sprawling facility. Also, don't let the RU defenders escape with their T-90A here, otherwise they'll have two tanks they can use to defend the next set of objectives. Once the depot is secure, move out toward M-COM Station A. Instead of splitting your forces and attacking both objectives simultaneously, overwhelm the defenders at M-COM Station A with your full team, attacking aggressively with the M1 Abrams and AMTRAC to secure the area while infantry plant a charge. After destroying M-COM Station A, leave the AMTRAC nearby to serve as a mobile spawn point for troops attacking M-COM Station B to the west. This is a great staging area for the attack, allowing troops to flank the next objective from the south.

RU DEPLOYMENT

Base Assets	NAME	T-90A	9M133 Kornet Launcher
	QUANTITY	1	2
	RESPAWN TIME	60 sec.	60 sec.

Spawning along the highway, south of the objectives, the RU team has some significant ground to cover if they hope to reach the M-COM stations before the US team. Surviving RU troops loitering at the depot can buy defenders some time by harassing the US team at their new deployment area. This allows the defenders to secure both objectives before the US team can launch an attack. Consider deploying the T-90A along the highway between the two objectives. From this location it can target vehicles racing down the roads to the north. The eastern road by M-COM Station A is also a good spot for the tank, as it help secure the objective's eastern flank by engaging incoming traffic to the north. In any case, defenders should expect armored vehicle attacks at both objectives and prepare accordingly. Engineers armed with rocket launchers and mines are ideal for countering these threats.

ZONE 4: BUS DEPOT

US DEPLOYMENT
- 1x Growler ITV
- 1x AAV-7A1 AMTRA
- 1x M1 Abrams

RU DEPLOYMENT
- 1x T-90A
- 2x 9M133 Kornet Launcher

N

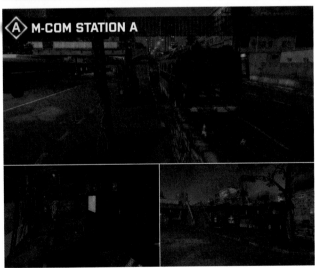

Ⓐ M-COM STATION A

Sandwiched between a bus and a bus stop shelter, M-COM Station A can be a tough objective both to attack and to defend. However, the various hiding spots at the bus depot definitely favor the RU defenders; they can pick off US infantry attempting to access this narrow choke point. This is obviously a great spot for booby traps like Claymores and C4. The foot bridge to the southwest offers the best elevated vantage point of the bus depot as well as the objective. So before approaching the M-COM station, attackers should make an effort to sweep the nearby foot bridge to eliminate any defenders. Securing both ends of the bus stop is important, too. If any doubts persist, deploy smoke at the bus stop before attempting to set a charge.

Ⓑ M-COM STATION B

M-COM Station B is inside a small garage-like structure west of the bus depot. The property is surrounded by a high stone wall, but this can easily be breached by attackers. So when attacking this site, use the M1 Abrams or rockets fired by engineers to bring down this perimeter wall for easy access to the objective. Eliminating this wall also denies the defenders cover and opens sight lines to the objective. When possible, attack from the east side to catch the defenders off guard—blast a hole in the garage's eastern wall to set a charge on the back of the objective. Hiding within the perimeter wall won't help the RU defenders here. So establish a defensive line on the north side of the objective and pick off attackers that filter in from the US deployment area. The T-90A can be a huge help in locking down this location, but be ready to repair it as it's likely to take heavy damage from the attacking M1 Abrams, not to mention US engineers.

Base Assets	NAME	Growler ITV	AAV-7A1 AMTRAC	M1 Abrams
	QUANTITY	1	1	1
	RESPAWN TIME	20 sec.	30 sec.	60 sec.

For the final stage of this battle, the US team deploys on the west side of the highway near the Construction Site. At the earliest opportunity, use the Growler ITV spawned here to launch a raid on M-COM Station B to the south. By traveling along the road to the west, you can reach this objective quickly, possibly before RU defenders can. So waste no time blasting your way through the perimeter wall here and setting a charge on the objective. If the RU team manages to put up a fight here, attack with the full weight of your team, including the M1 Abrams and AMTRAC. Once M-COM Station B is destroyed, park the AMTRAC near the smoldering objective and use the armored vehicle as a mobile spawn point for your team's attack on M-COM Station A at the bus depot. Use your remaining vehicles and infantry to establish a perimeter around M-COM Station A before planting the final charge.

RU DEPLOYMENT

Base Assets	NAME	T-90A	9M133 Kornet Launcher
	QUANTITY	1	2
	RESPAWN TIME	60 sec.	60 sec.

This is the end of the line for the RU team. Securing a victory here hinges on holding out at the final two objectives positioned near the bus depot. As usual, the RU team must make the most of their T-90A to hold off the onslaught of US vehicles and infantry. Consider positioning the tank along the street north of M-COM Station B to counter raids by vehicles approaching from the US deployment area. This objective is most likely to come under attack first, so get the tank here as quickly as possible at the beginning of the stage. But don't neglect M-COM Station A, either. Fortunately, defenders can use plenty of sneaky hiding spots at the bus depot to prevent the US attackers from setting a charge on M-COM Station A. Although the RU deployment area isn't far away, consider placing Radio Beacons near each objective to give your team spawn points closer to the action. But don't forget to spawn back at the deployment area if the T-90A is destroyed—bring a freshly spawned tank to the front lines as soon as possible.

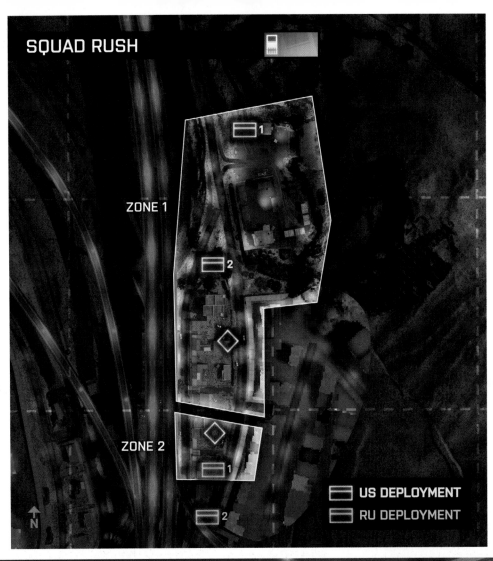

SQUAD RUSH

ZONE 1

ZONE 2

US DEPLOYMENT
RU DEPLOYMENT

N

During the Squad Rush match, the action is limited to the small neighborhood on the east side of the map. While long-range combat is a possibility along the street to the east, it's wisest for the attacking team to avoid this route, as it's most likely being watched by the defending squad. Whether attacking or defending, your squad doesn't need more than one sniper. Most of the action occurs at close quarters among the buildings, alleys, and yards at the center of the map. Assault troops and engineers armed with carbines, shotguns, and submachine guns all fare well in these close-quarters engagements. Attackers may want to bring along some smoke, too, which is useful for obscuring the objectives while planting charges.

ZONE 1: BACK YARD

The Back Yard is the site of this skirmish, as the US squad attempts to destroy the M-COM station inside the garage. Deploying from the depot to the north, the US team should avoid advancing along the street to prevent being spotted and picked off by RU defenders posted near the objective. Instead, cut through the buildings and alleyways on the west side of the street. When the garage is within view, instead of rushing toward the objective, circle around the south side of the structure to sweep the area for defenders. Always assume defenders are hiding in the garage, so toss grenades inside before approaching the objective. When defending this position, don't move too far away from the objective. Establish a perimeter around the garage and always make sure the south side is monitored to prevent sneak attacks from the rear. The roof of the garage is accessible via the staircase next to the objective. The roof provides a great view of the eastern street as well as the open area on the north side of the garage—this spot can serve attackers as well while defending the charge on the objective. But if you're on the roof, remain prone to avoid silhouetting yourself.

ZONE 2: TRADING CO.

The next objective is in the same neighborhood as the Back Yard on the east side of the highway. This M-COM station is positioned inside a small garage within a commercial structure. The garage opens onto a wide courtyard and the objective is visible from the street to the east. The RU team can effectively lock down this location simply by covering this small garage from the perimeter of the courtyard. But cover is very sparse here, so stay low in an effort to conceal your position. It's a good idea to post at least a couple of squad members around the garage while the rest of the team covers the northern approach. Once again, attackers should avoid rushing down the street. The buildings and yards to the north offer much more protection, but they also serve as good ambush points for the defenders. So move through this area slowly with your weapon raised. When you reach the Trading Co. building, circle around the western and southern sides, performing a through sweep of the courtyard before approaching the objective. It may be necessary to kill the entire defending squad before it's safe to plant a charge on the M-COM station.

SQUAD DEATHMATCH

If you're familiar with the Conquest variants of Tehran Highway, you'll have an easier time getting your bearings in this chaotic match. The action here is restricted to the areas around the Back Yard, Truck, Foot Bridge, and Construction Site. While the highway makes up a large portion of this map, avoid this area if you're on foot. Three of the four potential IFV spawn locations are positioned along the highway—the fourth is on the north side of the map, near the depot. Given the wide roads and long sight lines, the IFV has an easy time operating along the highway. But if you're on foot, it's a good idea to stay within the neighborhood on the east side of the highway. This gives you a better chance to confront other squads at close to intermediate range. This neighborhood also sits on higher ground, so your squad fires down at opponents on the highway to the west.

TEAM DEATHMATCH

The combat zone in this map is similar to Squad Deathmatch, but now the highway area is off limits, restricting action to the small neighborhood to the east. So prepare for plenty of close-quarters, house-to-house fighting in the map's center. The long narrow streets on the east and west sides of the neighborhood offer flanking opportunities, but prepare to come under fire by recon opponents positioned to the north and south. Implementing a team strategy on this map is difficult due to the tight quarters. But make an effort to control either the northern or southern ends of the map. This allows your team to take advantage of the long sight lines along the streets to the east and west while occupying buildings in the center. Consolidating your team on one end of the map is a great way to overwhelm less organized teams consisting of small squads and lone-wolf players. So set up camp to the north or south and dig in. If your whole team can stick to the game plan, you have a strong chance of walking away with a win.

●● [CO-OP]

A CRASH COURSE IN COOPERATIVE PLAY

The co-op Mode in Battlefield 3 is an interesting hybrid of the smaller maps from the Campaign and a simplified version of the persistent reward system from Multiplayer. It offers a separate, but parallel, storyline that runs alongside the efforts of Black, Dima, Miller, and Hawkins that provides an alternate take on the fight.

Though there are shared environments from the Campaign, they're often presented in new or slightly differing ways. And like the Multiplayer experience, enemy fire deals far more damage. There's no shrugging off multiple rounds here; if you come under fire, even on the easiest difficulty levels, it's quite easy to go down. Stick to cover, use teamwork, and above all else, communicate constantly.

THE BASICS

SEMPER FI

Being a good Marine is more than just shouting "Hooah" and gunning down tangos left and right. You have to work as a unit, supporting and covering your fellow squadmates with absolute precision. Grabbing cover should be the first thing you think about when entering a firefight. The second should be controlling the kick from any weapon, be it an assault rifle, light machine gun, or machine gun. Burst fire is key; not only will it keep your view from bucking from the recoil, but it allows for quickly reaction to changes in the combat situation should an enemy take cover or if more of his friends join the fray. Remember, too, that bullets in Battlefield are modeled just like the real thing. You need to lead far-off targets while accounting for bullet drop over long distances.

SERVICE HAS ITS REWARDS

Starting the co-op campaign offers a chance at acquiring several Achievements/Trophies. In addition, it offers the lasting benefit of unlocking new weapons for use in Multiplayer. They are:

MP412 REX Revolver

Available For:	All Kits
Points Required:	63,000

KH2002 Assault Rifle

Available For:	Assault Class
Points Required:	126,000

MP7 Machine Gun

Available For:	All Kits
Points Required:	189,000

M39 EMR Assault Rifle

Available For:	Recon Class
Points Required:	262,000

93R Pistol

Available For:	All Kits
Points Required:	315,000

SG553 Assault Rifle

Available For:	Engineer Class
Points Required:	378,000

G3A3 Assault Rifle

Available For:	Assault Class
Points Required:	441,000

These exclusive weapons are a mix between those that are class-specific and others which can be used with any kit. Earning them requires plenty of practice and a firm knowledge of each level. It is highly recommended that all Achievement/Trophy runs be attempted on Easy. It's also a good idea to stick to Easy for your first time playing through co-op so you can learn the layout of the levels: enemy placement, surprise threats, the flow of the missions, and so on.

MAKING THE MOST OF A DIFFICULT SITUATION

Notching up the difficulty has a number of key effects: enemy gunfire does more damage, the aim assist is reduced or completely disabled, and when in Man Down state, you're given less time to be revived by a teammate. There's no significant difference in the number of enemies or the points earned per mission. Nevertheless, on higher difficulties, enemy aim improves and their AI level increases, making them far more lethal. Patience becomes increasingly important, as does familiarity with the mission at hand. It's highly recommended that you and your teammates make an Easy run-through before attempting the tougher stuff.

■ [TIP]

The Art Of Bleeding Out

It's going to happen: you're going to be surprised by a grenade or a close-quarters enemy and enter the Man Down state. This is not the end, however; you can still fire your sidearm and you're still mobile enough to crawl towards buddies and capable of firing your sidearm. Use this to your advantage by crawling over to heavy cover, allowing a co-op partner to assist you without coming under fire himself. There's nothing worse than going from support to a liability in the middle of an intense battle. Take the time to settle yourself into a position to get patched up without getting your friends killed.

■ [TIP]

Eyes On

Verbal communication during missions is crucial, but comments like "second tango from the left, your 12 o'clock" isn't as helpful as simply spotting the target for your teammate. Spotting works exactly as in multiplayer, with the added benefit of being able to see which player has marked a target thanks to a handy little number next to the orange blip over an enemy's head. It only takes a second, and helps identify targets with great efficiency. On harder difficulty levels, this can be the difference between drawing a bead on a target before they can take out your buddy or watching them get gunned down in front of you, necessitating a revive.

OPERATION EXODUS

VITAL STATISTICS

The enemy has gotten wind of the camp's weakened condition and the PLR are poised to take full advantage of the situation. Reports of a large invasion force moving in on the camp's position from all sides has pushed tensions to the breaking point for the small detachment tasked with the camp's defense. History is filled with examples of numerically inferior forces triumphing over their adversaries through superior strategy and tactics; these are the moments where a soldier's training is put to the ultimate test. With the support of five Humvees armed with .50 cal machine guns, hold back the enemy surge set to converge this critical urban junction until the extraction choppers arrive.

MISSION SUMMARY

A number of high valued POWs are being detained at a US camp. A recent earthquake has weakened the camp's defensive perimeter and made it vulnerable to PLR attacks. An evacuate order of the camp has been given. You and a handful of marines are assigned to defend the camp until all personnel have pulled out.

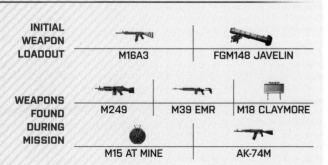

INITIAL WEAPON LOADOUT	M16A3		FGM148 JAVELIN

WEAPONS FOUND DURING MISSION	M249	M39 EMR	M18 CLAYMORE
	M15 AT MINE		AK-74M

◈ DEFEND THE US CAMP

TAKE UP POSITION AT THE WALK BRIDGE

Once the mission begins, all available units are called to scramble toward the walk bridge that spans the north section of the broad thoroughfare. While the Humvees hold position to the south, your squad moves to the front lines to meet the inbound hostiles. Once you reach the bridge, take a defensive position around the bridge at street level and prepare for the troop onslaught swarming through the far end of the street.

The walk bridge may seem like a good spot to hold position, with its elevated perspective and sandbag barriers installed along the railing. However, the metal sheets placed in front of these barriers only offer a brief tactical advantage. After the metal sheets are gunned down, you are only safe from enemy fire while prone behind the sandbags. Peeking in and out in this state to attack is difficult and can allow multiple enemies can advance under the bridge out of your line of sight. Keep them at bay before they reach and engage the Humvees.

The bridge columns under the walkway offer superior cover and more mobility for your squad. This area is close to the Ammo Crate, both columns are close enough for you to support to any overwhelmed squad member and the position can halt the PLR's progress on both sides of the street.

HOLD THE DEFENSIVE LINE

Once in position, look down your iron sights past the smoke and haze to the northern horizon. Be patient and aim carefully at the first wave coming over the rise in the road. Try to take them down while they charge in and look for cover behind the cars parked along the street. Although the targets are harder to tag from far away, don't pass up this opportunity to clear them out while they are still out in the open. Cover both sides of the street, but anticipate the bulk of the invaders to charge in from the street's left side. The right side of the street has fewer parked cars and enemies eventually run out of cover as your teammate covering that side funnels them over to the

left side of the street. After gunning down several waves of PLR forces, a low rumble shakes the street. It is not an aftershock, but a BMP moving in to take out the Humvees.

There is barely a moment to think after clearing the north side of the street. Scouts report more hostiles moving through the rubble-filled alley, west of the walk bridge. Grab a mine from the Ammo Crate and place it at the mouth of the alley in anticipation of later threats. Find a secure spot to stop all the soldiers advancing into the small market next to the walk bridge. There is good cover near either wall under the bridge stairway, or stay put at the nearby bridge column.

Watch out for the RPGs camping on the top floor of the northwest building—both you and the Humvees are wide open to attack from the high ground. They are tricky to take down but you don't have much choice unless you're willing to expose the Humvees to considerable damage. Luckily, the proximity of this alley to the Humvees gives their gunners a chance to provide covering fire, allowing you to easily flank the hostiles.

As you weed out the last of the gunmen, the mine placed earlier goes off and signals a BMP's arrival through that narrow alley. Immediately switch to the Javelin and blow up the infantry fighting vehicle before it travels out of the market. If it clears the market stalls, it will almost certainly will blow up one of your Humvees. Annihilating the BMP leaves both the north and west ends of the street clear, but the fight is far from over.

REINFORCE THE EAST PERIMETER

Replenish your weapons ammo at the Ammo Crate before following the Humvees to the east side perimeter. It's hard to shake an ominous feeling while repositioning as several aftershocks rock the area. To prepare for the incoming heavy vehicles that precedes the regular PLR troops, grab a mine or claymore. They can be acquired from one of two Ammo Crates, either on the roof of a nearby buildings or inside the open garage door inside the building on the right. After setting the explosives, seek out an optimal defensive position and get ready for the PLRs last—albeit largest—attack battalion.

■ [TIP]

Location, Location, Location

There are many worthy spots that allow your team to ambush the numerous hostiles populating the east side, but the best defensive formation hinges on a bird's eye view that covers a street level teammate. Climb the ladder on the building right next to the archway that leads into the east side perimeter. Equip the sniper rifle on the Ammo Crate and lie down in the corner of the building next to the sandbag barriers and the metal sheet. While

you scope out the scene from above, your teammate can take a prone position behind the second white car on the street and draw most of the enemy's attention.

The scouts from the chopper above inform your team that several squads are about to pour out of the other end of the street. Opposition forces arrive in the area from the left corner of the intersection. From this location, they either charge forward from cover to cover as they inch their way to the Humvees, or hang back and dig into defensive positions behind the row of parked cars at the end of the street. Your teammate covering the street level can strafe behind the white car and spot targets from either side. Aggressively unloading bullets on the encroaching enemies successfully draws the majority of PLR attention and eases enemy pressure on the sniper's high perch. This allows the sniper to easily pick off any soldiers out of his teammate's view without fearing for his safety.

After several squads are mowed down, the action shifts to an alleyway to the right of the cars. From the high ground, keep an eye out for these troops and warn your teammate of the approaching hostiles. Your partner on the ground should shift position in order to keep the white car between him and the PLR soldiers. Things get cooking as the troops continue to flood the area. While your teammate is busy with the troops trying to flank his position, scan the roof and top balconies of the buildings directly facing you. RPG units are hiding along the concrete lips of the buildings, waiting for a chance to fire a rocket at you or your teammate. Catch them in the act as they pop up to aim their rockets and nail them with a quick head shot.

Once the majority of the PLR troops are taken care of, the enemy battalion is reinforced with a final BMP that drives down the street toward the Humvees in a last ditch attempt to break through the convoy to the camp. Switch to the Javelin for the last time and fire and unleash multiple missile payloads at the Russian vehicle until it is immobilized. With the last heavy vehicle disposed of, return to the cross street behind the Humvees and board the transport helicopters for extraction from this hostile area.

FIRE FROM THE SKY

VITAL STATISTICS

MISSION SUMMARY

An American convoy escorting a general privy to classified intel has been ambushed on their way back to base. The general is being held captive in a remote mountain village. You will be providing close air support for a strike team sent in to rescue him.

Finally, a taste of the Battlefield series' hallmark vehicles without having to actually deal with the chaos of online multiplayer. Unfortunately, the vehicle being offered on this mission is *easily* the most difficult of the bunch: the simultaneously feared and loved helicopter. If you're looking for a bit of training before putting the lives of your online brethren at risk, this is the way to do it. Just don't expect to become an expert your first time through this lengthy mission. When playing as the pilot, your gunner is counting your flying skills to keep the helicopter level and help them line up targets. Steering the craft takes a light touch and a steady hand, so this guide focuses on the pilot's perspective during the mission. Compared to navigating this valley intact, operating the main guns and guided missiles is a piece of cake.

ESCORT FIRE TEAMS TO LZ

■ [CAUTION]

A Crash Course in Heli Piloting

Your first time flying a helicopter is bit like trying to ride two bikes at once; the thing just wants to get back down to the ground, pilot and crew be damned. The key to getting a handle on things is to start slowly and remember a few basic strategies. Your top priority is mastering the throttle control and learning to pitch the rotors in the direction you want to go. Apply the throttle sparingly; your heli is incredibly nimble while fuel is being applied to the rotors, but that power also amplifies minute changes in direction. Start slow, learning to pitch your view down to pull the aircraft forward, then back to slow it down. Remember that this also increases altitude, so feather the controls at first and experiment with pitching the aircraft forward and back *without* applying more throttle afterward.

The second lesson is in actually steering the whirlybird. The main controls used to turn left and right on-foot apply here to rotation around the helicopter's central axis. The normal look controls guide the ability to pitch, allowing you to strafe the helicopter side to side and move forward and backwards. Successful navigation uses a combination of these controls; rotation to actually change direction and pitching the craft to help level out and counter excessive momentum in undesired directions. There's no hard and fast way to teach this; like learning a clutch in a stick shift, it must come naturally in time after practice. Eventually, things like slow banking turns or even quick 180 degree snaps will become second nature.

Of course, there's also the matter of your gunner to consider. Although the forward turret they command can rotate quite freely, it doesn't do much good if the heli is traveling in the wrong direction. Use those first lessons to get a handle on hovering as evenly as possible, and above all *communicate* with your gunner to let them know when you need to make an abrupt change. The less you move, the more precise their shots will be. Since the pilot only has a limited supply of rockets before reloading, keeping the helicopter steady is the single most important technique for taking out ground troops.

As a gunner, you have far more range of movement. Use this to call out targets that you'd like the pilot to swing around to get a better position on. The gunner's ability to switch to an enhanced vision mode makes picking out those last few stragglers and spotting them for the pilot much faster, and can mean the difference between losing Alpha or Bravo squads or seeing them charge forward toward the next objective.

[ACHIEVEMENT | TROPHY]

Untouchable

Despite the name, you *can* indeed take a little incoming fire—from small arms, mostly—and still earn this Achievement/Trophy. What you can't do, however, is withstand too many sustained attacks from the mobile anti-air vehicles and BMPs that appear throughout this mission. If facing ground troops, feel free to venture close to allow your gunner to take out the targets. But when engaging a vehicle, attack from afar and don't be afraid to beat a hasty retreat if you've drawn too much attention. If that pounding from the ground becomes too much for the engines, a fire warning will sound for the pilot, necessitating the use of the Fire Extinguisher, which instantly kills the chances of becoming Untouchable. As with all co-op Achievements/Trophies, attempting this on the Easy difficulty is absolutely recommended.

Start by taking off from the landing pad and cruising at relatively high altitude through a narrow canyon that spills out into a small farm village. Your helicopter is faster and more agile than the troop transports moving Fire Teams Alpha and Bravo into the combat zone, so use the opportunity to move out into the farmland just past their landing zone. Here you can turn to face them and practice leveling out and hovering. The pilot's external view here comes in handy when first wrapping your head around the concept of controlling the pitch of the aircraft. Watch how the whole helicopter responds to each subtle adjustment to the controls to acclimate to their sensitivity.

Once the Fire Teams get their boots on the ground, the mission proper begins.

SUPPORT THE FIRE TEAMS

The first target the air support is tasked with is a pair of mortar batteries on opposite ends of the river that snakes through the middle of the map. As a pilot, resist the temptation to unload with rockets since lining up the target requires that the helicopter pitch downward, which will in turn cause the craft to lose altitude and begin moving forward. Instead, the gunner should take out the targets by switching to infrared and targeting the mortars with the main cannon. The pilot's rockets' explosive payload might seem a good way to make a strafing run, but the cannon is far more effective. As a gunner, concentrate fire on the targets until they're turned from HUD blip to non-issue. You can save ammunition by targeting the nearby vehicles and catching the mortars in the ensuing explosion.

After removing the mortar threats, the Fire Teams will come under attack from multiple tangos in the tilled field directly ahead of them. Use the same techniques here as before, hovering as a pilot with minimal altitude changes or lateral movement to let your gunner get the best position. Try to hover parallel to the lines of the field, as the trees between them offer ample cover for the enemy ground forces. It's critical that gunners take note of the infrared scope's incredible usefulness. It lights up targets that would otherwise be almost completely camouflaged against the backdrop of the brown soil and leafy trees below.

When the initial threats have been gunned down, Alpha and Bravo will move up a short distance. They don't get very far before coming under fire again from more enemies in the twin fields ahead, as well as enemies in the modest structures bordering the fields. While responsibility for taking these enemies out still falls to the gunner, pilots can finally make use of those rocket volleys to completely destroy the structures tangos are firing from. Unload with a salvo, then manually reload as you would on foot instead of waiting for the current rocket supplies to dwindle to nothing. Reload on your terms to avoid being caught with less than a full complement of firepower in fights to come.

Only once the threats near the fields have been removed can Alpha and Bravo move up again, this time to the bank of the river. A pair of RPG-wielding PLR are waiting on rooftops to the right and left of the gas station in the middle of town. Unload on them with the gunner or make use of the rockets' ability to collapse the rooftops entirely, robbing the RPG troops of their footing. Having eliminated the threats to the heli, assist the Fire Teams with the PLR that pour out of buildings on the other side of the river. Take things slowly, clearing each squad of enemies in an area before slowly moving to the next group. Always keep in mind the many nearby vehicles can be destroyed to provide some explosive deterrence. Look for a large explosion at the gas station as a sign that enemy numbers are dwindling and take out any remaining ground forces so the Fire Teams can continue pushing up.

As they do, a pair of BMPs will roll out of the main compound at the far end of the map. Taking these armored vehicles out is best done at a distance, with the gunner switching to the guided missiles the helicopter is packing. These aren't fire-and-forget weapons; the missiles must be guided toward their target by keeping them painted in the center of the targeting reticule, so ask your pilot to hover from afar to allow a clear line of sight toward the BMPs. It may take multiple tries to hit home as the vehicles are constantly on the move.

Strafing runs are generally not recommended here, though the pilot's rockets can help pour on the damage to eventually take out the enemy. However, getting close to these armored mobiles is a risky proposition than can cost you the Untouchable Achievement/Trophy before you know it.

The Teams will come under fire again as they push up the street cutting through the middle of town—the most dangerous targets being a pair of RPG PLRs. Take them out as you and your co-op partner did before, then switch to hovering alternately near the buildings on the left side of the street and the grassy areas on the right to help thin out the opposition.

A trio of threats present themselves as the teams move up: a pair of BMPs and a far more dangerous mobile anti-air vehicle with its sights trained directly on your helicopter. Focus on the AA first, using guided missiles as available. Note that the pilot's own missiles and the gunner's cannon fire are more effective on the AA than the BMPs. Once the AA has been dealt with, concentrate on the BMPs, hitting them with everything you and your partner have got. With the major threats eliminated, move on to take out any remaining ground forces with the cannon, including gun trucks. You can pick them out easily from their surroundings with the infrared view.

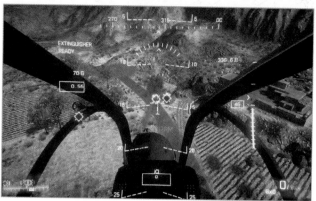

REPEL THE ATTACK

The Fire Teams may have infiltrated the compound and found the general, but the PLR aren't going to let him go without a fight. A pair of BMPs and a mobile anti-air appear on opposite sides of the map and must be dealt with quickly. Focus on the single BMP coming out of the tunnel near the river on the right side of the map first, watching out for its gun truck escort. Then take out the remaining BMP and AA moving toward the compound, dusting any nearby gun trucks as your strafing runs allow. Remember that while distance is important here, so is line of sight for those guided missiles. The catch is that whenever a gunner has a clear shot toward the mobile anti-air, it can fire back just as cleanly so work quickly. Any remaining

gun trucks and ground troops that weren't taken out while attacking the trio of main threats will take up position near the compound, so gun them down to help with the extraction effort.

ESCORT THE FIRE TEAMS TO EXTRACTION ZONE

As the Fire Teams move out of the compound and begin pushing right toward another field, a mass of ground troops and gun trucks attempt to route them. Pilots should hover around the open plain to the right of the compound to allow gunners to lay down heavy fire on the enemies there.

Before the fight is over, yet another pair of armored vehicles spills out from the tunnel near the river where the single BMP emerged before. Quickly move to eliminate the anti-air, then the BMP to allow the Fire Teams to move to the extraction point.

Keep eyes on the twin troop transports as the teams board and dust off, then enjoy a well-deserved high five from your co-op buddy or buddies for a job well done.

EXFILTRATION

VITAL STATISTICS

MISSION SUMMARY

Thanks to extensive intelligence work, we've been able to locate El Zakir. He was not expected to give himself up, but when local agents located and captured his immeadiate family, he agreed to negotiate his surrender. El Zakir is awaiting extraction in an apartment complex in the outskirts of Baghdad. You need to secure him and bring him back to the Green Zone.

Although El Zakir has contacted the US and is willing to surrender himself, the PLR is not willing to give up one of their own so easily. Several PLR troops guard the complex he's being held in. Once he is freed, the entire army reacts and engages the extraction team with a full-on assault through the streets of Baghdad.

INITIAL WEAPON LOADOUT	M9 SUPP	M16A3		

WEAPONS FOUND DURING MISSION	870MCS	AK-74M	SAIGA 12K	RPK-74M
	G3A3	SVD	KH2002	C4

LOCATE EL ZAKIR

ESCORT EL ZAKIR TO THE HUMVEES

[ACHIEVEMENT | TROPHY]

Ninjas

Baghdad doesn't exactly mirror feudal Japan, but the extraction team can execute their plan quietly like the notorious asssassins of that era. To obtain this co-op Achievement/Trophy, reach El Zakir without comprimising the extraction team's presence. To avoid detection, crouch and quietly move through the complex, eliminating any guards or security systems that may reveal your position. When you encounter a PLR post manned by several hostiles, kill the guards swiftly and quietly using the silenced pistol or save ammo with the knife when their backs are turned. Most of the rooms and halls in the area have more than one guard posted, and all must be eliminated simultaneously to remain hidden. Failing to coordinate attacks with your teammate results in a PLR guard tripping the alarm and alerting

the entire complex to your presence. With those alarms blaring, the complex becomes the center of an intense firefight rather than a swift, stealthy extraction.

Hop off the Humvee, pass by all the garage doors and enter the complex through the door on the west side of the building. As you enter the complex, crouch to stalk carefully through the garage until you reach a pair of guards lounging in front of a television. While they watch the latest news reports, aim your pistols from just outside the door or through the entryway window and take them out.

■ [TIP]

Quantity, Not Quality

While aiming for a headshot is nice for perfectionists out there, a missed shot can screw up a perfectly good stealth mission and any chance at that Ninjas Achievement/Trophy. Unloading several shots at the enemy's center of mass while their backs are turned may not be elegant, but it beats having to restart the mission.

With the garage clear, continue your search for El Zakir, traveling through a hallway that leads to the laundry room. Take position in the small room just before the laundry room and carefully aim your pistols at the next set of guards posted there. After putting some permanent bloodstains in the guards' clothes, watch out for the Closed Circuit TV (CCTV) camera installed in the hallway ahead. Take a cautious peek at the CCTV as you go around the storage shelf in the center of the room, place the device between your sights and disable it with a shot or two.

There are two more CCTVs placed in the storage hall ahead. To be absolutely sure you don't get caught in either cameras' view, aim at each CCTV through the storage grates. Slowly edge past the first storage grate to spot the camera installed in the second corner of this storage hall and uninstall it with authority. With one camera down, set your sights on the next one placed in the corner near the door at the end of the hall.

Now that those voyeuristic viewfinders are out of commission, go through the door at the end of the storage hall to reach the apartment's stairway. A PLR guard, with his back turned away from you, is standing at the base of the stairway. There is no need to waste any bullets on this guard; simply sneak behind him and silently put him down with your knife. Intel says El Zakir is on the third floor of this building, but the path up to his apartment is dense with heavy security. Keep those sights trained ahead as you quietly climb the first flight of stairs. A single guard and a CCTV are positioned next to the second floor doorway. Stay out of view near the top of the first set of stairs and decide with your teammate who takes down which hostile. Get a precise bead on your designated target and coordinate a simultaneous attack to continue the journey upward undetected.

Don't congratulate each other just yet; there is another security post occupied by two guards and a CCTV near the third floor doorway. Follow the same strategy that worked for the last set— one person handles the CCTV and the other tackles the guards. However, whoever is charged with taking care of both guards has the tough task of finding the precise angle to carefully line up both guards in their sights. In order to maintain the team's cover,

the bullets must penetrate the first target and take out the one behind him. Fire multiple bullets to ensure that both targets go down to clear out the stairway.

Enter the third floor and sneak down the hall to find El Zakir's apartment, where two more guards are stationed in front of the door. Move into a good firing position without alerting them and aim for a headshot this time. Since both targets have their backs to the wall, shooting at center of mass and right into their body armor does not take them out fast enough to remain hidden. Eliminate the door guards in one shot, and your team is awarded this mission's Achievement/Trophy.

With ninja status obtained, breach the the apartment door and surprise the last two guards inside the living room. Now that all hostiles have been cleared out of the building, get to the frightened El Zakir cowering in the kitchen. After he equips himself with a weapon, escort the PLR defector to the stairway at the other end of the hall, down the stairs to the ground floor, and finally out of the building and to the waiting Humvees.

◆ PROTECT THE HUMVEE CONVOY

TAKE POINT

The asset is secure and all that is left is to escort the convoy out of Baghdad. Of course, an exit strategy out of Baghdad is never a simple proposition. Move ahead of the convoy and trek down the street to scout for any threats. Turn left at the first corner, load up at the Ammo Crate on the left sidewalk and equip the sniper rifle next to it. Travel south down this short road and hang another left onto the narrow street ahead. Upon reaching the corner, the waiting PLR springs their trap. Suddenly, dozens of soldiers flood out from the far end of the street and begin firing upon the convoy. They're backed by additional hostiles camping out along the rooftops and balconies on the buildings on the south (right) side of the street.

■ [TIP]

Bait and Hook
Since multiple targets are advancing down this single street, it's best to split up your forces between both sides of it in order to spread out the incoming fire. While your partner rushes out to the walkway on the right side of the street and finds cover between the support columns, stay on the corner of the street on the left side and cover him by sniping the rooftop soldiers—especially any that are carrying an RPG. As your partner draws enemy fire from the street level, pick off any targets moving  down the left side of the street that try to flank him or encroach on your position. Methodically locate and eliminate each target until the street is clear of all hostiles.

The Humvee convoy begins moving again once the PLR trap is thwarted and the opposition eliminated. Before trudging ahead to the next area, take this opportunity to replenish your supplies from the Ammo Crate located in a small gap on the north (left) side of the street. Now that you are rearmed and ready to go, head down the street and turn right at the next road to find a gate blocking the end of it. Wait for the Humvees to arrive and apply their ample horsepower to crashing through the gate.

Follow them into a construction work site where another PLR ambush takes out several Humvee gunners. Without their gunners, the vehicles are extremely vulnerable to attack and your team has to provide immediate support. Find cover behind the crane at the north end of the area while your teammate locates some cover on the opposite side to cover your flank. The PLR ground troops can only enter the site through the corner on the south end. Fire on any enemy that comes through the corner, and scan the two buildings for any RPG equipped enemies. If you spot one on any of the balconies, focus your full attention on dropping those targets before they can blow up a Humvee.

TAKE GUNNERS POSITION

After your team survives the PLR's second ambush, the extraction team orders you and your partner to replace the Humvees' vacant gunner cabs. Run over to an open transport and get in the vehicle. The team is off scouting detail and now in the relative safety of the Humvee, but the exposed 50. cal turret reminds you that this is no leisurely drive to the extraction point. The convoy starts to move again through the streets, but is interrupted when the lead Humvee is destroyed by a hidden IED. Open fire on the PLR troops' fortified position on the corner in front of the convoy while the Humvees regroup on the road to the left. Spray bullets at the enemies camping upon the building balconies above as the Humvees pick up speed down the narrow market road.

◇ REACH THE EXTRACTION POINT

DETONATE C4 ON THE GATE

A domed structure ahead houses several parked cars and a heavily-reinforced wooden gate blocking the convoy from reaching the extraction point. Tasked with clearing the obstruction with a C4 charge, your team exits the vehicles. While inside the building, stock up on supplies from the Ammo Crate before you place the charge on the gate and blow it up. Once you open up the path, PLR troops arrive to cut your team off from the convoy. They take positions in the alleyways flanking the stretch between you and the Humvees, laying down heavy fire. Utilize the Ammo Crate in the garage and lob enough grenades into both alleys until the coast is clear for the team to return.The convoy continues its run for the extraction point once the team reaches the Humvees.

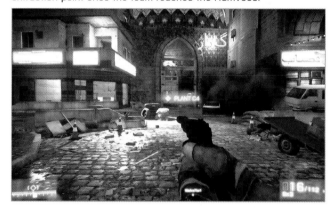

■ [TIP]

Point Man

There's no need for everyone to pile out of the Humvees to tackle the objective. Leave your partner in their forward-most Hummer and proceed on foot, sprinting over to the gate to lay down the C4, but hold off on detonating it. Sprint back to the cover of the Humvee convoy, letting that forward gunner unload on any enemies that might try to stop your sprint back to the trucks. Once under cover, detonate the C4 and climb back into your vehicle.

◇ SECURE THE EXTRACTION POINT

CLEAR THE AREA

The path has reopened and the convoy burns rubber as they blaze a trail to the extraction point. Unfortunately, the open square ahead is swarming with PLR troops. Before the evac choppers can land and dust off El Zakir and the extraction team, the area has to be cleared of all hostiles. Doing so is easier said than done. The PLR have secured positions both in the center of the square and inside the Iraqi Union building to the south. Even worse, reinforcements are pouring in from both the east and west end of the square. With the multiple hostile contacts firing and attempting to flank the team, this firefight is going to take plenty of skill and endurance to survive.

■ [TIP]

Rock the Rockets

As the extraction team drives into the square, there are only a few seconds until you are forced to exit the vehicle. Use those precious moments to mow down as many enemy troops as possible. Two juicy targets to consider before you part with the 50. cal are the pair of BM-21s, or rocket equipped trucks, in the cen-

ter of the square. Other than providing a spectacular explosion, blowing up both targets takes out nearby enemies caught in the blast and destroys some of their vital cover.

El Zakir and the rest of the extraction team have taken refuge, but are pinned down in a small storage garage in building on the northwest corner of the square. If you are running low on supplies, an Ammo Crate is in front of the northern building, directly behind the remaining Humvees. In fact, the most secure cover in the area is found behind the Humvees. Crouch or lay prone while keeping the Humvee between you and the enemy. Alternate between firing from the rear or the front of the vehicle to retaliate against the numerous enemy PLR.

Focus on weeding out the ground forces around the square first before even attempting to tackle the troops firing from the Iraqi Union Building. Staying behind the Humvees keeps you protected from the high ground, but the street level threats are constantly trying to flank your position. Only after taking down the bulk of the forces down here should you shift attention to the targets above. Once the main ground forces have been thinned to a more manageable number, be on the lookout for the RPG-toting enemies scattered across multiple floors in the building ahead. By launching a couple of rockets, they can virtually obliterate most areas of cover in the square.

Once the Union building and the ground troops are cleared, the extraction chopper arrives to remove El Zakir and the extraction team from the PLR forces. Climb into the chopper and give the team that long awaited congratulations.

HIT AND RUN

VITAL STATISTICS

MISSION SUMMARY

The company El Zakir referenced is Levin Cooperative. It's located in central Paris. You need to go in and retrieve everything you can from their offices. A private security team has been alerted to your presence and is headed to the offices to stop you. You need to secure and extract whatever evidence there may be.

In an interesting reversal of the Campaign level Comrades, you and your co-op partners must infiltrate the Parisian financial district and then exit *from* the garage that Dima, Kiril and Dimitri infiltrated through. Your reward for making it through an absolutely insane series of firefights is the chance to take brief control of a car as it careens through the levels of the garage.

INITIAL WEAPON LOADOUT		
MP7 Supp.	M9 Supp.	

WEAPONS FOUND DURING MISSION			
MP7	PDW-R	DAO-12	USAS-12
UMP-45	RPK-74M	AEK-971	

NEUTRALIZE ALL ENEMY FORCES

[ACHIEVEMENT | TROPHY]

Push On

This is quite possibly the hardest Achievement/Trophy in the game. It cannot be overstated enough: this should be attempted on an Easy difficulty run. It's hard enough to get through this fight at all, much less without entering a Man Down state that requires a revival from a buddy.

Move quickly as soon as the level kicks off, dropping a claymore at one of the doorways leading into this small office while your buddy does the same with the other doorway. As soon as they're down, quickly retreat to the desk at the back of the room and go prone, looking out toward the windows. If the desk becomes too crowded, your teammate can hold position in south corner of the room where a lip provides cover from the windows. A trio of enemies crash through the windows, throwing flashbangs as soon as they do. From your prone position, gun them down, then rise to assist your partner with the other entryways. The claymores may not even be triggered, but their presence can hold back the enemy. Make sure to stick to cover and fire at any flashlights that come into view before heading out into the room beyond to finish off any stragglers.

Shortly after removing the rest of the breaching team, the double doors in the room outside the starting office will be blown open, and a few more enemies will try to pour in. Lob a grenade here to disperse and hopefully take out a few more enemies, then get ready for a real firefight.

ESCAPE WITH THE INTEL

EXTRACT THRU THE GARAGE

The hallway beyond the double doors is absolutely teeming with enemies. Stick to the cover on the right side of the doorway or the planters on the left to thin the number of enemies along the length of the hallway. Duck back into cover often or risk losing the chance at that Push On Achievement/Trophy.

Once the more immediate threat of the enemies in the hallway are dealt with, things get more dangerous; a team of snipers have taken up position just outside and will fire in with laser-sighted precision on anyone attempting to make their way down the hallway. Sprint toward the left side of the display case directly ahead, and keep a watchful eye for more enemies before pushing on diagonally to the right near another display case. On harder difficulty levels, grenades will be a constant threat, so stay on your toes. Use your co-op buddy or buddies to leapfrog up, providing covering fire for them as they move to the next bit of cover.

Sprint back to the left and go prone behind a third display case and get ready for more enemies to try to crash the party from the doorway at the far end of the hall. Take them out, then sprint through the doorway. Avoid trying to take on the snipers; it's better to concern yourselves with the immediate threat in the hallway than a far-off hostile that can end your mission prematurely.

The next room is mercifully free of windows and offers a brief respite from the enemy sniper fire—at least until the end of the hallway. Use the planters and display cases to continue to push forward and down the stairs to the lobby below, where a multi-tiered firefight erupts. Sprint into the room across from the staircases to grab a valuable bit of cover, but be prepared for plenty of tangos to storm in through the entrance facing into the main lobby. Gun them down methodically, then turn your attention to the fire coming from the upper level across the lobby. Be ready for inbound grenades; thankfully this room is large enough that you can sprint away from any explosions near the doorways. Look for flashlights up above and

snub them out with a little lead before moving on up a set of stairways to the right. Keep watch for any enemies that might try to ambush you at the top of the first set of stairs.

Take things cautiously ahead; those fleur-de-lis-stamped walls are extremely poor cover. In fact, almost *all* of the objects in the room designated by the waypoint will crumble away under gunfire—something to keep in mind as you discover the door out is blocked. Make note of the Ammo Crate to the left and stock up for a big firefight.

A False Sense of Security

Though it might appear the desks and computers here can offer some semblance of protection, they're no match for the heavy firepower coming from the east. Tons of enemies are unloading on this office complex, and there are only a handful of real pieces of cover. There's a filing cabinet to the left of the doorway facing east and a copier to the right of it. A small chunk of wall on the far right side of the room can be used for cover, but only as a last resort due to exposure from enemies on the left side of the room outside.

On easier difficulty levels, the bottom-less reserves of the Ammo Crate at the back of the room can make for a fun game of grenade toss. Unload with gusto lobbing grenades until incoming fire subsides, but remember that there's no real cover behind the desks, so don't get grenade happy lest you lose your chance at that Push On Achievement/Trophy.

When the incoming fire finally dies down, that locked door suddenly becomes a bit more cooperative. Head toward it, but be ready for it get kicked open by a masked hostile and unload on him before he can take you out. Head down the stairs and into a chance for some multi-level mayhem.

The squad needs to briefly split to stack up at two doors on different staircase landings before both teams can breach at the same time. The upper floor is rife with enemies, but the DAO-12 offers a meaty means of dealing with these close-quarters threats. Gun them down, then stock up with the Ammo Crate at the far left end before firing down on enemies that are going after your buddies below.

For those on the ground floor, immediately take cover behind the circular columns on the left or right side of the room. Though this fight is meant to be something of a dual-level shootout, it's actually much more advantageous to double-back up the stairs and deal with the threat from above. Aside from being a better vantage point from which to snuff out all those flashlights, the Ammo Crate up there means easy refills of grenades

Keep in mind that this upper level's only real sources of cover are the circular columns jutting up from below and a small wall directly to the right of the entrance. However, the latter position is vulnerable to incoming fire from enemies on the left side of the room below. The low edge of this upper floor provides almost no cover, so stay near the door leading back to the staircase and retreat there to recover health.

More shooting kicks off as soon as you and your buddies press forward into the next set of offices. More fleur-de-lis walls here are chipped away by even glancing fire. Stay mobile, going prone as needed to recover health, or consider falling back to the rooms on either side of the office behind you. It can be tough to spot enemies here, but keep a lookout for flashlights and fire in that direction. The multiple angles here make cross-fire quite common, so be sure to gun down enemies in office to the east before peeking out to take out more to the south.

Again, the DAO-12 shotgun is astoundingly good at quickly putting out buckshot spreads that have a surprising amount of range. Move slowly down these hallways, dealing with enemies as they move into your line of fire. If need be, fall back to the Ammo Crate behind you to restock. Remember that there are two south-facing hallways where you can find additional hostiles. Don't let them get the drop on you here.

Both south-facing hallways eventually converge into a single hallway. The doorway out of these offices and down toward the garage is tantalizingly close at the far end, but the rooms to the right and especially the large glass-walled room to the left are still chock full of enemies. Thankfully, the walls of this hallway are quite solid. Proceed slowly, gunning down enemies with precision and burst fire. You're incredibly close to the end here, so don't let impetuousness or impatience ruin this run; if you die here, you have to start the mission from the very beginning.

Only when all the enemies in these rooms have been mowed down should you breach the doorway. Once through, head down the staircases into a small room with an Ammo Crate. Don't be fooled into thinking it's safe; quite a few enemies in the room beyond can open fire from afar, and even more will stack up on the doorway and try to rush in. Take cover near the Ammo Crate, gunning down the close-range enemies with plenty of shotgun fire. Then deal with the enemies behind cover in the other room—say, perhaps, with the bottomless supplies of grenades in that Ammo Crate?

When the room has been cleared, pass through it into a series of zig-zagging hallways, stocking up with the Ammo Crate along the way. Take care in breaching the next doorway, as more enemies wait on the other side. Gun them down with everything you've got, then hop in the waiting car ahead.

GET INTO THE ESCAPE VEHICLE

When everyone is inside, put pedal to the metal and crash through the gate directly ahead. Once through, make a hard right and gun it. Veer left around a white van, cutting across the garage and heading up the ramp on the left side. Hang a hard right and drive up the circular ramp dead ahead. Veer left again around a set of concrete barriers, charging ahead to bust through the post and on to the end. Whatever you do, don't let up here; the incoming RPG fire can cut short the mission seconds before it ends.

DROP 'EM LIKE LIQUID

VITAL STATISTICS

With the intel received in the last mission, the French police are doing there best to wrangle up most of the terrorists. Those still at large have taken hostages all over the city, including several buses and the embassy where we suspect Abu Muhammad himself is running the show. The sniper team is going to dropped on the other side of the the engagement zone and they can provide the strike team with long range support and scouting.

MISSION SUMMARY

A hostage situation has developed in Paris. It's confirmed that Abu Muhammad is on site orchestrating the operation. French Police has requested out help. We are sending you in to assist. You need to provide sniper support, free the hostages and neutralize Abu Muhammad.

INITIAL WEAPON LOADOUT	MK11 MOD 0	M9 SUPP	
WEAPONS FOUND DURING MISSION	M1014	AK-74M	UMP-45

REACH THE APARTMENT

The mission begins on a street where the French police have apprehended some of the terrorist forces. Pass through the scene, moving south down the street to enter the manhole ahead. Climb down the ladder into the sewer system to sneak right under the terrorist forces and reach an optimal sniper position. Head down the grimy tunnel and slow down before reaching the single terrorist pacing the end of it. Scope out the lonely terrorist through your scope and deliver the coup de grace.

At the end of the sewer tunnel, take the ladder back up to the street level. The team is a short distance from the apartment's location, but there are several hostiles keeping watch over the streets. Two hostiles wait on the street a couple of feet from the team's position. Sneak over to the top of stairs southwest of the manhole to get an overview of your targets. While prone, each team member should select a guard and aim for the kill. After taking out those two guards, move down the stairs into the street and secure their former positions. Once again go prone and swing your sights west to another pair of guards at the other end of the street, inside an archway. Repeat the same sniper tactics on this duo and run down the street, under the archway into the following street that brings the team in front of the apartment's entrance.

Pick a spot, look straight at the entryway, and scope out two more guards stationed at the entrance. Swiftly dispatch them and move into the building. Take the stairs up to the designated apartment. Open the apartment door and quickly eliminate the last two guards inside. While one person opens the door the other covers it as it swings open. Permanently relieve the enemy guards from active duty and take a moment to replenish the sniper rifle rounds.

LOCATE AND SUPPORT ALPHA TEAM

Pick a window and survey the tense hostage situation taking place across the river. Look over to the south east section of the canal (to the right of the ferry boat) to see the strike team. Operating under the call sign "Alpha", they emerge from the tunnel and hold position there. The Alpha team is tasked with getting to each bus without alerting the terrorists watching over the hostages inside. There are several guards roaming around the bus site and its up to the sniper team to quietly eliminate those targets, allowing the strike team to close in on the buses.

■ [CAUTION]

DO Kill the Messenger

If any of these patrols gets wind of the operation taking place, they immediately break into a sprint toward the buses to warn them of the attack. It's vital you eliminate these scouts before they reach the buses to prevent the terrorists onboard from executing the hostages, effectively ending the mission in failure.

The first set of terrorists stroll out into view from the southeast end of the canal, a short distance to the left of Alpha Team. Wait for the pair to stop moving, pick out a target and coordinate the kill shots. As the Alpha team moves up the stairs into the street above, survey the van directly ahead of them to the left of the buses. Another enemy patrol reveals themselves from behind the van. Steady your scope and wait until the targets stop moving before taking the shot. With that patrol down, Alpha team is clear to move in on the buses undetected.

RESCUE THE HOSTAGES

The strike team secure themselves in a low a hidden spot next to the bus. Upon receiving your team's signal, they toss flashbang grenades into each bus. Before your team hits the action button and begins the rescue operation, plan out the attack in advance. Each team member should choose one of the buses (Charlie or Delta) to cover. Spot the two terrorists watching over the hostages inside each bus to mark them on everyone's HUD. When your team is ready, signal Alpha team to toss the flashbangs. The second they go off, swiftly and systematically shoot down each terrorist while they are distracted. Remember that this rescue mission ends in failure if a terrorist executes a hostage.

◇ TACTICAL ADVANCE

MOVE OUT

The bus is clear of terrorists, but there are more hostages in the embassy down the street west of Alpha team's position. Exit the apartment, go down into the street, and follow the strike team as they advance down the street parallel to yours. Stay alert to any movement on both streets and position yourself in front of the bridge railing. The strike team stops moving when they spot two patrols—one directly west of their position and the other in a standing in front of a railing directly above them.

■ [TIP]

Sharpshooter

Each patrol is comprised of two soldiers but, luckily, they are not yet aware of the attack on the bus. Use this advantage to pick out which patrol your team targets and shoot each pair down so the team can move forward. Dropping the two draws the attention of some previously unseen hostiles. These troops suddenly appear and converge on Alpha team. Kick into high gear and clear the incoming enemies that begin to swarm. After your team clears the reinforcements, a final trio of guards appear on the

west end of the street. Choose a guard to eliminate first and take a "first come, first served" approach with the remaining terrorist.

With this section of the street cleared of terrorist threats, resume following the westward bound strike team down the street until they stop at a plaza. Both snipers should take position on the opposite ends of the street because the enemy troops are now fully aware of your presence and surround Alpha team as they reach the center of the plaza. Three patrol squads (in groups of three) move in from

multiple areas including: from the east end coming down a long set of stairs next to a large Hotel sign, from the southwest street above the plaza down the stairs and straight into the group, and from the west end of the street. After dispatching the patrol groups watch out for any rival snipers camping out in the buildings directly south of the strike team's position.

◇ PROCEED TOWARDS VANTAGE POINT

The Alpha team is ready to continue to the embassy, a short distance from the plaza. Head back down the street and follow it as it curves north. Before moving up to the balcony, be prepared to fight some terrorists that have already secured the spot. They arne't about to give it up without a fight. They run down the stairs and take cover among the cars scattered on the street level. Split

up, find adequate cover and pick off the targets from a distance before heading up the long staircase to the final sniper's nest.

◇ EMBASSY

SUPPORT ALPHA TEAM

Resupply the team from the Ammo Crate before taking positions on the west end of the balcony. Alpha team plans to move in on the embassy from the south end through the garden entrance. Two guards block the stone gate to the embassy garden. Aim, coordinate and take them both out so the team can press on. As the team marches into the main stairway located west (directly in front of your position), a pair of enemy soldiers walk down the northern lawn toward the stairs. Wait for them to stop at the base of the stairs, line them up on your scopes and take them down. The stairs are free and Alpha team go up toward the front of the building, but stop when three guards emerge from the center entrance behind the fountain. Use the same tactics employed on the last trio you team encountered—assign a target to each sniper and then converge your sights on the last terrorist.

The remaining terrorists are still inside the embassy, and the ring leader can be seen in the large window on the second floor of the building. Before Alpha team can get up there, shoot through the window at the two guards on the first floor to the left of the fountain. The strike team enters the embassy at last, moving into an attack position just outside the large window. While they secure their position, press the spot button to label the terrorist targets, who are gathering the hostages into one area. There are four terrorists total—three of them are standing still, while the fourth is pacing the room. When you decide which targets to take out first, prioritize the pacing guard because he is harder to hit when the action begins. When everyone's ready, hit the action button to signal the Alpha team to throw the flashbangs through the window and disorient the enemy. Quickly shoot down all the targets while the Alpha team moves in to secure the hostages.

KILL THE HTV

Abu Muhammad escapes Alpha team's siege and runs out of the embassy through the first floor window next to the fountain. Ignore the multiple hostiles that exit the building and focus exclusively on tracking the leader down. Take him out with precision fire before he leaves the compound. It only takes a few rounds before Muhammad gets wise to the sniper fire and occasionally ducks into cover. Be patient and tag him when he is out in the open. Once your team has brought him down the mission is over with zero civilian casualties. Well done.

THE ELEVENTH HOUR

VITAL STATISTICS

MISSION SUMMARY

The attack has started. We're confident this is the main attack referred to by El Zakir. Witnesses claim bomb-like devices have been left in the metro and the Paris Stock Exchange. If Abdul Rahman is behind this attack, we expect it to be similar to the one that took place in London several years ago. You will be assisting the French police to locate and disarm the bombs and neutralize Rahman if the opportunity presents itself.

It all comes down to this, a subway shootout that could mean the difference between saving a city and the loss millions of lives. The clock is ticking, but thankfully this final mission offers one of the easier Achievements/Trophies in the game—if you're quick about it and you play this mission first on Easy. The mission begins with the donning of gas masks and a drop into an empty elevator car...

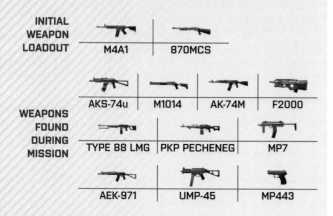

INITIAL WEAPON LOADOUT	M4A1	870MCS		
WEAPONS FOUND DURING MISSION	AKS-74u	M1014	AK-74M	F2000
	TYPE 88 LMG	PKP PECHENEG	MP7	
	AEK-971	UMP-45	MP443	

◈ LOCATE AND DISARM THE SUBWAY BOMB

LOCATE THE BOMB

■ [TIP]

Blinded by the Light
Though the flashlights you and your partner are equipped with are great at illuminating the darkened tunnels of the subway system, it's important to pay attention to where they're pointed. Accidentally shining them in the face of your co-op comrade will fill their screen with nothing but white light, blinding them for as long as your flashlight's beam is trained on them. On the higher difficulty levels, this moment's distraction is all the enemy needs to put your teammate down. Avoid sweeping of the flashlight too wildly and keep in mind that the flashlight can be toggled on and

off at will. When taking cover from hostile fire, turn off the flashlight or turn away from your teammate rather than towards them.

This breezy entrance to the subway system is littered with enemies that have ample opportunities to take cover. Have either you or your buddy sprint across the room to take up a position on the opposite side to cover the maximum number of angles. These enemies are crack shots and aren't shy about exhausting their plentiful supply of grenades. Spread out the team to avoid bumping into them while running from a grenade, offsetting the chance that a single grenade catches both of you in its blast.

Hang back in this area, methodically taking out the enemy one at a time and assisting a downed comrade if needed before pushing up.

As you push forward, a few more enemies will try to stop your progress by taking up position near the turnstiles. A set of enemies to the left of the small platform above try to mount a surprise attack, but they can be quickly taken out so long as you're prepared. Stick to the available cover as you move up and take them out, then stop in the ticket booth to stock up at the Ammo Crate before heading down the escalators ahead.

Upon arriving near a stopped subway train, more enemies will pour out from the right up ahead, some of which will take cover in the train itself. There's enough cover in these cars to go around, so feel free to head into the trains yourself. Stay crouched while ducking between seats to limit exposure. The windows between cars can be fired through to take out threats, but the bulk of them will be to the right. If you opt not to hop aboard, stick to the right wall of the subway tunnel and peek out from behind the modest pieces of cover strewn about only to gun down enemies. Take the time to recover any depleted health as needed before pushing on toward another set of escalators.

Be ready for a small ambush as you move slowly up the escalators. A set of enemies to the left of the small platform above try to mount a surprise attack, but they can be quickly taken out so long as your squad is prepared. Head back down via the escalators ahead just as cautiously in anticipation of another firefight breaking out immediately upon reaching the bottom.

DISARM THE BOMB

[ACHIEVEMENT | TROPHY]

In the Nick of Time
Designate someone as bomb defuser and immediately have them sprint toward the bomb indicated by the waypoint. The bomb defuser should ignore all enemy threats and charge straight toward the bomb. As the defuser, use the Action Button to kick off a lengthy series of Quick Time Event button presses. Be quick, but efficient with your button presses here; the sequence is long, and uses no less than six different inputs. You only have one crack at this, so make sure those inputs count.

Those who opt to provide cover should apply as much forward suppression as possible. Plenty of enemies will come down the escalators across the way, so grab some cover and be efficient with your shots. Use burst fire on the approaching targets and aim for headshots to quickly take them out before they can pose a threat to the defuser, using the nearby Ammo Create to restock if needed. When the bomb has been defused, clear out the room and press onward up the escalators.

Don't let the sucessful defusal cause you to relax your guard and sprint up the escalators blindly. There are plenty of enemies are waiting to put a stop to the next part of your mission.

Take them out methodically, backing away from the hot lead flying through the air and down the escalators if your health is running low. After thinning out the opposition, push forward and take cover behind the tiled walls of the ticket booth. The nearby columns here can be used for cover in a pinch, but they're susceptible to being chipped away by the abundant gunfire during the fight. Opt for a more resilient barrier to provide protection when the opportunity presents itself and the coast is clear.

Push up when the forward enemies are cleared out. A set of smoky explosions in the distance signal more threats, and unfortunately there's not as much cover here as before. Use the columns, pushing up slowly and watching your flanks as you do. These columns work well enough for forward cover, but don't forget you're just as exposed from the sides as the enemies you're trying to take out.

Push through the rest of the thankfully empty subway tunnels and up the stairs into the blindingly bright daylight of the streets above.

◇ LOCATE AND ELIMINATE THE HVT

ENTER THE STOCK EXCHANGE BUILDING

The massive building ahead is your next objective, already under fire from the Police. The stone steps mark the entrance to another heavy gunfight. Push down the streets toward the building and stack up near the solid walls on either side of the huge entrance.

A small contingent of enemies greet your arrival with gunfire, but they can be easily taken out as long as cover is stuck to. Their friends firing from the upper level, however, need to be dealt with using a long-range weapon. Plenty of grenades are lobbed out here, so don't venture into the building until the lobby has been completely cleared. Skirt the middle of the room to avoid being crushed by the large chandelier crashing down as you head toward the stairs on the far side of the lobby.

LOCATE THE HVT

Take cover near the extreme left and right sides of the lobby. Enemies have taken up positions on the other side of the information counter and more of their friends will try to rush from the sides. The positions on either side will make for the best firing angles and assure maximum coverage.

Continue searching for Rahman after securing the lobby. Head through a few rooms and past the elevators to a waiting Ammo Crate preceding the start of another firefight. If possible, make sure you have a well-balanced loadout with a close-range weapon like a shotgun and another capable of striking down enemies at long range. Both will be needed in the fight to come.

Once you're locked and loaded, breach the door leading into the trading floor of the Parisian stock exchange. There are enemies immediately on the other side of the door, but the more pressing threat are the ample angles of attack avaialble to the enemies on the higher floors. One team member should head up the stairs on the left side of the room and quickly take out the threats on the upper level. Be careful, however, as there are enemies across the way that can quickly cut short this assault. Don't leave a wounded teammate stranded up here by staying close enough to provide a critical revive if needed.

The upper level offers little in the way of cover, so the threats across the trading floor should be dealt with quickly. Keep a watchful eye on the staircase, as tangos will actively use them to try and flank you. From the elevated position, firing down on the enemies below is rather easy. If you opted to engage the hostiles down below, make sure to grab cover near the many desks here where you can drop into a prone stance if needed to refill health. Generally, speaking, this fight becomes much easier if both squad members can get upstairs and cover the flanking positions. An Ammo Crate at the base of the staircases offers a chance to reload, but should only be used once the room is cleared due to it being completely out in the open. Stock up and stack up at the waypoint to press onward.

This next room is similarly filled with threats spread across multiple floors. The ground forces are easy enough to take care of, but their allies up above are harder to draw a bead on. Of course, they're just as dangerous when they jump down from the upper level to ambush unsuspecting Marines. Split up and have one teammate concentrate fire on the right side of the room while you sprint under the overhanging lip where the enemies are firing (and jumping) down. Hang back, waiting for them to land before taking them out. Your reward after surviving this fight is well worth it.

ELIMINATE THE HVT

Only one objective remains for you and your squad. Take a deep breath, then stack up near the door. The person to kick the door open is powerless to react initially, as the first person into the room is attacked by Rahman. What follows is a Quick Time Event where the person being held captive by the terrorist must press the correct button to knock away Rahman's gun. This leaves Rahman briefly exposed, long enough for the breaching teammate to follow his own button prompt to take the villain out with a pistol. Be ready to perform the button press before the circular meter fills to finally end this threat once and for all.

●[CAMPAIGN]

SEMPER FIDELIS

VITAL STATISTICS

LOCATION New York City

MISSION SUMMARY

Well *that* was certainly a way to make an entrance. Whatever's going on, it's clear this subway train isn't filled with the usual passengers—at least not ones that normally open fire on a guy sporting a pair of handcuffs who comes crashing in from the roof. Take out all hostile threats and make your way toward the front of the train.

Let it never be said that you (whoever you are) aren't one to make an entrance. After taking the express entrance into the train and "borrowing" one of the masked tangos' firearm, it's time to clear our the rest of the car before they decide you're better left like the rest of the poor, doomed passengers on this express car to... somewhere. Follow the on-screen prompts for the basic controls to draw a bead on the fleeing masked combatants, drop them, and then proceed slowly toward the next car.

◇ STOP THE TRAIN

GET TO THE ENGINE

A mess of broken ladders and debris requires ducking, conveniently affording a clean shot at another of the masked men. Take him out before carefully scooting left, using the wall for cover if the first few shots don't connect with the pair of enemies at the far end of the car. Once they're dealt with, proceed forward with caution.

At the end of the car waits the oh so helpful M1014—an Italian semi-automatic shotgun capable of laying down startling amounts of wide-area fire.

■ [TIP]

Close-Quarters Combat

Almost immediately upon entering the next car, a knife-wielding, gas-masked threat makes itself known with gusto. Study the on-screen prompts here as closely as possible; in most cases, these surprise Quick Time Events will use the same few buttons, namely the Fire, Grenade, and the Action Buttons. This isn't *always* the case, but more often than not, it's best to have those fingers ready to quickly tap to avoid an unfortunate end. Regardless, that handy semi-auto shotty isn't in your poses-

sion for long; the masked combatant steals it, but not before you can do the same, helping to introduce him to the delights of New York City's light rail system at high speed.

Keep pushing forward toward the next car and ever-closer toward a rather bold, unmasked threat that has wired the car with explosives—explosives that are quickly counting down. Look to the shattered window on the left and press the Action Button to slip outside the moving car.

■ [CAUTION]

With the Quickness

The Quick Time Event that kicks off explosively is one of many to come, but this one is especially dire. After being shot by the unmasked mystery man, you'll need to quickly mash the on-screen button to climb up the side of the train and onto the roof. The threat of immediate death may have been skirted, but that doesn't mean things are going to get any easier. Three different tangos will attempt the same move you did, leaning out the window and opening fire directly toward the only non-metallic object on this subway car's roof. Because there's no cover here,

quickly acquiring the targets and taking them out with quick, short bursts of fire will ensure they end up where you don't want to be.

Another explosion rocks the car up ahead, sending debris screaming toward you. Don't worry about taking too much damage here, just keep battling the gale force winds as you march ever-closer to the front of the train. Just before dropping into the entrance, a AKS-74u offers an extremely rapid-fire reward for surviving not one but two close-range explosions. Yes, you are a badass. Drop down into that train to continue to prove it.

More masked bandits pour in from the front of the car, but are quickly dispatched with the new weapon you just acquired. Be particularly careful to grab cover with the small outcropping to the left, as there are numerous enemies here and their combined fire can be extremely dangerous on the harder difficulty levels. Move forward slowly past the first set of seats to discover a few more threats taking cover to the left. They're well covered here, and can completely duck out of sight. Proceed slowly until you've gunned them all down.. A few more masked enemies wait in the next car, but they can be easily taken out from the previous car with careful aim and judicious use of burst fire. Continue forward slowly, sticking to cover and reloading after each firefight before popping out to re-engage.

STOP THE TRAIN

One more enemy waits, using the flapping door as both cover and disguise. It can be rather dark here, so move carefully. Squeeze off a few shots between the doors as you move up to avoid the enemy getting the drop on you. After moving forward a little more, the target objective behind the abrupt train-jumping becomes clear: those are *big* bombs, and they look ready to go off. The goal here isn't to disarm them, though, it's to stop this train from arriving wherever it's headed, and fast. Keep moving forward, following the on-screen prompt to open the door, and get ready for a confrontation.

There's nothing to be done here but to wonder what the hell is even going on. Thankfully, things will become quite a bit clearer in the hours to come...

OPERATION SWORDBREAKER

VITAL STATISTICS

UNIT	1st Recon Marines
CALLSIGN	Sgt. Henry "Black" Blackburn
LOCATION	Al Sulaymaniyah, Iraq
DATE	March 15th
TIME	1300hrs Zulu Time

MISSION SUMMARY

The 1st Recon Marines have been diverted to an escalating situation in the town of Al Sulaymaniyah, a dense environment choked with as many PLR insurgents as innocent locals. Contact with Viper Squad was lost just a few hours prior while they were investigating a possible IED. The urban landscape makes snipers and other PLR threats a very real, very dangerous likelihood. You and your fellow Marines are to locate Viper Squad and call in CASEVAC if needed.

INITIAL WEAPON LOADOUT	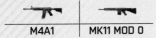				
	M4A1	MK11 MOD 0			

WEAPONS FOUND DURING MISSION					
	G3A3	AK-47M	RPK-74M	M249	M16A3

RENDEZVOUS WITH COLE

MOVE OUT WITH SQUAD

Al Sulaymaniyah's opening view is a rather breathtaking one. Light spills through a massive set of arches on the way to the staging area, and a clear military presence has been established to confront the PLR streaming across the border from nearby Iran. As the SITREP was rather vague, it falls to the 1st Recon Marines to gather more intel about the coming mission. Follow the other Marines through a covered alleyway to get the full briefing and prepare for trouble.

■ [KNOW YOUR JARGON]

CASEVAC

Short for Casualty Evacuation, CASEVAC differs from the more common MEDEVAC in that it is only used in extreme situations where immediate extraction from the battlefield is necessary. CASEVACs are strictly for extraction, meaning much of the medical equipment found in MEDEVAC vehicles are not present, and urgent care must wait until the final destination is reached.

FOLLOW SQUAD

Continue along with the rest of your squad down the alleyway and into a small hookah bar. Campo will breach, allowing entry into another tight alleyway. A lone dog at the end of the alleyway only serves to highten the sense that what should be a bustling market is entirely devoid of other human life. Not a good sign.

After pressing forward into another building, the squad will experience the first sign that Iraq is hardly a tranquil place. A tremor rolls through, but doesn't do much in the way of damage. Still, it's an unsettling feeling when even good ol' terra firma can't sit still. Head up the stairs and hang a left to arrive near a gate leading into a wide open street. Wait for a carload of PLR insurgents to pass, then wait for Chaffin, Montes, and Campo to cross before following behind Matkovic. Don't drag your feet here, Marine; double-time it to stack up on the door to the right with Matkovic while the rest of the squad sweeps around to the left. Inside, a small garage sits empty, forcing another trip through a doorway and out into a far more open (and exposed) parking lot.

■ [KNOW YOUR JARGON]

SITREP
Situation Report, a literal up-to-the-moment breakdown of the current conditions of the squad or nearby allies.

Before you can even make it outside, Chaffin is tagged by a sniper. The wound isn't fatal, but a downed Marine in the middle of an open area isn't going to last long against a sniper. Rush up to grab your squadmate and hammer the Action Button to pull them back into the relative safety of the garage. This is hardly an easy task; PLR forces quickly stream into the parking lot, and there's precious little cover here to hide behind.

HOLD OFF ENEMIES TO THE EAST

Regardless of where you choose to make a stand, make sure you're crouched—or even better, prone—if under heavy fire. The less of you that's exposed, the better chance you'll have at holding off this wave of enemies. Make slow, measured attempts to breach cover, just long enough to acquire a target before popping back down into cover. Pop up, unload with bursts rather than spraying bullets, and dispatch each of the enemies as cleanly as possible.

■ [CAUTION]

An Imperfect Circle
Keep an eye out for grenade indicators during this fight. When one lands nearby but not in your field of view, it will appear as a small glowing orb surrounded by a circle. The PLR in this fight aren't shy about using explosives, particularly on harder difficulty levels. Pay attention to the environment and scope outa secondary cover location that you can fall back to if things start to heat up.

TAKE OUT RPGS

Almost immediately after delivering a combined SITREP, a pair of RPG-wielding PLRs unleash their payload on a nearby van from the south. Don't let it throw you off balance and move up quickly, making sure to take out both rocket men as they pop up from cover. You'll have a precious few seconds to take them down, so make those shots count. Go for headshots if either of the enemies is foolish to expose their noggins.

■ [CAUTION]

Explosive Consequences

Rocket-propelled grenades are dangerous in their own right, but they have the nasty habit of turning a normally safe bit of cover like a car or van into a powerful explosion. Heed the advice of your squadmates and keep clear of the cars while the RPGs are still a threat, but remember that your weapons can deliver the same kind of results. If multiple insurgents are bunching up near a vehicle, unload on it or lob a grenade to take out multiple enemies at the same time.

■ [TIP]

Center Mass

Use the western- and northern-facing sheets of corrugated metal to shield yourself while taking out the PLRs that swarm the area. Not only is it semi-solid cover (dropping completely prone offers genuine cover for refilling health if needed), but offers a direct line of sight to enemies that might enter from east. Crouch here and unload much like you did earlier: burst fire, quick pops in and out of cover, and make sure you acquire

a target **before** sneaking out of cover. It only takes a few stray shots to mark a rather bloody end to your service record.

Eventually, the PLRs entering the parking lot will subside, but there's still the issue of what to do with that sniper. Regroup with the rest of the squad back in the garage to figure out a better way to take on the scoped threat.

◆ TAKE OUT SNIPER

REGROUP IN GARAGE

Chaffin is definitely in a bad way. Thankfully another squad moves in to help provide medical support while yours deals with the sniper personally.

FOLLOW SQUAD

Another dizzying trip up a staircase inside the garage leads toward the rooftop, but not before another tremor rocks the whole structure and the group is forced to sprint past the exposed windows on the west side of the building. The second you arrive at the far end of the room, more PLRs open fire from behind a desk. Take them out quickly, then continue to follow the rest of the squad up more stairs. Stack up with your squadmates and head onto the roof to get a better look at the POS that took out Chaffin.

That sniper isn't some rookie pushover, and your squad has only made it easier to get picked off by ascending to his level. Before even rounding the corner, the telltale sound (and impact) of a .50 cal sniper rifle makes it obvious the insurgent knows you're there. Tuck in close behind Montes, waiting for each member of the squad to move from one piece of cover to the next.

PICK UP RPG

■ [CAUTION]

Deadly Precision

Under no circumstances should you attempt to sneak a peek at the shooter even after everyone has crawled their way into the relatively protected corner of the roof. Popping up here for even a second means instant death. Instead, wait for Matkovic to roll over a little explosive firepower of his own, tap the Reload Button when prompted to equip the RPG and get ready for some fireworks. There's no need to actually manually rise here; it's done for you, so wait for the signal and resulting adrenaline-fueled bit of slow-motion. Keep an eye out for the glint of the scope, and send the business end of your single-use AT4 right into the sniper's spider hole. The resulting explosion offers some measure of vindication as it takes out Chaffin's attacker.

◆ COVER EXTRACTION OF CHAFFIN

GET INTO POSITION

The PLR aren't the only ones with some serious sniping talent. Black is just as adept, and he's packing a rifle of his own—perfect for covering the wide-open streets below for Chaffin's extraction. Head to the edge of the rooftop and look down toward a group of burned-out cars in the middle of the street.

PROTECT SQUAD

Directly northwest of the debris, PLR troops begin streaming out of an alleyway. More soon join the fight from the right, taking cover near car frames and dumpsters. When this first wave has been dispatched, another group appears on the rooftops across the street. Because of their higher vantage point they actually *can* hit you, so take cover behind the nearby satellite dish if need be. The enemies on the topmost floor are particularly dangerous, so dispatch them as quickly as possible. To mitigate the the scope sway when zoomed in, click and hold the Left Stick to take a big gulp of air and steady the shot. Black can only hold his breath for so long, so make sure to take a few seconds to let Blackburn catch his breath between shots when targeting enemies.

A third group of tangos will try to rush the extraction squad as they move up to another car, pouring into the street and popping out from the rooftops. Deal with this threat like the others, holding your breath if needed. A final group streams out of the very same gate your squad left a while back. Bear in mind that this group has seen you taking out their friends and will be just as concerned with attacking your squad as the rescue one—especially the PLR in the alcove-like upper floors of the nearby building. Unload on them to finally clear the way for Chaffin's escort to get him to safety.

FOLLOW SQUAD

Just as Doc Holiday reaches safety, the PLR comes tearing out of the woodwork, utterly swarming the streets on the way to the very building your squad is sitting atop. It's not really necessary or even prudent to attack these insurgents as they'll just keep coming. Follow the rest of the squad back toward the door you entered from, this time sweeping around to the left side. Campo and Matkovic grab a nearby plank and use it to create a makeshift bride to the nearby rooftop. Cross slowly and drop down into the neighboring courtyard.

■ [KNOW YOUR JARGON]

Oscar Mike

A combination of two military letters Oscar for O and Mike for M, used during radio communication to clearly designate letters that might be otherwise confused (M/N, S/F, etc.). "O M" means "On the Move", so the squad is Oscar Mike toward the site where Viper Squad last made contact.

■ [KNOW YOUR JARGON]

Break

Used during radio communiques to indicate a pause in the conversation (as opposed to "Over" to mean preparation for a response, or "Out" to signal the end of the communication at the time). Because warzone radio chatter is often cluttered with multiple types of broadcasts, "Break" lets everyone on the same channel know there is room for more high-priority conversations to slip through as needed.

■ [TIP]

Salvation in a Box

As the squad makes their way through the courtyard and into a nearby building, they gain access to one of the most valuable objects in the field: the lowly Ammo Crate. Sometimes hard to see, utilize these boxes whenever possible—simply walk up to it and all ammo for the currently equipped weapons will be replen-

ished. Bear in mind that Ammo Crates also often contain specific weapons that can make the fights immediately ahead a bit easier, so swap weapons as needed.

More insurgents make you grateful for that Ammo Crate as they clog the nearby hallway to the left. Take a cue from the rest of your squad and stack up next to them, crouching to stay out of the line of fire. Sneak out, pop off a few shots, then get back into cover as needed. There are quite a few PLR insurgents in this tight hallway, and more move in as the squad moves up (including some that may fire prone).Stick to the generous bits of cover littering the floor while advancing. When the group rounds the corner at the end of the hallway, they come upon a difficult sight: two of Viper Squad's men have been slain, and as Montes kicks open the nearby door, the screams of the locals make it obvious something big is about to happen.

FOLLOW SQUAD

The meat market is anything but a pleasant place to go shopping. Viper Squad's Humvee shows the signs of a brutal ambush, with a Viper squad member in grave condition. After radioing for a CASEVAC, the discovery of an IED attached to the nearby van only makes things worse. While the rest of the squad is exposed, it falls to Black to investigate where the wires attached to the IED actually start.

■ [KNOW YOUR JARGON]

IED/Secondaries

Most explosives, like Improvised Explosive Devices, use secondaries—materials that aren't themselves volatile but will add explosive force to a nearby explosion. In the case of Matkovic's discovery, he's found a bomb that's primed to explode, but still needs that detonation force before it will go off. In other words, those wires leading... somewhere

TRACE WIRE TO SOURCE

Black's just been nominated for an emergency game of "follow the wire." Use the Action Button to bust through the nearby door the wire runs under, into a laundromat and down a set of stairs to a decidedly dingy back room. Both doors are locked, so you'll have to go prone and crawl through the duct work to find out where the wire leads again. Yet another tremor makes the crawl a little more interesting, but eventually the ducts lead to a hole that drops Black into the building's basement. Head toward the wire and get ready to do a little disarming.

CUT THE RED WIRE

Before there can be any dismantling, an ominous shadow falls across Blackburn. It quickly reveals itself as a hostile that engages Black ina tense fistfight. Follow the on-screen prompts to knock this PLR goon out cold, but be quick about it. The IED's trigger is quickly counting down and if this fight isn't over quickly, the rest of Blackburn's squad will have front row seats to a Marine barbeque.

REACH THE TOP

Things topside haven't gotten any less tense now that the bomb has been defused. Race up the stairs and then head back toward where you dropped in from the vent. Hang a left and jump over the fallen shelving to arrive back at the crashed Humvee and van, steeling yourself for what is bound to be a huge fight in a very open, compromising market.

◈ CLEAR THE LZ OF ENEMIES

CLEAR THE WALKWAY AREA

CASEVACs may be used to extracting troops from dangerous areas, but no flying support can actually touch down to pull the injured Marines out without a clear, relatively safe place to land. As Black exits the laundromat, more Marines are gunned down in front of him by serious weapons fire. Take up a position using the now-disarmed van as cover, taking out any PLR forces on the street. Eventually, you'll get the call to take up some heavier arms of your own.

HOLD THE WALKWAY AREA

■ [KNOW YOUR JARGON]

LMG

Contrary to their name, Light Machine Guns are anything but underpowered. Their name comes from the ability to provide heavier firepower than a standard assault rifle, but they're "light" enough to be deployed with a simple bipod near the barrel. Bigger machine guns may require a tripod for more stability, making them Medium Machine Guns. An LMG's ability to be quickly deployed to provide covering fire or bursts of hot lead at multiple targets makes them an extremely good tool for evening the odds.

Quickly move Black up the nearby stairs toward the waypoint on your screen. Grab the LMG and get ready to push back against the PLRs flooding the streets. If needed, the corrugated sheet metal offering paper-thin cover can be knocked out with a burst from the LMG. Once it's cleared out,you can go prone and pop the bipod to steady the LMG while looking through it's scope. Gun down as many of the insurgents as possible, making careful note of ones that are grouped near the building to the left. As the crude cover disintegrates under a barrage of gunfire, move to another sheet of metal to allow the color to seep back into Black's world. A pair of explosive threats must be mitigated as best you can; grenades will be lobbed up onto the walkway even as RPGs are deployed to add even more pain. Take out the RPG grunts first, as they present the most pressing danger. Don't forget to keep an eye out for that grenade indicator; these guys have better throwing arms than you might think.

■ [TIP]

Big Gun, Big Clip

One of the LMG's best traits is that it has a monster-sized clip to deal with threats. The downside? It takes much, much longer to reload than other weapons; the case must be opened and a new belt of rounds inserted. In all, the process takes several seconds that can feel like an eternity, and can leave you open to incoming fire. Make the most of the 100 bullet belt by staying the urge to reload after every firefight. Nothing's worse than getting gunned down while in the middle of a reload.

GET ON 50 CAL

Eventually, a pair of enemy vehicles with some heavier firepower will show up. Even with the LMG, Black's not going to last long against them, so head back near the Humvee and hop in the .50 cal turret highlighted on the HUD to begin repelling more insurgent forces.

DEFEND

The most immediate threat that must be dealt with are a few PLRs directly in front of the turret and a few more near some cars to the right. Both are capable of attacking Black quickly, so deal with them before turning the barrel on the stream of enemies pouring out of the street—at least until a real earthquake putting the previous tremors to shame rips through the streets of Al Sulaymaniyah. Not only does it crinkle the concrete streets like so many sheets of paper, but the building dead ahead starts to pitch... and then tumble directly toward Black.

UPRISING

VITAL STATISTICS

UNIT	1st Recon Marines
CALLSIGN	Sgt. Henry "Black" Blackburn
LOCATION	Al Sulaymaniyah, Iraq
DATE	March 15th
TIME	2036hrs Zulu Time

MISSION SUMMARY

Mission Summary: After an impromptu nap, Blackburn wakes to find Al Sulaymaniyah in ruins. The quake has absolutely ravaged not just Iraq, but neighboring Iran as well. The whole border area is left in shambles while a madman and the PLR occupy the former Iraqi town en masse. If Black is to have any chance of surviving, he must make his way under the cover of night to first find a weapon, then reach the extraction zone without becoming another POW—or worse.

INITIAL WEAPON LOADOUT

 Tactical Blade

WEAPONS FOUND DURING MISSION

AEK-971	AKS-74u	SAIGA 12K	KH2002	G3A3

◇ AVOID PLR AND REACH SAFE AREA

RETRACE STEPS TO BAZAAR

Despite the raw troop numbers and generally unfavorable lighting conditions, there's still plenty of shadow here to hide within. Stay out of sight of the PLR as they scour the area. Move slowly along the channel created by the quake, sticking to the right wall where the lip above keeps Black out of the light. Crouch under the downed heli's skids and continue to stay to the right within the shadowy passage created by the overhang.

A lone guard with a flashlight complicates things a little as you inch farther ahead. Fortunately, the sweep of his light follows a pretty simple path. Wait for it to sweep toward Black, then to the left to inch underneath the guard, hugging the wall to the right. Another sweep back to the left allows further movement toward a pipe in the distance reveals some startling news: a dead Marine tumbling out of the wreckage of a Humvee has a radio quietly broadcasting that the allied forces here are leaving—and soon. Time to get to that RZ.

All Misfit victors, this is Misfit Actual. Regroup at extraction point "Lima", we are pulling out, over.

Upon nearing the pipe, a prompt to go prone appears, allowing access away from the PLR patrols. Head through the pipes, dealing with a surprisingly tenacious rodent, then head toward the open door in the distance by using the familiar Action Button prompt.

■ [CAUTION]

Rats!

For a particularly entertaining death, simply spare the rat from the business end of your blade. It means having to repeat this short little sequence again but trust us, it's absolutely worth it for Black's last few moments before shuffling off this mortal coil.

SECURE A WEAPON

An oblivious PLR combatant is too busy studying something on top of all those rugs to notice Black's presence until his blade opens up the opportunity to pilfer his weapon. Quickly draw a bead on the alerted soldiers and take them out if possible, but taking cover is the absolute priority here. At such close range, these enemies can easily end your game even on lower difficulty levels, and on the harder ones? Forget it. Pop up quickly to spot a target, line up a shot, then drop to recover any health if needed. Squeeze off quick double-taps to the targets' centers of mass or quick headshots to end this bit of resistance. Once they're eliminated, gear up for their backup to arrive.

◆ FIGHT YOUR WAY BACK TO EXTRACTION POINT

RETRACE STEPS TO PARKING LOT

A few latecomers will round the corner to the right. Deal with them similarly, using low cover to sneak out and add a few more headshots to Black's total. As soon as they're dealt with, proceed down the darkened hallway toward a blaze at the far end toward another short encounter with a few more PLRs before rounding the corner to the left.

An ominous chopper patrol and a few far-off troops are still scouring the area. Deal with them from the relative safety of the nearby crates, then move forward toward even more quake-riddled streets and a handy Ammo Crate.

CLEAR THE AREA OF ENEMIES

This parking lot is far more rife with threats than it first appears. A pair of PLR patrols are busy snaking their way through the few cars that haven't been completely destroyed by the quake down below.

Unseen, more wait to the right, obscured by a small outcropping of concrete and burned-out car frames. Obviously, dropping down into this lower area would be a bad idea. For one, the upper area provides a terrain advantage. But more importantly, there's only one place that the enemy can actually flank you: on the far right past the cars, there's a small ramp allowing enemies up. Keep this in mind while going for a fairly easy Achievement/Trophy—easy as long as none of the PLR actually catch sight of Blackburn.

[ACHIEVEMENT | TROPHY]

Heads Up
Head right while staying crouched to avoid the patrols below. Scoot around the fire toward a precariously positioned taxi. Look down to the left, waiting for the two-man patrol to slowly make their way toward the cab. They'll never walk directly underneath it, but that's fine; they aren't the ones that are going to made into Liberation pancakes. When they've swept back out into the parking lot, mash the Action

Button to kick the cab down onto the poor sap below to snag the Achievement/Trophy, then quickly shift left to grab a bit of cover, as the cab has now left this landing exposed.

Check Your Six

As mentioned before, this little area is great for firing down on enemies, but it can be easy to get tunnel vision while gunning down the troops below. Keep your head on a swivel here; as the first few enemies are taken out, more will come pouring in from the garage, and they're well aware of your position. Move back toward the white car next to the fire and use it for cover before enemies can get the drop on you. Alternately, cut off their only means of getting up to your perch by using the rubble as cover while slowly moving forward to deal with the enemies in the garage.

Whatever your strategy, make sure all the enemies are cleared out of this area before following the waypoint marker back into the garage. A small aftershock rocks the building, killing the lights and offering a few audio cues that things are about to get dicey again. Hit up the Ammo Crate to the right of the rolling doors, but quickly beat a path back into the small side room in the northwest corner of the building. Keep your eyes on the leftmost door for a few more PLR interlopers. After the investigative unit is taken out, proceed from cover slowly, gunning down any other PLRs in the open— there's one near the white car, and another next to the planters in the street.

◇ RETRACE STEPS TO SCHOOL

The surprisingly intact bus ahead is blocking the main path. There's no way to get to the upper landing where its back end sits, so it's time to hop on the bus and investigate.

As Black nears the edge of the vehicle, an RPG strike tears open the roof and creates a second point of entry. Stay crouched to avoid incoming fire, popping out to zero in on the flashlights the PLR are carrying. Take them down one at a time, ducking back into cover as needed. Once all the lights have been permanently extinguished, make note of the next waypoint objective and keep your sights trained on the distance. After another, more powerful aftershock hits, there's precious little time to gun down the two targets in the distance.

After making your way back through a familiar gate, an insurgent will kick open the very same door Black's squad moved through what seems like ages ago. Gun him down quickly, then retrace your steps back through the choked (and now half-destroyed) rooms on the way to the original rallying point before everything went to hell.

Involuntary Euthanasia

Speed is absolutely critical here; the falling building ahead offers just a scant few seconds to acquire the twin targets before the building pancakes the pair as only tons of falling debris can. The first begins sprinting away to the left more or less out in the open, while the second is frozen in

his tracks next to the wreckage of a car. Go for the target on the left first and then move on to the right before debris can claim them.

Montes makes for an unlikely reunion Black spills out into a hallway, delivering a grim bit of news: the dust-off of the extraction vehicle is quickly approaching. Time to race back to the extraction point— and fast.

FOLLOW MONTES

■ [KNOW YOUR JARGON]

MILNET

MILNET is the first spin-off from ARPANET, one of the packet-switching pillars of the original Internet. The Military Network allows unclassified information to flow between various global military operations overseen by the Department of Defense, using much of the same underlying technology as the Internet. However, MILNET is understandably walled off from civilian Internet applicationsthat otherwise piggyback off the ARPANET foundation.

> **IF I WAS A BETTING MAN, I'D SAY WE'RE GOING TO BE GETTING A TOURIST VISA IN THE NEAR FUTURE.**

The initial sprint back toward the Ospreys should feel eerily similar. In the darkness, the small alleyways crowded with covered shops just a few hours ago looks quite a bit different now. Duck into the hookah bar and wait for Montes to raise the door just enough to duck under, then keep on his tail as he sprints back toward freedom. Hardly a few seconds go by before yet another firefight breaks out, this time between departing Marines and more PLR insurgents. Sprint down toward the flares and take cover behind the left Humvee to assist Montes and the others with the extraction.

◇ SECURE EXTRACTION

REACH EXTRACTION POINT

ENTER HUMVEE TURRET

HOLD OUT FOR OSPREY

There's really nothing the Marines can do but lay down enough suppressing fire to hold back the swarms of PLR that threaten to compromise the extraction landing zone. Hop in the nearby Humvee's turret and swivel the mounted .50 cal turret around easily to acquire targets. Thankfully, there are really only a few places the PLR seem to be coming from. The first is dead ahead; a set of cars, one with its lights still on, offer a steady trickle of PLR targets to mow down. The second is a small covered camp-out spot near the central lighting towers on the street. The third is a wall near a white car offering cover to the PLR streaming out of the alleyway behind it. Avoid taking out the car if possible; while it makes for a satisfying explosion, the flames and smoke it spews out help to obscure the PLR coming out of the alleyway. Quickly find and take out the various targets as they continue to leak into this area while waiting for the arrival of the Ospreys.

■ [CAUTION]

Fire, Don't Forget
The .50 caliber turret's ammo is effectively unlimited, but the gun heats up rapidly during bouts of sustained gunfire. It doesn't take much; if you start to hear the rate of fire slowing accompanied by a heavier chugging sound, ease off the trigger and allow the gun to cool. It takes several seconds for it to cool off, which is why it's extremely important to avoid letting it happen in the middle of a firefight. It only takes a single round to take down a ground troop with a weapon this mighty, so fire in single or few-round bursts rather than simply opening up with everything the turret has. Nobody likes taking a bullet to the dome because they were stuck waiting for their own weapon to cool down.

■ [KNOW YOUR JARGON]

Know Your Jargon: Osprey
The MV-22 Osprey, a variant of the Bell-Boeing V-22 is a staggeringly agile, resilient Vertical Takeoff and Landing (VTOL) and Short Takeoff and Landing (STOL) tiltrotor aircraft. It's capable of setting down almost anywhere and taking off just as easily thanks to its ability to swivel the rotors from a normal helicopter-like position parallel to the main fuselage to one perpendicular, allowing full forward thrust. This allows the aircraft to descend more or less straight down like a helicopter, yet also achieve far faster forward speeds than a conventional heli. This versatility is thanks to its turboprop engine that combines normal rotor blades and a jet-like turbine engine. This combination of helicopter and airplane technologies gives the MV-22 a clear advantage at both high-altitude deployment and low-clearance loading, making it a perfect extraction vehicle for the Marines currently under fire.

The Osprey takes a little small arms fire while beginning its descent into the LZ, but shrugs it off. It's not until an incoming RPG from the nearby rooftops smacks into it that the pilot must find a more secure LZ to pull everyone out. While it relocates, concentrate fire to the front of the Humvee, down a darkened alleyway where plenty of PLR targets offer a chance to really unload with the .50 cal. After a gunning down a wave of enemies, a well-placed RPG will streak straight towards Black and the Humvee, knocking him clear.

■ [CAUTION]

Make Like Usian
The final part of this mission is a simple and clear-cut one: get your ass into that Osprey, Marine. Of course, the hail of gunfire coming from the left isn't going to make it a leisurely stroll—especially on the hardest difficulty level. Don't even think about returning fire here; there's far too much incoming fire, and the Osprey is already beginning its dust-off. Instead, employ a combination of sprints and dives to maintain forward momentum at all times. It's going to be a seriously difficult push to make it through the open, but the small channel through the crumbling street offers just a bit more protection from flanking fire. After that, a straight sprint should be more than enough to grab Montes' outstretched hand and kiss Al Sulaymaniyah goodbye.

GOING HUNTING

VITAL STATISTICS

UNIT
CALLSIGN Lt. Jennifer "Wedge" Coleby Hawkins - WSO
LOCATION USS George H.W. Bush, Persian Gulf
DATE October 31st
TIME 0600hrs Zulu Time

MISSION SUMMARY

Mission Summary: The Marines on the ground need a little airborne firepower to help assist with operations in Tehran in the search for a high value target. Unbeknownst to Lt. Hawkins, her sortie has a direct link to Blackburn's operations on the ground, albeit from a few thousand feet up.

■ [KNOW YOUR JARGON]

CAG, WSO

The Commander, Air Group, is responsible as the chief pilot for organizing any air operations onboard an aircraft carrier. In this case, operations are being handled by the U.S. Navy. Hawkins is actually a "wizzo" or Weapons Systems Operator that can be a member of the Marines or Navy. The WSO handles the actual firepower in the back seat of an F/A-18 Hornet while the pilot takes care of maneuvers.

■ [KNOW YOUR JARGON]

Whisky Delta

Literally "weak dick," this indicates an operation that is not for the faint of heart or flaccid of extremity. In other words, this is not going to be a normal flight op, and is of extremely high priority.

■ [KNOW YOUR JARGON]

DASC

A Direct Air Support Center is an ad-hoc, ground-based setup to allow coordination between forces on the ground and air operations underway overhead, including operating unmanned UAVs and drones. During this mission, you'll hear plenty of chatter from the DASC as they relay intel from troops on the ground, making this easily one of the most chatter-rich parts of Battlefield 3's campaign.

■ [KNOW YOUR JARGON]

ELINT

In combat, the single most important element is information. The more one side knows about the other, the better prepared they are in nearly all operations. This is precisely why Electronic Signals Intelligence is so valuable. ELINT is essentially a cross-section peek at the detectable spectrum of electronic signals. It can create a surprisingly detailed construct of various radar, electronic, communications and even GPS frequencies that reveal installations, vehicles, and more. Anaylzing all the signal noise coming from an enemy location, ELINT provides critical informationthat even satellite or infrared observations may miss.

■ [KNOW YOUR JARGON]

Cat Shot

Despite their impressive length, aircraft carriers are still markedly shorter than most runways. To assist with takeoff, a catapult mechanism is attached to the front landing gear of a plane which literally "shoots" them similarly to a crossbow down a channel cut into the deck, rapidly bringing an aircraft up to takeoff speed. The entire steam-powered process goes from standstill to cruising velocity in seconds, and allows multiple aircraft to be deployed in rapid-fire fashion.

◇ PREPARE FOR CAT SHOT

COMPLETE PRE-FLIGHT CHECKS

Sometimes being aboard an aircraft carrier almost seems magical—aside from the cramped quarters, lack of personal space, long deployments and cacophonous ambience, of course. Still, the ramp-up to this flying op is nothing short of an audiovisual overload in the best possible way. Sit back and enjoy the brief tour of the bowels of the USS George H.W. Bush before heading up onto the deck. Amid choppy seas and the constant spray of the Persian Gulf,follow the on-screen prompts to complete the pre-flight check. Lower the canopy, check flaps/stabs, spin up the main cannon, check that missiles and countermeasures are good to go, and then hold on for the coolest roller coaster ride ever made.

■ [KNOW YOUR JARGON]

HMD

A Head-Mounted Display is one of the most lethal tools a wizzo has available to them, allowing targeting through the simple action of looking at (more specifically, turning one's head toward) a target. With it, weapons can be deployed without ever taking eyes off the target. When dogfighting, keeping tabs on a target is absolutely paramount. Constant breaks, dives, ascents, and rolls are used to help shake pursuers, and all it takes is a second of lost focus to turn the predator into prey.

■ [KNOW YOUR JARGON]

Angels

Altitude in thousands of feet. "Angels" precedes the actual measurement, so "angels 3" indicates an altitude of three thousand feet.

After turning to a proper heading, you and your wingman punch through heavy clouds on the way toward potential targets. There's not much to do here save for admire an incredible view, but things are quickly going to change. Take a deep breath and prepare for the most expensive game of cat and mouse on the planet.

■ [KNOW YOUR JARGON]

IFF

Identification, Friend or Foe is a simple system for verifying if a target is a friendly. Contrary to the name, it does not necessarily mark targets that do not or cannot respond, or respond with an invalid code as a foe. This is due to the myriad reasons why an IFF response may not be received (damage, interference, etc.). That said, a negative or incorrect response most definitely *is* a valid reason to be on guard for the potential for an enemy threat.

The two unidentified bogeys decide it's best to shoot first and ask questions never, forcing a hard break to the left to re-acquire the targets. The pair of fighters break formation, forcing your wingman to follow the left bogey. Meanwhile, you and your co-pilot track the right one, which almost immediately begins dumping countermeasures. Time to go hunting.

■ [KNOW YOUR JARGON]

MiG-29

It's a testament to just how powerful the Soviet aircraft counter-design efforts really were that a jet fighter conceived at the height of the Cold War is still in service today. The MiG-29 was designed as to directly counter to the US' F-15 Eagle and F-16 Fighting Falcon. It sports similar capabilities in terms of firepower, agility, and range.In addition, it is more than capable of holding its own as a formidable escort, air-to-surface combatant, and air-to-air threat. Simply put, Hawkins' and her wingman's planes aren't the only dangerous thing in the sky.

In a brilliant move, the pilot of the MiG dumps flares, immediately pulls up, punches his air brake, and sheds enough speed to swap places. Yes, that means there's a bogey on your six. Thankfully, this is precisely what a wizzo is trained to handle. Swivel your head around to keep the enemy in sight while your pilot performs evasive maneuvers to re-establish the natural order of things where *you* are the aggressor rather than the other way around.

It's a simpler task than it may sound, though that doesn't mean it's especially easy. Keep your eyes trained to the rear at all times and listen for the sound of a missile lock. When it turns into a steady tone, get ready to deploy flares. They are designed to throw off the heat-seeking missiles the enemy jet will try to unload with precision. There's a limited window of time to react, but deploying the flares is a multi-stage process that releases multiple flares to mask your jet's engines. A smattering of incoming fire from the 30 mm cannon forces your pilot to mimic the bogey's evasive maneuvers. He turns hard, dumps speed much like his opponent, and finally drops in behind the hostile craft even as it begins expelling out flares of its own. Keep eyes-on, as this is practice for protracted dogfights that may play out in the moments to come.

Have patience here; both your flares and those of the enemy MiGs are used heavily for a very good reason: they *work*—and work well provided they are used properly. Their deployment period is fairly lengthy; plenty of flares are shed in a single go, though they don't take terribly long to reload. That reload time is the absolute key to taking down these fighters with a carefully-paced shot. Most pilots will try to break away as they dump flares, creating a wide wake of heat that confuses the missiles. If you see a target beginning to bank, hold off on firing until they've leveled out—and likely after they've dumped yet another set of flares.

When being pursued, play the waiting game. Your HMD prominently indicates when a missile has actually been launched by lighting up as red as Satan's generous ass. Refrain from deploying flares until **just** after the display turns red. Generally speaking, if your pilot is turning and burning during a lock, it's a good idea to bust out the flares. If flying along a relatively straight trajectory, wait for the crimson hum.

FARUK AL-BASHIR IS ABOUT TO HAVE A REALLY BAD DAY.

◇ SECURE ENEMY AIRSPACE

TAKE OUT ENEMY FIGHTERS

Finally, a chance to turn the tables on these airborne aggressors. Hawkins' HMD goes into effect, locking onto any target that she (and you) can keep relatively centered in view. It's important to get off a clean shot here without letting enemy flares render your missiles useless. Play the waiting game and listen for the ticking sound to stop. Again, if the target jet is banking, prepare for their flares to fill the screen. Wait for them to subside, then launch and pray for a proper impact.

After a few more dogfights, the opportunity to unload with your own cannons comes into play. Press the weapon switch button just as you did during the pre-flight check, then get ready to finish things old-school. The engagement becomes all about classic dogfighting mechanics here; unload as the target is crossing *into* the line of fire. If you hesitate or wait for a perfect position, it will already too late and you'll have to switch back to missiles.

After finally finishing off his targets, your wingman moves back into formation from behind with orders to proceed to the original target. Unfortunately, a radar lock comes from out of nowhere and a bogey cuts the transmission short as your wingman is shot out of the sky. After a hard brake to avoid the same fate, *two* bogeys appear on your six. This is not going to be easy.

◇ CLEAR SKY

TAKE OUT REMAINING MIGS

A pair of missile locks is a bad situation to find yourself in, so respond quickly with flares to break both locks. Don't be stingy with the flares here when dealing with these close-range pursuers. After a few close scrapes, the enemies break formation and split up. This creates an opportunity to avenge your lost wingman. Hit them **hard** here, punching missile fire as soon as the lock alarm sounds to avoid deflections by their countermeasures. If the missiles don't take, fall back to the usual tactics, playing patiently to bring this cat and mouse game to a close. After taking out the first target, his buddy quickly slips in behind you and another bout of missile evasion begins. Deftly avoid the incoming attacks and down the last enemy fighter while pulling some intense Gs.

The skies may be clear of bogeys, but they most definitely aren't free of danger. While linking back up with the strike force, heavy anti-air and surface-to-air missile threats make it clear this isn't going to be a cakewalk. Perhaps its time this nimble fighter takes care of those SAM batteries...

◇ SECURE AIRFIELD AIRSPACE

CLEAR SAMS USING HARM MISSILES

■ [KNOW YOUR JARGON]

HARM Missiles

The AGM-88 High-speed Anti-Radiation Missile is a true marvel at turning an enemy strength into their greatest weakness. By homing in on the radiation produced by radar signals, this missile is able to snuff out a communications network hub with ease. Tracing the transmissions back to their source, the impressive payload literally follows a signal to its genesis and detonates. An enemy's transmissions become a bullseye that the HARM can target with incredible precision.

❝ HERE WE GO, HAWKINS. ❞

Follow the on-screen prompts to switch to the HARM, then look for the brightorange targets to come into view. Use the zoom button if needed, then center a target in the reticule until a hard lock is acquired. After firing, keep the target painted as the missile races toward it. Repeat with the other two targets to secure the airspace for strafing and bombing runs to come, and then move on to something a little more challenging.

■ [KNOW YOUR JARGON]

JDAM

Nothing says "teamwork" like the Joint Direct Attack Munition. The JDAM is an Army/Navy co-developed combination of GPS tracking strapped to conventionally "dumb" (read: unguided) bombs that allows them to seek out targets that have been painted by another source. In this case, it's the guiding hand of Lt. Hawkins that marks targets from high above, directing the bomb-equipped planes on their strafing runs. So long as a target is held in view, the deployed munitions will easily hit the bullseye every time.

◆ SECURE AIRFIELD SPACE

CALL IN JDAM TO DESTROY ALL PARKED PLANES

The second phase of the airport strikes is similar to the first, but requires more effort tokeep the target centered in view despite any sudden maneuvers your pilot might have to make. Switch to infrared view to see a smattering of warm jet bodies all around the airport. Wait for the flashing targeting reticle to turn solid, then center it on a plane in view and punch that fire button. Correct the aim as needed to keep the target centered until the air strike run is completed. Zooming in and out here definitely helps; pull out wide to look for the target, then zoom in to make sure the target is painted until the last second. Repeat for the other three planes on the field, then gear up for even more challenging target practice.

DESTROY PLANES BEFORE THEY CAN GET AIRBORNE

Three hangars hardened against normal air strikes are hiding a dangerous threat. Multiple jets parked there will complicate the mission significantly if they are allowed to take off. Thankfully, they glow in infrared just as brightly as the stationary ones that were taken out. Use the same wide view to first find the planes, then zoom in and paint them, holding on the target until they've been hit. There's only a short amount of time before they can throttle up and tear down the runway, so make the shots count. Take out three more planes to ensure complete air supremacy.

■ [TIP]

Playing the Waiting Game

It's tempting to try to take out the planes immediately as they expose themselves coming out of the hangars, but with so many hardened surfaces around them, some shots may not hit their mark. Instead, wait for the planes to fully clear the hangar's outer walls and begin turning onto the long stretch of tarmac. By the time the strafing run begins, the planes will be completely clear of obstructions yet won't have enough time to reach takeoff speed. Just don't forget to *keep them centered* to avoid a missed strike.

◆ TAKE OUT POSSIBLE HVT

TAKE OUT HELICOPTER USING 30 MM

■ [KNOW YOUR JARGON]

HVT

High-Value Targets are, just as the name implies, mission-critical or otherwise extremely important persons, resources or objects that are given the utmost priority in operations. In this case, the HVT may be somewhere in the convoy and will try to board the helicopter in hopes of escaping the allied forces on the ground. HVT persons are prized for their information, and as such are often wanted alive to be used for interrogation later rather than dead where their role in enemy operations can be transferred to another person.

■ [KNOW YOUR JARGON]

A-10 Thunderbolt

Filling the US military's need for close air support during the early 70s, the A-10 Thunderbolt is equipped with a staggeringly quick, Gatling-style 30 mm nose cannon that fires armor-piercing shells made from depleted uranium at a blistering average of 65 rounds per second. This ensures every strafing gun run is equally effective against ground forces and more heavily-shielded targets like transports and even tanks. At its heart, the A-10 Thunderbolt is an almost exclusively ground-attack aircraft designed to quickly light up a target area and get out. This specialized focus makes it ill prepared for air-to-air combat against specialized craft like the MiG-29s seen earlier in the mission.

Marking the A-10's gun run is similar to the previous support you've provided thus far with one important distinction: this time the target is marked wherever the crosshairs are at the time; no correcting the target or needing to track it here. When given the go-ahead, use the on-screen controls to switch to targeting for the Thunderbolt's run, line things up and press the trigger.

TAKE OUT THE RUNNERS

The helicopter and its PLR passengers will be completely obliterated, causing the rest of the ground forces to scatter almost immediately. Pick out the small group running away from the pack and lead them ever so slightly, then call in one last run and enjoy the show. Once the runners have been dealt with, the mission is marked as successful. As Hawkins and her pilot can head back to the USS George H.W. Bush, sit back and enjoy a first-person view of a carrier landing in the dead of night.

OPERATION GUILLOTINE

VITAL STATISTICS

UNIT	1st Recon Marines
CALLSIGN	Sgt. Henry "Black" Blackburn
LOCATION	Tehran, Iran
DATE	October 31
TIME	0645hrs Zulu Time

MISSION SUMMARY

Despite the military's best efforts, there are no specifics regarding the valuable intel believed to be in Tehran. Black and the rest of the 1st Recon Marines must push past heavy defenses in the Iranian capital in the hopes of seizing vital information. What Black doesn't know is just how valuable that information will be...

INITIAL WEAPON LOADOUT		
SCAR-H	870MCS	

WEAPONS FOUND DURING MISSION				
M320	UMP-45	M16A3	KH2002	G3A3
AK-47M	PKP PECHENEG	M98B	M1014	

◇ SECURE APARTMENT BLOCK

SET UP MORTAR

Seeing Tehran lit up by both buildings and weapons fire alike almost gives you pause to take in the beauty... if not for the fact that, in just a few seconds, Black and company will be sprinting for their lives through incoming fire. After getting orders from HQ, a mass of Marines gears up and charges down the hill. Their destination is a site for Black to set up the mortar he's carrying and provide light for the invading forces. The enemy strikes aimed at slowing the advance have their targets dialed in. This helps Black avoid taking damage by skirting the areas that areregularly hit. Travel along a slightly zig-zagging path right down the middle to arrive the mortar site without a scratch. Once in place, Campo assists Black in deploying illumination rounds to shed a little light on the situation. After that, Black gets boosted over the nearby wall by a helpful fellow Marine.

CLEAR RIVER BANK

Immediately after scaling the wall, all hell breaks loose. The PLR has set up a generous complement of ground forces and, farther up, machine gun nests to really complicate things. Deal the most immediate threat first: the enemies on the other side of the canal. Move left behind the cover afforded by the large rocks, and then drop to a knee or go prone. Sneak out slowly to the right while scoped to take out the bridge targets as they come into view. If you come under fire, simply scoot back to the left to recover health before resuming your attack. Once all four enemies on the far side have been taken out, it's clear to charge down the hill into the riverbank itself.

Danger in this next section can come from multiple angles; PLR up above will fire down into the canal as their friends use the staircase at the far end of the canal to push back at ground level. Deal with the upper enemies first, using the boulders and wall to the left to avoid incoming fire as needed. Gun down the enemies in the creek bed next, pushing up toward the stairs where a waiting MG nest blocks further progress.

ELIMINATE MG NESTS

■ [TIP]

Hot Potato

The easiest way to take the machine gun and its PLR operators out of commission is to lob a grenade. Aim a little above the sandbags that protect the emplacement, arcing the grenade just over them and into the nest. With luck, the grenade will take out

the whole group in one fell swoop. But if you don't trust your aim, you can always try holding the grenade button to cook it a bit and shorten the fuse—just don't hang on for too long!

With the first MG nest taken out, the second is now within striking distance. Though it's wise to use the walls underneath the first MG nest to push forward, even the crumbling bits ahead don't offer the best angle to take out the nest. Use the wall to take cover from the second nest, then , sprint left around the barriers back toward the canal, dive behind a small group of rocks just to the right of a light post. A PLR on the other side should be taken out before concentrating fire on the group surrounding the second MG nest directly ahead. Keep laying down suppressive fire to allow other Marines to move forward and lob grenades into the pit. Alternatively, you can attempt it yourself if you still have grenades. Once the second nest is taken out, push forward toward it by approaching around its left side.

There's a good chance Black and the other Marines will come under heavy fire as soon as they crest the hill, so dive into a prone position behind the sandbags of the second MG nest. Sweep left, diving as needed, to a large rock that provides cover from the enemy forces. Keep an eye out for PLRs up on the top of the wall that might fire down, but focus on the bulk of incoming fire coming from directly ahead. A few PLRs are standing, mostly stationary, off in the distance and can tag you quite well when in the open. Use the wall to the left as a guide and move up, leapfrogging over the nearby boulders that provide cover while watching your right flank for any PLRs that might still be up. After taking out any remaining combatants near the stairs, push up them to reunite with more Marines as they lob a grenade into the nearby apartments.

The grenade's explosion has thoroughly cleared the first few rooms of PLR. After bypassing an insurgent that met an unfortunate, fiery end, move through the buildings until reaching a door that requires button mashing to breach. Beyond wait more empty corridors and rooms, and another door to breach.

■ [CAUTION]

Itchy Trigger Finger?

As Black tries opening this second door, a PLR insurgent on the other side knocks him back, kicking off a slo-mo sequence. Unload on the armored grunt, then get ready for two of his buddies to return fire, one in first room ahead on the right and another behind a bit of makeshift cover. If you're quick enough in this section, all three enemies can be taken out without them ever getting off a shot of their own. Black's second default weapon, the 870MCS semi-auto shotgun, works great here. If it comes to an exchange of bullets, just use the wall on Black's side of the door to get a breather as needed before pushing on.

REGROUP WITH BRADY

Moving through the rest of the apartment complex is blessedly free of PLR encounters. Eventually, the corridors spill out into a garage where the rest of the Marines are being led by Captain Brady. Black and his squad are ordered to jump into a Humvee convoy on the way into the heart of downtown Tehran. Obey orders by jumping into the passenger seat of the second Hummer in the convoy. Enjoy a brief respite as the group of vehicles winds its way through what's left of the captial on the way to the financial district.

◆ DRIVE TO FINANCIAL DISTRICT

FOLLOW BRADY IN HUMVEE

The Humvees meander through the wreckage of Tehran's highway system without incident, though Captain Brady's talk of trying to catch the PLR off-guard by driving right into the middle of an ambush is a little disconcerting. The convoy finally reaches an impasse due to a car parked right in the middle of the road. Ordered to investigate the blockade, Black and buddies hop out of their armored transports and into a potential trap.

◆ CLEAR BLOCKADE

MOVE VEHICLES BLOCKING THE ROAD

Oh, hey, a stalled vehicle, this *definitely* isn't a trap or anyth-

Oh, yep, that was a trap alright. Well, if it's a fight the PLR want, the United States Marine Corps can most definitely provide it.

FLANK ENEMIES

Follow your fellow squadmates' lead and sprint as if your life depended on it because it does. Speed is of the essence here. When you arrive at the wall formed from the (literally) jacked-up street, make sure to duck or go prone and scoot under the overhang. If you're standing, the PLR on the overpass above can still snipe you well before you get a chance to get the drop on them. After a few seconds, another sprint up the stairs and under the overpass begins. Follow your squad through the belly of the bridge, up a couple flights of stairs and to a door leading out to the overpass itself. Campo kicks open the door, and the counter-attack is on.

While this bridge provides plenty of cover, it's also populated with some crack shot PLRs. Use the distraction of the convoy below to get the drop on the pair of PLRs on the left side of the bridge, then quickly duck back into cover behind the large truck nearby.

◆ SECURE THE BRIDGE

CLEAR THE BRIDGE

There are quite a few PLR tangos downrange, both on the bridge itself and on an elevated bit of rubble far off in the distance. Take this shootout slowly; just a few shots from these enemies can end Black's career quickly (especially on higher difficulties). Peek out, squeeze off a few shots if a target hasn't already acquired you, then get back into cover. When there are no clear targets from your position, sprint forward and find another safe piece of cover. Keep taking out threats here and advancing until nothing stands between the squad and that ledge at the far end of the bridge.

◆ PROCEED TO BANK

FOLLOW SQUAD

Head toward the wall and use the Jump Button to climb up, then quickly take stock of the situation down below on the other side. There are plenty of cars to use as cover, so resist the temptation to use this lofty perch to take out enemies. There's nothing in the way of quality cover here, and Black will be just as exposed as the PLR troops stationed here. Jump down and slowly make your way up through the makeshift parking lot, making sure to drop to full prone if you take too much fire. These enemies are well hidden by darkness, so look for muzzle flash and do a little medium-range sniping as needed before moving up a bit more. As the squad makes its way to the top of the hill, something far more dangerous crashes through the wall to the left.

FLEE TANK

Yep, that's a friggin' *tank*. Without anti-tank weaponry to even the odds, the only smart move is retreat. Run toward the rest of the squad as they make their way through a small channel cut out of the earthquake-riddled street and do not stop sprinting until you reach safety. The tank is seconds from completely obliterating the entire squad, so this is most definitely a run for your life scenario.

■ [KNOW YOUR JARGON]

T-90

The T-90 tank is the third generation evolution of the technology that turned the tide during World War II. It's capable of laying down staggering amounts of firepower, resisting RPG attacks with heavily armored front and sides. Massive 125 mm rounds for the main cannon, anti-air and anti-tank capability, laser detection systems and more all combine to make something extremely dangerous to other tanks, to say nothing of a set of four fleshy humans trying to outrun its main cannon. Black and his squadmates must have somebody watching out for them because that was a one-in-a-million escape.

FOLLOW SQUAD

Worm your way through the darkened building with your buddies until finally reaching the outside again and one hell of a view. A massive bank looms overhead, dwarfing the other buildings nearby and allowing a small breather... right before a familiar friend shows up to spoil the sightseeing tour. Thankfully, that air support that was called in seconds before the squad emerged from the building does its thing in the nick of time, reducing the tank to a burning mess of rended metal. Count your blessings while following the rest of the squad toward the bank, taking heed of the warning that this wasn't the last tank the PLR has at their disposal.

SUPPORT JAVELIN TEAM

Sprint across the street, leaping over the low dividing walls between lanes and up the stairs to encounter a trio of PLR goons that have overwhelmed the Javelin team. A fourth insurgent attempts a flanking attack by kicking open the door to the portable building to the right after his friends are down. Show him what waits for those that try to surprise a Marine before considering what's next.

DESTROY REMAINING ARMOR

■ [KNOW YOUR JARGON]

Javelin

The FGM-148 Javelin represents the continued advancement of American military firepower, capable of fire-and-forget ease upon acquiring a lock-on. By opting to shoot *up* instead of directly toward a tank, the Javelin is able to pick up tremendous speed thanks to gravity's help and plunge straight down into the comparatively unprotected top of a tank. Once a Javelin's operator has acquired a direct line of sight lock on a target, they need only fire and find cover while the missile heads straight up, then straight down.

With heavy armor quickly approaching, securing a means to remove them in lieu of a dedicated team is vital to the success of the mission. Thankfully, there's a Javelin waiting near the sandbags. The only problem? The tank guarding the bank is pointed right at the squad, meaning standing up with a giant anti-tank weapon is only going to make Blackburn a priority target. Drop to the ground and listen for the tank's main cannon to fire, then stand, aim, and lock on before firing. *Immediately* drop back down into a prone position to avoid the tank's inevitable return fire while the Javelin completes its roller coaster trip toward that lock-on target. Once the tank is out of the way, it becomes a little easier to pop Black's head up to scope out the situation, but things are going to change, and fast.

If one tank is bad news, then two is akin to getting bathroom duty for a year. While the head's in constant use. In Hell. The strategy here isn't wildly different from last time, but the importance of keeping your ass *down* most definitely is. The only time you should be doing anything other than laying down and listening is when you're getting

ready to fire. Keep an ear out for the main cannon's fire (bearing in mind it's more than capable of destroying any nearby walls to get at the squad), pop up, lock on and then flatten yourself immediately. Try to slide to the right or left a ways while listening for the second tank's cannons to fire, then pop up and repeat. The first tank will roll from the main street to the left, right up into the center of the bank's courtyard, allowing a precious few seconds to lock on before it can swivel the main gun around to take aim. The second tank isn't nearly as forgiving, steaming straight toward the squad down the street to the right of the bank. Take your time here and stay mobile even while on the ground; if Black goes down here, the entire three-tank disposal sequence must be repeated.

REGROUP

When all three tanks have been taken out, sprint across the street below toward the bank's courtyard. There's plenty of incoming fire from the PLR sitting in the upper windows of the bank, so use cover as needed until crouching with the rest of the group and awaiting orders. The push toward the bank was only the first part of the mission. Now it's time to find the back way into the massive building.

FLANK THE BUILDING

With so much firepower coming from the bank, a frontal assault would be suicide, but perhaps a smaller group of Marines could sneak by and slip in through a different entrance. Follow the squad, making sure to sprint by the staircases as the group rounds the plaza. When everyone stacks up near the left set of stairs, wait with them, then make a run for the sandbags near the middle of the plaza. Pop up when the other Marines offer suppressing fire and continue sprinting up the stairs directly ahead, slipping around the left side of the building toward a few more PLR obstacles. Gun down these grunts and continue skirting the left side of the building, getting a boost over the wall toward the next obstacle.

ENTER THE BANK UNDETECTED

After dropping into this back area, head toward the waypoint marker and get ready to give your buddy a boost. He'll climb up and kick down the ladder so you can join him in a seriously precarious bit of gymnastics. After watching him climb in through the bathroom window, it's time to do the same. Almost immediately after dropping into the room, a PLR insurgent attacks your ally. Follow the on-screen prompts to quietly and gruesomely eliminate this threat before getting ready to punch into the bank proper.

CLEAR THE ATRIUM

Giant, open structures might make for an awe-inspiring sight during normal business hours. But trying to re-take an occupied bank in the dead of night when every building occupant is packing assault rifles is a completely different story. This shootout is going to be more difficult than any you've faced so far, but by taking things very slow and picking off one enemy at a time, it can be done with minimal frustration. The most immediate threat is that of the PLR at the end of the short hallway beyond the last knifed guard. One insurgent will come to investigate things, but he's quickly joined by a couple more buddies. The shootout here is a matter of carefully peeking out of cover just long enough to fire off a burst or two. Since your buddy is already using the copier, hang back inside the doorway and pop out to gun down the PLRs at the end of the walkway. Once they're gone, things get *really* interesting.

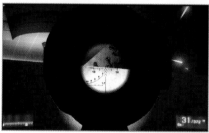

After taking out the trio of baddies, avoid the temptation to push forward just yet. The threats ahead attack from above, positioned throughout multiple floors across the way. Hug the left wall and pop up just long enough to acquire a target before grabbing cover again. One particularly pesky tango waits on the second floor from the top all the way to the right of the room, giving him a great angle to fire down on you. He's hardly alone up there. Multiple PLRs dot that level, sniping from just about every angle. Take your time here, either popping up very briefly to find a target or by staying prone and slowly inching backward until one is revealed. This leaves Black's legs rather exposed, so it's best to use this only when you're sure you're lined up for a headshot.

After removing the upper-level threat, there's still plenty of forces on this floor to contend with, so stay low and inch around toward the rows of cubicles. These flimsy walls offer hardly any real protection. Instead, use the more solid stone walls to the left to block incoming fire as needed. Enemies will bunch up near a set of crates and a pillar around the opposite side of where you came in. Retrea to the walkway where you knifed the guard and pop up long enough to reduce their numbers from a distance before inching forward.

Patience is key here. If Black dies, everythinghas to be done again, starting with the knifed guard. There's simply too many enemies here to try to blast your way through on the easier difficulty

levels, to say nothing of the challenge of doing this on the hardest. If a scoped assault rifle isn't doing the trick, try the M98B sniper rifle resting next to a table to the left of where the cubicles start.

Even with the opposite hallway cleared of enemies, don't start breathing easy just yet. Backup is waiting for you and your buddy down below, but there's still plenty of danger about. A few straggling PLRs appear on the opposite side just one floor above where you first entered this massive shootout. Take them out the same way as you have until now with slow, deliberate progression. Rather than trying to fire down into the open area below, pause near the stairs leading down to the other squad and snipe at enemies that are exposed to the right and left. A few PLRs will try to stick to cover near the columns on either side of the room. Once they've finally been cleared out, it'll be safe to move on.

REGROUP

Head down the stairs and bunch up with your fellow squadmates near the door leading deeper into the bank. After a bit of coordination, Black's squad is told to find the vault and hopefully with it, Al-Bashir. Montes kicks down the door and the way forward is revealed.

◇ SEARCH THE BANK

GAIN ENTRY TO THE VAULT

Signs of violence only grow more grim as the Marines head lower into the depths of the building. Bodies are strewn everywhere and an open elevator shaft isn't making things any easier. It falls to Blackburn to lead the charge down the shaft. Follow the on-screen prompts to hook up the rapelling gear and then slowly slide down toward the floor below. A pair of flashlights betrays a PLR presence and, after lobbing a QTE-assisted flashbang down into the room below, a slo-mo flying kick starts yet another shootout.

Deal with the closest enemies first, then sidestep right to use the wall ahead and columns to the side for cover. Shoot through the shelves to take out enemies down the hallway, but don't forget to monitor the hallway to the left. There are a few columns here where enemies will bunch up for cover, though they can be chipped away with enough weapons fire to allow for easier shots. Always maintain a solid wall rather than a column between you and enemy fire. Pop out quickly and unload, then duck back into cover to reload and recover health if needed. Once these small rooms have been cleared out, Black and his squad can make their way into the vault—and the terrifying discovery within.

COMRADES

VITAL STATISTICS

UNIT	GRU
CALLSIGN	Dimitri "Dima" Mayakovsky
LOCATION	Paris, France
DATE	November 13
TIME	1320hrs Zulu Time

MISSION SUMMARY

With precious little time before Solomon puts his nuclear plans into effect and Russia is blamed for the incident, Dima and his cohorts from the GRU must find the nuke and recapture it before it can be detonated. This is a mission that must succeed at any cost—even if that means the lives of French police officers.

INITIAL WEAPON LOADOUT				
AKS-74u	AK-47M			

WEAPONS FOUND DURING MISSION				
M1014	AEK-971	F2000	G36C	UMP-45

■ [KNOW YOUR JARGON]

GRU

The Glavnoye Razvedyvatelnoye Upravleniye was formed just days before the armistice that marked end of the first World War. This resilient agency has survived Russia's transitions from military superpower to hotbed of revolution to civil war to thriving communist superpower to the fall of communism. As a military intelligence agency, the GRU had a bitter and long-lasting rivalry with the KGB that lasted up until the KGB was dissolved after a botched coup against Gorbachev in 1991. Through it all, the GRU has survived, and its operatives are every bit as tough.

❞ YES, TODAY A FEW PEOPLE WILL FIND OUT WHAT WE DID FOR HUMANITY. ❞

GAIN ENTRY TO THE EURONEXT BUILDING

Nothing like a leisurely drive through the claustrophobic streets of Paris to help hit home just how bad a nuclear blast in a densely populated capital would be. Dima and his fellow GRU agents discuss the threat as they steel themselves for the fight to come. They power-up a signal jammer to remove the possibility of remote detonation and prepare to infiltrate the Euronext exchange to take down Solomon and retrieve the suitcase nuke. After plowing through an already-occupied front gate, the trio cuts the power to the parking garage and heads down into the depths of the Parisian version of Wall Street.

A pair of masked enemies stands near a parked car on the far right side of the parking garage. Move up to the white van, crouch, and wait for orders to take down the terrorists with a pair of carefully (but quickly) executed bursts to their center mass. The whole garage turns into a flurry of gunfire, with Dima's friends sweeping to the right side columns. Do the opposite: run to the left and apply fire toward any masked enemies that may try to push back. Scoot along the left wall, using available columns and cars as shielding to close the distance to the enemies on the left side. With luck, they'll be too distracted by the two other Russians shooting at their friends to the right to notice you.

Flank the enemy wherever possible without creeping too far forward. Moving past the first column is a bad idea; instead, stick to this position and take your time, whittling away at the enemies in the middle and left sides before attempting to help out with the rightmost enemies. After the first few have been taken out, more masked menaces will join the party and should be dispatched in the same way. Keep in mind that Dima has multiple grenades that can be used to detonate the nearby cars to help clear out enemies. Use the limited grenade supply sparingly, as this will be one of the most protracted battles yet. When the floor is clear, the trio can proceed down to Floor B to continue the assault.

■ **[TIP]**

Lights Out

The headlights from the parked cars all through this garage are very good at obscuring enemies that might be nearby. Extinguish the glare by shooting out the lights while safely behind heavy coverto help get a clearer view of the situation.

Floor B seems deserted as the GRU proceed onward, only to have a machine gun open fire on the group. Thankfully, the van and cars nearby form a nice shield. Pop the headlights to get a clearer view ofthe gunner between two cars in the back-right. He can be sniped from between your vehicular shield's crack if you're quick and precise about it.After he's taken care of, follow your teammates down farther into the garage.

A sudden RPG strike against a stationary vehicle forces the team to sprint past the burning wreckage to the leftmost column similarly to the first shootout. *Unlike* the first shootout, there are quite a few more exposed angles here—just popping out to fire shots at enemies down range on the left can leave Dima open to hits from the right. Deal with these enemies on the right first, looking for muzzle flashes when they pop out of cover. Then swing your aim back to the left to catch enemies taking cover near the back columns and cars closer to your position.

After clearing out the first wave, more will pour in from the back corner of the room, largely protected by a waist-height wall. Most of the enemies will dash toward cover near the columns on the left and middle parts of the garage. However, a few eagle-eyed masked men stay put at the back of the room to take pot shots near the giant EXIT sign. Deal with the closer threats first to avoid being shot at while aiming at the longer-range targets, then pop them with a couple carefully-placed headshots. Push on toward the exit and into the exchange.

Threading through the pipe work and right angles of the garage's exit, the trio finally comes to a closed door at the end of a long hallway. It falls to Dima to breach, and the other two quickly swoop in to take down the unsuspecting goons inside. Almost instantly, they realize the area is choked with gas and all three don their gas masks. The restricted field of vision creates a tense atmosphere that can cause you to miss a handy Ammo Crate along the right wall. Stock up on ammo and consider switching to a more close-quarters weapon like the extremely quick AKS-74u that serves as the default secondary weapon. It may not have the scope of the AK-47M, but it makes up for it with little recoil and plenty of precision.

MAKE YOUR WAY TO SECOND FLOOR

Ascend out of the basement via a series of stairs, taking point when ordered. Before Dima can enter the doorway, a masked fighter starts a fistfight. Bad idea. Follow the single prompt after slamming his head into the wall to offer a one-way ticket back down from whence you came before pushing on into the exchange itself.

This office has become a tomb for the poor employees that used to work here. After navigating the walkway, hostiles appear when the trio makes its way to the first junction. Let your comrades deal with the enemies on the left and swing right, taking out a tango before he can draw a bead.

More enemies will join the fray, pouring in from the adjacent room ahead. Several find cover among the cubicles near the windows to the right. Be patient here, waiting for them to show their heads, then send a few carefully-placed bullets to their final resting place in your foes' noggins.

Keep pushing forward as enemies are taken out, sweeping right to hug the windowed wall where light is pouring in as your teammates edge into another part of the office. The wall emblazoned with MB is a great place to take cover from the enemies firing down from the upper ledge at the far end of the room. Keep an eye out for a few more tangos that will try to ambush and flank the team from the rooms on the other side of the cubicles. Deal with them before the enemies in the elevated positions, and then edge ever closer to the main target by dashing through a doorway on the far side of the room.

Another set of stairs and another door that must be breached. Stack up to the left of the door, allowing Kiril to kick it down and into—you guessed it—another shootout.

LOCATE DEVICE

Things quickly turn hairy as soon as the trio makes their way to another set of desks. Take the same approach as last time, splitting off from the main assault group. While Kiril and Vladimir proceed down the right corridor, get the drop on enemies from the left. Cover here is rather flimsy and thus fleeting. Be quick with your shots, capitalizing on the distraction that your teammates create as they move deeper into the gas-choked office.

Enemies will swarm in from a lower floor, but this shouldn't change your strategy. Continue hugging the leftmost path, getting the drop on enemies distracted by your buddies. After clearing out any remaining threats, head down the stairs into a sun-drenched lobby toward the main trading floor. The nuclear device is located here, accompanied by a heavily-armed security detail. Don't expect the fight to secure it will be easy. Check your mags, be ready to grab cover as needed, and get that friggin' nuke!

Stack up with Kiril and Vladimir, breach the door to the main floor and get ready for a serious firefight.

CAPTURE NUKE CARRIER ALIVE

The nuke carrier doesn't hesitate to flee the scene, covering his escape with a flashbang. While he makes his escape, scads of enemies swarm the trio. Quickly drop into a crouch and use the desks on the trading floor as cover while sweeping your sights to the right. Plenty of enemies will try to use the columns in this room for cover, so make sure they're dealt with quickly. If you can sprint over to the back-right column and go prone, you can catch enemies off-guard as they try to use this column for cover while they're distracted by your friends. Slide out and take a few shots at the enemies that seem to stream in endlessly, picking them off as they take refuge behind the upturned desks. Eventually, the reinforcements will subside, and the trio can proceed through the exit where all the enemies originated from.

In an unlucky turn of events, the signal jammer begins to run out of batteries. No time to waste here, then. The nuke carrier will take a couple wild shots at his pursuers as he flees, but the real threat here is waiting in one of the elevators to the right. The hostile within bursts out in a misguided attempt to stop Dima. Follow the on-screen prompts to give him a little taste of his own medicine. Continue the chase down into the lobby of the exchange, taking out a pair of guards while the rest of the masked men flee behind them. They arrive to discover a scene of utter chaos: the French police and the terrorists are embroiled in an all-out street shootout, meaning there are now *two* sets of hostile forces that must be considered. This is going to take some careful planning...

◇ NEUTRALIZE NUCLEAR THREAT

CAPTURE NUKE CARRIER ALIVE

MAIN TRADING FLOOR, THROUGH THERE. LET'S GO, DIMA.

Follow Kiril as he jumps over a railing and continues through a few back alleys. There's no point in engaging any hostiles along the way; the nuke carrier has gained valuable distance and must be stopped at all costs. Dash through the warzone, shrugging off crossfire and a few explosions as you tail the terrorist. After vaulting over a low cluster of wood, the duo finally catches sight of the carrier crossing a street to the train station. Again, avoid confrontation here; the nuke is the target. Sprint across the street and up the stairs. As they reach the top, a surprise Quick Time Event puts it all on the line. Watch for the familiar prompts and put an end to this chase once and for all before making a tragic discovery.

THUNDER RUN

VITAL STATISTICS

UNIT	1st Marine Tank Battalion
CALLSIGN	Sgt. Jonathan Miller
LOCATION	Near Tehran, Iran
DATE	October 31st
TIME	0915hrs Zulu Time

MISSION SUMMARY

Jumping back in time a little, Jonathan Miller's tank mission takes place before the events of Operation Guillotine, outside of Tehran. The tank battalion is charged with first clearing a path toward, and then into Tehran itself when a distress call from a certain Sgt. Blackburn changes things dramatically...

INITIAL WEAPON LOADOUT M4A1

■ [KNOW YOUR JARGON]

LOD

A Line of Departure is just that, a forward line where attack elements (in this case a tank battalion) can move to in preparation to move out for a combined assault or to coordinate with other attack or defensive elements. Miller's the tank battalion is en route to a jumping off point for the rest of the mission, as they patrol the wide open, high-altitude, unforgiving Iranian plateau desert.

■ [KNOW YOUR JARGON]

BM-21s

Though comparatively ancient compared to the military might thundering across the Iranian desert, the Russian BM-21 truck-mounted multiple rocket launcher is not to be trifled with. Their salvos are quite capable of putting down a huge amount of damage when they reach their target. Despite lacking modern refinements like laser guidance systems, the ability to launch up to 40 M-210F rockets within seconds means anything caught in the blast radius is almost certainly reduced to rubble. Being built on a truck platform, they are highly mobile and can be quickly deployed and fired before moving to a new location for reloading.

■ [KNOW YOUR JARGON]

Actual

Due to the complexity of communications, chain of command,and other factors, commanding officers infrequently issue radio communications themselves. Instead, orders and intel are relayed by operators to multiple units simultaneously. When a radio broadcast is identified as "Actual", it means the commanding officer, not an operator, is speaking directly to the unit. In short, your unit is being addressed by the commander directly, and you'd best listen up.

■ [KNOW YOUR JARGON]

REDCON

The Readiness Condition of a unit is broken down into four levels (five including REDCON-1.5) in descending numerical value indicating increasingly higher levels of preparedness. REDCON-4 means the unit is ready to move out within the hour, but radio communications are still kept open. REDCON-1, by contrast, means the unit is fully ready for engagement. The engines are running, everyone is at their post with weapons manned and hot, communications are relegated to mission-critical, and the operation is officially ready to begin.

After a brief bit of introspection brought on by homesickness, Miller is snapped back to reality by the mission at hand. After a bit of brief chatter while the battalion pushes forward, everyone is called inside and the mission officially starts with a bang.

◇ CROSS THE KAVIR DESERT

ENGAGE AND DESTROY THE ENEMY TANKS

The tank directly to the left of Miller's is hit by a surprise blast, revealing an enemy battalion of no less than six rival tanks heavily armed and bearing down on the Marines' position. Time to return fire and show these rolling hunks of metal how the USMC deals with enemy armor.

■ [TIP]

Trial By Fire

There's plenty of new stuff to manage here in the midst of this fight. For one, it provides a crash course on controlling and firing a tank at the same time. In the belly of this beast, zooming and firing buttons have been *swapped*, which can make things confusing in the heat of a shootout. The second is that a tank's extraordinary range allows it to engage enemies whiley they're little more than specks on the horizon. Unfortunately, that also means a bit of trial and error in leading targets. As a general rule of thumb, the farther a target is, the more it must be led in the direction it's traveling.

■ [TIP]

Tank Armor 101

It's easy to assume that tanks are well-armored all around. However, the composite materials used for plating are not only expensive, but heavy. In order to outmaneuver opposition, tanks must sacrifice some protection to allow for mobility and speed. As a result, front armor is considerably stronger than the sides and especially the back. It's best to try to flank or even get behind around a tank, as their armor is weakest at the back. Use this to your advantage both offensively and defensively. By turning into incoming fire, damage is minimized, while shots on enemy tanks from the side or back will produce a much more rewarding effect.

Use this knowledge to get an early jump on the pack of tanks by firing well ahead of the direction they're traveling in. Every reload means a dangerous bit of down time, and tanks aren't especially known for their maneuverability. Thankfully, as the enemy tanks roll closer, they become easier to hit, but the same goes for Miller and company. Keep moving, especially when the distance between battalions starts to shrink. If you don't have to adjust much to hit those tanks, they don't have to either.

> ❝ MILLER, PUT THE DINOSAUR DOWN. IT'S GO TIME. ❞

After polishing off a half-dozen enemy tanks, radio communication is cut short by a pair of T-72 tanks. Follow the on-screen prompts to switch over to thermal view to counter these tanks' camouflage paint jobs offer and take them out quickly.

■ [KNOW YOUR JARGON]

Say Again

No military organization will *ever* use the word "repeat" to confirm a command via broadcast. "Repeat" is used to indicate that a previous firing order on a position should be attempted again. To repeat a command, the military uses the far less confusing "Say Again," which is meant to overcome possible interference during the initial order.

As the battalion prepares to resume their original run toward Anvil Actual's commanded objective, things suddenly get a bit more complicated. A nearby camp is laying down a considerable amount of explosive rocket deterrence in the battalion's path, forcing the tanks to stop for a moment while the eyes in the sky are able to take a look at things.

An umanned aerial vehicle above allows Miller in his tank to take a peek the rocket battery, allowing him to lase the rockets for a gun run by close air support. After a little infrared-tinted feedback, it's obvious those rockets aren't going to be causing any present danger. Time to push forward and into the enemy camp.

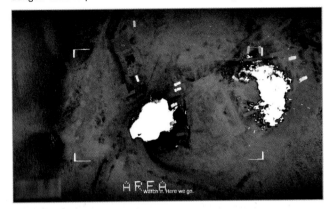

■ [KNOW YOUR JARGON]

Bingo

The only thing keeping aircraft airborne is their fuel. "Bingo" indicates fuel has fallen to a minimum level with enough remaining to comfortably return to base. While there are reserves allocated for extended sorties, bingo is usually considered the point at which an airborne vehicle should avoid staying out in the field, lest they risk dire gravity-based consequences. That incredibly helpful A-10 Thunderbolt has just hit E and needs to head back to base to refuel. No more convenient gun runs for Miller and his tank buddies from here on out.

The crew inside Miller's tank gears up for the oncoming wave by loading in new ammo and spooling up the machine gun turret mounted in parallel to the barrel. Aiming through the sights, Miller can contend with both ground forces and enemy armor without breaking a sweat, easily alternating between cannon rounds and rapid turret fire. The enemy camp won't know what hit them.

■ [KNOW YOUR JARGON]

HEAT, Sabot

Modern technology has enabled tanks to adapt easily to different combat roles. In addition to offering the ability to operate remote vehicles, their on-board armaments can be swapped out as needed. These Marines can switch the main cannon between Sabot rounds for long-distance targets and High Explosive Anti-Tank rounds for shorter ranges. HEAT rounds have a cavity in their nose that allows the full payload behind it to melt a shaped charge liner. As it melts, the shaped charge compresses the liner into a high velocity "jet" stream of metal that is funneled into a very small area to almost "drill" into the point of impact with maximum force . By contrast, Sabot rounds have a casing (the sabot itself, named after a fitting like a shoe) that keeps the dart-like depleted uranium penetrator rod centered within the wider tank barrel. The casing also provides a larger area for the propellant to push against, causing the dart to have even greater velocity right before the sabot casingis shirked upon leaving the barrel. The friction of this high-speed projectile against the tank's metal armor generates spall, metal flakes that are extremely dangerous to the tank crew within. By moving to HEAT rounds, it's a sign that hardened, armored targets will be in very close range. Something to keep in mind, perhaps?

ASSAULT THE DESERT ENCAMPMENT

Push hard and fast toward the camp. Multiple incoming RPG fire will make it difficult, but remember that tanks were literally *made* to handle explosives impacts to their front. The M1 Abrams tanks Miller's unit uses are capable of laying the hammer down to boost their normal cruising speed a bit higher at the expense of valuable fuel. Punch up the speed to spill over the berm protecting the encampment. Make note of the controls for swapping between the main cannon and a machine gun, as both will be needed in the upcoming breach. An air strike thankfully takes care of the forward RPG threat, but there's sure to be more inside.

The single biggest threat in this choked series of roads is RPG teams. The main cannon is quite adept at turning their positions into craters, but opening up the 7.62 mm machine gun provides excellent suppression fire to make them think twice about popping out. Deal with RPG teams to the right of the entry point with whatever weapon feels right, then roll around to the left to unload on the rocket batteries themselves. With the ground forces scattering, move on to the next objective dead ahead.

◆ REACH HIGHWAY 1

As the battalion surges across the open plains, they come across a mysterious dust cloud—an almost sure sign that there are enemy vehicles nearby. Just seconds later, a T-72 is spotted, followed by a friend, rolling across the horizon at high speed. Time for a bit more tank hunting.

CHARGE THE RIDGE

The enemy tanks' seemingly erratic behavior is soon explained when *four* new threats make themselves known directly on the Marines' left flank. Engage and destroy all six tanks using the same techniques as earlier; lead far off targets more than close ones, turn into incoming fire as needed and punch as many rounds as possible in to the sides or rear of the tanks. The entire enemy battalion will quickly disappear over a ridge, sending Miller and his battalion in pursuit. Keep in mind that a tank *cresting* a hill is at a disadvantage since its main cannons will be pointing skyward for a second, leaving the vehicle open to attacks without fear of retaliation. A smarter strategy is to roll over the hill at an angle, quickly getting the tank onto the downward slope to re-acquire targets with speed and precision.

DESTROY THE TRUCK COLUMN

A small convoy worms its way across the desert ahead, and orders come down to destroy them. Do so at range, switching to infrared and waiting for the convoy to eventually stop and spill out a anti-tank team heavy with RPGs. They are backed by a trio of enemy tanks that should be dealt with quickly before tending to the ground troops. Using the directional buttons, switch to the tank's 7.62 mm machine gun and take out the RPG crew as they sprint from one vehicle to the next to set up for rocket volleys. When they're gone, the remaining individual vehicles of the convoy can each be destroyed with a single shot from that 120 mm main cannon with ease.

FOLLOW 3-4 ONTO THE HIGHWAY

After that succession of attacks, the Marines finally get something of a break as they discover a surprisingly smooth main road for travel. Follow the rest of the tank convoy, admiring the scenery until further orders come in.

■ [KNOW YOUR JARGON]

B-1

Originally designed to replace the ailing and equally massive eight-engine B-52 Stratofortress bomber, the B-1 Lancer is a considerably faster, more agile, less radar-obvious and more modern way of delivering precision payloads in a variety of locales. Though its original designs didn't include such now-common innovations as smart guided bombs and advanced targeting systems, the later revisions of the B-1 have added these technological advances to keep the B-1 a critical component of modern deployments.

◇ CONNECT WITH THE MAIN FORCE

FOLLOW 3-4 TO HIGHWAY OVERPASS "ALTER"

The scope of the conflict's destructive repercussions is made readily apparent as the Marines finally link up with the main highway. Burning, twisted messes of metal litter the road. Continue on mission, following the convoy to Alter. When the convoy comes upon an overpass where heightened activity has been observed, Miller is ordered to move on ahead to investigate.

Push forward until Miller automatically hops out, then charge forward to meet up with an engineer from Hatchet Company to get the SITREP. Apparently, the unit was ambushed by PLR before they could properly detonate explosives planted farther up the road. It falls to Miller to brave intensive crossfire to retrieve the trigger mechanism.

◆ CLEAR THE MINEFIELD

PICK UP THE TRIGGER FOR THE LINE CHARGE

Thankfully, Miller can take cover behind his tank escort for a short distance. It can't move up all that far, however, so eventually you'll have to sprint from behind the tank to a bit of burning rubble. Sprint speedily from there to another burning Humvee to find the abandoned trigger sitting on a structure just to the left. After pressing the Action Button when near to pick it up, retrace your steps and sprint back, using the same pieces of cover to protect from incoming fire.

BLOW THE LINE CHARGE

Head back to the sandbag waypoint and use the Action Button again to detonate the mines and clear a path for the tanks to push on toward their objective. Head toward the lead tank while watching out for incoming fire, and press the Action Button to climb into the gunner's seat.

◆ CLEAR THE HIGHWAY TO TEHRAN

PROTECT THE TANK

The roughly straight path directly into Iran's capital seems relatively quiet, but it's actually peppered with multiple RPG teams and plenty of cover for them to hide behind. The .50 cal turret you're manning won't cut through the cover, but it can take out a normal PLR in a single shot. Remember the basics of heavy weaponry: fire in bursts, zoom as needed, and ease off the gun when it audibly slows to avoid overheating.

The first rocket troops pop out directly in front of Miller from behind some barriers. Another group waits along more barriers in the middle of the road, near a burning bus. Don't bother firing on the white car that crosses the road next, but continue to track it until more PLR run out into the open and gun them down. Past them, a group of RPG troops wait on top of a pair of buildings with red entrances. Take them out quickly by aiming just above the roofline and burst firing as the crosshairs pass over them.

Another vehicle starts moving on the right, a red van that you most definitely *can* blow up. Keep your eyes peeled for more ground troops around the vehicles until coming up on a tank near a gas station ahead. Simply shoot the pumps to cause a chain reaction that takes out troops and armor in one fell swoop.

Just ahead and to the right is a small covered building housing a couple of PLR and a vehicle that can be blown up. Don't spend too much time waiting on them; another RPG trooper waits, sandwiched between a length of stone blocks and a white house. Be sure to take him out quickly to avoid complications as the convoy finally arrives at objective Alter.

■ [KNOW YOUR JARGON]

V-BIED
Vehicular-Borne Improvised Explosive Devices like the white car that just barreled into 3-3 and turned it into rubble are particularly dangerous. They're mobile, pack a large amount of explosive material and blend in with other nearby vehicles. It's often hard to spot a V-BIED until it begins making a kamikaze run toward its target, so keep your head on a swivel to spot them before they can do to Miller's tank what they just did to 3-3.

■ [CAUTION]

A Chain of Explosive Events

The first V-BIED rolls up from the direction of the overpass, racing down Miller's lane. Wait for it to draw close to maximize the effectiveness of the .50 cal and unload as it crosses the threshold of the overpass. This is a life or death showdown, so open up that turret and let the full force of its firepower come to bear once the car is squarely in the crosshairs. At the same time, a pair of RPG troops will take up position around the rightmost car on the overpass. Gun them down quickly.

Another car roars up from 3-3's lane, but crosses through the median to head straight for Miller's tank. Follow the same rules as before: get it sighted in and unload with everything the turret has. If Miller fails to destroy it, he and his tank crew are miraculously spared as the vehicle careens off to the right of the tank, slamming into a wall and detonating.

From the same direction, another car comes barreling over the hill in the distance. This time there will be no close calls, so keep your aim true and gun the bomb down before it can make an impact. Be careful not to overheat the turret because *another* V-BIED crests the same hill after the first is destroyed, obscured by the smoke of the last car's explosion. Tear into it with everything left in the cannon before it can find its target, then quickly swivel left, back toward the overpass.

A final pair of RPG PLR take up spots near the leftmost car, intent on smacking as many of their rockets into the tank's side as possible. Take them out cleanly and precisely to put an end to this tense showdown at the overpass.

Move out toward Tehran to link up with India Company for resupply and an even more tense mission in the heart of the captial.

FEAR NO EVIL

VITAL STATISTICS

UNIT	1st Marine Tank Battalion
CALLSIGN	Sgt. Jonathan Miller
LOCATION	Tehran, Iran
DATE	October 31st
TIME	1045hrs Zulu Time

MISSION SUMMARY

As Miller and his fellow Marines make their way into Tehran, Blackburn and his squad are already there, deeply entrenched in the bank where they've made a grave discovery. If Black and company are to survive, they're going to need some serious help from Miller's battalion, which is precisely why Miller is heeding the distress signal and heading straight for the bank.

There's little to do as the battalion cruises through the heart of downtown besides drinking in the sheer level of destructive force a combined PLR coup and a massive earthquake have wreaked. It's not a pretty sight, but Blackburn and his Marines are in trouble, and a pair of tanks are just what the doctor ordered. Once the tanks move through a choked alleyway, Miller ducks down to avoid sniper fire and steer operation of the tank from the safety of the enclosed interior below.

◇ DRIVE TO BANK PLAZA

FOLLOW FRIENDLY TANK

Keep fairly close to the tank ahead as the convoy turns left, then left again, coming under fire from RPG-equipped PLR. One group spills out to the right of your tank buddy ahead, while another emerges from the rubble to the left.

MOVE OUT OF AMBUSH

Another group waits just ahead near the shops to the right. Bypass them by simply turning right and charging *through* those shops to find the main drag to the plaza and bank directly to the right. Though there are troops here, they don't pose a significant threat as long as you keep moving. However, the hostile tank near the bank across the street can. Tag it before it reaches its destination, it will make this fight a bit easier.

Switch to infrared to get a better picture of what the PLR armor situation ahead looks like. Aside from the aforementioned tank that was coming up the left, there's another sitting on the right side of the main plaza. As you inch forward, another tank is revealed on the main roadway in front of the plaza. Take all three out as quickly as possible, then push forward toward the bank and up into the familiar plaza setting.

Though the lighting conditions may be a little different, this indeed the same area seen at the conclusion to Operation Guillotine, and Black needs the Marines' tank support badly. As the tank rumbles up the steps, it's hit by something with far more oomph than a normal RPG, crippling the engines. Miller and his crew must fend off the converging PLR with the .50 cal. Get topside and start searching for targets; this plaza isn't going to stay calm for long.

◇ DEFEND MARINES

DEFEND BLACKBURN

Things seem calm initially. Miller and Black have a little conversation on a private channel about the nuke that makes the gravity of what they found in the bank vault that much more obvious.

The Marines have called for a helicopter evacuation, but it's going to take time. There's nothing to do now but stay put, keep your eyes open for enemies, and take them out with extreme prejudice. As the heli evac's radio chatter makes obvious, there are plenty of enemies closing in on this position to re-secure the nuke. Continue to lay down fire toward the left near a set of sandbags, to the middle (also near sandbags), and to the right near the stairs.

◇ DEFEND EXTRACTION HELICOPTER

DEFEND EXTRACTION HELICOPTER

More PLR swarm the plaza in hopes of stopping the helicopter. Given that Miller and his crew are stuck without working hydraulics, they have no choice but to continue to push back the enemy from their static position. PLR continue to advance from the same positions as before, forcing Miller to keep the .50 cal trained on those locations to hold them off for 15 minutes until help can arrive.

Anvil 6-6. Anvil 3-4. Status on QRF, over?

■ [KNOW YOUR JARGON]

QRF

A Quick Reaction Force is a unit designed exclusively for mobilization at a moment's notice, and are capable of everything from medical to engineering to bomb disposal and more. Except during times of intense fighting, QRFs may be kept at a lower REDCON level to reduce the resource burn of being at constant REDCON-1. However, QRFs still operate on the idea that they can respond in minutes—in this case, a rather harrowing 15 minutes. If Miller and company can just hold out long enough, the tank will be back up and running and they will be mobile soon.

◇ HOLD OUT UNTIL QRF ARRIVAL

HOLD OUT UNTIL QRF ARRIVAL

With no means to move out and heavy resistance, a call is made to check on support's estimated time of arrival, but it's not looking good. Continue to pour on the .50 cal diplomacy while holding out for support. Miller and his fellow Marines are literally sitting ducks here, so keep that turret hot. Eventually, the conflict will resolve itself in a surprising—but hardly welcome—way...

> **TANK IS IMMOBILIZED, WE ARE NOT COMBAT EFFECTIVE!**

NIGHT SHIFT

VITAL STATISTICS

UNIT	1st Recon Marines
CALLSIGN	Sgt. Henry "Black" Blackburn
LOCATION	Tehran, Iran
DATE	November 2nd
TIME	0358hrs Zulu Time

MISSION SUMMARY

The bank nuke is secured, but the question of the third nuke's location weighs heavily on Black and Campo as they prepare for their next mission. Under the cover of night, the two Marines plan to assist another team currently en route to capture Al-Bashir and gain his valuable intelligence.

INITIAL WEAPON LOADOUT		
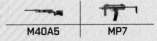		
M40A5		MP7

WEAPONS FOUND DURING MISSION				
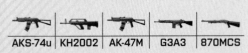				
AKS-74u	KH2002	AK-47M	G3A3	870MCS

A rainy, dark rooftop serves as the introduction to Black's mission at hand. After a bit of radio chatter and some misgivings from Campo, it falls on Black to snuff out any lights near the landing zone.

 SECURE MARINE INSERTION

DISABLE THE LIGHTS IN PARKING LOT LZ

[ACHIEVEMENT | TROPHY]

 Army of Darkness

The LZ is too bright thanks to those swinging, bouncing lights down below. To snag the Army of Darkness Achievement/Trophy, Black must take out all four lights with just one shot each. The key is to aim not for the lights themselves, but their small, conical coverings. Observe the way the lights sway and bounce for a moment before firing, then hold your breath and tag the light boxes one at a time. Using breath control here to minimize scope sway is absolutely important. Although Campo might harp about the timeline, getting these shots right the first time means ignoring his impatience and making each shot count.

With the lights out, the Osprey is clear to land, and deposits a quintet of Marines into the dark parking lot. Though nearly invisible to the naked eye, the Marines' body heat makes them quite obvious through Black's sniper scope. Track the Marines as they drop in and take up position along a nearby wall.

CONFIRM COLE'S IR SIGNATURE

After using the scope to view Cole's infrared flash, make sure Black and Campo have moved to the right side of the roof above the Marines. Track their progress as they move to another area of cover.

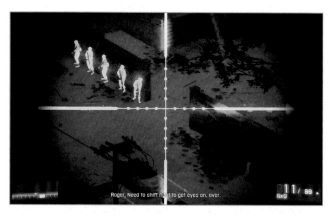

ELIMINATE LOOKOUT

A lone PLR strolls out into the balcony of a nearby apartment. He should be fairly obvious through the scope, but if you're having trouble finding him, just track right and slightly up from the Marines' position. The clueless PLR lookout will have no idea what hit him...

◆ REACH RV POINT BRAVO

RAPPEL TO STREET LEVEL

There's nothing like running down the side of a building to get the blood pumping. After making it to ground level, the mission becomes all about stealth.

AVOID ALERTING PLR PATROLS

Follow Campo through a gauntlet of enemy avoidance, starting with crouching by the same car Campo drops near to avoid the oncoming truck. Sprint with him down the street, then duck right into an alley and climb over a nearby wall.

ELIMINATE SENTRY

Another PLR lookout waits here, but is easily taken out with a little held breath and a clean shot.

FOLLOW CAMPO TO ROOFTOPS

As you push forward, a partrol emerges from a nearby alleyway. Wait until they pass, then sprint toward a ladder and climb it to another vantage point to help out the Marines below.

◆ SECURE MARINE CROSSING

ELIMINATE THREAT

The Marines down on the ground level cannot do anything until you take down the two guards below. Use the scope to locate them on the right side of the street, dead ahead.

[ACHIEVEMENT | TROPHY]

Twofor

Nailing this Achievement/Trophy isn't especially hard. But like the parking lot lights, there's only one chance at it without having to reload a checkpoint. Move as far to the right as possible along the roof to get the two tangos nice and lined up. Then crouch and steady your breath, aiming for the

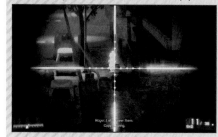

front PLR's head. Take the shot and you'll drop both at the same time, as the bullet whizzes through one skull and into the neck of his buddy behind him.

ENSURE THE MARINES CROSS STREET SAFELY

This is arguably the easiest objective in the game to complete. Just keep your eyes on the Marines as they use cover cross and move past barriers into the building formerly guarded by those two PLR you eliminated. When they're clear, head down the ladder to the right.

AVOID ENEMY PATROLS

There's not much to say about this objective either. Once you and Campo are on the ground, a big ol' PLR convoy decides to rumble through the rain-drenched streets. Take cover next to Campo at a nearby vehicle until it passes. Then follow him up onto the overpass and back down, heading left into a building to avoid further patrols. Once inside, they discover a PLR, necessitating his quiet termination. Creep forward with your blade drawn and stealth attack him, which leads into a lengthy, and unfortunately noisy, death that alerts a PLR patrol. Time to run.

ESCAPE PLR

With enemies on your tail, there's no option left other than to run—and run like hell. Follow Campo, moving in a serpentine fashion to reach a blown-out hole leading down to the sewers. After descending, Campo places a charge near the entrance before sprinting ahead down the tunnel. Follow and listen for an oh-so satisfying explosion behind you.

REACH STREET LEVEL

Thankfully, the PLR haven't yet infiltrated Tehran's sewer system, but that doesn't mean they aren't close. Listen in on a conversation between a few of the insurgents above while making your way toward Campo's position by a ladder at the end of the sewers. Sharp ears will pick up on the fact that Al-Bashir is *indeed* here in Tehran, which explains the sheer numbers of patrols in the area.

ELIMINATE HOSTILE SQUAD

In fact, one of the many patrols is right on top of Black's position. This shootout is particularly rough because there's not a huge amount of clear cover and the enemies are extremely hard to spot. In addition, they appear to be better trained, firing more accurately than previously encountered enemies. It's important to take note of that from here on out, firefights will be significantly more dangerous. Use either the low wall dividing the street to the left or the burning wreck in front to take cover, but know there are numerous enemies here. A small group waits to the right of the burning wreck, while still more open fire from the mound of broken concrete ahead. Take care when acquiring and firing on targets here; it can be tough to draw a bead *and* engage an enemy in the same pop-up from cover. These enemies know exactly where you are, and they'll all open fire the second you rise up. Use the old techniques from before: pop up, sight an enemy, then drop again to recover health if needed. Keep in mind that health recovery is tough when using the scope, as the normal blood spatter and color-draining effects aren't there. Repeat to take out all threats and move forward.

REGROUP WITH MARINES

Okay, so Cole has a bad habit of broadcasting very obvious, clear landmarks over open radio waves. That makes him something of a bad CO, but it also means the support Black and Campo so desperately need is at least in a clear place. Time to head there, but not before getting a peek backstage for Miller's execution video.

Though the mood is somber, Campo and Black can't afford the time to mourn. A PLR group makes a ruckus heading up the steps on the other side of the room, through the windows. Follow Campo's lead and drop to a knee in preparation for the enemies coming up the stairs. Campo is covering the left, so concern yourself with the enemies that spill in to the right of the large pillar in the middle of the room. They'll take cover behind that column and an overturned desk to the right, so quickly snap your crosshairs to the targets and fire. Move to the left to take cover behind the door as needed. Look for flashlights to betray enemy positions when firing back. Keep a watchful eye for grenades; there's little room to maneuver away from their blast radius that isn't compromised by those open windows. When it's all over, follow Campo down to ground level and the mall's entrance.

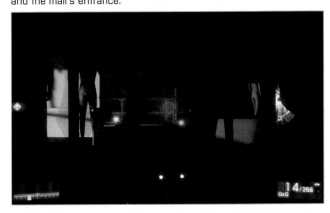

Cole could use some pointers to improve his motivational speeches. He actually *mentions* the possibility of things turning out poorly as you move through the mall, but at least he's right about it being a good place to fall back. Push onward with the other Marines on the way to capture Al-Bashir—alive, as Cole insists.

REACH OVERWATCH POSITION

Follow Campo to a sniping spot where he and you can offer a bit of cover for Cole's squad that's about to turn a small apartment complex into a warzone. This is not going to a be a quiet or easy op, so stay frosty.

COVER MARINE ADVANCEMENT

The squad comes to a sudden stop due to a PLR that doesn't see the group just yet. They move in from a structure to the right that Cole calls a "playground". Mark this as a point of reference as it'll be one of many places the PLR will mobilize from.

Cole's Marines stack up on wall below the main apartment complex, then push forward. Matkovic grabs a fellow Marine and plays babysitter while Cole's squad punches into the apartments from the ground floor.

DEFEND MISFIT 1-4

■ [TIP]

Night Vision

From your elevated position and with an infrared scope, you're capable of quickly finding and dispatching the PLR that will race to the defence of Al-Bashir. Campo will call out positions that should be kept in mind. The playground you already know about; however, there are more structures just up and to the right of that entrance. Ground level shows enemies in the parking lot straight ahead, but also on the walkways leading into the apartment complex from the playground.

PLR almost instantly starts flowing in, both around the same outside wall that Cole's team stacked up on before the parking lot and another, low wall just inside the lot above. To make matters worse, your position is compromised fairly early on by PLR that will fire on your position from the various levels of the apartment complex itself. Keep sweeping with the scope to spot their heat signatures and take them out as fast as possible. There's no core strategy here beyond just finding and eliminating targets as quickly as possible, with the priority being those in elevated positions that can actually hit you and Campo. Whenyou need to take cover, scoot right to hug a bit of rubble before popping back out to take out more tangos.

After Cole breaches the second apartment, things really go to hell. PLR know you're there and have positioned enemies on the roof of the building near the playground entrance. Deal with them quickly and cleanly before moving your sights down to the parking lot and playground, which are quickly erupting into a firefight.

A truck will roll in from the leftmost street, deploying even more PLR into the area. Take your time here and pick them off as best you can, but the playground nearby has plenty of threats, too. Stay calm and imagine being at a carnival shooting gallery. Scope targets, pick them off, then quickly sweep over to other areas where known PLR will group. There's the same low wall as before, the exit from the playground and the entrance of the parking lot now invaded by more PLR. One shot, one kill. Take your time and pull out of scope view every so often to make sure you're not in dire need of cover.

An RPG PLR shows up atop the apartment complex the roof when enough enemies have been downed. He can actually be taken out from between the areas of cover to the right of the normal, open sniping position. From here, it's also possible to gun down more PLR that are taking positions near the walls leading out of the playground. Eventually, Cole will scream about Al-Bashir making a break for it. No more sniping for you.

STOP HVT'S CAR ESCAPING

Follow Campo back to the right, sprinting over rooftops until you can both drop down to the street level below. A slo-mo event lets you tag Al-Bashir's car as it escapes, causing the HVT to swerve around a corner and crash, allowing you and Campo to scoop up the terrorist.

SECURE HVT

Al-Bashir is immeasurably more valuable alive than dead, and a wrecked car is a precarious place to leave him in. Sprint over to the wreck of his vehicle and grab him with Campo before attempting an extraction back near the start of the mission.

HOLD OFF PLR ATTACK

PLR are absolutely swarming your position, intent on bringing their leader back. Crouch near the low barrier next to Al-Bashir's wreck, wait for Campo to carry the HVT toward the open doors on the opposite side of the road, and then sprint to meet him there. The PLR in the streets are nothing if not numerous, making this a textbook target-rich environment. Grab a spot near the door and open fire on anything foolish enough to have a light. Use your scoped rifle if finding targets is difficult, as the PLR tends to group near cars for cover. After you dramatically increase the number of PLR that are KIA, Campo eventually radios that he's found a good place for the weakened Al-Bashir.

REGROUP WITH CAMPO IN RV POINT CHARLIE

Head back through the darkened ground floor of the mall and up an escalator to rejoin Campo in a small shop riddled with debris. Al-Bashir is not doing well, and certainly won't last long under the current conditions. He's weak, barely conscious and the PLR are moving in. Time to make a stand.

DEPLOY DEFENSIVE PERIMETER

The first priority is to use your best judgment in deploying claymores where you anticipate the enemy *might* show up. This isn't exactly an easy task with so many points of entry, and the clock is ticking. Throw down claymores near the top of the elevator entrance and position the remainder down the corridor where you've taken up position. Place one near the planter about halfway down the hall and another at the far end, near a bit of cover to the left, then high-tail it back toward the room where Al-Bashir waits, slowly dying.

The Waiting Game

This will be the single hardest part of the Campaign, and there's no clear strategy here beyond "shoot them before they shoot you." The first wave of PLR will make their entrance from the door you dashed through just a few moments ago. Look down the escalator and toward the door to pick off targets with your sniper rifle as they move in. At the same time these grunts move in, another team will blast their way in on the floor below, hidden by the escalator system and some walls. Take your time here, picking off the glowing bodies of troops as they move behind a long planter, behind a column to the left and a car down below. Take care to watch for enemies that will try to move up from below and to the right. They tend to take cover near the railings below before charging up the escalator, so be ready with a quick shot to their torso if they do so.

After the first wave on the ground floor, another will breach the floor you are on and will begin moving in from the far end of the mall. Thankfully, they are slightly funneled by the walkway leading from their side of the floor to yours. Take extreme care in dealing with these enemies, as they fire from the opposite side of the mall and can hit you even while you're crouched. Wait for the PLR to move up the hall toward you before taking them out. It's important not to stray out of the room with Al-Bashir. Not only does it provides ample protection from enemies outside, but some PLR can sneak by you if you aim down toward the back side of the mall. Look for telltale flashlights that appear at close-range and gun them down rapidly. Failure here means restarting this whole sequence again, right down to placing the claymores. An Ammo Crate just outside the room provides critical refills your survival will be depending on.

Clearly, your position has been compromised and it's time to relocate. Campo hefts Al-Bashir's slack, weakened form and carries him to a secondary position in the mall. Follow him into a shop across the very walkway in which you just gunned down seemingly endless waves of PLR. While he does, a series of explosions too close for comfort are heard as the PLR breach deeper into the mall. Despite the promise of an extract chopper on the way, things are quickly going from bad to worse. Make sure you have a weapon with a infrared scope on hand, like your sniper rifle, and get prepped for another battle from this new room.

Although it's certainly a factor, the threat this time isn't so much the PLR on your current level as much as the troops on the *upper* levels. Peek out from behind the bookshelf in this new room, acquire them, then duck back into cover. They're fixed in their firing positions, so it's most important to get your sights level with where they are first. After lining up the shot, duck back into cover, peeking out to take them down one by one during lulls in their bombardment. Keep an eye out for forces on your level, too. Some hostiles will descend the escalator nearby to make things complicated, so go slow here. Fix a target, take cover if needed, then dispatch them. The sheer number of enemies and their skill at drawing a bead means this is incredibly difficult on normal levels, and lethal on the hardest one.

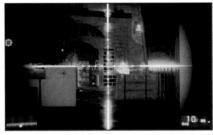

After whittling down the PLR numbers, Campo gets the call that the extraction vehicle is here. Only one problem: it waits outside with a sea of hostile opposition between here and there. Gun down as many targets at the far end of the mall as possible while staying alive, then let Campo do his thing. Even more PLR move in behind him, and sprinting to the exit will only end in a fatal hail of gunfire. Instead, try to push forward from one bit of cover to the next, making note of all the enemies to your right flank and those above. Push or sprint to the main, central planter before dealing with the immediate threats above. After eliminating them, catch your breath and recover health before sprinting out and around the planter, then right back through the exit from this mall.

DO NOT charge out ahead despite the enticing attraction of the helicopter rescue. You must supply covering fire as Campo brings the VHT into the Osprey's bay. PLR will assault the LZ from above with RPGs that can bring things to a swift end. You will have to restart the whole section following Al-Bashir's reclocation over if you die. Hold them back until things have subsided for a moment, then sprint like you've never sprinted before toward the bay of the VTOL. Once inside, things become just a bit more clear as Faruk Al-Bashir explains the seemingly cozy relationship between himself and Solomon.

ROCK AND A HARD PLACE

VITAL STATISTICS

UNIT	1st Recon Marines
CALLSIGN	Sgt. Henry "Black" Blackburn
LOCATION	Araz Valley, Iran
DATE	November 9th
TIME	0810hrs Zulu Time

MISSION SUMMARY

Black is on the tail of a Russian arms dealer by the name of Amir Kaffarov, who may have helped in moving the final missing nuke elsewhere around Iran. If there is to be any hope in finding Solomon, it must start with using Kaffarov to track him down. With Al-Bashir dead, the Marines are out of options.

INITIAL WEAPON LOADOUT	M16A3	SMAW
WEAPONS FOUND DURING MISSION	AN-94	

What starts as a downright tranquil trek through a small Iranian forest quickly turns dangerous as the convoy comes under fire from RPGs and ground forces alike.

 **RECON ARAZ VALLEY**

REPEL ENEMY ATTACK

> **THIRTY FOUR MINUTES. I'VE BEEN ALSEEP FOR THIRTY FOUR MINUTES. DRINKING A VANILLA MILKSHAKE. DOES THAT MEAN SOMETHING?**

One would certainly be forgiven for thinking this is just another routine ambush, but these skilled enemy marksmen demonstrate more extensive training than most.

Immediately grab cover behind the uprooted tree next to a fellow Marine. Duck safely under cover of the tree roots in response to incoming fire as the enemies here are extremely lethal. A few tangos can be eliminated by poking out behind the roots' right side. One takes up a position near the trees to the right, while another grabs cover near the burning wreckage of the first part of the convoy.

Still more enemies wait to the right of the roots, but trying to fire around the Marine here is problematic at best. The wall of rocks to the left can provide cover, but only when you're absolutely flush. Although the outcropping might seem safe, it's vulnerable to flanking fire from the right. Pick off these enemies one at a time and take the time to recover your health fully before exposing Black again. The hostiles are incredibly hard to spot, forcing you to rely on their muzzle flares to give them away—which often means they're firing at *you*.

When the first group is taken care of, push forward but don't make the mistake of staying in the open. More enemies pour in ahead, and one of them has an extremely deadly RPG. The bulk of the threats will take positions on the left side, but make the RPG bearer the absolute priority. These troops' superior aim means even the splash damage from an RPG can force you to start this whole fight over again. Take out the RPG by moving up and crouching or going prone behind the rock just ahead of the uprooted tree. There's a slight ledge created by some earth ahead, but this should be considered a fall-back position rather than somewhere to fire from. The threats to the right aren't of significant concern, but there is a clump of enemies waiting on the left side of the road that might be hard to spot without crossing over to grab cover elsewhere. Take things *slowly* here; nobody needs to hear about vanilla milkshakes more than once.

INVESTIGATE

On the plus side, these aren't PLR. The bad news? They're Russians, and that means the opposition is going international. Follow the rest of the squad up the path and back toward some semblance of safety.

◈ FIGHT THROUGH VALLEY

REPEL ENEMY ATTACK

The firefights ahead are unlike anything seen thus far. The sheer numbers of parachuting Russian forces are staggering to say the least. Stick to cover on the way down the hillside to confront the troops here. There's no real strategy beyond simply thinning their numbers. Push forward and gun down some targets, making sure to push up as the waypoint indicators change. Eliminate the tangos that take up positions behind cover ahead. Trying to gun down every Russian streaming into this battlefield is a foolish and possibly costly idea. Focus your fire on the forward operating enemies nearest Black's position. Continue to lay them out as efficiently as possible, moving up when the situation presents itself. Take care not to find yourself behind cover that can be easily destroyed. As a general rule of thumb, if it's metal, it's cover—at least until the softer stuff surrounding it is removed by heavy gunfire from those mounted turrets, leaving only a metallic skeleton.

After putting a sufficient dent in the enemy troops, a pair of mounted machine gun vehicles will show up. Their gunners are extremely dangerous, and must be taken out as quickly as possible via headshots. Once both are removed, the unit can regroup and figure out their next move.

With no other options, the unit proceeds onward and presses forward. The series of walls ahead are good place to drop to a knee and gun down as many enemies as possible—at least until they bring those god-forsaken turret vehicles into the picture. They present a significant threat, but they're nothing compared to the armored vehicle that rumbles in. Use the directional buttons to swap to a proper anti-tank weapon and lay the rumbling beast out.

SMAW

A Shoulder-Launched Multi-purpose Assault Weapon is far more than just a means to take out some enemy armor. Designed to be a bunker buster as much as an anti-armor weapon, the SMAW is capable of taking out both hardened structures and vehicles alike. Unfortunately, its limited capacity here means it must be deployed to take down something quite mobile and present. Once the armor has been removed, take out any remaining tangos and push forward toward another conflict.

The enemy heavies might be taken care of, but this new group of enemies is nothing to scoff at. Use the nearby rocky outcropping to go prone when in need of cover and eliminate every single enemy in this small camp. As they are taken out, a massive tower in the distance comes crashing down, snapping cables and no doubt causing considerable damage to those underneath is baleful shadow.

Charging down the road, another conflict erupts near a set of silos near a farm. The Russians here are relentless, but clear them out and push into the farm-like area ahead to quell their numbers. More occupy the neighboring areas to the north and northwest, so proceed slowly. Stick to cover and eliminate any hostiles that try to charge in. Push forward on your own if need be to hit the next checkpoint.

Before the unit is in the clear, a pair of the same armored BMP tanks seen earlier decide to make things more complicated. Thankfully, you're well-equipped. Bust out the SMAW when near a reliable piece of cover Black can go prone behind. Pop up and send a few shots apiece into those would-be dangers.

Follow the group toward a series of low cover near a car. Take your time here eliminating threats and moving up as cover provides; it's about to get far more explosive...

After some vocalized objections from Campo and Montes to the current op and its overwhelming odds against the Russians, things get far more pressing. A jet fighter shows up, all too ready to offer some serious air-to-ground complications. Sprint as fast as possible to assume position beside Cole for the time being and get ready to run for your life as the plane circles for more strafing runs.

The first buzz is simple enough to avoid. Sit next to Cole near the pipe for moment while the plane flies overhead, then begin making sprints toward the bridge. Behind you lies another pipe and the next piece of cover. From there, advance to the flipped car on the left side of the bridge, and then into an open cargo container. After the plane crosses again, head out and sprint toward safe cover behind the destroyed APC farther down the bridge. When the plane makes another run, sprint toward the burning wreckage at the end of the bridge in search of a way to take down the plane.

 DEFEAT RUSSIAN FAST AIR

SEARCH THE GROWLER WRECK

Sprint forward toward the objective while staying mindful of the plane's position. Eventually the location of the anti-air ordnance will be revealed.

GRAB STINGER AND TAKE OUT SU25

Scoot around to the side of the vehicle and hold the prompted button to grab the missile.

[ACHIEVEMENT | TROPHY]

Float like a butterfly...
Like Achievements/Trophies in the past, this one is for all the marbles; a one-shot assault on the plane currently buzzing you and your friends. The difficulty comes in getting a hard lock on the plane. If you try to get a lock as the plane is flying away, you're guaranteed to lose it as it's jet turbines carry it off in to the distance. Instead, take a hard stand amidst the wreck-

age of the Growler Black retrieved the rocket from. Turn and wait for the plane to come into range, get the lock, and then let loose, watching the missile find its target far off in the distance.

After all that fighting, this mission comes to a tragic and violent close. Let the memories and accomplishments of those that died in the line of duty live on in our hearts and minds.

KAFFAROV

VITAL STATISTICS

UNIT	GRU
CALLSIGN	Dimitri "Dima" Mayakovsky
LOCATION	Araz Valley, Azerbaijan
DATE	November 9th
TIME	0830hrs Zulu Time

MISSION SUMMARY Dima and the GRU have precious little time left to reacquire and secure the nuke or risk an international incident over presumed involvement with Solomon. Even as Blackburn is crossing the valley, Mayakovsky plans to drop in on Kaffarov—literally.

INITIAL WEAPON LOADOUT	MP7		

WEAPONS FOUND DURING MISSION	DAO-12	F2000	USAS-12	SCAR-H
	M60E4	AEK-971	AK-74M	RPK-74M
	M27 IAR	M39 EMR	PKP PECHENEG	

In the dim red glow of a cargo plane's belly, Dima and his friends check each other's equipment and set their height sensors in preparation for the drop. After a few moments, Dima punches a button and the back of the plane opens. Looks like you're taking the express route down to Kaffarov's compound. When the green jump light comes on, take up a position alongside the supplies and push the whole thing right out the back before joining it in a thrilling free-fall.

> **ASSAULT BATTALION IS CURRENTLY DESCENDING, NOBODY LEAVES OR ENTERS THE VALLEY.**

GAIN ENTRY TO KAFFAROV'S COMPOUND

HALO JUMP

■ [KNOW YOUR JARGON]

HALO

When your objective is getting boots on the ground stealthily, there's nothing like a High Altitude-Low Opening jump. They are designed to deploy units at extreme altitudes with minimal exposure to the plane and jumpers, who often require oxygen masks due to the thin atmosphere. HALO jumps typically involve pulling the parachute ripcord very shortly before pancaking the ground. This minimizes the risk of being spotted by cutting down on the time spent slowly gliding downward. Despite the relative safety of the insertion altitude, the rapid change in atmospheric pressure can have the same effect as divers get when ascending too quickly: the bends. As Dima and crew are racing the clock to find Kaffarov before the Americans, they've set the altitude to pull the cord at a gut-wrenching 500 feet.

After tumbling earthward for a few moments, enjoying one hell of a view, listen for a steady tone and use the Action Button to pull the ripcord. Once on the ground, stick close to the rest of the team and push onward through the forest.

RETRIEVE WEAPONS DROP

The canister that was pushed out of the plane along with Dima's crew was a weapons drop, a canister with serious firepower that will make getting into Kaffarov's villa much easier. Unfortunately, as you'll discover when following the other GRU operatives, the canister has been discovered by a small group of Russians. When your buddy drops to a knee next to a small mound, follow his lead but scoot around the *right* side to get a good firing position on the enemy below. Listen for the count to coordinate with your teammates, then simultaneously open up with small, quick bursts into the crowd. The idea is to eliminate as many of these curious grunts in the opening salvo as possible. The moment the small group is fired upon, their friends near the cars to the south will quickly return fire. Carefully drop down and open the ammo case to procure something a little beefier than your starting weapon.

The enemies near the car can be surprisingly deadly thanks to their shotguns and eagerness to lob grenades right into whatever cover you're currently using. Grab cover behind the smallish rocks closest to the vehicles. Either pop up just long enough to find a target or scoot slowly around the rocks themselves to get a good firing position. Polish off the last of the threats before looking toward the vehicles themselves as a way in.

GAIN ENTRY TO KAFFAROV'S COMPOUND

INFILTRATE KAFFAROV'S VILLA

Hop in to the SUV's back seat on the driver's side and sit back while enjoying the privacy provided by the car's tinted windows. Once inside the compound, get ready for a serious show of resistance. Wait for the button prompt, then pull the trigger on the guard standing just outside the window and slip out of the vehicle.

The door to the control room is forced open, allowing the team to split up. Punch the switch on the wall to open your door and a sliding door for the other two GRU operatives.

FIND KAFFAROV

ADVANCE THROUGH POOL HOUSE

A guard waits at the top of the stairs, alerted by the sound of the doors opening. Gun him down, then head up the stairs and immediately take cover near the stone wall ahead rather than one of the vehicles. The reason becomes clear just seconds into this firefight: a RPG trooper up on the hill fires down at the cars whenever Dima takes cover near one. Pick off the RPG from your current position behind cover before taking aim at the many troops nearby. They have no qualms about tossing an abundance grenades, so don't be afraid to return the favor. Keep pushing up, gunning down more enemies as they spill out of more SUVs, but keep an eye out for more RPG fire as you push forward. Slip into the small channel near the wall on the right side of the road and take out the tangos up above before pushing on.

Your GRU buddies move up quickly, taking cover near another series of walls and firing on the hostiles running down the hill. Although they mention a pipe nearby that can be crawled into to flank the enemy, it's possible to just wait out the firefight here, pushing up as your teammates do, though it's not nearly as sneaky or interesting as using the pipe to flank enemies. Regardless, continue pushing toward the pool house. As Dima and squad near the house, they discover the garage door is sealed shut and take a detour to the front door. After entering, your teammates will stack up near one door, while you can take the one leading to the garage. Just as you breach, a guard tries to overpower Dima who shrugs the attack off without incident.

After Dima and the GRU bound up the stairs onto the pool house's roof, another group of tangos opens fire from Kaffarov's main villa. Deal with them easily using a scoped weapon with an infrared sight like the AEK-971 dropped by the guard in the garage below. Stay low behind the planters here on the roof and pick off the enemies one at a time before moving up with your two buddies when the opposition starts to pull back.

Their retreat wasn't a concession; snipers spill out onto the roof of the villa, and should be taken out as quickly as possible. Continue to counter them with the infrared scope. The snipers come in waves, and can set up on the upper-most floor as well as the roof, so keep that scope moving to find the next target. Once all threats have been eliminated, it's time to move into the villa and find Kaffarov. Before moving on, keep the sniper rifle and swap out your other weapon with one of the DAO-12s laying around. The combination of short-range stopping power and infrared scope on this drum-fed semi-automatic shotgun is too useful to be overlooked.

CAPTURE KAFFAROV

The second the trio nears the front door, all hell breaks loose. Enemies try to push in from the left side of the room, so direct Dima's shotgun spread to quickly take out the two guards on the right. Flank any remaining enemies that are still engaging your buddies near the front door. When all hostiles have been cleared out, take a multi-story approach to tracking down Kaffarov; Dima heads up the stairs while the other two deal with ground-level threats. A single guard waits at the end of the hall after heading up the stairs. Take him out, then move into the next room, keeping an eye out for a guard that's standing on the deck. If he retreats to the adjacent room off the deck, just take him out through the windows before he can draw a bead. An Ammo Crate is your reward, as is an empty set of hallways for the rest of this upstairs trip.

After heading back down the stairs ahead to meet up with your buddies, swing around the corner facing the sunny deck outside and gun down a few more guards in the room ahead. The staircase leads up to an even sunnier pathway, but there's a hidden danger lurking here, so proceed slowly.

■ [CAUTION]

Rocket-Propelled Surprise
The second Dima makes it up the stairs, an RPG is launched directly at him. Whatever you do, don't stay in the open. Use the metal framing of the windows as cover if needed, or try to snipe the RPG troops from the stairs. An RPG to the face means having to repeat this *entire* villa shootout from the front door checkpoint, so proceed slowly. The RPG fire is coming from the opposite side of the house, from behind a small bar.

Once the room is clear, your buddies will stack up on the door and wait for you to breach. Unfortunately, there's another surprise waiting on the other side: a shotgun-armed grunt blows holes in the door when you draw near. Keep clear of the line of fire while Kiril tosses in a grenade the team breaches the room.

There are quite a few enemies in this darkened room, which makes having an infrared scope that much more important. Drop to a knee to use the many couches here for some cover, then sweep the outside of the room to take out as many guards as possible. Head up the stairs and watch the left door at the end of the room for a surprise guard. The other two squadmembers will stay on the lower level, leaving the upper floor all yours. The door on the right leads out to another set of furniture being used for cover. Eliminate the guards up here before helping your buddies below to avoid being tagged in the back while providing support. When all the guards are dealt with, head downstairs to regroup.

Head into the red room, restocking on supplies at the Ammo Crate as needed. This is it, the final push toward the fleeing Kaffarov. Head down through the blackened corridors before turning left into a long hallway absolutely swarming with enemies. Infrared scopes are invaluable here, particularly on a sniper rifle. But in a pinch, the enemy's own flashlights can be used to target and take them out before they can fire. Move up slowly, using the columns as cover while eliminating as many enemies at long range as possible. It's extremely easy to get flanked or to have cover blown away, so move between cover often and don't be afraid to go prone behind a buddy to recover health.

One of your comrades will kick open a door revealing a room beyond bathed in flames. There's no point in trying to push through this area; the two lethal machine gunners laying down fire at the far end are protected by a wall. Instead, follow the waypoints downstairs into a training area. This low-light section is filled with automated targets *and* hidden guards with laser sights that will blind if pointed directly at Dima's face. Move from room to room slowly, thoroughly eliminating each area's threats before moving on. Be mindful of enemies that can appear on the upper catwalks.

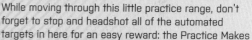

[ACHIEVEMENT | TROPHY]

 Practice Makes Perfect

While moving through this little practice range, don't forget to stop and headshot all of the automated targets in here for an easy reward: the Practice Makes Perfect Achievement/Trophy—just don't forget to concentrate on  any enemies that might be in the room first. Traverse the whole course, and don't be afraid to head upstairs to make sure you've tagged everything before moving on.

After dealing with the threats in the firing range rooms, head up the stairs to confront a few more guards in the room beyond the glass door. Inside wait the two machine gunners from that long, fiery hallway where your buddies have been waiting for you to flank the protected gunners. Gun down all the guards in this room to open the way for your friends to regroup before pressing onward. One of your GRU teammates will kick open a door leading to another staircase revealing a few guards at the top. Rush the staircase, unloading on any tangos as you push through the fire and explosions. At the top of yet another staircase wait a few more guards, but they can be taken down in a similar fashion as the last, especially if you're still rocking that DAO-12. Gun them down, then head for daylight.

 Kaffarov is getting away! Sprint toward the helicopter and press the Jump Button to grab onto one of the struts before the chopper can fully lift off. A simple Quick Time Event plays out, revealing an awesome mid-air bail-out and some parting words of disappointment.

THE GREAT DESTROYER

VITAL STATISTICS

UNIT	1st Recon Marines
CALLSIGN	Sgt. Henry "Black" Blackburn
LOCATION	Long Island, USA
DATE	November 14th
TIME	1755hrs Eastern Time

MISSION SUMMARY

This is it. This is for all the marbles. If the two government morons that have been grilling Blackburn for hours won't listen to the evidence, Black will have to deal with matters himself. Solomon is *not* going to do to New York what he did to Paris, not while this Marine is still breathing.

INITIAL WEAPON LOADOUT	None		
WEAPONS FOUND DURING MISSION	UMP-45	M1014	AK-74M
	AKS-74u	MP7	SAIGA 12K

When the interrogators return, wait for the on-screen prompt to take the first one out, then help Montes out with his captor. When both are down, head for the door, then out into the hallway.

◆ FLEE THE BUILDING

JUMP OUT THE WINDOW

With more misguided fools coming, there's no other option than to crash through the window at the end of the hallway. Sprint toward it and press the Jump Button when you get near for a spectacular escape.

◇ ESCAPE

REACH THE STREET

No time to dawdle, now; there's automatic gunfire behind you and a train that's right on time. Follow Montes up the stairs, then head down and toward the waypoint marker, watching for traffic.

REACH THE TRAIN

This should all look rather familiar by now. Just make a bee line for the objective and wait for the train to arrive.

JUMP!

When the train draws near, press the Jump Button to vault over the railing and onto the speeding cars below.

◇ STOP THE TRAIN

GET TO THE ENGINE

You ever get the feeling you've seen all this somewhere before? Yep, this is the very first level all over again, but this time, things aren't going to end so abruptly. Gun down the masked men as soon as you're given control of the situation, then repeat the process you did all those hours ago: duck under the rubble, push through the second car, pick up a shiny new weapon, lose it to a guard, leap to the next train car, gun down the enemies at the top of the train, jump back down, unload with automatic weapons fire through the next few cars, then, finally, reach the door where Solomon is waiting with a guard. Time to make things play out a little differently.

SECURE THE DETONATOR

Press the Action Button to kick off a scripted sequence that will be all too familiar. The unsuspecting guard is ambushed, then Black is ambushed and a Quick Time Event plays out. Follow the on-screen prompts, fighting off Solomon and taking his guard hostage. Commit to taking this terrorist down via any means necessary, even if that means doing yourself in in the process.

> **YOU'RE GOOD, SOLDIER. YOU'RE GOOD. WHAT'S NEXT? I'M NOT AFRAID TO DIE. HOW ABOUT YOU?**

◆ SEWER CHASE

CHASE DOWN SOLOMON

When Black comes to, Solomon has already gotten some ground on him. Groggily grab the AKS and gun down the guard in the same car, then move forward toward the fleeing Solomon, stopping to pick up the MP7 dropped by the guard. Its night vision scope will be invaluable in the minutes to come. Down below, a tango is busy pulling his buddy to safety. Though they can't be hurt until the injured man is put down, Black can drop in on them by just edging close to the hole. Be *extremely* tactical in this and every fight ahead; grab cover quickly, pop out only long enough to acquire a target, and unload with quick double-tap bursts to make sure enemies are down before moving on.

This first room has multiple enemies with laser sights that will blind Black if he catches them in the face. On top of that, flashbangs and frag grenades are being thrown like they're going out of style, so keep an eye out for the next bit of cover that can be run to, and check your six for enemies that might be hiding on the other side of a piece of cover as you move up. When the tunnel is cleared, push onward toward a small, watery lip that must be climbed onto, kicking off another fight.

Immediately run for cover, grabbing the slab of stone on the right side of the canal. Move quickly here, peeking out long enough to take down a tango before ducking back into cover and making sure to watch for grenade indicators. When the enemies in this room have been taken care of, check your mags, take a deep breath, and move *slowly* up the stairs.

■ [CAUTION]

Barrel o' Laughs

The goon waiting up these stairs is ready for you. He'll kick down a flaming barrel that will explode if it touches Black or is shot, so back away, letting the barrel roll out into the waterway below. Get some distance on it and detonate it to prevent an untimely end to this chase. If you die at any point during these battles, you'll have to do them all over again, starting with waking up on the crashed train, so be methodical here.

Past the flaming barrel and guard is a short ladder leading into another waterway and an inviting ladder. Head up it to kick start the final moments of Blackburn's valorous pursuit of Solomon.

Black can only watch as Solomon piles into a white SUV across the street and begins to escape. From out of nowhere, Montes comes through with a "borrowed" cop car and gives chase, headed straight for Times Square in the mother of all chase sequences. Eventually, Montes is able to catch up, allowing Black to poke his head out the window and take some pot shots at the SUV. Aim for the tires while unloading on the vehicle, and eventually a spectacular crash will play out, with Black and Solomon left in the open streets to slug it out.

[ACHIEVEMENT | TROPHY]

Between A Rock and a Hard Place
This Quick Time Event sequence is the last in the game, but it carries a heavy burden: you can't mess up a single button press during this knock-down, drag-out fight or the Trophy goes bye-bye (though you can always try restarting the checkpoint). Thankfully, the same buttons used time and time again throughout other QTEs, so take your time in making *sure* you're pressing the right button, then beat the shit out of this

terrorist scum and save the day while New Yorkers look on with no idea of the kind of bravery Sgt. Henry Blackburn has just demonstrated. But you know. And you're not the only one...

BATTLEFIELD COMPENDIUM

Multiplayer Scoring System

ACTION	POINTS	DESCRIPTION
ATTACK ORDER FOLLOWED	20	Have a squad mate follow the attack order
AVENGER BONUS	10	Kill an enemy within 2 seconds of him killing a friendly
COMEBACK	TBD	Comeback from a streak of 5 or more consecutive deaths. Score is number of consecutive deaths x10
DEFEND ORDER FOLLOWED	20	Have a squad mate follow the defend order
DESIGNATED TARGET HIT	TBD	Score based on how much damage the locked missile does
DESTROYED EXPLOSIVE	20	Destroy an enemy explosive (claymore, mine or C4)
DOGTAG SAVIOR	50	Rescue a teammate just as he is about to be stabbed
DOUBLE KILL	40	Kill two enemies in 0.8s of each other
DRIVER ASSIST	10	Have a passenger in your vehicle kill an enemy
ENEMY DOWN	100	Kill an enemy
EQUIPMENT DESTROYED	20	Destroy a stationary weapon that is occupied by an enemy or equipment placed by an enemy. This includes EODBots, MAV, Mortar, Radio beacon, SOFLAM and UGS
FLAG CAPTURE ASSIST	50	Participate in a flag capture
FLAG CAPTURED	100	Capture a flag
FLAG DEFEND	20	Kill someone while you or the victim is in the radius of a flag owned by your team
FLAG NEUTRALIZE ASSIST	50	Participate in a flag neutralize
FLAG NEUTRALIZED	100	Neutralize an enemy flag
HEADSHOT BONUS	10	Kill an enemy with a headshot (with a non-sniper rifle)
HEAL	10	Heal points awarded for every 10% health healed on a friendly
KILL ASSIST	50-100	Do at least 50 points of damage to an enemy and have a team mate finish them off. Note that this caps out at 100 as healing can restore the enemies hit points.
KILLSTREAK STOPPED	TBD	Kill an enemy who has made 6 or more kills without dying. The score awarded is the number of kills in the enemies streak x10
MARKSMAN BONUS	1-50	Score a headshot with a sniper rifle. Score increases over range
M-COM ARMED	100	Arm an mcom station
M-COM ATTACK KILL	20	Kill an enemy that is disarming the crate
M-COM DEFENCE KILL	20	Kill an enemy that is arming the crate
M-COM DESTROYED	200	Destroy an mcom station
M-COM DISARMED	100	Disarm an mcom station
MOTION SENSOR ASSIST	20	Enemy was killed while in your MAV's motion sensor range
MOTION SENSOR ASSIST	20	Enemy was killed while in your T-UGS motion sensor range
MULTIPLE KILL	100	Kill four or more enemies within 0.8s of each other
NEMESIS KILL	TBD	Kill the same enemy 6 or more times. The score awarded is the number of kills x 10
NEMESIS PAYBACK	TBD	Kill your nemesis. The score awarded is the number of times your nemesis has killed you x10
REPAIR	10	Repair vehicle points given for every 10% of damage repaired
REPAIR	20	Repair vehicle points given for every 10% of damage repaired
RESUPPLY	10	Resupply a teammate
ROAD KILL	10	Run over an enemy
SAVIOR BONUS	20	kill an enemy within 2 seconds of him dealing 50-99% of damage to a friendly
SPOT BONUS	10	Spot an enemy and have a team mate kill them
SQUAD ATTACK ORDER	20	Attack an objective that the leader has designated
SQUAD DEFEND ORDER	20	Defend an objective that the leader has designated
SQUAD DRIVER ASSIST	20	Have a squadmate who is a passenger in your vehicle make a kill
SQUAD ELIMINATED	10	Kill all members in a squad
SQUAD HEAL	20	Heal a squad mate
SQUAD PASSENGER ASSIST	20	Have a squadmate who is driving your vehicle make a kill
SQUAD RESUPPLY	20	Resupply a squadmate
SQUAD REVIVE	110	Revive a squad mate
SQUAD SPAWN ON YOU	10	Have a squadmate spawn on you
SUPPRESSION ASSIST	50	Suppress an enemy and have a team mate kill them
TARGET DESIGNATED	10	Lock on to an enemy vehicle with the target designator
TEAM PASSENGER ASSIST	10	Have the driver in your vehicle kill an enemy
TEAM REVIVE	100	Revive a team mate
TRIPLE KILL	60	Kill three enemies within 0.8s of each other
VEHICLE DESTROY	50	Destroy a vehicle within 10 seconds of an enemy leaving it
VEHICLE DESTROY ASSIST	50-100	Do at least 50 points of damage to an enemy vehicle and have a team mate destroy it. Points awarded are based on how much damage was done.
VEHICLE DISABLED	100	Disable a vehicle

Ranks

INSIGNIA	RANK	NAME	POINTS	UNLOCK	IMAGE	INSIGNIA	RANK	NAME	POINTS	UNLOCK	IMAGE
	1	Private First Class	1,000	870MCS Shotgun			24	Master Sergeant I	510,000	Desert Khaki Camo	
	2	Private First Class I	8,000	Sprint Specialization			25	Master Sergeant II	550,000	M9 SUPP. Pistol	
	3	Private First Class II	18,000	Woodland Camo			26	First Sergeant	590,000	Squad Ammo Specialization	
	4	Private First Class III	29,000	G17C Pistol			27	First Sergeant I	630,000	Urban Camo	
	5	Lance Corporal	41,000	Ammo Specialization			28	First Sergeant II	670,000	MP443 SUPP. Pistol	
	6	Lance Corporal I	54,000	Ranger Camo			29	Master Gunnery Sergeant	710,000	Squad Flak Jacket Specialization	
	7	Lance Corporal II	67,000	PP-2000 PDW			30	Master Gunnery Sergeant I	760,000	G18 SUPP. Pistol	
	8	Lance Corporal III	81,000	Flak Jacket Specialization			31	Master Gunnery Sergeant II	810,000	Squad Explosives Specialization	
	9	Corporal	96,000	Army Green Camo			32	Sergeant Major	860,000	PDW-R PDW	
	10	Corporal I	111,000	M9 TACT. Pistol			33	Sergeant Major I	910,000	Squad Suppression Specialization	
	11	Corporal II	130,000	Explosives Specialization			34	Sergeant Major II	960,000	SAIGA 12K Shotgun	
	12	Corporal III	150,000	Expeditionary Force Camo			35	Warrant Officer One	1,010,000	Squad Suppression Resist Specialization	
	13	Sergeant	170,000	MP443 TACT. Pistol			36	Chief Warrant Officer Two	1,060,000	.44 Magnum Pistol	
	14	Sergeant I	190,000	Suppression Resist Specialization			37	Chief Warrant Officer Three	1,110,000	Squad Grenades Specialization	
	15	Sergeant II	220,000	Paratrooper Camo			38	Chief Warrant Officer Four	1,165,000	DAO-12 Shotgun	
	16	Sergeant III	250,000	UMP-45 PDW			39	Chief Warrant Officer Five	1,220,000	Veteran Kit Camo	
	17	Staff Sergeant	280,000	Suppression Specialization			40	Second Lieutenant	1,280,000	P90 PDW	
	18	Staff Sergeant I	310,000	Navy Blue Camo			41	First Lieutenant	1,340,000	G18 Pistol	
	19	Staff Sergeant II	340,000	G17C SUPP. Pistol			42	Captain	1,400,000	Spec Ops Black Camo	
	20	Gunnery Sergeant	370,000	Grenades Specialization			43	Major	1,460,000	USAS-12 Shotgun	
	21	Gunnery Sergeant I	400,000	Jungle Camo			44	Lieutenant Colonel	1,520,000	.44 Scoped Pistol	
	22	Gunnery Sergeant II	430,000	M1014 Shotgun			45	Colonel	1,600,000	AS VAL PDW	
	23	Master Sergeant	470,000	Squad Sprint Specialization							

Ranks (continued)

INSIGNIA	RANK	NAME	POINTS	INSIGNIA	RANK	NAME	POINTS	INSIGNIA	RANK	NAME	POINTS
	46	Colonel Service Star 1	1,830,000		82	Colonel Service Star 37	10,110,000		118	Colonel Service Star 73	18,390,000
	47	Colonel Service Star 2	2,060,000		83	Colonel Service Star 38	10,340,000		119	Colonel Service Star 74	18,620,000
	48	Colonel Service Star 3	2,290,000		84	Colonel Service Star 39	10,570,000		120	Colonel Service Star 75	18,850,000
	49	Colonel Service Star 4	2,520,000		85	Colonel Service Star 40	10,800,000		121	Colonel Service Star 76	19,080,000
	50	Colonel Service Star 5	2,750,000		86	Colonel Service Star 41	11,030,000		122	Colonel Service Star 77	19,310,000
	51	Colonel Service Star 6	2,980,000		87	Colonel Service Star 42	11,260,000		123	Colonel Service Star 78	19,540,000
	52	Colonel Service Star 7	3,210,000		88	Colonel Service Star 43	11,490,000		124	Colonel Service Star 79	19,770,000
	53	Colonel Service Star 8	3,440,000		89	Colonel Service Star 44	11,720,000		125	Colonel Service Star 80	20,000,000
	54	Colonel Service Star 9	3,670,000		90	Colonel Service Star 45	11,950,000		126	Colonel Service Star 81	20,230,000
	55	Colonel Service Star 10	3,900,000		91	Colonel Service Star 46	12,180,000		127	Colonel Service Star 82	20,460,000
	56	Colonel Service Star 11	4,130,000		92	Colonel Service Star 47	12,410,000		128	Colonel Service Star 83	20,690,000
	57	Colonel Service Star 12	4,360,000		93	Colonel Service Star 48	12,640,000		129	Colonel Service Star 84	20,920,000
	58	Colonel Service Star 13	4,590,000		94	Colonel Service Star 49	12,870,000		130	Colonel Service Star 85	21,150,000
	59	Colonel Service Star 14	4,820,000		95	Colonel Service Star 50	13,100,000		131	Colonel Service Star 86	21,380,000
	60	Colonel Service Star 15	5,050,000		96	Colonel Service Star 51	13,330,000		132	Colonel Service Star 87	21,610,000
	61	Colonel Service Star 16	5,280,000		97	Colonel Service Star 52	13,560,000		133	Colonel Service Star 88	21,840,000
	62	Colonel Service Star 17	5,510,000		98	Colonel Service Star 53	13,790,000		134	Colonel Service Star 89	22,070,000
	63	Colonel Service Star 18	5,740,000		99	Colonel Service Star 54	14,020,000		135	Colonel Service Star 90	22,300,000
	64	Colonel Service Star 19	5,970,000		100	Colonel Service Star 55	14,250,000		136	Colonel Service Star 91	22,530,000
	65	Colonel Service Star 20	6,200,000		101	Colonel Service Star 56	14,480,000		137	Colonel Service Star 92	22,760,000
	66	Colonel Service Star 21	6,430,000		102	Colonel Service Star 57	14,710,000		138	Colonel Service Star 93	22,990,000
	67	Colonel Service Star 22	6,660,000		103	Colonel Service Star 58	14,940,000		139	Colonel Service Star 94	23,220,000
	68	Colonel Service Star 23	6,890,000		104	Colonel Service Star 59	15,170,000		140	Colonel Service Star 95	23,450,000
	69	Colonel Service Star 24	7,120,000		105	Colonel Service Star 60	15,400,000		141	Colonel Service Star 96	23,680,000
	70	Colonel Service Star 25	7,350,000		106	Colonel Service Star 61	15,630,000		142	Colonel Service Star 97	23,910,000
	71	Colonel Service Star 26	7,580,000		107	Colonel Service Star 62	15,860,000		143	Colonel Service Star 98	24,140,000
	72	Colonel Service Star 27	7,810,000		108	Colonel Service Star 63	16,090,000		144	Colonel Service Star 99	24,370,000
	73	Colonel Service Star 28	8,040,000		109	Colonel Service Star 64	16,320,000		145	Colonel Service Star 100	24,600,000
	74	Colonel Service Star 29	8,270,000		110	Colonel Service Star 65	16,550,000					
	75	Colonel Service Star 30	8,500,000		111	Colonel Service Star 66	16,780,000					
	76	Colonel Service Star 31	8,730,000		112	Colonel Service Star 67	17,010,000					
	77	Colonel Service Star 32	8,960,000		113	Colonel Service Star 68	17,240,000					
	78	Colonel Service Star 33	9,190,000		114	Colonel Service Star 69	17,470,000					
	79	Colonel Service Star 34	9,420,000		115	Colonel Service Star 70	17,700,000					
	80	Colonel Service Star 35	9,650,000		116	Colonel Service Star 71	17,930,000					
	81	Colonel Service Star 36	9,880,000		117	Colonel Service Star 72	18,160,000					

1	Defibrillator		4,000
2	M320		11,000
3	M416		22,000
4	M26 MASS		38,000
5	AEK-971		60,000
6	M16A3		89,000
7	F2000		124,000
8	AN-94		166,000
9	M16A4 (for RU)		220,000
9	AK-74M (for US)		220,000

1	C4 Explosives		4,000
2	M249		11,000
3	M18 Claymore		23,000
4	M224 Mortar		40,000
5	PKP Pecheneg		60,000
6	M240B		90,000
7	M60E4		130,000
8	M27 IAR (for RU)		170,000
8	RPK-74M (for US)		170,000

Engineer Unlock Progression

UNLOCK	NAME	IMAGE	ENGINEER SCORE
1	FIM-92 Stinger (for US)		3,000
1	SA-18 IGLA (for RU)		3,000
2	M15 AT Mine		7,000
3	SCAR-H		14,000
4	EOD Bot		25,000
5	M4		40,000
6	A-91		58,000
7	FGM-148 Javelin		82,000
8	G36C		110,000
9	M4A1 (for RU)		145,000
9	AKS-74u (for US)		145,000

Recon Unlock Progression

UNLOCK	NAME	IMAGE	RECON SCORE
1	T-UGS		5,000
2	SV98		13,000
3	SOFLAM		26,000
4	MAV		45,000
5	SKS		71,000
6	M40A5		104,000
7	M98B		146,000
8	MK11 MOD 0 (for RU)		195,000
8	SVD (for US)		195,000

Co-Op Weapon Unlocks

UNLOCK	NAME	IMAGE	ASSAULT SCORE
1	MP412 REX Pistol		63,000
2	KH2002 Assault Rifle		126,000
3	MP7 PDW		189,000
4	M39 EMR		252,000
5	93R Pistol		315,000
6	SG553 Carbine		378,000
7	G3A3 Assault Rifle		441,000

Camo Patterns

IMAGE	NAME	UNLOCK CRITERIA	IMAGE	NAME	UNLOCK CRITERIA
	Woodland	Rank 3 (Private First Class II)		Jungle	Rank 21 (Gunnery Sergeant I)
	Ranger	Rank 6 (Lance Corporal I)		Desert Khaki	Rank 24 (Master Sergeant I)
	Army Green	Rank 9 (Corporal)		Urban	Rank 27 (First Sergeant I)
	Expeditionary Force	Rank 12 (Corporal III)		Veteran Kit	Rank 39 (Chief Warrant Officer Five)
	Paratrooper	Rank 15 (Sergeant II)		Spec Ops Black	Rank 42 (Captain)
	Navy Blue	Rank 18 (Staff Sergeant I)			

	Ribbon	Description	Points
	Assault Rifle Ribbon	In a round, kill 7 enemies with assault rifles	200
	Carbine Ribbon	In a round, kill 7 enemies with carbines	200
	Machine gun Ribbon	In a round, kill 7 enemies with light machine guns	200
	Sniper Rifle Ribbon	In a round, kill 7 enemies with sniper rifles	200
	Handgun Ribbon	In a round, kill 4 enemies with handguns	200
	Shotgun Ribbon	In a round, kill 7 enemies with shotguns	200
	PDW Ribbon	In a round, kill 7 enemies with personal defense arms	200
	Melee Ribbon	In a round, kill 4 enemies with melee weapons	200
	Disable Vehicle Ribbon	In a round, disable 4 enemy vehicles	200
	Anti Vehicle Ribbon	In a round, destroy 3 enemy vehicles	200
	Accuracy Ribbon	In a round, get 5 headshots	200
	Avenger Ribbon	In a round, get 2 avenger kills	200
	Savior Ribbon	In a round, get 2 savior kills	200
	Nemesis Ribbon	In a round, get 2 nemesis kills	200
	Suppression Ribbon	In a round, get 7 suppression kills	200
	MVP Ribbon	In a round, be the best player	500
	MVP 2 Ribbon	In a round, be the 2nd best player	400
	MVP 3 Ribbon	In a round, be the 3rd best player	300
	Ace Squad Ribbon	In a round, be part of the best squad	500
	Combat Efficiency Ribbon	In a round, get 3 streak bonuses	500
	Anti Explosive Ribbon	In a round, destroy 2 enemy explosives	200
	Squad Spawn Ribbon	In a round, get 7 squad spawn bonuses	200
	Squad Wipe Ribbon	In a round, get 2 squad wipe bonuses	200
	Transport Warfare Ribbon	In a round, kill 4 enemies with transport vehicles	200
	Ground Warfare Ribbon	In a round, kill 7 enemies with land vehicles	200
	Stationary Emplacement Ribbon	In a round, kill 2 enemies with emplaced weapons	200
	Air Warfare Ribbon	In a round, kill 6 enemies with air vehicles	200
	M-COM Attacker Ribbon	In a round, blow up 3 M-COM stations	200
	M-COM Defender Ribbon	In a round, defend 4 M-COM stations	200
	Rush Winner Ribbon	Win a Rush round	500
	Conquest Winner Ribbon	Win a Conquest round	500
	TDM Winner Ribbon	Win a TDM round	500
	Squad Rush Winner Ribbon	Win a Squad Rush round	500
	Squad Deathmatch Winner Ribbon	Win a Squad Deathmatch round	500
	Rush Ribbon	Finish a Rush round	200
	Conquest Ribbon	Finish a Conquest round	200
	Team Deathmatch Ribbon	Finish a Team Deathmatch round	200
	Squad Rush Ribbon	Finish a Squad Rush round	200
	Squad Deathmatch Ribbon	Finish a Squad Deathmatch round	200
	Flag Attacker Ribbon	In a round, get 4 flag captures	200
	Flag Defender Ribbon	In a round, get 5 flag defends	200
	Resupply Efficiency Ribbon	In a round, get 7 resupplies	200
	Maintenance Efficiency Ribbon	In a round, get 7 repairs	200
	Medical Efficiency Ribbon	In a round, get 5 revives	200
	Surveilance Efficiency Ribbon	In a round, get 5 motion sensor assists	200

Medals

MEDAL	NAME	CRITERIA	POINTS	MEDAL	NAME	CRITERIA	POINTS
	Assault Rifle Medal	Obtain the Assault Rifle Ribbon 50 times	20,000		Rush Medal	Obtain the Rush Ribbon 50 times	20,000
	Carbine Medal	Obtain the Carbine Ribbon 50 times	20,000		Conquest Medal	Obtain the Conquest Ribbon 50 times	20,000
	Light Machine Gun Medal	Obtain the Light Machine Gun Ribbon 50 times	20,000		Team Deathmatch Medal	Obtain the Team Deathmatch Ribbon 50 times	20,000
	Sniper Rifle Medal	Obtain the Sniper Rifle Ribbon 50 times	20,000		Squad Rush Medal	Obtain the Squad Rush Ribbon 50 times	20,000
	Handgun Medal	Obtain the Handgun Ribbon 50 times	20,000		Squad Deathmatch Medal	Obtain the Squad Deathmatch Ribbon 50 times	20,000
	Shotgun Medal	Obtain the Shotgun Ribbon 50 times	20,000		Flag Attacker Medal	Obtain the Flag Attacker Ribbon 50 times	20,000
	PDW Medal	Obtain the PDW Ribbon 50 times	20,000		Flag Defender Medal	Obtain the Flag Defender Ribbon 50 times	20,000
	Melee Medal	Obtain the Melee Ribbon 30 times	20,000		Resupply Medal	Obtain the Resupply Ribbon 50 times	20,000
	Anti Vehicle Medal	Obtain the Anti Vehicle Ribbon 50 times	20,000		Maintenance Medal	Obtain the Maintenance Ribbon 50 times	20,000
	Accuracy Medal	Obtain the Accuracy Ribbon 50 times	20,000		Medical Medal	Obtain the Medical Ribbon 50 times	20,000
	Avenger Medal	Obtain the Avenger Ribbon 50 times	20,000		Surveilance Medal	Obtain the Surveilance Ribbon 50 times	20,000
	Savior Medal	Obtain the Savior Ribbon 50 times	20,000		Mortar Medal	Kill 300 enemies with the Mortar	20,000
	Nemesis Medal	Obtain the Nemesis Ribbon 50 times	20,000		Laser Designator Medal	Kill 300 enemies with the Laser Designator	20,000
	Suppression Medal	Obtain the Suppression Ribbon 50 times	20,000		M18 Claymore Medal	Kill 300 enemies with the M18 Claymore	20,000
	MVP Medal	Obtain the MVP Ribbon 50 times	20,000		Radio Beacon Medal	100 spawns on your Radio Beacon	20,000
	2nd MVP Medal	Obtain the 2nd MVP Ribbon 50 times	20,000		US Service Medal	Spend 100 hours in the US Marines	20,000
	3rd MVP Medal	Obtain the 3rd MVP Ribbon 50 times	20,000		RU Army Service Medal	Spend 100 hours in the RU Army	20,000
	Ace Squad Medal	Obtain the Ace Squad Ribbon 50 times	20,000		Assault Service Medal	Spend 50 hours as Assault	20,000
	Combat Efficiency Medal	Obtain the Combat Efficiency Ribbon 30 times	20,000		Engineer Service Medal	Spend 50 hours as Engineer	20,000
	Transport Warfare Medal	Obtain the Transport Warfare Ribbon 30 times	20,000		Support Service Medal	Spend 50 hours as Support	20,000
	Ground Warfare Medal	Obtain the Ground Warfare Ribbon 30 times	20,000		Recon Service Medal	Spend 50 hours as Recon	20,000
	Air Warfare Medal	Obtain the Air Warfare Ribbon 30 times	20,000		Tank Service Medal	Spend 20 hours in Tanks	20,000
	Stationary Emplacement Medal	Obtain the Stationary Emplacement Ribbon 30 times	20,000		Helicopter Service Medal	Spend 20 hours in Helicopters	20,000
	M-COM Attacker Medal	Obtain the M-COM Attacker Ribbon 30 times	20,000		Jet Service Medal	Spend 20 hours in Jets	20,000
	M-COM Defender Medal	Obtain the M-COM Defender Ribbon 30 times	20,000		Stationary Service Medal	Spend 2 hours in stationary weapons	20,000

Specializations

IMAGE	NAME	UNLOCK CRITERIA	DESCRIPTION
	Sprint	Rank 2 (Private First Class I)	Lightweight load-bearing equipment that reduces soldier fatigue and allows a higher sprint speed.
	Ammo	Rank 5 (Lance Corporal)	Additional MOLLE tactical ammunition pouches allow the player to carry a greater amount of primary and sidearm ammunition.
	Flak Jacket	Rank 8 (Lance Corporal III)	Reduces the damage taken from explosives and shrapnel by providing additional coverage to high-risk body parts.
	Explosives	Rank 11 (Corporal II)	An EOD vest that increases the total amount of explosive and rocket ammunition.
	Suppression Resist	Rank 14 (Sergeant I)	The combined effect of field experience and advanced training reduces the suppressive effect of incoming rounds.
	Suppression	Rank 17 (Staff Sergeant)	Advanced marksman training gives the soldier's rounds a greater suppressive effect on his targets.
	Grenades	Rank 20 (Gunnery Sergeant)	Additional MOLLE grenade pouches allow the soldier to carry a larger amount of hand grenades and 40mm grenades.
	Squad Sprint	Rank 23 (Master Sergeant)	Lightweight load-bearing equipment that reduces soldier fatigue and allows a higher sprint speed. This specialization will be granted to your entire squad.
	Squad Ammo	Rank 26 (First Sergeant)	Additional MOLLE tactical ammunition pouches allow the player to carry a greater amount of primary and sidearm ammunition. This specialization will be granted to your entire squad.
	Squad Flak Jacket	Rank 29 (Master Gunnery Sergeant)	Reduces the damage taken from explosives and shrapnel by providing additional coverage to high-risk body parts. This specialization will be granted to your entire squad.
	Squad Explosives	Rank 31 (Master Gunnery Sergeant II)	An EOD vest that increases the total amount of explosive and rocket ammunition. This specialization will be granted to your entire squad.
	Squad Suppression	Rank 33 (Sergeant Major I)	Advanced marksman training gives the soldier's rounds a greater suppressive effect on his targets. This specialization will be granted to your entire squad.
	Squad Suppression Resist	Rank 35 (Warrant Officer One)	The combined effect of field experience and advanced training reduces the suppressive effect of incoming rounds. This specialization will be granted to your entire squad.
	Squad Grenades	Rank 37 (Chief Warrant Officer Three)	Additional MOLLE grenade pouches allow the soldier to carry a larger amount of hand grenades and 40mm grenades. This specialization will be granted to your entire squad.

Basic Dog Tags (Left)

DOG TAG	NAME	CRITERIA	DOG TAG	NAME	CRITERIA
	Carbine Dog Tag	Obtain Carbine Efficiency Ribbon 10 Times		Rush Dog Tag	Obtain Rush Ribbon 10 Times
	Light Machine Gun Dog Tag	Obtain Light Machine Gun Efficiency Ribbon 10 Times		Conquest Dog Tag	Obtain Conquest Ribbon 10 Times
	Sniper Rifle Dog Tag	Obtain Sniper Rifle Efficiency Ribbon 10 Times		Team Deathmatch Dog Tag	Obtain Team Deathmatch Ribbon 10 Times
	Handgun Dog Tag	Obtain Handgun Ribbon 10 Times		Squad Rush Dog Tag	Obtain Squad Rush Ribbon 10 Times
	Shotgun Dog Tag	Obtain Shotgun Ribbon 10 Times		Squad Deathmatch Dog Tag	Obtain Squad Deathmatch Ribbon 10 Times
	POW Dog Tag	Obtain POW Ribbon 10 Times		Flag Attacker Dog Tag	Obtain Flag Attacker Ribbon 10 Times
	Melee Dog Tag	Obtain Melee Ribbon 10 Times		Flag Defender Dog Tag	Obtain Flag Defender Ribbon 10 Times
	Anti Vehicle Dog Tag	Obtain Anti Vehicle Ribbon 10 Times		Resupply Dog Tag	Obtain Resupply Efficiency Ribbon 10 Times
	Accuracy Dog Tag	Obtain Accuracy Ribbon 10 Times		Maintenance Dog Tag	Obtain Maintenance Efficiency Ribbon 10 Times
	Avenger Dog Tag	Obtain Avenger Ribbon 10 Times		Medical Dog Tag	Obtain Medical Efficiency Ribbon 10 Times
	Savior Dog Tag	Obtain Savior Ribbon 10 Times		Surveillance Dog Tag	Obtain Surveillance Efficiency Ribbon 10 Times
	Nemesis Dog Tag	Obtain Nemesis Ribbon 10 Times		Private First Class Dog Tag	Reach rank Private First Class
	Suppression Dog Tag	Obtain Suppression Ribbon 10 Times		Private First Class 1 Star Dog Tag	Reach rank Private First Class 1 Star
	MVP Dog Tag	Obtain MVP Ribbon 10 Times		Private First Class 2 Star Dog Tag	Reach rank Private First Class 2 Star
	2nd MVP Dog Tag	Obtain 2nd MVP Ribbon 10 Times		Private First Class 3 Star Dog Tag	Reach rank Private First Class 3 Star
	3rd MVP Dog Tag	Obtain 3rd MVP Ribbon 10 Times		Lance Corporal Dog Tag	Reach rank Lance Corporal
	Ace Squad Dog Tag	Obtain Ace Squad Ribbon 10 Times		Lance Corporal 1 Star Dog Tag	Reach rank Lance Corporal 1 Star
	Transport Warfare Dog Tag	Obtain Transport Warfare Ribbon 10 Times		Lance Corporal 2 Star Dog Tag	Reach rank Lance Corporal 2 Star
	Armored Warfare Dog Tag	Obtain Armored Warfare Ribbon 10 Times		Lance Corporal 3 Star Dog Tag	Reach rank Lance Corporal 3 Star
	Stationary Dog Tag	Obtain Stationary Ribbon 10 Times		Corporal Dog Tag	Reach rank Corporal
	Air Warfare Dog Tag	Obtain Air Warfare Ribbon 10 Times		Corporal 1 Star Dog Tag	Reach rank Corporal 1 Star
	M-Com Attacker Dog Tag	Obtain M-Com Attacker Ribbon 10 Times		Corporal 2 Star Dog Tag	Reach rank Corporal 2 Star
	M-Com Defender Dog Tag	Obtain M-Com Defender Ribbon 10 Times		Corporal 3 Star Dog Tag	Reach rank Corporal 3 Star
	Rush Winner Dog Tag	Obtain Rush Winner Ribbon 10 Times		Sergeant Dog Tag	Reach rank Sergeant
	Conquest Winner Dog Tag	Obtain Conquest Winner Ribbon 10 Times		Sergeant 1 Star Dog Tag	Reach rank Sergeant 1 Star
	Team Deathmatch Winner Dog Tag	Obtain Team Deathmatch Winner Ribbon 10 Times		Sergeant 2 Star Dog Tag	Reach rank Sergeant 2 Star
	Squad Rush Winner Dog Tag	Obtain Squad Rush Winner Ribbon 10 Times		Sergeant 3 Star Dog Tag	Reach rank Sergeant 3 Star
	Squad Deathmatch Winner Dog Tag	Obtain Squad Deathmatch Winner Ribbon 10 Times		Staff Sergeant Dog Tag	Reach rank Staff Sergeant

DOG TAG	NAME	CRITERIA	DOG TAG	NAME	CRITERIA
	Staff Sergeant 1 Star Dog Tag	Reach rank Staff Sergeant 1 Star		FIM-92 Stinger AA Proficiency Dog Tag	Obtain FIM-92 Stinger AA Service Star 1
	Staff Sergeant 2 Star Dog Tag	Reach rank Staff Sergeant 2 Star		SA18 IGLA AA Proficiency Dog Tag	Obtain SA18 IGLA AA Service Star 1
	Gunnery Sergeant Dog Tag	Reach rank Gunnery Sergeant		M15 AT Mines Proficiency Dog Tag	Obtain M15 AT Mines Service Star 1
	Gunnery Sergeant 1 Star Dog Tag	Reach rank Gunnery Sergeant 1 Star		SG553 Proficiency Dog Tag	Obtain SG553 Service Star 1
	Gunnery Sergeant 2 Star Dog Tag	Reach rank Gunnery Sergeant 2 Star		M27 IAR Proficiency Dog Tag	Obtain M27 IAR Service Star 1
	Master Sergeant Dog Tag	Reach rank Master Sergeant		RPK-74M Proficiency Dog Tag	Obtain RPK-74M Service Star 1
	Master Sergeant 1 Star Dog Tag	Reach rank Master Sergeant 1 Star		M240B LMG Proficiency Dog Tag	Obtain M240B LMG Service Star 1
	Master Sergeant 2 Star Dog Tag	Reach rank Master Sergeant 2 Star		M249 Proficiency Dog Tag	Obtain M249 Service Star 1
	First Sergeant Dog Tag	Reach rank First Sergeant		M60E4 Proficiency Dog Tag	Obtain M60E4 Service Star 1
	First Sergeant 1 Star Dog Tag	Reach rank First Sergeant 1 Star		PKP Pecheneg Proficiency Dog Tag	Obtain PKP Pecheneg Service Star 1
	First Sergeant 2 Star Dog Tag	Reach rank First Sergeant 2 Star		Type 88 LMG Proficiency Dog Tag	Obtain Type 88 LMG Service Star 1
	Master Gunnery Sergeant Dog Tag	Reach rank Master Gunnery Sergeant		MK11 Mod 0 Proficiency Dog Tag	Obtain MK11 Mod 0 Service Star 1
	Master Gunnery Sergeant 1 Star Dog Tag	Reach rank Master Gunnery Sergeant 1 Star		SVD Proficiency Dog Tag	Obtain SVD Service Star 1
	Master Gunnery Sergeant 2 Star Dog Tag	Reach rank Master Gunnery Sergeant 2 Star		SKS Proficiency Dog Tag	Obtain SKS Service Star 1
	Sergeant Major Dog Tag	Reach rank Sergeant Major		SV98 Proficiency Dog Tag	Obtain SV98 Service Star 1
	Sergeant Major 1 Star Dog Tag	Reach rank Sergeant Major 1 Star		M98B Proficiency Dog Tag	Obtain M98B Service Star 1
	Sergeant Major 2 Star Dog Tag	Reach rank Sergeant Major 2 Star		M40A5 Proficiency Dog Tag	Obtain M40A5 Service Star 1
	Warrant Officer One Dog Tag	Reach rank Warrant Officer One		MUAV Proficiency Dog Tag	Obtain MUAV Service Star 1
	Chief Warrant Officer Two Dog Tag	Reach rank Chief Warrant Officer Two		C4 Expl Proficiency Dog Tag	Obtain C4 Expl Service Star 1
	Chief Warrant Officer Three Dog Tag	Reach rank Chief Warrant Officer Three		Laser Rangefinder Proficiency Dog Tag	Obtain Laser Rangefinder Service Star 1
	Chief Warrant Officer Four Dog Tag	Reach rank Chief Warrant Officer Four		M18 Claymore Proficiency Dog Tag	Obtain M18 Claymore Service Star 1
	Chief Warrant Officer Five Dog Tag	Reach rank Chief Warrant Officer Five		M39 MBR Proficiency Dog Tag	Obtain M39 MBR Service Star 1
	Second Lieutenant Dog Tag	Reach rank Second Lieutenant		M98B Proficiency Dog Tag	Obtain M98B Service Star 1
	First Lieutenant Dog Tag	Reach rank First Lieutenant		MP443 Proficiency Dog Tag	Obtain MP443 Service Star 1
	Captain Dog Tag	Reach rank Captain		G18 Proficiency Dog Tag	Obtain G18 Service Star 1
	Major Dog Tag	Reach rank Major		.44 Magnum Proficiency Dog Tag	Obtain .44 Magnum Service Star 1
	Lieutenant Colonel Dog Tag	Reach rank Lieutenant Colonel		G17C Proficiency Dog Tag	Obtain G17C Service Star 1
	Assault Dog Tag	Obtain Assault Service Star 1		M9 Suppressed Proficiency Dog Tag	Obtain M9 Suppressed Service Star 1
	Engineer Dog Tag	Obtain Engineer Service Star 1		MP443 Suppressed Proficiency Dog Tag	Obtain MP443 Suppressed Service Star 1
	Support Dog Tag	Obtain Support Service Star 1		M1911 Proficiency Dog Tag	Obtain M1911 Service Star 1
	Recon Dog Tag	Obtain Recon Service Star 1		93R Proficiency Dog Tag	Obtain 93R Service Star 1
	DICE Dog Tag	The wearer of this tag contributed to making this game		MP412 REX Proficiency Dog Tag	Obtain MP412 REX Service Star 1
	Co-op Dog Tag	Obtain Co-op Service Star 1		PDW-R Proficiency Dog Tag	Obtain PDW-R Service Star 1
	M16 Proficiency Dog Tag	Obtain M16 Service Star 1		PP-2000 Proficiency Dog Tag	Obtain PP-2000 Service Star 1
	AK-74M Proficiency Dog Tag	Obtain AK-74M Service Star 1		UMP-45 Proficiency Dog Tag	Obtain UMP-45 Service Star 1
	40MMGL Proficiency Dog Tag	Obtain 40MMGL Service Star 1		P90 Proficiency Dog Tag	Obtain P90 Service Star 1
	AEK-971 Proficiency Dog Tag	Obtain AEK-971 Service Star 1		MP7 Proficiency Dog Tag	Obtain MP7 Service Star 1
	AN-94 Proficiency Dog Tag	Obtain AN-94 Service Star 1		870MCS Proficiency Dog Tag	Obtain 870MCS Service Star 1
	KH2000 Proficiency Dog Tag	Obtain KH2000 Service Star 1		DAO-12 Proficiency Dog Tag	Obtain DAO-12 Service Star 1
	M416 Proficiency Dog Tag	Obtain M416 Service Star 1		M1014 Proficiency Dog Tag	Obtain M1014 Service Star 1
	Mortar Dog Tag	Obtain M224 Mortar Medal		USAS-12 Proficiency Dog Tag	Obtain USAS-12 Service Star 1
	F2000 Proficiency Dog Tag	Obtain F2000 Service Star 1		SAIGA 12K Proficiency Dog Tag	Obtain SAIGA 12K Service Star 1
	G3A3 Proficiency Dog Tag	Obtain G3A3 Service Star 1		Main Battle Tank Proficiency Dog Tag	Obtain Main Battle Tank Service Star 1
	M4A1 Proficiency Dog Tag	Obtain M4A1 Service Star 1		Infantry Fighting Vehicle Proficiency Dog Tag	Obtain Infantry Fighting Vehicle Service Star 1
	AKS-74u Proficiency Dog Tag	Obtain AKS-74u Service Star 1		AA Vehicle Proficiency Dog Tag	Obtain AA Vehicle Service Star 1
	SMAW Proficiency Dog Tag	Obtain SMAW Service Star 1		Attack Helicopter Proficiency Dog Tag	Obtain Attack Helicopter Service Star 1
	RPG-7V2 Proficiency Dog Tag	Obtain RPG-7V2 Service Star 1		Scout Helicopter Proficiency Dog Tag	Obtain Scout Helicopter Service Star 1
	G36c Proficiency Dog Tag	Obtain G36c Service Star 1		Jet Pilot Proficiency Dog Tag	Obtain Jet Pilot Service Star 1
	SCAR-H CQB Proficiency Dog Tag	Obtain SCAR-H CQB Service Star 1		Assault Rifle Dog Tag	Obtain Assault Rifle Ribbon 10 Times
	FGM-148 JAV Proficiency Dog Tag	Obtain FGM-148 JAV Service Star 1		AS-Val Proficiency Dog Tag	Obtain AS-Val Service Star 1

Advanced Dog Tags (Right)

DOG TAG	NAME	CRITERIA
	Carbine Mastery Dog Tag	Obtain Carbine Medal 1 time
	Light Machine Gun Mastery Dog Tag	Obtain Light Machine Gun Medal 1 time
	Sniper Rifle Mastery Dog Tag	Obtain Sniper Rifle Medal 1 time
	Handgun Mastery Dog Tag	Obtain Handgun Medal 1 time
	Shotgun Mastery Dog Tag	Obtain Shotgun Medal 1 time
	PDW Mastery Dog Tag	Obtain PDW Medal 1 time
	Melee Mastery Dog Tag	Obtain Melee Medal 1 time
	Anti Vehicle Dog Tag	Obtain Anti Vehicle Medal 1 time
	Accuracy Dog Tag	Obtain Accuracy Medal 1 time
	Avenger Dog Tag	Obtain Avenger Medal 1 time
	Savior Dog Tag	Obtain Savior Medal 1 time
	Nemesis Dog Tag	Obtain Nemesis Medal 1 time
	Suppression Dog Tag	Obtain Suppression Medal 1 time
	MVP Dog Tag	Obtain MVP Medal 1 time
	2nd MVP Dog Tag	Obtain 2nd MVP Medal 1 time
	3rd MVP Dog Tag	Obtain 3rd MVP Medal 1 time
	Ace Squad Dog Tag	Obtain Ace Squad Medal 1 time
	Combat Efficiency Dog Tag	Obtain Combat Efficiency Medal 1 time
	Transport Warfare Dog Tag	Obtain Transport Warfare Medal 1 time
	Armor Warfare Dog Tag	Obtain Armor Warfare Medal 1 time
	Air Warfare Dog Tag	Obtain Air Warfare Medal 1 time
	Stationary Dog Tag	Obtain Stationary Medal 1 time
	M-Com Attacker Dog Tag	Obtain M-Com Attacker Medal 1 time
	M-Com Defender Dog Tag	Obtain M-Com Defender Medal 1 time
	Rush Dog Tag	Obtain Rush Medal 1 time
	Conquest Dog Tag	Obtain Conquest Medal 1 time
	Team Deathmatch Dog Tag	Obtain Team Deathmatch Medal 1 time
	Squad Rush Dog Tag	Obtain Squad Rush Medal 1 time
	Squad Deathmatch Dog Tag	Obtain Squad Deathmatch Medal 1 time
	Flag Attacker Dog Tag	Obtain Flag Attacker Medal 1 time
	Flag Defender Dog Tag	Obtain Flag Defender Medal 1 time
	Resupply Dog Tag	Obtain Resupply Medal 1 time
	Maintenance Dog Tag	Obtain Maintenance Medal 1 time
	Medical Dog Tag	Obtain Medical Medal 1 time
	Surveillance Dog Tag	Obtain Surveillance Medal 5 times
	M224 Mortar Proficiency Dog Tag	Obtain Mortar Medal 1 time
	Laser Designator Dog Tag	Obtain Laser Designator Medal 5 times
	M18 Claymore Dog Tag	Obtain M18 Claymore Medal 1 time
	Radio Beacon Dog Tag	Obtain Radio Beacon Medal 1 time
	US Service Dog Tag	Obtain US Service Medal
	RU Army Service Dog Tag	Obtain RU Army Service Medal
	Assault Service Dog Tag	Obtain Assault Service Medal 1 time
	Engineer Service Dog Tag	Obtain Engineer Service Medal 1 time
	Support Service Dog Tag	Obtain Support Service Medal 1 time
	Recon Service Dog Tag	Obtain Recon Service Medal 1 time
	Tank Service Dog Tag	Obtain Tank Service Medal 1 time
	Helicopter Service Dog Tag	Obtain Helicopter Service Medal 1 time
	Jet Service Dog Tag	Obtain Jet Service Medal 1 time
	Stationary Service Dog Tag	Obtain Stationary Service Medal 1 time
	Second Lieutenant Dog Tag	Reach rank Second Lieutenant
	First Lieutenant Dog Tag	Reach rank First Lieutenant
	Captain Dog Tag	Reach rank Captain
	Major Dog Tag	Reach rank Major
	Lieutenant Colonel Dog Tag	Reach rank Lieutenant Colonel
	Colonel Dog Tag	Reach rank Colonel

DOG TAG	NAME	CRITERIA
	Colonel Service Star 5 Dog Tag	Obtain Colonel Service Star 5
	Colonel Service Star 10 Dog Tag	Obtain Colonel Service Star 10
	Colonel Service Star 25 Dog Tag	Obtain Colonel Service Star 25
	Colonel Service Star 50 Dog Tag	Obtain Colonel Service Star 50
	Colonel Service Star 100 Dog Tag	Obtain Colonel Service Star 100
	Assault Service Star 5 Dog Tag	Obtain Assault Service Star 5
	Assault Service Star 10 Dog Tag	Obtain Assault Service Star 10
	Assault Service Star 25 Dog Tag	Obtain Assault Service Star 25
	Assault Service Star 50 Dog Tag	Obtain Assault Service Star 50
	Assault Service Star 100 Dog Tag	Obtain Assault Service Star 100
	Engineer Service Star 5 Dog Tag	Obtain Engineer Service Star 5
	Engineer Service Star 10 Dog Tag	Obtain Engineer Service Star 10
	Engineer Service Star 25 Dog Tag	Obtain Engineer Service Star 25
	Engineer Service Star 50 Dog Tag	Obtain Engineer Service Star 50
	Engineer Service Star 100 Dog Tag	Obtain Engineer Service Star 100
	Support Service Star 5 Dog Tag	Obtain Support Service Star 5
	Support Service Star 10 Dog Tag	Obtain Support Service Star 10
	Support Service Star 25 Dog Tag	Obtain Support Service Star 25
	Support Service Star 50 Dog Tag	Obtain Support Service Star 50
	Support Service Star 100 Dog Tag	Obtain Support Service Star 100
	Recon Service Star 5 Dog Tag	Obtain Recon Service Star 5
	Recon Service Star 10 Dog Tag	Obtain Recon Service Star 10
	Recon Service Star 25 Dog Tag	Obtain Recon Service Star 25
	Recon Service Star 50 Dog Tag	Obtain Recon Service Star 50
	Recon Service Star 100 Dog Tag	Obtain Recon Service Star 100
	Tank Service Star 5 Dog Tag	Obtain Tank Service Star 5
	Tank Service Star 10 Dog Tag	Obtain Tank Service Star 10
	Tank Service Star 25 Dog Tag	Obtain Tank Service Star 25
	Tank Service Star 50 Dog Tag	Obtain Tank Service Star 50
	Tank Service Star 100 Dog Tag	Obtain Tank Service Star 100
	Co-op Service Star 5 Dog Tag	Obtain Co-op Service Star 5
	Co-op Service Star 10 Dog Tag	Obtain Co-op Service Star 10
	Co-op Service Star 25 Dog Tag	Obtain Co-op Service Star 25
	Co-op Service Star 50 Dog Tag	Obtain Co-op Service Star 50
	M16 Master Dog Tag	Obtain M16 Service Star 5
	AK-74M Master Dog Tag	Obtain AK-74M Service Star 5
	40MMGL Master Dog Tag	Obtain 40MMGL Service Star 5
	AEK-971 Master Dog Tag	Obtain AEK-971 Service Star 5
	AN-94 Master Dog Tag	Obtain AN-94 Service Star 5
	KH2000 Master Dog Tag	Obtain KH2000 Service Star 5
	M416 Master Dog Tag	Obtain M416 Service Star 5
	M224 Mortar Master Dog Tag	Obtain M224 Mortar Medal
	F2000 Master Dog Tag	Obtain F2000 Service Star 5
	G3A3 Master Dog Tag	Obtain G3A3 Service Star 5
	M4A1 Master Dog Tag	Obtain M4A1 Service Star 5
	AKS-74u Master Dog Tag	Obtain AKS-74u Service Star 5
	SMAW Master Dog Tag	Obtain SMAW Service Star 5
	RPG-7V2 Master Dog Tag	Obtain RPG-7V2 Service Star 5
	G36c Master Dog Tag	Obtain G36c Service Star 5
	SCAR-H CQB Master Dog Tag	Obtain SCAR-H CQB Service Star 5
	FGM-148 JAV Master Dog Tag	Obtain FGM-148 JAV Service Star 5
	FIM-92 Stinger AA Master Dog Tag	Obtain FIM-92 Stinger AA Service Star 5
	SA18 IGLA AA Master Dog Tag	Obtain SA18 IGLA AA Service Star 5
	M15 AT Mines Master Dog Tag	Obtain M15 AT Mines Service Star 5
	SG553 Master Dog Tag	Obtain SG553 Service Star 5

Advanced Dog Tags (Right) continued

DOG TAG	NAME	CRITERIA
	M27 IAR Master Dog Tag	Obtain M27 IAR Service Star 5
	RPK-74M Master Dog Tag	Obtain RPK-74M Service Star 5
	M240B LMG Master Dog Tag	Obtain M240B LMG Service Star 5
	M249 Master Dog Tag	Obtain M249 Service Star 5
	M60E4 Master Dog Tag	Obtain M60E4 Service Star 5
	PKP Pecheneg Master Dog Tag	Obtain PKP Pecheneg Service Star 5
	Type 88 LMG Master Dog Tag	Obtain Type 88 LMG Service Star 5
	MK11 Mod 0 Master Dog Tag	Obtain MK11 Mod 0 Service Star 5
	SVD Master Dog Tag	Obtain SVD Service Star 5
	SKS Master Dog Tag	Obtain SKS Service Star 5
	SV98 Master Dog Tag	Obtain SV98 Service Star 5
	M98B Master Dog Tag	Obtain M98B Service Star 5
	M40A5 Master Dog Tag	Obtain M40A5 Service Star 5
	MAV Master Dog Tag	Obtain Surveillance Medal
	C4 Expl Master Dog Tag	Obtain C4 Expl Service Star 5
	Laser Rangefinder Master Dog Tag	Obtain Laser Designator Medal
	M18 Claymore Master Dog Tag	Obtain M18 Claymore Service Star 5
	M39 MBR Master Dog Tag	Obtain M39 MBR Service Star 5
	MP443 Master Dog Tag	Obtain MP443 Service Star 5
	G18 Master Dog Tag	Obtain G18 Service Star 5
	.44 Magnum Master Dog Tag	Obtain .44 Magnum Service Star 5
	G17C Master Dog Tag	Obtain G17C Service Star 5
	M9 Suppressed Master Dog Tag	Obtain M9 Suppressed Service Star 5
	MP443 Suppressed Master Dog Tag	Obtain MP443 Suppressed Service Star 5
	M9 Master Dog Tag	Obtain M9 Service Star 5
	M1911 Master Dog Tag	Obtain M1911 Service Star 5
	93R Master Dog Tag	Obtain 93R Service Star 5
	MP412 REX Master Dog Tag	Obtain MP412 REX Service Star 5
	PDW-R Master Dog Tag	Obtain PDW-R Service Star 5
	PP-2000 Master Dog Tag	Obtain PP-2000 Service Star 5
	UMP-45 Master Dog Tag	Obtain UMP-45 Service Star 5
	P90 Master Dog Tag	Obtain P90 Service Star 5
	MP7 Master Dog Tag	Obtain MP7 Service Star 5
	870MCS Master Dog Tag	Obtain 870MCS Service Star 5
	DAO-12 Master Dog Tag	Obtain DAO-12 Service Star 5
	M1014 Master Dog Tag	Obtain M514 Service Star 5
	USAS-12 Master Dog Tag	Obtain USAS-12 Service Star 5
	SAIGA 12K Master Dog Tag	Obtain SAIGA 12K Service Star 5
	Main Battle Tank Mastery Dog Tag	Obtain Main Battle Tank Service Star 1
	Infantry Fighting Vehicle Mastery Dog Tag	Obtain Infantry Fighting Vehicle Service Star 1
	AA Vehicle Mastery Dog Tag	Obtain AA Vehicle Service Star 1
	Attack Helicopter Mastery Dog Tag	Obtain Attack Helicopter Service Star 1
	Scout Helicopter Mastery Dog Tag	Obtain Scout Helicopter Service Star 1
	Jet Pilot Mastery Dog Tag	Obtain Jet Pilot Service Star 1
	Alienware Teeth Dog Tag	Provided exclusively by Alienware
	6 Wolf Moon Dog Tag	Dr. Pepper promotional offer
	Bye Kitty Dog Tag	Dr. Pepper promotional offer
	Roar Dog Tag	Dr. Pepper promotional offer
	Pile o Bones Dog Tag	Dr. Pepper promotional offer
	Opener Dog Tag	Dr. Pepper promotional offer
	Had to be Snakes Dog Tag	Provided exclusively by Act of Valor
	Flaming Skull Dog Tag	Provided exclusively by Act of Valor
	Metal Dog Tag	Provided exclusively by Act of Valor
	Rabbit Duck Dog Tag	Provided exclusively by Act of Valor
	Death's Hand Dog Tag	Provided exclusively by Act of Valor

DOG TAG	NAME	CRITERIA
	Ace of Spades Dog Tag	Obtained by purchasing the Dog tag DLC package
	...and Counting Dog Tag	Obtained by purchasing the Dog tag DLC package
	Bringer of Death Dog Tag	Obtained by purchasing the Dog tag DLC package
	Cause of Death Dog Tag	Obtained by purchasing the Dog tag DLC package
	More Dinosaurs Dog Tag	Obtained by purchasing the Dog tag DLC package
	Haggard Dog Tag	Obtained by purchasing the Dog tag DLC package
	Mayan Dog Tag	Obtained by purchasing the Dog tag DLC package
	Yarrr Dog Tag	Obtained by purchasing the Dog tag DLC package
	Edgy Dog Tag	Obtained by purchasing the Dog tag DLC package
	Todo Dog Tag	Obtained by purchasing the Dog tag DLC package
	Need for Speed - The Run Dog Tag	From Need 4 Speed - The Run
	Battlefield Play4Free Dog Tag	From the Play4Free remake of the classic BF2
	N7 Dog Tag	A gift from the Mass Effect 3 development team
	Mass Effect 3 Dog Tag	A gift from the Mass Effect 3 development team
	Dice Dev Team Dog Tag	The wearer of this tag contributed to making this game
	Battlefield 1943 Dog Tag	The wearer of this is a grizzled Battlefield Veteran
	Battlefield 2142 Dog Tag	The wearer of this is a grizzled Battlefield Veteran
	Battlefield Bad Company Dog Tag	The wearer of this is a grizzled Battlefield Veteran
	Battlefield Bad Company 2 Dog Tag	The wearer of this is a grizzled Battlefield Veteran
	Battlefield 2 Dog Tag	The wearer of this is a grizzled Battlefield Veteran
	Battlefield Vietnam Dog Tag	The wearer of this is a grizzled Battlefield Veteran
	Tournament Winner Dog Tag	Win an official tournament
	Tournament Runner Up Dog Tag	Be runner up in an official tournament
	Tournament 3rd Place Dog Tag	Be third place in an official tournament
	Assault Rifle Mastery Dog Tag	Obtain Assault Rifle Medal 5 times
	Attack Helicopter Service Star 5 Dog Tag	Obtain Attack Helicopter Service Star 5
	Attack Helicopter Service Star 10 Dog Tag	Obtain Attack Helicopter Service Star 10
	Attack Helicopter Service Star 25 Dog Tag	Obtain Attack Helicopter Service Star 25
	Attack Helicopter Service Star 50 Dog Tag	Obtain Attack Helicopter Service Star 50
	Attack Helicopter Service Star 100 Dog Tag	Obtain Attack Helicopter Service Star 100
	Scout Heli Service Star 5 Dog Tag	Obtain Scout Heli Service Star 5
	Scout Heli Service Star 10 Dog Tag	Obtain Scout Heli Service Star 10
	Scout Heli Service Star 25 Dog Tag	Obtain Scout Heli Service Star 25
	Scout Heli Service Star 50 Dog Tag	Obtain Scout Heli Service Star 50
	Scout Heli Service Star 100 Dog Tag	Obtain Scout Heli Service Star 100
	IFV Service Star 5 Dog Tag	Obtain IFV Service Star 5
	IFV Service Star 10 Dog Tag	Obtain IFV Service Star 10
	IFV Service Star 25 Dog Tag	Obtain IFV Service Star 25
	IFV Service Star 50 Dog Tag	Obtain IFV Service Star 50
	IFV Service Star 100 Dog Tag	Obtain IFV Service Star 100
	Jet Service Star 5 Dog Tag	Obtain Jet Service Star 5
	Jet Service Star 10 Dog Tag	Obtain Jet Service Star 10
	Jet Service Star 25 Dog Tag	Obtain Jet Service Star 25
	Jet Service Star 50 Dog Tag	Obtain Jet Service Star 50
	Jet Service Star 100 Dog Tag	Obtain Jet Service Star 100
	AA Service Star 5 Dog Tag	Obtain AA Service Star 5
	AA Service Star 10 Dog Tag	Obtain AA Service Star 10
	AA Service Star 25 Dog Tag	Obtain AA Service Star 25
	AA Service Star 50 Dog Tag	Obtain AA Service Star 50
	AA Service Star 100 Dog Tag	Obtain AA Service Star 100
	AS-Val Mastery Dog Tag	Obtain AS-Val Service Star 10
	Razer Serpent Dog Tag	Equip your Battlefield 3 soldier with this Razer Serpent Dog Tag provided exclusively by Razer

Achievements/Trophies

IMAGE	NAME	DESCRIPTION	GAMERSCORE	TROPHY
	CAMPAIGN			
	FlashForward	Completed Semper Fidelis	10	Bronze
	Shock Troop	Survived the quake	15	Bronze
	Rad Loot	Found the nuke	20	Bronze
	SacreBOOM!	Failed to prevent the attack	20	Bronze
	Wanted: Dead or Alive	Captured Al Bashir	20	Bronze
	No Escape	Captured Kaffarov	30	Bronze
	Not on my watch	Protected Chaffin from the soldiers in the street in Operation Swordbreaker	25	Bronze
	Roadkill	Kicked the car and killed the soldiers in Uprising	20	Bronze
	Involuntary Euthanasia	Killed the 2 soldiers before the building fell on them in Uprising	25	Bronze
	You can be my wingman anytime	Completed Going Hunting in a perfect run	30	Bronze
	The Professional	Completed the street chase in All Russian in under 2 minutes 30 seconds without dying	30	Bronze
	Scrap Metal	Destroyed 6 enemy tanks before reaching the fort in Thunder Run	25	Bronze
	Army of Darkness	Shot out the 4 lights in 4 bullets in Night Shift	30	Bronze
	Twofor	Took down 2 enemies in 1 bullet in Night Shift	15	Bronze
	What the hell *are* you?	Took a russian Dog Tag in the forest ambush on Rock And A Hard Place	20	Bronze
	Float like a butterfly...	Took down the jet in one attempt in Rock And A Hard Place	25	Bronze
	Practice makes perfect	Headshot each of the targets in the gun range in Kaffarov	15	Bronze
	Between a rock and a hard place	Beat Soloman, flawlessly, in The Great Destroyer	15	Bronze
	Ooh-rah!	Completed the campaign story	30	Silver
	Semper Fidelis	Completed the campaign story on Hard	50	Gold
	CO-OP			
	Push On	Reached the garage without going into man-down state in Hit and Run	20	Bronze
	In the nick of time	Disarmed the bomb in under 20 seconds in The Eleventh Hour	20	Bronze
	Car Lover	Completed the mission without losing a humvee in Operation Exodus	20	Bronze
	Untouchable	Completed the mission without using the fire extinguisher in Fire From The Sky	20	Bronze
	Bullseye	Saved the hostages without alerting any enemies in Drop 'em Like Liquid	20	Bronze
	Ninjas	Reached the VIP without setting off the alarm in Exfiltration	20	Bronze
	Lock 'n' Load	Unlocked all unique co-op weapons	30	Silver
	Two-rah!	Completed all co-op missions	30	Silver
	Army of Two	Completed all co-op missions on Hard	50	Gold
	MULTIPLAYER			
	Vehicle Warfare	Recieved all 3 vehicle warfare ribbons	30	Bronze
	Support Efficiency	Recieved all 4 support efficiency ribbons	30	Bronze
	Infantry Efficiency	Recieved all 4 weapon efficiency ribbons	30	Bronze
	Decorated	Received one of each ribbon we have in the game	50	Gold
	M.I.A	Took your first enemy dogtag	20	Bronze
	It's better than nothing!	3rd MVP in a ranked match	30	Silver
	1st Loser	2nd MVP in a ranked match	30	Silver
	Most Valuable Player	MVP in a ranked match	30	Silver
	Colonel	Rank 45 achieved!	50	Gold
	PS3 EXCLUSIVE			
	Platinum Trophy	Collect all other Battlefield Trophies	N/A	Platinum

PRIMA Official Game Guide

Written by:

David Knight & Sam Bishop

PRIMA GAMES

An Imprint of Random House, Inc.
3000 Lava Ridge Court, Suite 100
Roseville, CA 95661
www.primagames.com

Associate Publisher: Andy Rolleri
Product Managers: Donato Tica and Fernando Bueno
Design & Layout: Marc W. Riegel
Additional Authoring: Ronald Gaffud
Copyedit: Sara Wilson and Off Base Productions
Manufacturing: Stephanie Sanchez

Prima Games and the authors would like to thank Kevin O'Leary, Gustav Enekull, Diego Jimenez, Tommy Rydling, Owen Johnson, Daniel Davis, Lorraine Honrada and Jim Stadelman for their help and support throughout the process!

ISBN: 978-0-307-89048-1

Printed in the United States of America

11 12 13 14 GG 10 9 8 7 6 5 4 3 2 1

THIS IS ONLY A CHOICE SELECTION OF WHAT'S
AVAILABLE FROM THE DICE™ STORE NOW. CHECK OUT
THE FULL RANGE OF T-SHIRTS, HOODIES, DOG TAGS,
PARACORD WRISTBANDS, KEYRINGS, POSTERS,
BOOKS, FULL-SIZE SOLDIER PRINTS, RAZER™
ACCESSORIES, VAULTS AND MORE. YOU'LL ALSO FIND
DESIGNS FOR MIRROR'S EDGE™, DICE™ & FROSTBITE™.
USE DISCOUNT CODE 'PGBF3' TO GET AN
INTRODUCTORY 10% OFF FOR THE FIRST 500 ORDERS
PLACED BEFORE 1ST DECEMBER 2011.